TO THE STUDENT

Citizens of the United States are also citizens of the state in which they live. For us, this means that we are both Americans and "Washingtonians." Most of us don't take much time to think about this. But we should, because we not only live in the best country in the world, but also in one of the best places in our country. People who live in Washington State have a better life in many ways than people who live in other places. We have higher than average incomes, mild weather, good crops, growing industries, good schools, wonderful scenery, and much more. However, this should not make us content; there is much that can be improved upon. So we should know about our state and the places around us.

You should study Washington — its people, geography, government, and history. There are many things to learn, so your study can be interesting as well as worthwhile. And, most important, you can be a better informed and more effective citizen because of what you learn.

A textbook is never long enough to include all that we know about the history of an area. An author must make many choices about what to include and what to leave out. This book covers some of the important things about the people who have lived and worked in our state and about their role in national and world affairs. The book also discusses some of the main issues that have been important in Washington from the earliest days to the present.

No book can be as detailed as you might wish in its treatment of some topics. Fortunately, it is possible to find more information about our state. Local newspapers and magazines carry interesting historical information every week. Books, photographs, letters, diaries, and official records are available at nearby libraries, museums, and public agencies. We are learning about our state all the time — especially in such areas as ethnic history and appreciation of the environment. This book can be a good starting place for learning more. If you wish, you can reach beyond this book for a greater appreciation of our state's history. You can also use your understanding to gain more insight into the challenges that lie ahead for you and for all of us.

David L. Moberly,
Superintendent

TABLE OF CONTENTS

The varied natural environment of Washington provides opportunities for boating, skiing, and many other outdoor sports. The mountains, the ocean, and other geographic features affect the weather. In what other ways does geography affect our daily lives?

UNIT 1

THE NATURAL ENVIRONMENT

There are many stories in the history of Washington State. People of several different races, cultures, and historical periods have lived here. They have all lived on the same land, but they used that land in very different ways.

This unit will cover the main features of Washington's natural environment: the climate, the location, the main land and water features, and the important natural resources. It also includes some stories about the history of the land and a description of the main geographic regions of our state.

To see how the people in Washington use their environment today, you can turn to Unit 11. In that unit you will learn about the many modern industries that depend on the natural resources of our state. This unit will focus more on the environment itself. In this way, it will set the stage for the historical units that follow. As you read those units, think about how geography has influenced the lives of people who lived here. How does it influence your own life today?

This unit has four sections:

1. The History of the Land
2. The Importance of Location
3. The Climate of Washington
4. Natural Regions

SECTION 1: THE HISTORY OF THE LAND

Geology And Our Changing Landscape

Can you imagine the State of Washington without Mount Rainier, Puget Sound, or the Grand Coulee? These features of the landscape seem permanent to most people. But millions of years ago, the land that we call Washington State looked very different. Much of it was under water at times. The climate was different, too. The land was once covered with tropical jungles, and animals such as rhinoceros, camels, and buffaloes roamed this part of North America.

Geologists are scientists who study how the earth was formed. Geologists know that the landscape is not as permanent as it seems. They know the earth's surface has been changing constantly ever since the earth was formed. During this long period of time, many mountains have been pushed up and then slowly worn away. Water has sometimes covered parts of the land and then retreated.

The processes involved in geological change are usually extremely slow. We don't have to worry that we will wake up in the morning and find that the mountains have disappeared. But it is true that they haven't always been here, and even now, little bits of them are worn away each year.

In other places the land is being built up. When volcanoes erupt, new rock is piled up on the surface of the land. Whenever there is a flood, a new layer of mud is deposited. These layers may build up until the land is much higher than it was before. Rivers and winds move small rocks and dirt and dust from one place to another.

1. What is a geologist?
2. Name some ways that the earth changes.

GINKGO PETRIFIED FOREST

The ginkgo is a tall tree with thick, fan-shaped leaves. For centuries, it has been planted near Chinese and Japanese temples, and it was considered a sacred tree. More recently, ginkgos have been imported from Asia and planted in the United States. No ginkgo trees have grown wild in historic times.

However, millions of years ago, a forest of ginkgo trees grew near Vantage, Washington. At that time, the climate was tropical and the land was swampy. Dead and fallen trees lay covered by the waters of the swamp. Then the whole forest was covered by lava. Slowly, over many, many years, minerals replaced the wood fibers. Finally, the whole log became petrified, or turned to rock. The Ginkgo Petrified Forest tells an unusual story about the geological history of this state.

Reading The Rocks

How do the geologists know about these geological changes? They study the rocks. The earth's surface has a language that geologists are learning to read, somewhat as a person might learn to read English, Spanish, or Japanese.

For example, the coal that has been found in Western Washington requires special conditions in order to form. It starts in a warm climate and a damp location. Here many plants must grow and die until there are layers and layers of them. The land must sink slowly so that tons of rock can settle, little by little, over the buried plants. The process takes many millions of years. When geologists find coal, they know that all these changes have taken place in that area.

In the language of geology, then, coal tells a lot about the history of an area. Other rock formations and mineral deposits can be "read" by geologists in a similar way. Each of them provides clues about how a part of the earth's surface was formed.

3. Why do geologists study rocks?
4. What do Washington's coal deposits tell us about the state's geological history?

How Were Mountains In Washington Formed?

Geologists have something surprising to say about the mountains in Washington State: they are very new. The Olympics are one of the youngest mountain ranges in the world. Both the Olympic Mountains and the Cascades were pushed up just a few million years ago. Most of the world's mountains are much older.

Geologists do not agree about how Washington's mountain ranges were pushed up, or uplifted. Many theories are being studied and tested. But most experts do agree about the formation of Mount Rainier and the other volcanic peaks of Western Washington.

Deep in the earth there is rock so hot that it has actually melted. This liquid rock is under pressure, and sometimes it rises through weak points on the earth's surface. The molten (melted) rock that reaches the surface of the earth is called lava.

Lava can emerge in different ways. Sometimes it seeps up slowly and spreads evenly over the land. Eastern Washington has been buried under many layers of slowly flowing lava in the past. Much of the rock that makes up the Cascades emerged in this way.

At times, lava erupts much more violently. This process could be compared to popping the cork on a champagne bottle. The lava shoots up suddenly with great force. As the lava falls and cools, it piles up into a giant cone. Mountains formed in this way are called volcanoes. Mount Rainier has popped its cork and erupted many times. Each time, fiery hot rock was thrown into the air and piled higher around its base. At one point, the mountain even blew its top. The peak exploded and collapsed, leaving Rainier about 2,000 feet shorter. That is why the mountain is somewhat flat on top today.

The Cowlitz Indians have a legend about this explosion. They say that White Mountain (Mount Adams) was a man who had two wives, the peaks we now call Mount St. Helens and Mount Rainier. Mount St. Helens started throwing fire at her rival, and Rainier threw it back. They kept doing this. Finally, Rainier got hit so badly that her head broke off. According to the legend, Mount St. Helens got the best of her.

We could say that the Northwest Indians were the first geologists in Washington. They wondered where the landforms came from and had explanations of their origins.

5. What is lava?
6. Name two ways that lava reaches the earth's surface. Give an example of each.

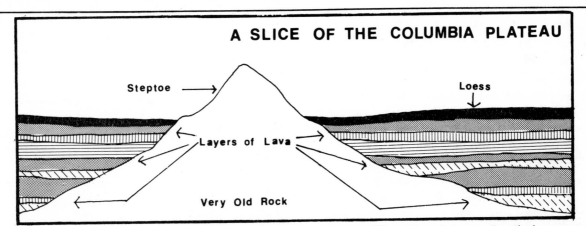

A SLICE OF THE COLUMBIA PLATEAU

Steptoe →

Loess ↓

← Layers of Lava →

Very Old Rock

The old rock of the Columbia Plateau was covered by layer after layer of slowly flowing lava. Some of these sheets of lava are only a few inches thick. Others range up to 200 feet in thickness.

Later, layers of dust were carried by the wind and deposited on top of lava flows. These dust deposits are called loess. The loess of Eastern Washington is very good farming soil.

Some of the old rock was not entirely covered by lava. Some of the high places, that used to be mountain peaks, still stick up above the lava rock. These half-covered, ancient mountain peaks are called steptoes, after Steptoe Butte in Eastern Washington.

The jagged shape of the Olympics and the Cascades shows that they are "young" mountain ranges. Older mountains, such as the Appalachians, have more curved and gentle slopes.

How Did The Ice Age Affect The Puget Sound Area?

At different times in its history the earth has experienced periods called ice ages. During these periods of time, great moving sheets of ice called glaciers covered large parts of the earth. Washington was partly covered by ice-age glaciers at least four times. These glaciers changed the surface of the land in many parts of the state, and their effects were especially important in the Puget Sound area.

Before the last ice age, Puget Sound did not exist as we know it now. The land between the Olympic Mountains and the Cascades probably looked like the river valleys south of Olympia. The glaciers acted like giant bulldozers in slow motion. As they moved, they scraped away soil, rocks, and even large boulders. They dug out valleys and flattened hills.

The glaciers that covered the Puget Sound area came from the north and moved south to about where Olympia now stands and then retreated to the north again as the climate grew warmer. It is no accident that Puget Sound, Lake Washington, and other nearby bodies of water stretch in a north to south direction. Before the glaciers came, both Puget Sound and Lake Washington were probably river beds. The glacier enlarged them as it moved southward.

At its greatest point, the ice was about 4,000 feet thick over the Seattle area. (That's about seven times the height of the Space Needle.) The heavy ice moved, crushed, and tumbled the rocks in its path. Small rocks and large boulders were carried great distances, and when the glacier retreated, it left behind patches of rocky trash called till. Today, these irregular layers of till cover much of the Puget Sound lowlands.

There are still some smaller glaciers in Washington today. They are found on the sides of the highest mountains. Mount Rainier, for example, has twenty-six glaciers — more than any mountain in the United States outside Alaska.

7. What is an ice age?
8. What part of Washington was most affected by the last ice age? Name some effects.

What Was The Spokane Flood?

Most geological changes take place very, very slowly, over millions of years. It is rare for the land to change much in a human lifetime. But Washington was once the scene of a highly unusual and dramatic event — a giant flood. It happened at the end of the last ice age (about 18,000 to 20,000 years ago). The climate was becoming warmer, and the glaciers were beginning to melt.

Usually the water from the melting glaciers would flow into existing rivers and then into the ocean. But during that time, the Clark Fork River became blocked with ice near the present Idaho-Montana border. Since the water could not escape, it began to back up behind the ice dam and formed a great lake. Geologists have

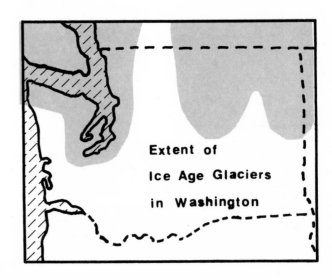

Extent of
Ice Age Glaciers
in Washington

called this Lake Missoula. The lake grew larger as it was fed by rain, mountain streams, and water from melting glaciers. It finally covered about 3,000 square miles — much larger than Puget Sound.

Water began to spill over the top of the ice dam, and the dam began to wear away. The warmer climate was beginning to melt the dam, and the lake water was putting great pressure on it. Suddenly (very suddenly in geological time) the ice collapsed, and the whole lake came crashing out! The lake was quickly emptied — possibly within just two days. It's hard to imagine so much water moving so fast. The flow of that water was about ten times as great as the flow of all the present rivers of the world combined!

The enormous power of the rushing water changed the landscape of Eastern Washington in many ways. In a very short period of time, the water dug out a channel 50 miles long and up to 900 feet deep. Today this channel is known as the Grand Coulee. The flood also washed away

Mount Rainier has more glaciers than any mountain in the United States, outside Alaska. This photo shows part of the Nisqually Glacier — one of Mount Rainier's largest. Notice how the glacier has scraped away land on both sides of the valley so that no trees grow there. Also notice the U-shaped curves of the glacial valley. Can you find any glacial valleys in the other photos in this book?

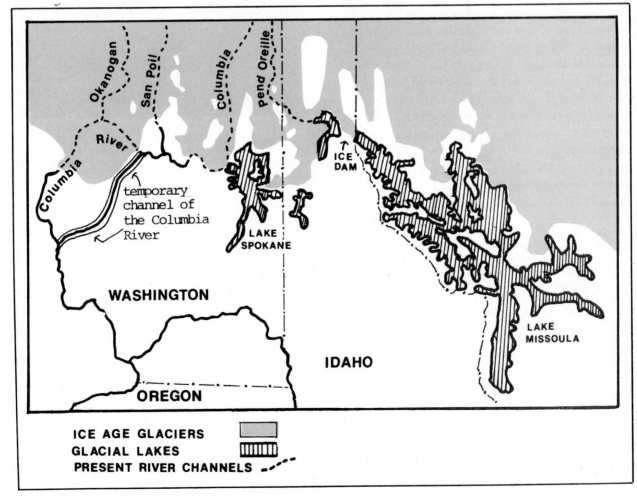

all the soil from parts of the plateau, leaving only the rock beneath. Today, this portion of Washington State is called the Channeled Scablands. From an airplane, it is easy to see why this name was chosen. The land seems to be covered with giant scabs, separated by old river channels.

Many of the Northwest Indian tribes have legends about a great flood. Perhaps the flood they were talking about was not this one. There is no proof that humans lived in this area at that time. But surely, if any humans witnessed the event, they would have found it worth describing in legends.

9. How were the Channeled Scablands formed?

How Is Geology Important Today?

For great drama, few things can compare with the floods and fiery explosions of Washington's past. But why is all this important today? First, understanding the history of our land can help us to predict its future and to use it wisely in the present. For example, it is important to study the structure of the earth before deciding where to locate buildings and roads. Geology is also important because it helps us understand how valuable resources are deposited and where they may be found. Knowing how long it takes for minerals such as coal to form should help us understand the need to use natural resources more wisely.

10. Why is geology important?

This photo shows the Grand Coulee as it looked before the Grand Coulee Dam was built. Can you pick out the old river channel? Imagine a huge river rushing through this desert. The force of the water carried away much of the soil from the land. The area in the front of this photo is an example of the Channeled Scablands.

MODERN GEOLOGICAL DRAMAS

Geological dramas are not just a thing of the past in Washington State. Scientists tell us that our volcanic peaks could still be active. Mount Rainier, Mount St. Helens, or the others might erupt again within our lifetime. It's also possible that mild volcanic activity might melt the ice on these peaks. The meltwater would pick up tons of soil and gravel and it could cause a disastrous mudflow. One mudflow that started on Mount Rainier covered land all the way to Auburn!

In the middle 1970's, steam began escaping from several places on Mount Baker. Part of the park was closed off for safety, and geologists set up instruments to study this activity. No one knew for sure whether an eruption or mudflow might follow.

Another dramatic geological event occurred in 1963. A huge chunk split off from the mountain called Little Tahoma, the small peak located at the foot of Mount Rainier. Several avalanches and rockfalls came after the first huge crash.

Floods still occur from time to time and cause a lot of damage. There were major floods here in 1876, 1894, 1948, and 1975. The 1948 flood destroyed the entire city of Vanport on the Columbia River. In 1975, waters covered most of the river valleys in Western Washington. Great numbers of farm animals drowned and many people lost their homes.

Another natural disaster that sometimes strikes the Northwest is the earthquake. A "quake" in 1949 caused 11 big breaks in Seattle's water mains. In 1965, a more serious earthquake shook the Space Needle, knocked out power lines, cracked buildings, and shattered windows around the city. Three people died, and there was 12.5 million dollars worth of damage.

SECTION 2: THE IMPORTANCE OF LOCATION

How Has Location Affected Washington's History?

Washington's relative location has been an important factor in its history. To understand why, find our state on a world map. How far is it from New York, Boston, Detroit, and Chicago? How far is it from the West Coast urban centers at Los Angeles, San Francisco, or San Diego? How far is it from Seattle/Tacoma or Spokane to the big cities of Europe? Compare these distances to the distance from New York to Europe.

Washington State is a long way from most of the world's big population centers. This is a problem even today, in an age of rapid transportation. It used to be a much bigger problem.

Try to imagine how difficult it was to travel from the East Coast of the United States to Washington without roads, railroads, airplanes, or even the Panama Canal! Suppose you chose to travel by ship. You would have to sail all the way around the tip of South America. That meant several thousand extra miles and many added dangers. What about travelling by land? Without roads, the Rocky Mountains and the Cascades — and even the gentle Appalachians — were difficult to cross. They acted as barriers to discourage people from travelling west during early periods of our history.

These travel difficulties caused Washington to remain an isolated, frontier area longer than most parts of our nation. People in the thirteen colonies knew nothing about Puget Sound, for example. It was almost 10 years after the United States had won its freedom that the first English ship sailed into Puget Sound. And, it was 300 years after Columbus first landed in the "New World" when an American ship sailed into the mouth of the Columbia River.

11. Why did Washington remain isolated for so long?
12. What is relative location?

How Has Location Affected The Economy?

Relative location has affected this state's economy in several ways. For example, location has had a great impact on Washington's trading patterns. There was little early trade between Washington and Europe or the Eastern United States. Travel was too difficult. But Washington

How did the high Rocky Mountains help cut Washington off from the rest of the country? What modern forms of transportation make it easier to cross these mountains today?

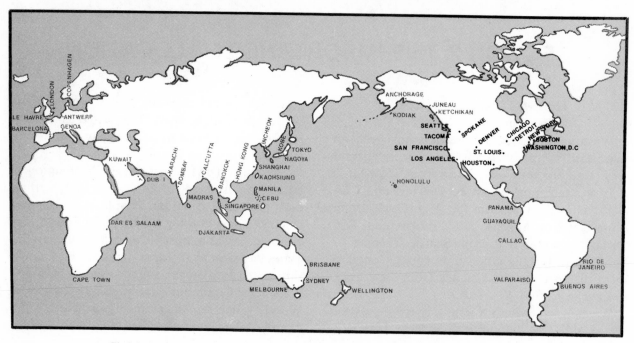

Find the land around the edge of the Pacific Ocean. This is the Pacific Rim. What big cities are located on the Pacific Rim? How is this map different from other world maps?

is relatively close to Alaska, Japan, and the port cities on the Pacific Ocean. A large part of Washington's trade is carried on with the states and countries of the Pacific Rim. The Pacific Rim is illustrated by the map on this page; it includes the lands that lie on the edge of the Pacific Ocean.

Pacific trade has been important to the Northwest ever since the first Europeans came here.

Natural resources and locations have affected the history of Washington and Alaska in somewhat similar ways. Few people were willing to make the long trip to Alaska until gold was discovered there in 1897. More recently, the discovery of oil has attracted people and businesses to this distant state. The photo above shows the town of Valdez, Alaska during the gold rush. It is now an important oil-shipping port. What natural resources attracted people to Washington?

Those early ship captains bought sea otter furs in the Northwest and sold them in Asia. Seattle is sometimes called the "Gateway to Alaska" or "Gateway to Asia." These nicknames show that Pacific trade is still important today.

Washington's relative location has affected its exploration and trading patterns. It has also helped determine how many people make their living here.

Washington industries could not compete with industries located near the big population centers. Prices for Northwest goods were too high. It was expensive to import raw materials (such as iron and cotton), and it was expensive to ship Northwest products out.

Because of this, many of the key Washington industries don't even try to compete. They sell their goods and services locally, or they specialize in industries based on local natural resources. These industries survive because they provide products that are not readily available in other areas. The forest-based industries such as lumbering and pulp mills are good examples.

13. What is the Pacific Rim?
14. Why is a large part of Washington's trade carried on with lands of the Pacific Rim?
15. Why was it difficult for Washington industries to compete with industries located near the big population centers?
16. Why are natural resource industries so important to Washington's economy?

PLATE 1 — The Washington coast.

PLATE 2 — The state capitol building in Olympia.

PLATE 3 — Highway across the Cascades.

PLATE 4 — The Olympic rain forest.

PLATE 5 — The San Juan Islands.

PLATE 6 — Wheat land in the Palouse Hills.

PLATE 7 —
The Palouse River Canyon.

PLATE 8 — The Grand Coulee Dam.

SECTION 3: THE CLIMATE OF WASHINGTON

What Causes The Different Climates Of Washington?

Ask people from out of state what they know about Seattle. They'll probably say, "It rains all the time." Mark Twain once said, "The nicest winter I ever spent was a summer in Seattle." He was talking about the rain, too. Lewis and Clark recorded 31 days of rain in a row, when they were here in the Northwest.

It is true that it rains many days each year in Western Washington. But Eastern Washington has quite a dry climate. The average rainfall varies a lot in different parts of the state.

The three main causes of the different Washington climates are the winds, the ocean, and the mountains. Most winds that blow over Washington come from the Pacific Ocean. Winds which blow in the same direction most of the time — as these winds do — are called prevailing winds. Washington's prevailing winds are also called westerly winds, because they come from the west.

As these westerly winds pass over the ocean, they pick up lots of moisture. The winds blow against the Olympic Mountains and the Willapa Hills. The air must rise to get over them. As air rises, it cools. This cooling causes the moisture in the air to condense, and it falls to the ground as snow or rain. This gives the land near the coast very heavy rainfall. Along the Wynooche

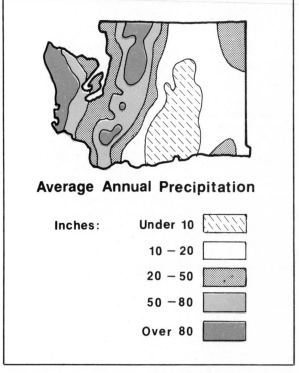

Average Annual Precipitation

Inches:

Under 10	⬚
10 — 20	⬚
20 — 50	⬚
50 — 80	⬚
Over 80	⬛

River north of the city of Aberdeen the average rainfall is over 150 inches. This is the highest average annual rainfall in the United States.

After the winds cross the Olympics, the air can drop again. Very little rain falls on the Olympics' eastern, or leeward slope (the side away from the wind). This is called a rain shadow.

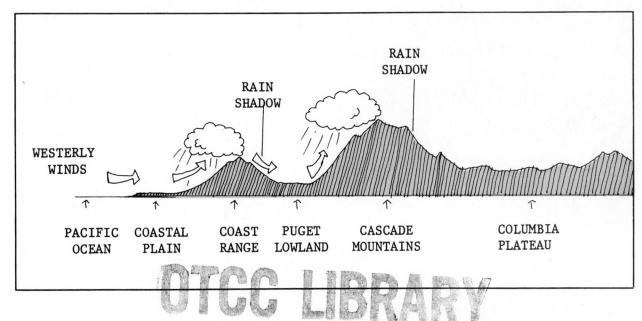

RAIN SHADOW

RAIN SHADOW

WESTERLY WINDS

PACIFIC OCEAN   COASTAL PLAIN   COAST RANGE   PUGET LOWLAND   CASCADE MOUNTAINS   COLUMBIA PLATEAU

The winds must rise again to get over the Cascade Mountains, and the process is repeated. The western side of the Cascades gets a lot of precipitation.

There isn't much moisture left in the air by the time it reaches the eastern side of the Cascades. Because of this, Eastern Washington is much drier than the western part. In some places, the average rainfall is less than 10 inches a year!

17. What is the rainiest area of the United States?
18. Explain why the west side of the mountains gets more rain than the eastern side.
19. Define these terms: prevailing winds, leeward, rain shadow.

Natural Heating And Air-Conditioning

The wind, ocean, and mountains influence our average temperatures as well as rainfall. Large bodies of water such as the Pacific Ocean stay at about the same temperature all year round. In winter, the ocean temperature is warmer than that of the land; in summer, the ocean is cooler. The prevailing winds bring the mild ocean temperatures to the coast. It's like natural heating and air-conditioning the year around.

As a result, Western Washington has mild temperatures. The summers are not too hot and the winters are rarely cold. Temperatures on Tatoosh Island — at the northwest corner of the state — are a good example of how the ocean can affect temperatures. This island is located quite far north, yet it has a growing season that is 306 days long! (The growing season is the average number of days between the last freezing temperatures of the spring and the first autumn frost.) There have been some years when there was not even a frost.

Geographers call this a marine climate. Its main features are mild temperatures and heavy rainfall. Marine climates are usually found in the middle latitudes (between 40 and 60 degrees) on the west coasts of continents. What are some other places in the world that you'd expect to have a marine climate?

20. Why does the Washington coast have mild temperatures?
21. What are the main features of a marine climate?

What Is A Continental Climate?

East of the Cascades, the ocean does not have much influence on temperature. Summers are much hotter in the eastern part of the state. Winter temperatures are near or below freezing for longer periods of time. Away from the ocean, there is a greater difference in temperature between day and night, as well as between summer and winter. This is because land areas heat and cool more rapidly than bodies of water.

Geographers call this a continental climate because of the inland location. Large areas of land in North America, Europe, and Asia have similar climates.

Look at the vegetation along the river, and see if you can tell which side of the Cascades this photograph represents. Is it Eastern Washington or Western Washington?

22. Why does Eastern Washington have hotter summers and colder winters than the Washington coast?
23. Why is this called a continental climate?

___

How Do Latitude And Altitude Affect Our Climate?

Geographers say that the continental United States has a middle latitude location, since it is about midway between the North Pole and the Equator. Temperatures usually get colder close to the poles and warmer close to the Equator.

In spite of our middle latitude location, there are mountains in Washington that are cold and snowy all year round. This is because altitude (the distance above sea-level) affects the climate, too. The average temperature drops about one degree Fahrenheit for every 300 foot increase in altitude. Moving higher up a mountain is like moving closer to the poles, in the way the climate is affected. Sometimes geographers use the term vertical climate (up and down) to describe this effect.

24. What does it mean to say that Washington State has a middle latitude location?
25. How does latitude affect climate?

Based on your understanding of vertical climate, explain why there is snow on tops of some mountains all year around. Why do the trees only grow at lower altitudes?

SECTION 4: NATURAL REGIONS

How Do Regions Help In Understanding Washington's Geography?

The earth's surface has a variety of physical environments. There are many contrasts, and it is often difficult to describe large areas. The job becomes easier when working with smaller parts. Geographers use the term region to talk about parts of the earth's surface such as the Pacific Northwest, Western Washington, or the Columbia Basin. A particular area that shares common geographical features makes up a natural region. For example, the land in a particular region might have light rainfall, extremely high or low temperatures, rolling hills, and poor soil. That region ends where those common features end.

Washington State is part of a natural region of North America called the Pacific Northwest. This region includes the states of Oregon, Idaho, and part of Montana, as well as Washington. Some geographers also include part of British Columbia. Find this region on a map. In the United States, the Pacific Northwest stretches from the Pacific Ocean east to the crest of the Rocky Mountains and from the Canadian border to the southern boundary of Oregon and Idaho.

The states which make up the Pacific Northwest share many things in common. For example, the Columbia River unites the region in an important way. Many rivers of the region flow into the Columbia. These rivers are called tributaries. Together, the Columbia and its tributaries drain most of the land in the Pacific Northwest.

26. What is a natural region?
27. What states make up the Pacific Northwest region?

What Are Natural and Political Boundaries?

The eastern and western boundaries of the Pacific Northwest region are formed by natural features of the environment. These are the Rocky Mountains and the Pacific Ocean. They are called natural boundaries.

The north and south boundaries of the region are not natural. They were created by people. Since these lines form the borders between different states or different countries, they are called political boundaries. (Other political boundaries include borders of cities and counties.)

28. What is a natural boundary?
29. What is a political boundary?

What Are The Geographical Regions Of Washington State?

Washington State is part of a larger natural region called the Pacific Northwest. But Washington can also be divided into smaller regions with common geographical features. Sometimes people think of Western Washington as a region because of a common climate, common resources, or common geological background. The eastern half of the state forms a similar region and is often called the Inland Empire. At times, it is more accurate to talk about even smaller regions. The five smaller geographic regions of Washington are the Puget Sound Lowland, the Cascade Range, the Coastal Region, the Columbia Plateau, and the Okanogan Highlands.

30. Name the five geographical regions of Washington.

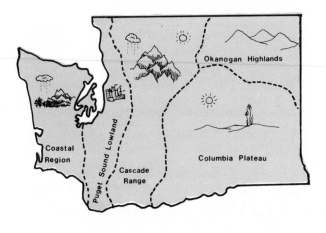

Coastal Region

The Coastal Region is bordered on the west by the Pacific Ocean, and it extends east to the Puget Sound Lowlands. It reaches from the Strait of Juan de Fuca to the Columbia River. This region is part of a larger natural region that continues down along the Oregon Coast and north into British Columbia. In Washington State, the northern part of the coastal region is called the Olympic Peninsula. The southern part is referred to as Southwest Washington or the Willapa Hills.

The Coastal Region has three parts: the Coastal Plain, the Olympic Mountains, and the Willapa Hills.

The Coastal Plain is a narrow strip of lowland that runs along the Pacific Ocean and the Strait of Juan de Fuca. There are miles of ocean

Many of Washington's beaches are marked by these huge rocks. Little by little, the force of the water is wearing these rocks away.

beaches and two sheltered bays: Grays Harbor and Willapa Bay. Around Grays Harbor and the Strait of Juan de Fuca are some areas where the plain is wider. This is the location of the best farmland in the Coastal Region. Shellfish such as oysters, clams, and crabs are found along the shoreline, inlets, and shallow waters. Salmon and sole are among the fish found in the waters offshore.

Behind the Coastal Plain are the Olympic Mountains and the Willapa Hills. These highland areas are part of the Coast Range which reaches down into Oregon and Northern California. Most of the mountains of the Coast Range are fairly low, but the Olympics are an exception. Several of the peaks are snowcapped year round. Mount Olympus, the tallest, rises to 7,954 feet above sea level. Glaciers helped to carve the sharp, jagged peaks and the valleys which extend outward in all directions from the center of the Olympic Range. At lower altitudes, there are forests of spruce, fir, hemlock, and cedar.

The western slopes of the Olympics receive the heaviest rainfall. Rain forests are found in some of the river valleys which open onto the ocean. There are few places in the world like these forests. The branches of trees are covered with moss. Ferns, fungus, and other plants cover almost every square foot of the forest floor.

The Chehalis River and Grays Harbor separate the Olympic Mountains from the Willapa Hills in the south. The Willapa Hills are much lower than the Olympics. Their highest point is less than 3,000 feet above sea level. They are less rugged than the Olympics, too. The Willapa Hills receive somewhat less rainfall than the northern part of the region.

The climate of the Coastal Region is mild except at higher altitudes. Westerly winds bring rain and fog. The Coastal Region is the wettest part of Washington State. Except in the rain shadows, there is heavy rainfall throughout most of the region. Many places on the Olympic Peninsula receive more than 100 inches of rain per year. Temperatures seldom fall below freezing, and snow is rare. Summers are cool. There are few days when the temperature gets above 70 degrees. Because of mild temperatures, the lowland areas in the Coastal Region have long growing seasons.

The vegetation of the Olympic rain forest is quite unusual. Few other places in the world get so much rain as the western side of the Olympic Peninsula.

31. Describe the three main parts of the Coastal Region.
32. Which part of the Coastal Region receives the most precipitation?

The Puget Sound Lowland

The Puget Sound Lowland is bordered on the west by the Coastal Region and on the east by the Cascade Range. This region stretches from the Canadian border on the north to the Columbia River on the south. It is actually part of a larger region called the Western Lowlands, an area which extends southward into the state of Oregon and northward into British Columbia. Most of the land has an altitude of less than 500 feet. The Puget Sound Lowland is also referred to as the Puget Lowland, the Puget Basin, or the Puget Trough.

Puget Sound is a large inland sea with many inlets and bays. There are several good, deep, protected harbors around Puget Sound, including Elliott Bay, Bellingham Bay, Commencement Bay, and Discovery Bay. The land around Puget Sound is an area of river valleys and rolling hills. Most of the land used to be covered by dense forest. After the forests are cleared, several of the river valleys offer wide areas of flat land covered with fertile soil. The surrounding hillsides are covered with evergreen forests of Douglas fir, hemlock, and red cedar. There are many fresh and saltwater fish and shellfish in this region.

Puget Sound is dotted with islands. The largest, Whidbey Island, is the second longest island in the continental United States (after Long Island, which is near New York City). The region also has many large and small lakes, including Lake Washington, Lake Sammamish, and Lake Whatcom.

The climate of the Puget Sound Lowland can be described as mild. Summer temperatures are usually in the 70's. In the winter, temperatures average between 40 and 55 degrees.

Clouds often cover the Puget Sound Lowland. It rains often, too, except in some areas located in rain shadows. Average precipitation ranges between 35 and 45 inches a year. (This is not actually very high. Chicago gets slightly more rain than Seattle, on the average.)

The Puget Sound Lowland has a long growing season. Some areas have an average of more than 250 days per year between frosts.

33. Name some deep protected harbors on Puget Sound.
34. List several natural resources of the Puget Sound Lowland.

The Cascade Range

The Cascade Range stretches across Washington State in a north to south direction. On the west it is bordered by the Puget Sound Lowland and on the east by the Columbia Basin and the Okanogan Highlands. Like the Coastal Region and the Puget Sound Lowland, the Cascade Range also extends into Oregon and British Columbia. In the north it is up to 100 miles wide, but in the south it narrows to about 50 miles in width. Altitude usually averages between 4,000 and 8,000 feet above sea level. The tallest and best-known peak is Mount Rainier which rises to 14,410 feet.

Mount Rainier is a volcano. So are several other outstanding peaks in the Cascades, including: Mount Adams (12,307 feet), Mount Baker (10,788 feet), Glacier Peak (10,658 feet), and Mount St. Helens (9,677 feet). Volcanic activity was important in forming the entire Cascade Range. And other great forces, deep within the earth, helped push up the mountains. (See Unit 1, Section 1 for more information.)

Glaciers and rivers have also helped form the Cascades, especially in the northern part of the region. Glaciers make curved or U-shaped valleys. River erosion causes V-shaped valleys, or trenches. There are many deep and narrow valleys with steep sides in the Cascades.

There are also many lakes of all sizes. Some are so small they don't even have names. Lake Chelan, the largest, is 50 miles long and 1,500 feet deep. ("Chelan" is an Indian word meaning "deep water.")

The Cascade Range divides the state into two almost equal parts. The Columbia River cuts a deep gorge through the range along the Washington-Oregon border, and there are natural passes through the mountains. Still the Cascades act as a barrier which separates eastern and western parts of the state. The western part has a rainy marine climate; the eastern part is dry and has more extreme temperatures.

The kinds of vegetation in the Cascades show differences in rainfall. The western slopes have thick forests of Douglas fir, hemlock, and other trees which need moisture. On the eastern side, the ponderosa pine is more common. It is a tree that grows well in drier climates.

This is a region that is rich in natural resources. The natural beauty of the Cascade Range and the vast evergreen forests are probably the resources that are first noticed. But there are also minerals within the ground that are not so easily seen. For example, beds of coal extend through the region. Sand and gravel are found in large amounts because of the glacial activity that has taken place in this area. There are also deposits of gold, silver, lead, zinc, and other minerals. Numerous streams and rivers carry off water from the melting snows and glaciers and provide spawning grounds for many kinds of fish.

What evidence of glaciers can you find in this photo of the Cascade Mountains? What natural resources do you see?

The Columbia River as it flows through Klickitat County. What features help to identify this area as part of the Columbia Plateau?

35. How are the climate and vegetation different on the east and west sides of the Cascades?

36. Name some forces that have helped shape the Cascade mountains.

The Columbia Plateau

The Columbia Plateau lies to the east of the Cascade Range. It covers most of the eastern part of Washington State except for the Okanogan Highlands in the north. The Plateau region reaches east to the foothills of the Rockies and south into Central Oregon and Idaho. The Columbia River, of course, is the major feature of the landscape. This is one of the great rivers of the world, both in length and in the size of the land area that it drains. Some important tributaries of the Columbia are the Snake, Yakima, Wenatchee, Cowlitz, and Spokane rivers.

This region is sometimes called the Columbia Basin or the Columbia Intermountain Region. (The region is not a true plateau because it is not flat and because no mountains rise steeply from the sides of it.) The land surface includes hills, small plateaus, and broad valleys. Most of the land is between 1,000 and 5,000 feet above sea level.

In the southeast corner of the state, the Blue Mountains rise above the plateau. They are lower than the Olympics or the Cascades, but they are very rugged. They are often treated as a separate geographic region.

The Columbia Plateau is one of the largest areas of volcanic rock in the world. During millions of years, many layers of lava flowed out over the old rock of the plateau.

Deep soil now covers the layers of volcanic rock. This soil was carried by the wind and deposited little by little, over a very long period of time. In some places in Southeastern Washington, the soil is as much as 150 feet deep. This makes it one of the world's best wheat-growing areas.

In many places, though, the soil has been eroded away by dust storms, rivers, human activities and, long ago, by the great Spokane Flood. (See Unit 1, Section 1.)

The soils of the Columbia Basin are generally fertile, but the climate is quite dry. The Cascade Mountains keep winds from bringing large amounts of moisture to the area. The western part of the basin is in the rain shadow of the Cascades, and it has an arid climate. Rainfall may be 10 inches or less a year. The natural vegetation is mainly sagebrush and bunch grass.

Rainfall increases toward the eastern part of the region. In this part, the climate changes from arid to semiarid. Yearly averages for precipitation can range up to 20 inches. Prairie grass is the common vegetation. There are forests of pine in areas having greater rainfall. Most farms in the region must use irrigation or special dry farming methods. (See Unit 11, Section 4.)

37. Discuss the climate and vegetation of the Columbia Plateau.

38. Name some important tributaries of the Columbia.

The Okanogan Highlands

The Okanogan Highlands Region of Northeast Washington is a region of hills and mountains. The landscape is not as rugged as the Cascades, and altitudes are lower. Summits of mountains range from 4,000 to 8,000 feet above sea level. This region reaches from the Cascades on the west to the Washington-Idaho border on the east. Included is all of the land between the Canadian border on the north and the Columbia and Spokane Rivers on the south. Sometimes the area is considered part of the Rocky Mountain Region which stretches across Northern and Central Idaho and into Western Montana and British Columbia. In fact, the Selkirk Mountains — in the eastern part of the highlands — are the beginning of the Rocky Mountains.

Important features of the Okanogan Highlands are the rivers which flow across the region from north to south. The chief rivers in this group are the Okanogan, the Columbia, the San Poil and the Pend Oreille. They begin in the mountains and run through long, narrow valleys. These valleys are often called trench valleys.

The geological forces that shaped the Okanogan Highlands also left many valuable minerals. Deposits of lead and zinc in the Pend Oreille Valley, for example, are among the largest in the world. Other metals of this region include copper, gold, and silver. In addition, there are large amounts of clay, sand, gravel, and limestone.

The Okanogan Highlands Region is partly in the Cascades' rain shadow. This location has a big effect on its climate. Look at the map on page 17 that shows precipitation in the state of Washington. It is easy to see that this region has a much drier climate than the regions of Western Washington. But it is not as dry as the Columbia Basin. This is due to the higher altitudes. Rainfall averages between 15 and 25 inches a year. Areas in the eastern part of the Highlands have heavier rainfall than places near the Cascade Range. Most of this precipitation falls during the winter and spring.

The Cascades also give the region a greater difference between summer and winter temperatures than is found in regions to the west. Mild winds from the Pacific are blocked by the Cascades. As a result, summer temperatures often climb into the 80's and 90's. In the winter, polar air enters the region, and temperatures drop below zero. Heavy snowfall is common.

The climate of the Okanogan Highlands, of course, affects the natural vegetation of the region. Since it is drier and since the growing season is shorter than in the regions of Western Washington, vegetation is not as dense. But there is enough rainfall for some kinds of trees to grow, and there are large forests of pine and some fir. Forests in the western part of the Highlands are sparse (thin) because of the light precipitation. Land in the eastern section is more heavily forested since it gets more moisture. In much of the region there is little underbrush. Instead, the forest floor is often covered with grasses.

39. How does climate affect the vegetation of the Okanogan Highlands?
40. What are the major natural resources of this region?

A farm in the Okanogan Highlands. How is the geography of this region different from that of the Columbia Plateau?

*At several locations in Washington State and along the North Pacific coast,
there is evidence of the cultures of the first people who lived here.*

UNIT 2

THE FIRST PEOPLE
IN WASHINGTON

The first people who lived on the land we now call Washington State were American Indians — the Native Americans. This unit deals with the Native American way of life before other people came to the Pacific Northwest.

This unit has three sections:

1. Origins and Names
2. Coastal Cultures
3. Plateau Cultures

As you read, compare the beliefs, values, knowledge, traditions, and skills of Native Americans to those of other cultures in America. Compare, for example, how Indians and non-Indians use the environment to fulfill their basic needs.

Ask yourself these questions: What can we learn from Native American cultures? What problems might develop from differences between Indian and non-Indian cultures?

SECTION 1: ORIGINS AND NAMES

Where Did The First People Come From?

Most people at some time in their lives ask the question: ''How did people first get here?'' The way that we answer this question is determined by our culture — a way of living with the environment, based on our knowledge, values, beliefs, and traditions.

You are probably aware that people have been living here in Washington for a long time. Have you ever wondered how the first people got here? The earliest inhabitants of this land were the people we now call Native Americans, or Indians. The many Indian cultures had different explanations of their origins. The Skagit legend below is one example. Another explanation, from Eastern Washington tribes, may be found in the legend about Coyote at the end of this unit.

1. What factors determine the way we explain our origins?

Other Possible Origins

Other cultures have different explanations of how people got to America. When Columbus first landed on a Caribbean island, he thought he was in India. This is why he called the people who lived here Indians. But Europeans soon realized that Columbus had actually landed on a new continent. They realized that this continent was inhabited by a race of people that Europeans knew nothing about. Based on European knowledge and beliefs about the world, European thinkers began trying to explain where American Indians had come from. One popular theory was that they were descendants of one or more of the ten lost tribes of Israel who were mentioned in the Bible.

Since then, there have been several other theories about the origin of the first Americans. Today there is a science that is concerned with the origins and cultures of the various humans who have lived on earth. This science is called anthropology. Most anthropologists believe that the first Americans migrated to this continent from Asia.

This is their explanation: During the ice ages, many thousands of years ago, more water stayed on land in the form of ice. (See Unit 1, Section 1 for more information on the ice ages in Washington State.) At these times, the oceans were shallower than they are now. It was almost like a very low tide around the world. Much land that is now beneath the ocean was above water during the ice ages. This probably included a large piece of land between Asia and Alaska. People could walk across this land bridge from one continent to another. Then they could have walked south from Alaska to all parts of North and South America. Anthropologists believe that these migrations took place during several ice ages, over a period of many thousands of years.

There is also evidence which suggests that a few people crossed the seas to the Americas from Asia, Europe, and the Middle East. Some of these visits may have occurred more than 2,000 years before Columbus! (See next page.)

CHANGER AND THE ORIGIN OF THE SKAGITS

Long ago there was a great flood. Only five people survived. A son was born to a man and woman among the survivors. He became the Changer, or New Creator.

When he was old enough, he was told to go to the lake, to fast and swim, and get his spirit power. But he did not obey, so his family deserted him. When he saw this, he realized he had done wrong, so he began to swim and fast for many days. No one can get spirit power unless he is clean and his stomach is empty. The boy kept swimming and fasting. The Old Creator came to the boy in dreams and gave him spirit power and told him what to do. The boy waved the Old Creator's blanket over the earth, and there was food for everyone. Then he gathered the bones of the people who lived before the flood. He waved the blanket over them and people were created. When he waved the blanket again, he created brains for the people from the soil of the earth. Then the people could talk. They spoke many languages. Doquebuth blew the people around to different parts of the land. Some he placed in the buffalo country, some by the saltwater, some by freshwater, some in the forests.[1]

[1]adapted from: Clark, Ella, *Indian Legends of the Pacific Northwest*, pp. 139-40. Copyright 1953 by The Regents of the University of California, reprinted by permission of the University of California Press.

---

2. How do most anthropologists believe people first came to North America?
3. Mention at least two other possible origins of North Americans.

DID ANCIENT SAILORS CROSS THE OCEAN LONG BEFORE COLUMBUS?

Many people who visit the ruins of ancient American cities are surprised at the similarities between the art and architecture of America and that of ancient cultures in China and the Mediterranean. The Mayan cities of Mexico and the Inca cities of Peru offer striking examples of these similarities. For example, the sculptural designs that decorate some ancient temples of Mexico closely resemble Chinese designs. Some pyramids of Mexico were found to contain burial rooms like the ones in Egyptian pyramids. Inca stoneworkers used tools and techniques similar to those of Mediterranean builders.

The stonework of these ancient American cultures was as advanced as that in any other part of the world at the time. These cultures were also very advanced in their knowledge of mathematics and astronomy. Some anthropologists are convinced that Native Americans developed their skills and scientific knowledge independently. Others believe they may have learned part of it from ancient visitors from other cultures.

Anthropologists have discovered many other cultural similarities between ancient civilizations in America and those of China and the Mediterranean. Several ancient cultures of the Americas had legends about a bearded white man or god who came from the east. Early non-Indian explorers left many reports of white-skinned American Indians. The Inca rulers were said to be whites, for example. In addition, the pre-Columbian (before Columbus) artists of Central and South America carved some faces that seem clearly to represent Asians, Africans, and white people. These facts suggest contact between the continents in ancient times.

Could this contact really have taken place? Were the ancient people of China and the Mediterranean really able to build and sail a ship across the oceans? Many anthropologists say yes. A few people have even tried to prove this theory by reproducing the voyages themselves. In 1969 and again in 1970, a Norwegian anthropologist named Thor Heyerdahl supervised the building of a very special ship called the "Ra." The structure, methods, and materials were as much as possible the same as those that Mediterranean ship-builders would have used more than 2,000 years before. Heyerdahl and his crew were able to sail such a ship from North Africa to the Caribbean islands.

A few years later, an Austrian named Kuno Knobl and his crew sailed from China in a ship called the Tai Ki. It was a copy of the kind of Chinese junk (a kind of ship) in use about 100 A.D. The Tai Ki only made it about two-thirds of the way to Mexico, due to storms and other problems. But the crew believed that such a ship could have finished the journey under better conditions. You will find more evidence to support this theory on page 49.

The Tai Ki and the Ra were both helped along by steady winds and ocean currents. Find these currents and winds on a world map. They seem to form natural highways across the oceans, and they are used by ships today to make voyages easier. Trace the routes that would be easy to follow across the Atlantic and Pacific Oceans. Where might a ship start? Where would it be likely to end up?

What Was The Marmes Dig?

In 1965, an archaeologist named Roald Fryxell discovered a piece of a human bone beneath the Marmes Rock Shelter on the Palouse River. The bone was estimated to be about 10,000 years old. Over the years, it had become buried under several feet of rocks and soil.

Digging beneath the earth for bones, tools, and other human remains is a method used by archaeologists to study past cultures. At the Marmes dig in Southeastern Washington, archaeologists found parts of skeletons of several people. They also found many tools, including the finest, oldest bone needle discovered in North America. As a result of this dig, scientists know that people have been living in Washington for at least 10,000 years.

4. What does an archaeologist study?
5. According to archaeologists, people have been living in Washington for at least how long?

PICTOGRAPHS AND PETROGLYPHS

Mysterious figures have been found on the smooth rock cliffs along the Columbia River. Some were pecked with a hard pebble. These are called petroglyphs. Others were painted using a mixture of ground rock and animal oil or pine resin. The painted figures are called pictographs. Why are they there? Modern Indians say simply that they were made by the "old people." Their origin and meaning are still a mystery.

Many Names, Many Peoples

Before Europeans came to America, the word "Indian" was never used by the people here. Instead, people called themselves by the name of the tribe or village to which they belonged. They were Duwamish, Snoqualmie, Spokane, and so on. Duwamish means "the people living on the river." Snoqualmie means "moon" which was considered the life source of this tribe. Spokane means "people of the sun." It is important to pay attention to the name of each village or tribe, because each group had its own culture. Different tribes spoke different languages and had some different customs.

Today, the word most commonly used for descendants of all the tribes is "Indian" or "American Indian." However, some people prefer the term "Native American," because it reminds us that these people were the native, or original, people of America. When people call themselves Native Americans, they are showing pride in their long cultural heritage. This book uses both "Indian" and "Native American," so that you can become familiar with both terms.

6. Why is the term "Native American" more accurate than "Indian"?

Coastal Indians And Plateau Indians

Although each tribe was different in some ways from all the others, some of the Pacific Northwest tribes had many things in common. In Washington, Native American cultures are often divided into two main groups: the Coastal cultures and the Plateau cultures. The Plateau Indians generally lived east of the mountains, on the Columbia Plateau. The Coastal Indians lived in Western Washington. The Cascade Mountains form a barrier which divides the state both geographically and culturally.

These cultures did not stop at the present Washington State borders, of course. In the early days, there were no state or national borders dividing the Pacific Northwest. Tribes who lived in the coastal areas of British Columbia and Oregon had many things in common with the Coastal Indians of Washington. Parts of the Plateau culture were shared by tribes to the north, south, and east of the Columbia Plateau.

7. What two main groupings are often used to describe Native American cultures in Washington?

Native American Cultural Regions

ESKIMO ■
SUB-ARCTIC
NORTHWEST COAST
PLATEAU
PLAINS
EASTERN WOODLAND
SOUTHEAST
CALIFORNIA
GREAT BASIN
SOUTHWEST
NORTHERN MEXICO
MIDDLE AMERICA
CARIBBEAN

North America

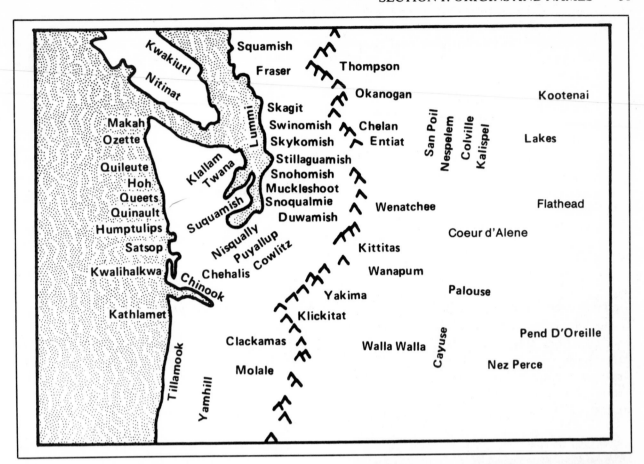

Kwakiutl
Nitinat
Squamish
Fraser
Thompson
Okanogan
Kootenai
Makah
Ozette
Skagit
Swinomish
Skykomish
Chelan
Entiat
San Poil
Nespelem
Colville
Kalispel
Lakes
Quileute
Hoh
Queets
Quinault
Humptulips
Satsop
Kwalihalkwa
Klallam
Twana
Lummi
Stillaguamish
Snohomish
Muckleshoot
Snoqualmie
Duwamish
Wenatchee
Flathead
Coeur d'Alene
Suquamish
Nisqually
Puyallup
Cowlitz
Kittitas
Wanapum
Palouse
Chinook
Chehalis
Kathlamet
Yakima
Klickitat
Walla Walla
Cayuse
Pend D'Oreille
Nez Perce
Tillamook
Yamhill
Clackamas
Molale

Contact Between Villages

It was common for village members to trade and intermarry with people from some of the neighboring villages. Coastal groups in what is now Washington State had frequent contact with some groups farther north. Plateau tribes had contact with Coastal tribes and also with Plains Indians from east of the Rocky Mountains. Influences of both northern and eastern tribes can be seen in Washington.

Plateau and Coastal villages also traded with each other. Some groups, such as the Chinook, specialized as traders. Some villages along the Columbia River — the main trade route — have much in common with both Coastal and Plateau villages.

Each year, Native Americans from many parts of the region would meet at favorite fishing grounds, such as The Dalles on the Columbia River. Here the different groups fished for salmon, visited, traded, and shared food and entertainment.

8. What was the special skill of the Chinook tribe?
9. What contact did Washington tribes have with the tribes to the north and east?

Totem poles were carved by tribal groups in the area that is now part of British Columbia, Canada. Groups in what is now Washington State traded with these northern tribes as well as their neighbors to the south and east.

SECTION 2: COASTAL CULTURES

What Were The Coastal Villages Like?

Coastal Indians lived in villages near the water. Some lived on the coast of the Pacific Ocean, the Strait of Juan de Fuca, or Puget Sound. Other villages were located up rivers, off the coast.

A typical coastal village was made up of several longhouses that faced the sea. The longhouses were made of overlapping cedar planks. Several related families lived in each one.

Cedar and cattail mats formed movable walls that separated the families. During ceremonies, the mats could be taken down so that all could participate. These mats were also used for rugs and mattresses. The floor was covered with cedar shavings. If the floor became soiled, the shavings would be swept out and new ones would be thrown on the floor. The beds were wooden platforms built into the wall like bunks.

10. What buildings made up a coastal village?
11. What tree provided material for the houses, mats, and floor coverings?

How Were Natural Resources Used?

The two most important resources in the Coastal Indians' lives were salmon and cedar. From different parts of the cedar tree, they made their houses, their clothing, their utensils, and their furnishings. Salmon was the Coastal peoples' chief food and the mainstay of their economy. It was essential to their way of life.

The Indians' attitude toward these natural resources was one of respect and appreciation. Animals and trees were like friends. They were other beings who shared the earth with their human neighbors. These attitudes are expressed in the following lines from a poem by Clarence Pickernell, a Quinault Indian.

> *This is my land*
> *From the time of the first moon*
> *Till the time of the last sun*
> *It was given to my people.*
> *Wha-neh Wha-neh, the great giver of life*
> *Made me out of the earth of this land*
> *He said, "you are the land and the land is you."*
> *I take good care of this land,*
> *For I am part of it,*
> *I take good care of the animals,*
> *For they are my brothers and sisters. . .* [1]

Salmon were treated with respect, too. Coastal Indians believed that the salmon were immortal and lived in a longhouse under the ocean. The "salmon people" lived exactly as the Coastal people did until spring, when they turned themselves into fish. They sacrificed themselves each year for the benefit of people.

[1] Pickernell poem: State Superintendent of Public Instruction, *The History and Culture of The Indians of Washington State - A Curriculum Guide*, Olympia, 1975, p. 3-42.

COASTAL VILLAGE ON THE BEACH
The pointed roof, shingles, and windows are recent additions to coastal houses. Which houses are more traditional?

Then the salmon people were reborn, and they returned to their underwater home until the next year's "run."

Native Americans threw the fish bones back into the river so that the salmon could take human form again. This would ensure a plentiful supply of fish the next season, they believed.

Each year, the first salmon was celebrated with a ceremony where the fish was thanked for its sacrifice. It was treated like an honored guest. The people would thank the salmon for allowing itself to be eaten in order to keep them alive.

12. Describe the importance of salmon to the Coastal people.
13. What was the Coastal people's attitude toward natural resources?

How Did The Coastal People Gather Their Food?

The lands and waters of the Coastal Region were rich with many kinds of seafood and edible plants.

After the first salmon ceremony, the salmon fishing season was opened for the year. Nets, traps, spears, and other methods were used to catch the fish that swam up the rivers in great

The tribal groups of the Pacific Northwest spoke seven different languages. Often, groups of the same language had quite similar cultures.

COASTAL TRIBES	Athabascan	Chemakuan	Chinook	Wakashan	Sahaptin	Coastal Salish
1. Chinook			■			
2. Hoh		■				
3. Klallam						■
4. Makah				■		
5. Ozette				■		
6. Queets		■				
7. Quileute		■				
8. Quinault						■
9. Cathlamet			■			
10. Chehalis						■
11. Chemakum		■				
12. Clakamas			■			
13. Copalis						■
14. Cowlitz						■
15. Duwamish						■
16. Humptulips						■
17. Kwalhaikwa	■					
18. Lummi						■
19. Muckleshoot						■
20. Nisqually						■
21. Nooksack						■
22. Puyallup						■
23. Samish						■
24. Satsop						■
25. Skagit						■
26. Skokomish						■
27. Skykomish						■
28. Snohomish						■
29. Snoqualmie						■
30. Squaxin						■
31. Stillaguamish						■
32. Suquamish						■
33. Swinomish						■
34. Twana						■

PLATEAU TRIBES	Chinook	Molale-Cayuse	Sahaptin	Interior Salish
1. Cayuse		■		
2. Chelan				■
3. Coeur d'Alene				■
4. Columbia				■
5. Colville				■
6. Kalispel				■
7. Kittitas			■	
8. Klickitat			■	
9. Kootenai				
10. Lakes				■
11. Methos				■
12. Nespelem				■
13. Nez Perce			■	
14. Okanogan				■
15. Palouse			■	
16. San Poil				■
17. Spokane				■
18. Wallula			■	
19. Wanapam			■	
20. Wenatchee				■
21. Wishram	■			
22. Yakima			■	

numbers. The fishing technology of the Coastal Indians was highly developed and included many of the techniques still in use today.

Part of the catch had to be stored, of course, to be eaten during the rest of the year. While the men were busy fishing, the women cleaned and dried or smoked the salmon and stored them in baskets lined with salmon skins.

The Coastal people ate many other seafoods too, including halibut, cod, herring, smelt, clams, and oysters. Some Indians ate sea mammals such as seals and otter, and the Quinault, Quileute, Makah, and Clallam hunted whales. People who lived near salt water ate some things that could not be found upriver. The freshwater people caught salmon and freshwater fish, and they also hunted animals.

Plentiful berries and roots were used to supplement (add to) their diet. The camas root was especially important. Camas has a taste similar to sweet potatoes when cooked. Roots and berries were formed into cakes and dried for storage. Each year, the people in a village would

The Native Americans of the Pacific Northwest developed many ways of catching salmon. They took advantage of the fact that salmon swim upstream to spawn. This man has built a simple fence, or wier, to block the salmon's progress. The salmon are trapped here, and he can spear or net them easily. This photo was taken in the early 1900's, after Native Americans had adopted non-Indian clothing.

travel to their traditional gathering grounds to collect these plants. Many groups also made yearly trips to traditional hunting and fishing grounds. The people lived at these spots in temporary shelters made of woven mats.

14. What other food besides salmon did the Coastal people eat?

15. Why did they travel each year to traditional gathering grounds?

All these objects were made from cedar by Indians of the Pacific Northwest coast. What other resources were important to the Coastal people?

How Were Canoes Important?

Canoeing was the chief means of transportation for the Coastal people. Canoes were so important to Coastal cultures that these people are sometimes called canoe Indians. Several types and sizes of canoes were made. Some were as much as 60 feet long and could carry a large crew and more than 1 ½ tons of cargo. (The Plateau people also used canoes, but theirs were smaller and less elaborate than the Coastal canoes.)

16. What was the Coastal people's main form of transportation?

This photo of a summer camp along the Skokomish River was taken by Edward Curtis in the early 1900's. (For more information, see page 176).

How Was Coastal Society Structured?

The Coastal Indians had a highly developed social structure. Wealth and status determined each person's place in the village. The wealthiest person held the highest rank followed by another person slightly less wealthy and on down the line. Those with the most wealth and status were the most important. However, there was no single chief or leader in the village.

Wealth included not only possessions but also family histories and the right to perform certain songs, dances, or ceremonies. These rights and possessions were usually inherited.

The lowest class of people in the village were the slaves. Several Coastal tribes (especially the northern tribes in what is now British Columbia) made raids and wars to get slaves. They cap-tured women and children from other villages for this purpose. Sometimes they sold the slaves to other groups for furs, dried foods, and other trade items.

Slaves had food and clothing and lived in the house with the families. They had to do the hardest work, and they had no inherited privi-leges or status. In some villages slaves might be killed and be buried with their masters. Children of slaves were often allowed to grow up free. Sometimes the home village would recapture or buy back a slave, but a person who was once a slave would carry that shame forever.

17. *How was a person's rank determined in tribal villages of the coast?*
18. *Which things might a wealthy Coastal person inherit?*

Some of the best photographs of North American Indians were taken by a former Seattle photographer named Edward Curtis. On these two pages are some of his portraits of the native peoples of the Pacific Northwest.

What Was The Potlatch?

The most important social event marking the rank and status of a person was the potlatch. Potlatches were given on special occasions, such as marriage and receiving an inheritance. In each case, the event was not official until the guests — who were also witnesses — were given a gift at a potlatch. The word potlatch comes from Chinook jargon and means "to give."

The main purposes of the potlatch were to confirm certain events such as to give names to children, to increase one's status in the village, or to announce one's social standing. Rank and status were observed throughout the potlatch. People were seated according to their status, and the highest ranking guests received the most valuable gifts.

Potlatches took as long as a year or more to prepare. Much time was spent in collecting food and possessions. Sometimes the hosts would give away all they had. Sometimes they would also borrow things to give away. The giving away served as a payment to the witness. It was also a competitive showing-off of wealth. The more the hosts gave away, the more status they would gain.

The potlatch was accompanied by a feast, and it was a time for visiting and entertainment, too. Often, many guests were invited from other villages. They would all arrive in decorated canoes, according to custom.

The Coastal Indians demonstrated their wealth through giving, rather than accumulating wealth for its own sake — as is common in most cultures. Today, giving is still important to the Coastal people. Indian festivals, such as Makah Days at Neah Bay, still incorporate some feasts, songs, and dances of the potlatch tradition.

THE WHALE HUNT

Whale hunting was the greatest test of canoeing skill among the Coastal people. A whale could crush a big canoe with a flip of its tail. All members of the crew had to be well-trained and highly skilled to avoid disaster.

Only a few tribes hunted whales. Everyone involved in the hunt prepared for it carefully. There were long training rituals, prayer chants, and ceremonies.

The harpooner was a very important person in the village. He was a man of wealth and status. His knowledge and privilege were inherited from his father or his wife's father.

When a whale was sighted, the harpooner's canoe would pull up swiftly and quietly along the huge animal's left side. The canoe had to be very close, for the harpoon was almost 20 feet long and too heavy to throw. It had to be thrust by hand into the whale's side, just behind the left flipper near the heart. The harpooning was the most dangerous moment of the hunt. The angry whale could overturn the canoe very easily. After the harpoon was placed, all the paddlers worked urgently and skillfully to back the canoe away from the wounded whale.

A second canoe then sped forward, and a crewman plunged a second harpoon into the whale. Sealskin floats were attached to the line to slow the whale down. The animal towed the boats until it was exhausted. The men then moved in for the kill. The flipper muscles were cut so that the whale could no longer be dangerous. The harpoonist then plunged a lance behind the flipper to the heart. The animal rolled, spouted blood from its blowhole, and died.

The dead whale's mouth was tied shut to keep it from filling with water and sinking. The tremendous animal was towed to shore. This effort might last several days. The whole village was waiting on the beach when they arrived. There were more ceremonies. The animal was hauled ashore and the blubber divided up: a special piece for the harpooner, large pieces for important villagers and guests, and smaller bits for the common people.

19. What were some of the purposes of the potlatch?

How Were Spirits Important?

In addition to having a highly developed society, the Coastal people also had strong religious beliefs. They believed that all living and non-living things had spirits. Some spirits were helpful; some were dangerous. There were spirits that could help a person become successful in fishing, whaling, securing wealth — or in whatever field this particular spirit was gifted.

To gain the aid of such a guardian spirit, a Coastal Indian would go on a spirit quest as a child. (A quest is a hunt or search.) The boy or girl would prepare for the journey by swimming or taking sweat baths and scrubbing the body with bark or nettles. They had to be clean and have empty stomachs for the quest. They stayed alone and did not eat while they waited for a spirit to come.

A person who was successful on the spirit quest might return with a special song or dance taught by the spirit. And later, he or she could call on the guardian spirit for help.

Coastal people believed that the wandering spirits came back each winter. During the short days of winter when there was no fishing or gathering to do, a village might have a spirit ceremony. People from other villages would be invited. For four or five days, there would be feasts and visiting. At night, everyone would sit together in a large building as the spirit songs and dances began.

20. According to the Coastal people, what things had spirits?

Who Were Shamans?

Sometimes on a spirit quest, a person might have a special vision that meant he or she could became a shaman. Shamans were healers and spiritual leaders. They had special powers. A shaman would have to prove these special powers by successes in spiritual tasks. Curing the sick was one of the shaman's most important duties.

The Coastal Indians used many native plants for medicines. When the first non-Indians travelled west, many of them got sick with scurvy. In those days, no one knew that scurvy was caused by lack of Vitamin C. But the Indians knew how to cure it. They brought thistles and

cranberries and other plants to the newcomers to cure the disease.

Coastal Indians also believed that diseases could be caused by spirits, or loss of spirit, or breaking tribal customs. Someone with a strong spirit, such as a shaman, could also make another person sick.

A shaman would examine the patient to determine the cause of the disease. Then he or she might perform a ceremony to bring back the person's spirit or remove the object that caused the disease.

A shaman's special powers could be used to harm as well as cure. If a patient died, the shaman was sometimes suspected as the cause of death. An unsuccessful shaman might be killed by the dead person's family. Sometimes the shaman would refuse to treat a patient at all.

21. What was the shaman's role in Coastal life?

How Were Oral Legends Important?

The Native Americans shared their culture through oral (spoken) legends. These legends were told, from memory, by the older members of the tribe. They included the history, values, and beliefs of the culture.

Oral legends were respected and sacred to the life of a village. They were also a form of family entertainment. On dark winter evenings, children and others would lie still and attentive as the stories were told.

In recent years, some of the oral legends have been written down. Here is an example of a legend with a lesson to teach. It was told by Helen Peterson of the Makah tribe.

THE FAMINE

A long time ago there was a great famine in all the land. There was nothing to eat. The tide would not go out, and it was stormy day after day. Soon there was nothing left to eat. In one house there was one little piece of salmon roe (fish eggs). The mother said, "Now I want you to all line up, the oldest one down to the youngest one." So, they lined up. She said to the oldest one, "You take a little bite," and onto the next one and to the next one, down to the youngest one. He ate all the rest. They looked at him sadly. They didn't scold him, but they looked at him as if to say, "Why did you do that? You took all that we had left to eat." He walked away and he felt very bad. He walked and walked and walked to a point. He stood there and began to pray to the Great Spirit. "Oh Great Spirit," he said, "forgive me for what I did. I ate all that we had left in our house and there is nothing left to eat. Now all my brothers and sisters and all my folks will die because there is nothing left to eat. Forgive me, Great Spirit."

This engraving shows The Dalles along the Columbia River as the area used to look. The Native Americans of the lower Columbia shared some parts of the Coastal culture and some parts of the Plateau culture.

from: *Pacific Northwest Economic Base Study for Power Markets.* Volume 1, U.S. Department of the Interior, Bonneville Power Administration, 1970.

While he was praying, fish began to come ashore. Every wave would bring hundreds and hundreds of fish ashore. The people of the village went down to the shore and filled their baskets up. This saved the people.[1]

22. What were the functions of oral legends in Coastal life?

Coastal Art

Native Americans of the Pacific Northwest coast are noted for their beautiful works of art, especially their woodcarvings and baskets. The most elaborate art work was done by northern tribes such as the Haida, Tlingit, and Kwakiutl. The most distinctive examples of northern woodcarving were the totem poles. The carved figures on a pole represented the history of the family who owned the totem pole.

Totem poles were not traditionally carved by most Native Americans of what is now Washington State. However, the Coastal Indians of Washington used carvings of animals to decorate canoes, tools, kitchen implements, and ceremonial objects. Many of the villages up and down the coast used carved wooden masks for ceremonial dances.

Native Americans from both sides of the Cascades were skilled basketweavers. From materials such as cedar root, bark, and cattails, they wove beautifully patterned baskets of many types. Coastal people also wove rainhats of cedar, and some Salish people wove blankets of dog hair, mountain goat wool, and other materials.

23. What do the figures on the northern tribes' totem poles represent?
24. Name some art objects that the Coastal people are famous for.

WHAT IS THE OZETTE DIG?

About 500 years ago, a great mudslide wiped out the busy fishing village of Ozette, on the Olympic Peninsula. It was the home of a tribe that was closely related to the Makahs. People had been living at Ozette for more than 2,000 years. Then, suddenly, the village and everything in it was all buried under 10 or 12 feet of mud.

Normally, a wooden object that was left outside for 500 years would be totally decayed. But the mud sealed off all objects in the village so that air could not get to them. Under the mudslide at Ozette, there were houses, tools, household equipment, artwork, and bones — all surprisingly well preserved.

Archaeologist Richard Daugherty first began uncovering the old village of Ozette in 1966. He was assisted by a team of archaeology students from around the country and a group of Makah Indians.

The archaeology team worked carefully, in order to learn and save as much as possible. They washed away the top layers of mud with powerful hoses. Then they switched to gentle hoses and small shovels. With these, they sorted carefully through all the mud. All buried objects were documented and soaked in a special solution to preserve them. Makah tribal members helped identify, label, and store the pieces. This whole project is known as the Ozette dig.

By 1975, more than 30,000 of these artifacts had been recovered. (An artifact is any object made by people. The word is most often used when referring to objects from past cultures.)

Many artifacts revealed the great artistry and skills of the people who lived there. The items discovered included tools such as harpoon hooks, looms, and steel knives. There were household goods, such as cedar mats, part of a blanket woven of cattail fluff and dog hair, and many wooden boxes. A great number of these objects were beautifully carved and decorated. One especially interesting artifact was a large cedar piece, carved in the shape of a whale fin and decorated with otter teeth.

[1]The History and Culture of the Indians of Washington State, revised edition, Olympia: Superintendent of Public Instruction, 1975, p. 3-27.

A drawing of the interior of a Coastal longhouse. It was here that the legends were told on winter nights.

SECTION 3: PLATEAU CULTURES

Who Were The Plateau Indians?

The many groups of Northwest Native Americans who lived east of the Cascades are sometimes called Plateau Indians. Although each group was independent and unique, they shared similar physical environments and similar cultures. They had somewhat different ways of filling their basic needs than the Coastal people, whose lands and cultures were different. (In a similar way, the people who live in Eastern Washington today share a geography, economy, and culture that are different from those of Western Washington.)

25. Where did the Plateau Indians live?

How Did The Plateau People Gather Their Food?

Like the Coastal Indians, the Plateau groups were hunters and fishers. They also gathered berries and camas root and other plants, and they ate salmon. But living in the interior made their lives different. The Plateau was not so richly supplied with food as the Coastal regions were. Plateau people usually had to travel greater distances for food. The yearly trips of some tribes included visits to places as far apart as The Dalles along the Columbia and the plains of Montana.

Each year, some of the villages would travel to fishing spots on the Columbia and Snake Rivers. Here, at places like The Dalles and Kettle Falls, many Plateau bands would gather not only for fishing but also for trade, festivals, and visits with old friends. During the spring season, there would be camps all along the river, all bustling with activity. The Plateau peoples' fishing technology was similar to that of the Coastal villages.

Since much seafood was not available in this area, Plateau peoples also hunted land animals such as deer, rabbits, and elk. Most people lived on the fringes of the plain, where wood and game were more plentiful.

In both the Plateau and Coastal cultures, hunting and gathering food were community activities. Everyone worked together to provide food for the whole village. Cooperation was necessary for survival. Living and working together also helped give the tribal members a strong sense of loyalty and belonging to the tribe.

26. How did geography influence food-gathering on the Plateau?
27. How are hunting and gathering related to a sense of loyalty to the tribe?

How Did Horses Change Plateau Life?

Sometimes the Plateau Indians are called the horse Indians, much as the Coastal people are called canoe Indians. Actually, the Plateau tribes did not have horses until the eighteenth century. Modern horses were not native to North America. They were all descendants of a few horses brought over by the Spaniards in the 1500's. Little by little, the horses multiplied, and they were traded from one Indian group to another until they reached the Columbia Plateau in the early 1700's.

With horses, the people could travel faster over greater distances. They could visit and communicate more often with other tribes. This led to greater unity among several tribal groups.

A Cayuse woman on horseback, dressed up for a special occasion.

INFLUENCE OF THE PLAINS INDIANS
East of the Plateau peoples lived the Plains Indians. This photo shows a dance of the Flathead tribe,
who lived in what is now Montana. After Plateau tribes got horses, they had more contact with the
Flatheads and other Plains tribes. Plateau people did not traditionally use tepees, travois, or feather
headdresses. These are some things they borrowed from their neighbors to the east, the Plains
Indians.

They could carry heavy loads more easily. They could race large game animals and tire them out or drive them over cliffs. This was the way they hunted buffalo.

Some of the Plateau tribes, such as the Nez Perce, Cayuse, and Spokane, began to send hunting parties over the Rockies on buffalo hunts. These expeditions lasted from a month or two to as long as two years. They allowed the Plateau Indians to meet and trade with the Plains Indians, their neighbors to the east. (Some of the Plains tribes were not friendly to the Plateau peoples. The Blackfeet especially were a warlike nation, and several Plateau tribes might band together to make sure their expeditions were more secure and safe.)

28. Name some ways that horses changed the lives of the Plateau Indians.

Houses And Clothing

The geography of the plateau influenced the dwellings that people built and the clothes they wore. Compared to Coastal people, the Plateau people needed extra protection from the cold and snowy winters.

Since wood was scarce, many villages built pit houses. They were about 30 feet in diameter and about 6 feet in the ground. A roof was made by laying mats, skins, grass, and soil on top of a circle of poles.

Other villages built long mat-houses shaped like tents. After the Plateau people came into contact with the Plains tribes, and got horses, they built houses by setting up pole frames and covering them with mats. It was a version of the Plains tepee.

The Plateau people made leather clothing. Men wore leggings, shirts, and moccasins. Women wore moccasins, leggings and dresses. These garments were often beautifully decorated with beads, fringe, and porcupine quills. In cold weather, Plateau Indians also wore robes of animal skins, and they made snowshoes for walking over deep snow. Bear claws, elk teeth, and feathers were some of the things they used for jewelry and decorations. In the summer months, inland women wove grasses into clothing.

29. How did the cold winter climate influence Plateau houses and clothing?

This photograph shows a type of mat house used by some tribes along the Columbia River. What details give clues about when this photo was taken?

How Were Plateau Tribes Organized?

The social organization of the Plateau Indians was somewhat different from that of the Coastal groups. Plateau tribes tended to be somewhat less concerned with social rank. Class differences were less important, and slaves were uncommon. Chiefs, or leaders, were chosen more because of their proven skills than because of their family heritage. Wealth and status were less important.

It is important to understand that each tribe and even each village might have several chiefs. One might lead the people in war, another in hunting, and so on. Decisions were made by a Tribal Council. The council was made up of several chiefs or respected leaders of the tribe. No single individual could speak for the entire tribe (as the President of the United States can represent all the people of the United States in certain situations).

The improved transportation made possible by the horse made communication between villages easier. Some of the groups began to work together at times as a large tribe which included several villages. Other groups, such as the San Poil, remained separate and independent in their own villages.

30. How were tribal decisions made in a Plateau village?
31. How were leaders chosen among Plateau people?

What Was The Religion Of The Plateau Indians?

The religious beliefs of the Plateau Indians were similar to those of the Coastal people. The Plateau people had great respect for the earth and a feeling of oneness with all of nature.

The Plateau people also had an awareness of the spirits in all things around them. They practiced spirit quests. Children prepared for these quests by cleaning themselves and fasting. Then they would go off alone to seek a vision in which a spirit (usually in the form of an animal) would appear and teach them special songs and dances. Later, they could call on their spirit for aid in war, in finding food, in fighting off dangers, or in curing sickness. January was the time for

Baskets were an important art form on both sides of the Cascades.

spirit dances in the Plateau regions. In later years, horse festivals took the place of some of the older religious ceremonies.

The Plateau Indians had special ceremonies to open the salmon season, the berry and root-gathering seasons, and the hunting season. The ceremonies expressed the people's appreciation and dependence on the natural resources so important to their lives.

32. How were the religious beliefs of Plateau and Coastal cultures similar?

The Importance Of Legends

Like the Native Americans of the coast, Plateau people shared their beliefs and values through oral legends. Tribal people from both sides of the Cascades believed that long ago, before people came, the earth was inhabited by animals who talked and acted like human beings. These animal people appear in legends from all over the Northwest. This story about Coyote is one of them.

33. How were oral legends important in Plateau cultures?

HOW COYOTE MADE THE INDIAN TRIBES

Long ago, when the animal people walked the earth, a giant beaver monster lived in Lake Cle Elum, high in the Cascade Mountains. His name was Wishpoosh. Under his red eyebrows he had eyes like fire. He had huge, fierce, shining claws, with which he seized everything that came near him.

Lake Cle Elum was full of fish, enough fish for Wishpoosh and all the animal people, too. But Wishpoosh would not let the people get any fish. Whenever they came to the lake, he seized them with his giant claws and dragged them down.

The people begged Coyote to help them. It was a hard task. Other animal people had tried to kill Wishpoosh, but he had killed them instead.

Coyote was very wise, but he couldn't think of what to do. He asked his sisters for help. According to their advice, he made a huge spear and fastened it to his wrist with a strong cord.

He went to Lake Cle Elum to fish with the spear. Wishpoosh tried to grab Coyote with his fierce, shining claws. But Coyote moved first. He plunged the spear into the monster's side.

Howling in pain, Wishpoosh began to fight. The two of them fought so hard, they tore a hole in the mountains. The water rushed out and formed a new lake. As they continued fighting they tore out more and more land, creating the Yakima River channel, Union Gap, the Columbia River, and many lakes.

When they reached the ocean, Wishpoosh was still very angry and very strong. He ate many salmon and whales. He threatened to kill everyone.

Coyote was very tired. He asked his sisters for help again. They told him to turn himself into the branch of a fir tree. In this shape, Coyote floated out to the monster. As he expected, Wishpoosh swallowed him.

Inside the monster's stomach, Coyote changed himself back into his animal shape. He took his sharp knife and began to hack at the heart of Wishpoosh. He hacked and he hacked until the beaver monster was dead.

Then Coyote made himself smaller and climbed out through the Monster's throat. Muskrat helped him drag the dead body up on the beach near the mouth of Big River. With his sharp knife, Coyote cut up the big body of the monster.

"From your body, mighty Wishpoosh," he said, "I will make a new race of people. They will live near the shores of Big River and along the streams which flow into it."

From the lower part of the animal's body, Coyote made the people who were to live along the coast. "You shall be the Chinook Indians," he said to some of them. "You shall live near the mouth of Big River and shall be traders."

"You shall live along the coast," he said to others. "You shall live in villages facing the ocean and shall get your food by spearing salmon and digging clams. You shall always be short and fat and have weak legs."

From the legs of the beaver monster he made the Klickitat Indians. "You shall live along the rivers that flow down from the big white mountain north of Big River. You shall be swift of foot and keen of wit. You shall be famous runners and great horsemen."

From the arms of the monster he made the Cayuse Indians. "You shall live along Big River." Coyote said to them. "You shall be powerful with bow and arrows and with war clubs."

From the ribs he made the Yakima Indians. "You shall live near the new Yakima River, east of the mountains. You shall be the helpers and the protectors of all the poor people."

From the head he created the Nez Perce Indians. "You shall live in the valley of Kookooskia and the Wallowa Rivers. You shall be men of brains, great in council and in speechmaking. You shall also be skillful horsemen and brave warriors."

Then Coyote gathered up the hair and blood and waste. He hurled them far eastward, over the big mountains. "You shall be the Snake River Indians," said Coyote. "You shall be people of blood and violence. You shall be buffalo hunters and shall wander far and wide."

adapted from: Clark, Ella, *Indian Legends of The Pacific Northwest*, pp. 172-175, by permission of the University of California Press.

This photo of the earth was made from a spaceship on its way to the moon. Can you pick out the continent of North America under the clouds? To the first European explorers, this continent was as strange and unknown as the distant planets are to today's astronauts. For what reasons do you think the first European explorers came to the Pacific Northwest? How do you think the Native American residents would have responded to them? Compare this to the situation of astronauts today.

UNIT 3

EXPLORATIONS AND CLAIMS

By the time of Columbus, Native Americans had been living in what is now Washington State for thousands of years. The land was comfortable and familiar to them. It was home. The idea that Columbus discovered America, or that Robert Gray discovered the Columbia River would probably seem ridiculous to them.

To Europeans, however, these lands were a complete mystery. Europeans didn't even know there was a continent here. When Columbus reached land, he assumed it was Asia. He was actually more than 7,000 miles away from that continent!

From the European point of view, the explorers were brave heroes. They were risking unknown dangers to bring benefits to their countries. They knew nothing about North and South America: the size, the climate, the physical features, the animals, or the people. For all they knew the land might be full of dangerous beasts, poisonous snakes, and hungry monsters. Perhaps no people could survive there. Or perhaps it was a rich paradise. Nobody knew.

The Pacific Northwest was one of the last parts of America to be explored by Europeans. Why did they come here? What did they hope to find? How did they interact with the Native American residents?

These are some of the central questions of this unit. The unit includes three sections:

1. Exploration by Sea
2. Exploration by Land
3. International Agreements

SECTION 1: EXPLORATION BY SEA

What Was The Northwest Passage?

The first Europeans to explore the Pacific Northwest were looking for a new route to Asia. This was the same goal that Columbus had when he accidentally landed on an island off the coast of North America. Asian products such as silks, rugs, dyes, perfume, and spices were valuable trade items. A country that discovered a new sea route to Asia could make lots of money by selling Asian goods in Europe. The discovering country was then able to control that route, so that no other ships could use it.

A few years after Columbus' first voyage, Europeans discovered that the huge continents of North and South America were blocking the route to Asia. But for many years, Europeans believed there was an all-water route through North America. They even had a name for this route they hoped to find. They called it the Straits of Anian, or the Northwest Passage. Some of the best explorers from Spain, France, England, and Holland went looking for the supposed Northwest Passage. The search went on for almost three centuries.

First, the explorers sailed the east coast of North America. They couldn't find a Northwest Passage. Other explorers decided to try looking for the other end of the passage, along the Pacific Coast. This was the search that brought the first Europeans to the Pacific Northwest.

1. What was the Northwest Passage?
2. Why were European countries so anxious to find a Northwest Passage?
3. Why did the first Europeans come to the Pacific Northwest?

Was Juan de Fuca's Story True?

The first European to sail up the Northwest coast in search of the Pacific end of the Northwest Passage was a Spaniard named Bartolome Ferrelo. In 1542, he sailed as far north as what is now Southern Oregon. In 1776, the British explorer, Captain James Cook, concluded that the Northwest Passage did not exist; and later explorers were more interested in exploring northwest resources than in finding the Passage.

Between Ferrelo's voyage and Cook's, several

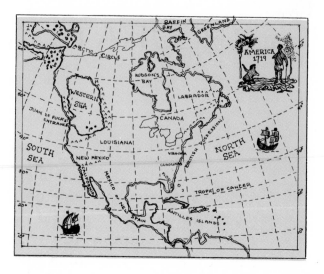

How is the map different from modern maps of North America? With which areas was the mapmaker least familiar?

explorers added to our knowledge of the Pacific Coast. During this period, there was one voyage that was unique. It is unique because no one knows for sure whether it actually took place or not!

This supposed voyage was reported by a Greek sailor named Apostolos Valerianos. Valerianos said that he used to sail for Spain under the name Juan de Fuca.

Valerianos claimed that in 1592 he had sailed northward from Mexico, looking for the Northwest Passage. He said that at 47 or 48 degrees north latitude, he had found a large strait. He added that there was "a great headland or island, with an exceeding high pinnacle, or spired rock, like a pillar, thereupon." This great rock pillar was supposed to mark the north side of the entrance to the strait.

Valerianos went on to say that his ship had sailed into the strait for twenty days. They had passed many islands, and found gold, silver, and pearls. Then they ended up at the Atlantic Ocean!

This is the story that Valerianos told to an Englishman named Michael Lok. The last part of the story is definitely false. What about the rest of it? Perhaps Michael Lok got the story confused. Perhaps Valerianos had actually said the great rock was on the south side of the strait. Then it could have been Mount Olympus. The strait that is now called Juan de Fuca is at 49 degrees latitude, and that's very close to Valerianos' report. But historians have found no mention of the name Juan de Fuca in Spanish records.

Lok seemed to believe the story and hoped that England could gain control of the route. He tried to interest the English government in de Fuca's story. He wanted a British exploring ship to check it out. Valerianos offered to guide the expedition himself. But the trip was never made.

4. What parts of Juan de Fuca's story seem accurate or true?
5. What parts of his story seem false?

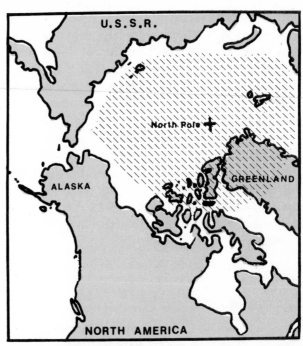

There actually is a Northwest Passage — an all-water route across North America. The route is usually blocked by ice, and Cook's ships could not get through. Can you find a possible route on this map? The lined area in the center is the polar ice cap.

WHO WAS CAPTAIN COOK?
James Cook was one of the outstanding sea captains of his time. He headed several exploring expeditions, including two important voyages in the South Pacific. On one of these voyages, he discovered New Zealand. On his 1776 voyage, he discovered Hawaii, which he named the Sandwich Islands, after his sponsor, the Earl of Sandwich. These islands became a regular stopping place for European ships that were crossing the Pacific.

What Other Ships Landed In The Pacific Northwest?

Ferrelo, Cook, and others came to the Northwest looking for a ship's passage to Asia. However, there is evidence that several Asian ships had already arrived on the Northwest coast by sailing from the other direction!

For example, official Chinese documents tell of a voyage made in the year 499. The captain of the expedition was Hui San, a Buddhist priest. Hui San's reports strongly suggest that his expedition visited the Aleutian Islands and the California coast. He described some tribal customs that were noticed by European explorers more than 1,000 years later.

The earliest European explorers were very surprised to find that some Northwest tribes had metal tools. Yet these tribes did not know how to make metal themselves. How did it get there? One theory was that some ships from Asia had been washed ashore on the North American coast.

Skilled Chinese metalworkers had been making beautiful bronze objects for more than 3,000 years before Cook's voyage. Asians were building ocean-going ships with some metal parts long before the 1700's. Perhaps some of these ships were blown off course and landed on the

North American coast long ago. As a matter of fact, many Asian boats were later discovered on American beaches. Seventy-five of them were noted before 1875. Sometimes, a few Japanese crew members were still alive on the boat when it landed. In 1834, three Japanese men were washed ashore in their ship near Cape Flattery.

Find a world map showing ocean currents and trade winds on the Pacific Ocean. Notice that the Japanese current flows almost directly from Japan to Washington State. It's quite possible that Asian ships, carried on these currents, were the first non-Indian ships to arrive in the Pacific Northwest.

6. What evidence supports the theory that Asian ships were washed ashore in the Pacific Northwest before Europeans arrived?

How Did Cook's Voyage Change The Purpose Of Exploration?

Captain Cook's voyage marked a key turning point in European exploration of the Pacific Northwest coast. Cook gave up on finding the Northwest Passage. But he made some other discoveries that turned out to be very important in this area's history.

While they were exploring the Northwest, Cook's crew traded with some of the Native Americans for sea otter furs. On their return trip to England, the crew discovered that they could sell each fur in China for three hundred dollars! Cook's voyage started a trade pattern that would bring many more ships to the Northwest. The pattern was: (1) trade with Northwest Indians for furs, (2) trade the furs in China for silks, spices, and other items, (3) sell the Asian goods in Europe for a large profit.

Cook himself did not live to finish the trip. But his journals contained notes on the fish and timber of the Pacific Northwest. What Cook had noted were the valuable natural resources of this area. After Cook, European and American explorers were not looking for a Northwest Passage. Instead, they were hoping to strengthen their country's claims to the rich land and resources of the Pacific Northwest.

7. What three important resources did Cook and his crew discover?
8. What was the profitable trade pattern that started after Cook's voyage?
9. How did the purpose of exploration change after Cook's voyage?

Who Were The Spanish Explorers?

When Balboa reached the Pacific Ocean in 1513, he claimed all the lands around it for Spain. A Spanish government was set up in Mexico. Spanish missions were later built in what is now the American Southwest. Many Indians in the Spanish Territories adopted the Spanish language and the Catholic religion. They began to intermarry with Spanish settlers. These people were the ancestors of many of the Chicanos who now live in Washington.

The Spanish felt they had a strong claim to the entire Pacific Coast of North America. They were disturbed by the growing interest of other countries in the Pacific Northwest. In order to strengthen the Spanish claims, several Spanish explorers sailed north along the coast in the late 1700's. They made detailed maps and gave Spanish names to the lands and waters they explored.

The following are some important Spanish voyages of exploration:

— 1774: Juan Perez commands an expedition up the coast to 54 degrees north latitude, but did not come ashore in the Pacific Northwest.

— 1775: Juan de la Bodega y Quadra and his crew sail to 58 degrees north latitude.

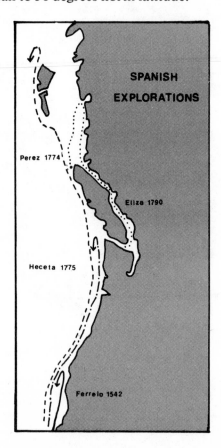

SPANISH EXPLORATIONS

Perez 1774

Eliza 1790

Heceta 1775

Ferrelo 1542

— 1775: Bruno Heceta notices what must be the mouth of a large river at 46 degrees north latitude. He names it the San Roque.

— 1790-1792: Lt. Francisco Eliza explores from Nootka Sound to the Gulf of Georgia. Many of the San Juan Islands still have the names given by Eliza's crew.

— 1790-1792: Lt. Manuel Quimper explores Haro and Rosario Straits and the Strait of Juan de Fuca. He establishes a Spanish colony called Nuñez Gaona at Neah Bay. (The colony was soon dissolved.)

— 1790-1792: Lt. Salvadore Fidalgo explores Prince William Sound.

10. Why did the Spanish feel they owned the Pacific Coast of North America?
11. Name five Spanish explorers of the Pacific Northwest.

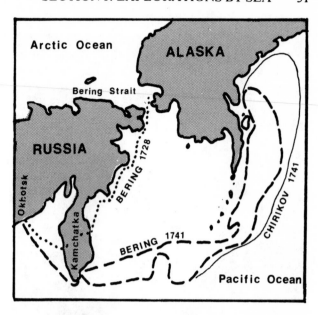

They traded the furs in China and also sold them in Russia.

Russian traders set up a network of fur trading posts along the Pacific Coast. For awhile, they were operating posts as far south as California. In fact, Russian traders used to own the land where gold was later discovered in 1848. (This discovery brought on the California gold rush.)

But the strongest Russian claims were in Alaska. For many years, Alaska was recognized as a Russian territory. The U.S. purchased it from Russia in 1867. Several Alaska cities still have Russian churches and Russian names.

12. What valuable resource did Bering's crew bring back from Alaska in 1741?
13. Where were the Russian trading posts?
14. What land was recognized as Russian territory until 1867?

Why Did Russians Explore North America?

Russia was a second country that competed for the land and resources of the Pacific Northwest. By the first half of the seventeenth century, Russia had extended its boundaries east to the Pacific Ocean. Some Russians were interested in expanding their territory even more.

Peter the Great, Tsar of Russia, hired a Danish explorer named Vitus Bering to see if Asia and America were joined together. Bering and his crew sailed from Kamchatka in 1728. They followed the coastline until it turned west. They concluded that the two continents were not joined by land. The water passage between Asia and North America is now called Bering Strait.

A second expedition left Siberia in 1740. Bering and Alexei Chirikov each commanded a ship. The ships became separated in a storm. Bering lost valuable time searching for the other ship. He was unable to make it back before winter. Bering and his crew were forced to spend the winter on Bering Island, where he and many of the crew died. The survivors returned to Siberia with large quantities of sea otter furs.

Bering had assumed that Chirikov was dead. But Chirikov had actually sailed farther than Bering. He sighted the American coast in 1741 and returned to Asia.

Under the leadership of Catherine the Great, Russia sent more explorers down the American coast. Russian ships also began making yearly trips to the Aleutian Islands of Alaska for furs.

What Land Did Vancouver Claim For England?

The British, too, were interested in claiming land and participating in the Pacific Northwest fur trade. The British government selected Captain George Vancouver to map and claim new areas of the Northwest.

Vancouver sailed up the coast from California, and into the Strait of Juan de Fuca. He spent the summer of 1792 exploring and mapping the Puget Sound area. Vancouver's maps were remarkably accurate. Vancouver commanded the exploration of the northern end of the sound and sent his lieutenant, Peter Puget, to explore the southern end. Later, of course,

Captain George Vancouver

the whole body of water took on Puget's name.

Near the present city of Everett, Vancouver went ashore and claimed the area for England. He named it New Georgia, after George III, King of England. The English claim to these lands would last for more than 50 years.

---

15. Identify the following: Peter Puget, New Georgia.

What Was The Important Claim Of The United States?

Like Cook before him, Vancouver failed to find the Columbia River. That discovery was to be made by a trading captain who became the most important American explorer in the Northwest: Robert Gray.

It was common for the nation that discovered a river to claim all the lands drained by that river. The Columbia drainage area is huge. It covers most of what are now Washington, Oregon, and Idaho as well as parts of four other states and two Canadian provinces!

In 1790, Robert Gray became the first American to sail around the world. In 1792, he discovered and claimed the huge Columbia River for the United States.

It was Gray's second voyage to the Pacific Northwest. On the first, he and Captain Robert Kendrick had stopped in the Queen Charlotte Islands to trade for furs before Gray continued his trip to China and then back to Boston. This time, Captain Gray set out to explore the Pacific Coast more thoroughly for furs.

Sailing north along the coast, he saw what seemed to be a river. But the seas were so rough, he couldn't enter it. He continued north. At about 47 degrees latitude, he saw an inlet "which had a very good appearance of a harbor." He entered a spacious harbor. The ship's officers named it Gray's Harbor, after their captain.

A few days later, they sailed south to try to enter the river again. This time they made it. A small boat found a channel into the fresh waters of the great river. The ship followed. Indians came from both sides of the river to trade. Gray and his crew spent nine days there, trading for furs.

Captain Gray named the river the Columbia, after his ship, *Columbia Rediviva,* which means "Columbus Lives Again." The United States now had a claim to the Northwest, too.

MR. AND MRS. BARKLEY FIND JUAN DE FUCA'S STRAIT
An English captain named Charles Barkley was the explorer who first accurately identified the strait between Vancouver Island and the Olympic Peninsula. His wife, Jane, accompanied him on this trip. She was the first white woman to visit the Pacific Northwest, and she kept a daily journal of their travels. On the day they found the Strait of Juan de Fuca, she wrote: ". . . to our great astonishment, we arrived off a large opening extending to the eastward. The entrance . . . appeared to be about four leagues wide (about 12 miles) . . . my husband immediately recognized (it) as the long lost Strait of Juan de Fuca. He gave (it) the name of the original discoverer . . . "

16. Why was discovery of the Columbia River so important to the United States?
17. Name some notable accomplishments of Captain Robert Gray.

How Did England And Spain Come Close To War?

George Vancouver was embarrassed to learn of Gray's discovery. The Americans had beaten him to a very important claim. Vancouver sent a British officer named William Broughton to explore the river. Broughton sailed farther up the river than Gray, and he claimed that Gray had not found the river's main channel. Broughton then claimed the river for England. The conflicting American and British claims would take many years to settle.

Meanwhile, Captain Vancouver was busy at Nootka Sound with a different problem. England was on the edge of war with Spain. Vancouver and Juan de la Bodega y Quadra had been selected by their governments to try to settle the dispute between the two countries.

The problems had started in 1788. The Spanish government was becoming alarmed that other countries were exploring and trading in the Northwest. The Spanish still felt they owned this whole area. They decided to take action to protect their claims. The government sent Don Estevan José Martínez to build a Spanish fort at Nootka Sound.

At Nootka, Martínez discovered two ships that were owned by a British trader named John Meares. Two more of Meares' ships arrived from China soon afterward. Martínez seized all four ships and sent them to Mexico. This was the beginning of what was called the Nootka Controversy.

18. Why were Vancouver and Quadra sent to Nootka Sound?
19. Why did the Spanish government want Martínez to build a fort at Nootka Sound?
20. What incident started the Nootka Controversy?

What Was The Nootka Agreement?

John Meares was furious at Martínez' action. He convinced many people that England should go to war against Spain.

The viceroy (Spanish ruler) of Mexico was also shocked by Martínez' move. Spain could

SOME CLAIMS TO FAME FOR JOHN MEARES

Captain John Meares, a retired British Navy officer, had many "firsts" in the Pacific Northwest. He brought over the first Chinese and Hawaiian workers. Together with Meares, these workers built the first ship here. Meares also exported some of the first lumber and he mapped new parts of the coast. He also claimed to be the first European to sail and name the Strait of Juan de Fuca — in 1788.

The last claim wasn't true. Captain Charles Barkley and his wife had been there the year before. Meares probably even had a copy of Barkley's chart!

not afford to go to war over its Northwest claims. The viceroy apologized, paid the ships' crews, and outfitted them for their return to England.

The British government did not want war either. Spain and England agreed to work out a peaceful solution. The two countries signed a treaty in October, 1790. It was called the Nootka Agreement. In the treaty, Spain agreed to let other countries trade on the Pacific Coast north of 42 degrees north latitude.

The treaty also provided that Spain and England would each send a representative to Nootka. These men would work out the final settlement. The British selected George Vancouver as their representative, and Spain selected Juan de la Bodega y Quadra.

They met at Nootka in 1792. Vancouver and Quadra were not able to settle all the disagreements. They agreed to let their governments decide.

In 1794, Spain and England signed a second treaty. They agreed that both countries could use the port at Nootka. Neither country would try to keep the other out.

Vancouver and Quadra showed their good feelings toward each other by naming the island Quadra's and Vancouver's Island. Today, of course, it is known simply as Vancouver Island. Quadra Island is now the name of a smaller island nearby.

21. What promises did Spain and England make in the Nootka Agreement?

SECTION 2: EXPLORATION BY LAND

Why Did President Jefferson
Want Americans To Explore The West?

Robert Gray was not the only American who was interested in the fur resources of the Pacific Northwest. Several other people hoped the United States would have a share in the riches of the region. One of these people was Thomas Jefferson, who became President of the United States in 1800. He planned an expedition to travel overland from St. Louis to the Pacific Coast. (See map.) This expedition would bring back as much information as possible on the geography of the region, including climate, physical features, and natural resources. The expedition was also supposed to establish friendly relations with the Native Americans so that trade could develop. Hopefully, the expedition would open up an overland fur trade route, and help support the United States claim to the Pacific Northwest. The expedition leaders were supposed to keep journals that noted all they observed.

In 1803, the United States bought a huge amount of land from France, known as the Louisiana Purchase. This territory extended from the Mississippi River to the Rocky Mountains. It almost doubled the size of the United States at that time. The price of the Louisiana Purchase was a real bargain: only 15 million dollars. Now that the U.S. owned Louisiana, Congress approved money for the exploring expedition that Jefferson had planned.

22. What was the Louisiana Purchase?
23. What land did President Jefferson want the expedition to explore?
24. What were some of the purposes of the expedition?

The Lewis And Clark Expedition
Gets Started

President Jefferson's choice for the expedition leader was Meriwether Lewis, his lifelong friend and personal secretary. Lewis asked his friend William Clark to serve as co-captain of the expedition.

Lewis and Clark spent the summer of 1803 recruiting army volunteers and selecting supplies and trade goods for wilderness travel. The men who were selected waited at a camp across the Missouri River from St. Louis.

The expedition started up the Missouri from camp on May 13, 1804. It was just two months after Louisiana officially became part of the United States.

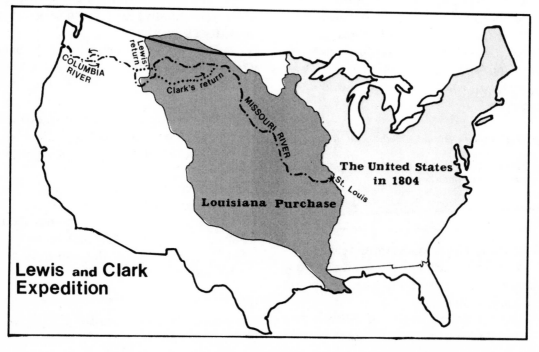

Lewis and Clark Expedition

25. When and where did the Lewis and Clark expedition start?

26. What kinds of boats did the expedition use on the Missouri?

27. What were some problems of the first part of the trip?

What Was the Trip Like?

The expedition had one big barge with a square sail and 22 oars. It was 55 feet long, and it was called a keelboat. They also had two smaller boats called peroques — a kind of dugout canoe that could be used with sails.

An experienced boatman, Pierre Cruzatte, navigated the keelboat. Seven soldiers and ten Creole boatmen also went along with the men on this part of the journey.

The trip up the Missouri was difficult, and all the extra men were needed. There were many sudden storms that tossed the boats about on the roaring river in the rain. It was all the men could do to keep the boats under control. Sometimes, they had to get out and wade through mud or water, and pull the boats along.

There were plenty of unwelcome visitors, too. Snakes, ticks, and mosquitoes attacked them constantly.

York Meets The Tribal People

Along the way, Lewis and Clark met with leaders of various tribes, including the Oto, Kickapoo, Omaha, Ponca, Yankton, Arikira, and Sioux. Lewis and Clark were careful to treat the Native Americans well, so that they would be friendly to American fur traders later on. They were very successful.

One expedition member who got along especially well with the tribal people was York. He was Captain Clark's slave. York "was an object of marvel among the natives, who had never seen a Negro, and who were amazed at his black skin, tremendous strength, and . . . dances." Often, an Indian would approach York and try to wipe the black color off his skin.

Captain Clark, too, was admired by the Native Americans. They called him the "red-haired chief, our brother."

Charles M. Russell is famous for his paintings of the American West. This is how he represented York in the Mandan villages. How would you picture this scene?

28. Why did the expedition want to start friendly relations with the Indians?
29. Who was York?

Who Was Sacajawea?

Near the end of October, the expedition reached the land of the Mandan Indians. The men selected a site for the winter and built a fort.

At Mandan, the expedition took on two valuable members. They were a Shoshone woman named Sacajawea and her French-Canadian husband, Toussaint Charbonneau. Sacajawea contributed much to the expedition. Having a woman in the party was a sign to Indians that the party was peaceful. She helped care for the sick. She taught the men about the culture of her people. She shared her knowledge about survival in the wilderness. Charbonneau was an experienced trapper. He served as a translator and guide.

Sacajawea's first child was born that winter. He was named Pompey, after a Roman general. When the expedition started up the Missouri again in the spring of 1805, Sacajawea carried the baby. Clark became very fond of the baby boy and nicknamed him Pomp. Years later, Pomp went to St. Louis and lived and studied with Clark.

30. How did Sacajawea help the Lewis and Clark expedition?

How Did They Get Horses?

As the expedition proceeded upriver, the water got shallower and shallower. The peroques were left behind. Then it became too shallow even for the canoes. The men needed horses.

Near Sacajawea's native country, they finally found a tribe with horses. But when the expedition members approached, the Indians ran

away. At one point, it seemed they were going to attack Lewis and two of his men.

Finally, Lewis was able to convince the tribe that he was friendly. He and some men were admitted to the Indian camp. Sacajawea translated as Lewis explained what they needed. The head chief began to speak. Sacajawea, they say, looked up in surprise and joy. The chief was her brother, Cameahwait. They had not seen each other since she had been kidnapped. The Shoshones helped the men get the horses they needed.

31. How did Sacajawea help the expedition trade with the Shoshones for horses?

Reaching The Pacific

That fall, the party was caught in the mountains with no food. Clark wrote: "I have been wet and as cold in every part as I ever was in my life, indeed I was at one time fearful my feet would freeze in the thin mockersins which I wore."

Finally the expedition crossed the Rockies and came to the Columbia Plateau. Plateau Indians helped them find their way to the great river, the Columbia. The men built more canoes, then, and went back to river travel.

They reached the Pacific Ocean late in November of 1805, and decided to spend the winter on the Pacific Coast. They selected a site and started building a fort. They called it Fort Clatsop, after the Indians in that area.

32. What river did Lewis and Clark use to get to the Pacific Coast?

Lewis And Clark Return

In March, 1806, the expedition started the return journey. This time, they were more familiar with the land. Native Americans helped them find a more direct route that was 600 miles shorter than their trip out. The return route to

EXPEDITION SALARIES
Records of the expedition show that Charbonneau received $409.16 for his services as an interpreter. Sacajawea received nothing.

The journals show that, "the monthly pay for sergeants was $8.00, that of privates $5.00, whereas interpreters received $25.00 per month."

An artist's conception of members of the Lewis and Clark expedition hunting grizzly bears.

St. Louis was 3,500 miles long.

The expedition arrived on September 23, 1806. They had been gone for over two years! Many people had thought they were dead.

Lewis and Clark had not found an easy route between the Columbia and the Missouri. But their maps helped later travelers find their way through the rugged mountains. And they gave the United States a stronger claim to the Pacific Northwest.

33. What were some important results of the Lewis and Clark expedition?

Exploration And Fur Trade Go Together

One of President Jefferson's important goals for the Lewis and Clark expedition was to pave the way for Americans to enter the fur trade. British fur trading companies were already exploring western North America for the same reason. As a matter of fact, the first person known to cross the continent north of Mexico was a British fur trader. His name was Alexander Mackenzie.

Mackenzie worked for the North West Company, a newcomer to the Canadian fur trade.

The "old-timer" was the Hudson's Bay Company. The King of England had given the Hudson's Bay Company a monopoly. No other British fur company could trade in any of their area. This included all the land drained by the rivers that run into Hudson Bay, or about half of what is now Canada! So any other English people who wanted to trade furs in Canada had to look for other places to work. In 1775, a number of these independent traders joined together to form the North West Company. The furs of the far west were still "up for grabs," and they hurried to take advantage of the opportunities. Discovery and exploration of new territory would mean more business for the company.

Between 1775 and 1811, several Canadian traders explored the rivers of Western Canada. They were looking for the source (beginning) of the Columbia River. They knew the Columbia was the most important route to the Pacific Ocean. In 1789, Mackenzie followed a river which he thought was the Columbia. It was a great river — the second largest river system in North America. But it was not the Columbia; it emptied into the Arctic Ocean, not the Pacific.

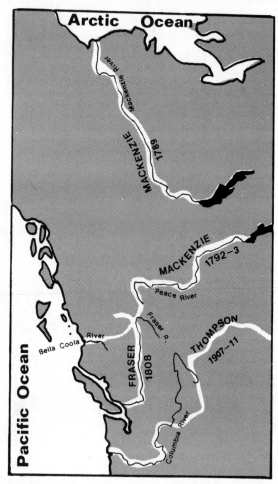

So Mackenzie named the river Disappointment. Today it is called the Mackenzie River, after the explorer.

34. Why did the North West Company need to develop fur trade in the far west?
35. What company was the "old-timer" in the fur trade business?
36. Why did explorers and traders want to find the Columbia River?

Who Finally Found The Columbia?

While Lewis and Clark were exploring farther south, another North West trader named Simon Fraser joined the search for the Columbia. He found a river that flowed to the Pacific, but it was not the Columbia. Mackenzie had found this river earlier, but he had decided not to follow it to the coast because it was too difficult. Today this river is called the Fraser.

The man who finally located the source of the Columbia was David Thompson. He was also a North West Company employee. Thompson had come west to the Rocky Mountains in 1800. His wife, Charlotte, and their children came with him. In 1810, he founded Spokane House, the first trading post in what is now Washington State. Thompson also set up several posts in the area. And he made excellent maps. The tribal people called him Koo-Koo-Sint, "the man who watches stars." He used the stars as points of reference when he surveyed the land. The maps that David Thompson made were so accurate that they were still used in the 1920's.

In July of 1811, Thompson and his party began canoeing down the Columbia. Near where the Snake and the Columbia flow together, Thompson put up a sign. It said, "Know hereby that this country is claimed by Great Britain as part of its territories. . ."

Probably, Thompson believed they were the only non-Indians in the whole river valley. He was wrong. A short time later, he met a group of American fur traders heading upriver.

37. What river did Simon Fraser explore?
38. Name some of David Thompson's accomplishments.
39. For what country did Thompson claim the Columbia River area?

Who Were The First American Fur Traders?

Were you wondering where the Americans were all this time? Well, they had arrived just a few months earlier. An American company had set up Fort Astoria, near the mouth of the Columbia River, in March of 1811. It was the first trading post on the U.S. Pacific coast.

The American company that built Fort Astoria was the Pacific Fur Company. It was established by a wealthy New York fur merchant named John Jacob Astor.

Astor already had a large fur trade east of the Rockies. He wanted to expand. Someday, he hoped to control all the fur trading in the west. Astor sent two expeditions to the Columbia River. He also sent a supply ship, called the *Beaver.* One expedition left New York on the *Tonquin,* a ship commanded by Captain Jonathan Thorn. The other group travelled overland and was led by Wilson Price Hunt. Both leaders were badly chosen. The result was tragic. Many members of both expeditions died.

40. What company built the first fur trading post on the Pacific Coast?
41. Who was John Jacob Astor?
42. Who led the sea and the overland expeditions of the Pacific Fur Company's trip to the Northwest?

The first trading post at Spokane was founded by David Thompson. What company did he work for?

Trouble On The Tonquin

There was trouble on the *Tonquin* almost as soon as it left port. The cause of most of the trouble was the captain.

Captain Thorn was a military man. He was used to military discipline and was intolerant of others' suggestions. There were constant arguments. At one point, Thorn left nine men stranded on an island. Another passenger named Robert Stuart had to hold Thorn at gunpoint in order to get him to turn around and go back for the men.

It was stormy when the *Tonquin* finally reached the Columbia River. They couldn't enter the channel. But Thorn was too impatient to wait for calmer weather. He sent five men ahead in a small boat to find the passage. Almost immediately, the boat was flipped over, and the men drowned. Three more men and a second boat were also lost before the *Tonquin* landed.

A few days later, the *Tonquin* managed to enter the river. They landed near the river's mouth. It was not a good location for the fort. But again, Thorn was impatient. He refused to sail upriver and look for a better place. He wouldn't even unload all the supplies. Instead, he took off for Nootka Sound to trade with the Indians. Several Pacific Fur Company employees went with him. The remaining men built a trading post, called Fort Astoria. And they began to trade.

Rumors reached Fort Astoria, later in the summer, that the *Tonquin* had been destroyed and that all members of the crew were killed. Apparently, Thorn had managed to make some local Native Americans so angry that they attacked the ship.

This was disastrous for Fort Astoria. Winter was approaching, and the *Tonquin* had carried badly needed men and supplies.

43. Why couldn't the Tonquin sail safely into the Columbia at first?
44. Why was Captain Thorn such a bad choice for the ship's captain?

What Happened To The Overland Party?

Meanwhile, the overland party wasn't doing much better. Wilson Price Hunt, the leader, had no experience in the wilderness. The party suffered because of it. They got lost. They ended up in steep river valleys with no way out. They ran out of food. Some men starved to death or drowned. They were attacked by hostile Indians.

During all this time, Marie Dorion, the brave Native American wife of the expedition's translator, managed to keep alive two children and to give birth to a third, who died. She kept up with the men and remained cheerful throughout the difficult journey.

Marie and Pierre Dorion were among the few people who made it to Fort Astoria. Nearly half the original party had died or deserted along the way.

45. What were some problems of the Pacific Fur Company's overland party?

NATIVE AMERICANS HELP THE EXPLORERS

Mackenzie might never have found the Bella Coola River without the help of friendly local Indians. The information and guidance of tribal people who knew the area well were very important to all the inland explorers. When they could, the tribal people also shared their food with hungry travellers. Pemmican, made of dried foods such as fish and berries, became the trail food of Indians and non-Indians alike. Explorers often bought canoes and horses from the Indians. The well-known Apaloosa horse was developed by the Nez Perce tribe.

How Did War Put An End To Astoria's Success?

Fortunately, the supply ship, the *Beaver,* arrived in May of 1812. For a few months, the Pacific Fur Company developed a good business. They traded by ship along the coast and set up posts along the rivers. The furs were traded in China, and Chinese goods were then sold in New York. Astor also traded supplies to the Russian fur posts and got more furs from them.

But Astor's success was over almost as soon as it began. Word reached Fort Spokane in January of 1813 that the United States and Great Britain were at war. This was known as the War of 1812. The Astorians were warned by members of the North West Company that a British warship was on its way to the mouth of the Columbia. The Astorians agreed to sell the fort to the British rather than lose everything. The company was dissolved. This marked the end of American fur trade in the Pacific Northwest for many years.

The British warship *Racoon* arrived at the mouth of the Columbia in November, 1814. Captain Black, the commander of the *Racoon,* took possession of Fort Astoria for the British and renamed it Fort George.

46. *How was Fort Astoria affected by the War of 1812?*

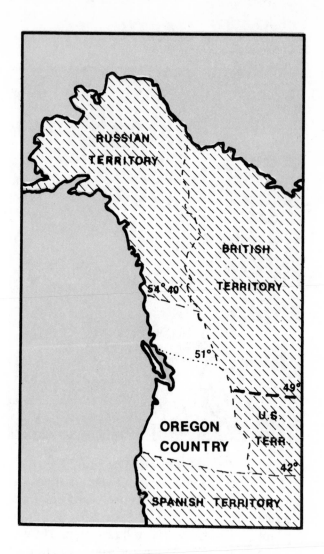

PLACE NAMES IN WASHINGTON

The place names of Washington State come from many languages. A great number of the names are English spellings of Indian words. A few examples are: Snohomish, Skykomish, Tacoma, Puyallup, Walla Walla, Klickitat, Mukilteo, Yakima, and Quinault. These names, and many others, came from the seven basic languages spoken by Native Americans here.

In some cases, the same place has been named many times. For example, San Juan Island was called Bellevue Island by the British and Rodgers Island by an American explorer. Each local tribe had its name for Mount Rainier before George Vancouver named it. Lieutenant Eliza named Bellingham Bay and Mount Baker with Spanish names, but neither of them stuck.

Other names still remind us of the explorers and settlers who named them. For example, several places still have the Spanish names chosen by the Spanish explorers. These include: San Juan, Sucia, Fidalgo, Lopez, Camano, and Orcas Islands; and Haro and Rosario Straits. Captain Vancouver and his officers named major land and water features around Puget Sound, such as Mount Baker, Mount Rainier, Puget Sound, Whidbey Island, Deception Pass, Dungeness, Bellingham, and Hood Canal.

French Canadian explorers and traders gave us Pend Oreille, Deschutes, The Dalles, and other names in French. American explorers were responsible for several Washington place names. The Columbia River and Grays Harbor are important names given by the American explorer, Robert Gray. Elliott Bay, Bainbridge Island, and Port Gamble are among the sites named by U.S. Naval Lieutenant Charles Wilkes in 1841. (Wilkes was commissioned by President Andrew Jackson to survey the rivers and bays of the Pacific Northwest, without attracting British attention. Wilkes recommended that the United States do all possible to win control of Puget Sound because of its excellent harbors.)

SECTION 3: INTERNATIONAL AGREEMENTS

What Were The Treaty Of Ghent Agreements?

In 1814, the United States and Britain signed the Treaty of Ghent, which ended the war of 1812. In the treaty, the two countries agreed to settle the borders between their territories.

Representatives of the two nations met several times in 1818. They decided that the 49th parallel of north latitude should form the U.S.-Canadian border from the Great Lakes to the Continental Divide.

But they were not able to reach a decision about who owned the Oregon Country. Instead, they agreed to meet to consider the issue again.

47. What was the Treaty of Ghent?
48. What parallel of latitude became part of the U.S.-Canadian border?
49. What did the United States and England decide about the Oregon Country?

What Border Agreements Did Spain Make?

In 1819, the U.S. Secretary of State, John Quincy Adams, and the Spanish minister, Luis de Onis, met to discuss their countries' claims. They settled the border between the Spanish Territories and the Louisiana Purchase. The United States purchased the Spanish lands called East and West Florida. And they agreed upon the 42nd parallel north latitude as the boundary between Spanish claims and Oregon Territory. Oregon now had three borders: the Continental Divide on the east, the Pacific Ocean on the west, and the 42nd parallel to the south.

50. Where did Adams and Onis agree to draw the boundary between Spanish territory and Oregon Country?

How Were Russian Claims Settled?

The northern boundary was more complicated. Russia wanted to claim more of the Pacific Coast. In 1815, Russian traders had a post in Hawaii and another one in California just north of San Francisco. Some Russians wanted to build a fort on the Columbia River.

In 1821, Czar Alexander of Russia claimed all land north of the 51st parallel of latitude. He prohibited all foreign ships from this part of the Pacific Coast.

The United States would not accept this. Adams and other Americans believed that U.S. claims might extend farther north. United States officials made an agreement with Russia in 1824. They signed an agreement which set the Russian border at 54° 40' north latitude. The two countries agreed to share the trade south of this line. The agreement was called the Russian-American Convention.

That same year, England signed a similar agreement with Russia. This was known as the Anglo-Russian Convention.

51. What were the Russian-American Convention and the Anglo-Russian Convention?
52. Where was the southern border of the Russian Territories established?

How Would England And The United States Settle Their Claims?

The borders of Oregon Country were now established. Only the United States and England remained to compete with each other, and with the Native Americans, for control of these lands.

The result of this competition would depend on several things. The early explorations by the U.S. and England gave each country certain claims. Gray's discovery of the Columbia River gave the United States a claim to that river's basin, for example. And Vancouver's exploration of Puget Sound gave a strong English claim to that area. As the fur traders explored and mapped the interior lands, they strengthened their country's claim to that area.

Settlement would also strengthen a country's claim. A large number of American settlers in the Northwest would give the U.S. a much better chance of winning these lands. For this reason, the English would try to keep Americans out of the areas they hoped to win.

The overall strength of each country was important, too. A powerful and independent nation would have a better chance of getting its way in international disputes.

53. Who still had claims to Oregon Country?
54. What things would determine who won the land?

Fort Vancouver was the center of fur trading activities in the Northwest for many years. What other businesses and activities seem to be taking place at the fort? Do you think this picture would have encouraged settlers to come to Oregon Country?

UNIT 4

FUR TRADERS AND MISSIONARIES

Fur traders were among the first explorers of the Pacific Northwest. They were also the first non-Indian settlers. Several of them married Native American women, became farmers, and raised their families here. They proved that settlement of this area was possible.

Missionaries made up the second group of settlers. The Protestant missionaries actively assisted and encouraged American settlement of the Oregon Country.

This unit talks about both of these non-Indian groups. It has five sections:

1. The Hudson's Bay Company
2. Later American Fur Traders
3. The First Missionaries
4. Catholic Missions
5. The American Board Missions

As you read, pay attention to the ways that these two groups influenced the non-Indian settlement of Oregon. Some questions to keep in mind are: How did the two groups use the environment? What were their attitudes toward the Native American residents?

SECTION 1: THE HUDSON'S BAY COMPANY

A Bloody Competition Is Ended

After the Pacific Fur Company left Fort Astoria in 1813, the North West Company had no competition in the Northwest. But on the east side of the Canadian Rockies, the North West Company had a powerful rival; the Hudson's Bay Company.

The contest between the two companies was often violent. Animals were destroyed; Native American trappers were bribed. There were even killings.

Finally, in 1821, the British government forced the two companies to merge (become one company). They would no longer be competing against each other.

The new company kept the name Hudson's Bay Company. This company controlled the fur business in what is now Canada and in Oregon Country. Sir George Simpson became the company's head in North America.

1. Which company competed with the North West Company on land east of the Canadian Rockies?
2. How was this competition ended?

Who Was The White-Headed Eagle?

The Hudson's Bay Company had to choose a Chief Factor, or director, for their business in the Oregon Country. This person would be business director, judge, governor, and policy-maker for the British citizens in the Territory. It was an important post.

The man they chose was Dr. John McLoughlin. McLoughlin had joined the North West Company as a post doctor when he was only nineteen. While he was working at the trading post near Lake Superior, he discovered that he was more interested in fur trading then doctoring because it was more profitable. He gained a good reputation as a trader during those years. In 1821, he was asked to help work out the merging of the North West and Hudson's Bay companies.

John McLoughlin was tall, strong, and bony. He had white hair and sharp blue eyes. So the Native Americans called him the "White-Headed Eagle."

3. What was John McLoughlin's first job with the North West Company?
4. What is a Chief Factor?

What Was Chief Factor McLoughlin Like?

McLoughlin always kept his word with Native Americans, and he ordered his employees to treat them with respect. In return, he won the Native Americans' respect and cooperation. In this way, he encouraged the tribes to trade only with the Hudson's Bay Company.

Chief Factor McLoughlin treated his non-Indian visitors well, too. He was famous for his excellent meals. He imported beautiful furniture for his house at Fort Vancouver. He welcomed and entertained settlers, trappers, and traders — even those who were competing with the Hudson's Bay Company.

McLoughlin's generosity sometimes got him into trouble. The company heads wanted to keep Americans out of Oregon. They felt that McLoughlin was encouraging them to come. But McLoughlin believed the Americans would come anyway. He said, "Where wheat will grow, settlers will go. Wheat will grow in Oregon." He hoped the American settlers might

CHIEF FACTOR JOHN MCLOUGHLIN
Do you think "White-Headed Eagle" was a good name for him? Why was McLoughlin's job so important?

become dependent on the Hudson's Bay Company.

McLoughlin's strong personality dominated non-Indian activities in the Northwest for many years. He was energetic and ambitious and had strong opinions. The Chief Factor had a stormy temper. But he often went out of his way to be helpful and kind. He was an unusual person to find in this rough, frontier environment.

5. What kind of relationship did McLoughlin have with the Indians?
6. How did he treat visitors? Who stopped at Fort Vancouver?

Why Did The Company Move To Fort Vancouver?

John McLoughlin came to his new job in 1824. He was accompanied by George Simpson, the director of the Hudson's Bay Company in North America. The two men immediately started looking for a better location for the company headquarters.

Since 1821, they had been using Fort George, the old Fort Astoria. But it could be too easily attacked. (Remember that the Pacific Fur Com-

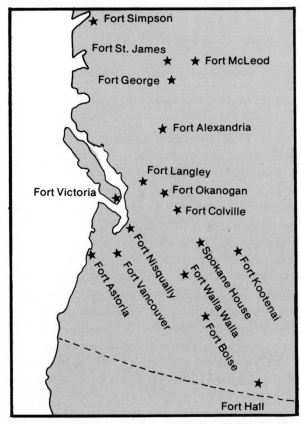

These were some of the most important forts of the Hudson's Bay Company. Which two forts were located near big company farms?

pany employees had not been satisfied with the location either. But Captain Thorn had been too impatient to look for a better site.)

Simpson wanted a place that would be closer to inland forts. He also wanted a site on the north side of the Columbia. He felt that England had no chance of winning the territory to the south. Simpson believed the Americans would get the Willamette Valley. But he wanted to be sure that England kept a strong claim to Puget Sound and the lands nearby.

McLoughlin chose a place 100 miles from the coast and called it Fort Vancouver. It is the present location of Vancouver, Washington. It was a safer location than Fort Astoria. It was close to the Willamette River and to rivers that flowed into Puget Sound. Also, there was rich farmland where the people at Fort Vancouver could raise food. This would allow the Company to raise its own food, instead of importing it.

7. Give several reasons why McLoughlin chose the new location of Fort Vancouver.

How Did Traders And Tribal People Depend On Each Other?

In addition to Fort Vancouver, the Company set up more than twenty other posts in all parts of the Oregon Country. Members of nearby tribes would hunt and trap beavers, sea otters, land otters, bears, and mink. Then they brought the skins to the posts to trade.

The trading session would start with the exchanging of gifts. Then the bargaining began. Only one or two Indian trappers were allowed in the fort at a time. This policy was designed to prevent conflicts and to help the company drive harder bargains. Trappers were given pieces of metal or wood "money" for the animal skins. These were then used to purchase goods such as blankets, beads, thread, buttons, knives, axes, and food.

The Hudson's Bay Company was careful to keep on good terms with the Native Americans. The company's business depended on Indian trappers. They tried to keep the tribes from trading with other fur companies. Often, the company built its forts close to tribal locations for this reason.

After a while, the Native Americans became more dependent on the company. The Indians'

Fort Walla Walla, a Hudson's Bay Company post. Why was the fort located near a tribal camp?

lives were changing. They grew accustomed to the new tools, clothing, and food that were available at the forts. The tribes were no longer meeting all their own needs from the resources around them.

8. Who did the Hudson's Bay Company depend on to trap the furs?
9. Why did the Company build its forts near tribal locations?
10. Why did Native Americans begin to depend on the fur company?

How Were Ships And Canoes Used?

Simpson wanted to trap all fur animals south and east of the Columbia River. This would discourage American trappers from coming to the area. Some parts of this area were far from the company forts. These distant areas were reached by boat. The Hudson's Bay Company sent ships up and down the coast to trade with some of the coastal tribes, for example.

The company would also send groups of trappers to remote (isolated, far away) river valleys. The most important — and most dangerous — expedition was the one to the Snake River area. This brigade was led by Peter Skene Ogden, the man that Ogden, Utah, was named after.

The men who accepted the challenge of these

expeditions were rough and adventuresome. They were often troublemakers. George Simpson called them "the very scum of the country." But they brought in some of the Hudson's Bay Company's best business.

11. What was the most important trading area that had to be reached by a canoe expedition?
12. Who was Peter Skene Ogden?

How Were Supplies Brought In?

The company used canoes for another important activity: the supply brigade. The supply brigade was made up of a large number of men and canoes. Each spring, the brigade would start out from Eastern Canada with important trading supplies. The men paddled and portaged their canoes along many rivers until they had crossed the continent and arrived at Fort Vancouver. They brought beads, blankets, tobacco, guns and ammunition, food, and other supplies. They also brought the mail. Other mail and supplies came by ship each year.

At Vancouver the brigade members loaded their canoes with the year's furs and started their long trip back to the East.

13. What did the brigade bring with them in the spring? What did they take back to Fort Vancouver?

WHAT WAS THE BRIGADE'S JOURNEY LIKE?

"In setting out on his journey, Mr. Ogden's practice, as well as that of all the Company's parties, is to go only a few miles the first day, in order that they may discover if anything has been neglected, and be able to return for it. . . Their brigade consisted of nine boats, rowed by sixty voyageurs, eight of whom had their Indian wives with them. . .The boatmen are Canadians, excepting about one-fourth, who are Iroquois Indians, all strong, active, and hardy men. They are provided only with a square sail, as the wind blows generally either directly up or down the river. . . .

"(During the portages) the load is secured on the back of a voyageur by a band which passes round the forehead and under and over the bale; he squats down, adjusts his load, and off he trots, half bent, to the end of the portage. . ."[1]

"Many years back, Mr. Ogden, while on his route, was attacked at the place where the fort (Walla Walla) stands, by the Wallawalla tribe, and was obliged to take refuge on the island near the fort, where he made a stand and completely routed the Indians. This occurrence took place twenty-three years before, and was the cause of this post being occupied; since which time no attack has been made.

"This will give some idea of the dangers the officers and men of the Hudson's Bay Company have to encounter; and although it is now safe on the Columbia River, yet there are many parts where they are still subject to these attacks: the voyageurs have a lot of toil and deprivation, yet few men are to be found so cheerful.[2]

[1] Gates, Charles Marvin, ed. *Readings in Pacific Northwest History*, Seattle: University of Washington Bookstore, 1941, pp. 54-55.

[2] Ibid., p. 59.

How Did The Forts Become Self-Supporting?

George Simpson believed strongly that the forts should be self-supporting (able to fulfill their own basic needs). John McLoughlin carried out this policy in the Pacific Northwest. Under McLoughlin's leadership, the Hudson's Bay Company became involved in farming, cattle-raising, shipbuilding, lumbering, and other enterprises.

At Fort Vancouver, for example, there were over 30 buildings, including carpentry shops, a blacksmith shop, a bakery, stores, a school, and a chapel. Outside the fort itself, there was a sawmill, a flour mill, and several hundred acres of farmlands. Wheat, corn, vegetables, and fruit trees were grown. The fort soon had herds of cattle, sheep, pigs, and horses. In addition, the company began salting and preserving large quantities of salmon.

Other Hudson's Bay Company forts in Oregon became involved in these activities. Soon, the company was producing a surplus (more than they needed). They began selling wheat to the Russian posts in Alaska in exchange for furs. They shipped large amounts of wool to England, and they also exported salted salmon and lumber.

By 1838, agriculture had become such a big business that the Hudson's Bay Company set up a separate agricultural company. Under McLoughlin's direction, the Puget Sound Agricultural Company operated two big farms, one on the Cowlitz River and another on the Nisqually River.

14. *What businesses besides fur trading did the Hudson's Bay Company become involved in?*

15. *What was the Puget Sound Agricultural Company?*

DAVID DOUGLAS

David Douglas, a Scottish botanist, visited the Northwest in 1824. (A botanist is a scientist who studies plants.) Everywhere he went, he collected samples and seeds of plants. He also studied the birds and animals and native customs of each area.

Douglas was a careful observer. His journals include notes on the landscape, types of vegetation, history, and Native American life of the Northwest. He introduced many new kinds of plants to Europe. The Douglas fir tree was later named in his honor.

SECTION 2: LATER AMERICAN FUR TRADERS

What Was The Rocky Mountain Fur Company?

After John Jacob Astor's company left Fort Astoria in 1813, British fur companies controlled almost all the fur trade in Oregon Country. The Hudson's Bay Company became successful and strong.

Yet some American trappers began moving into the Rocky Mountain areas to trade for furs. In 1823, two Americans set up the Rocky Mountain Fur Company with hopes of taking away some of the Hudson's Bay Company's trade.

The Rocky Mountain Fur Company did not build forts. There were no central trading houses. Instead, the Rocky Mountain Company trappers lived and traveled alone. They were called mountain men.

Some of them became famous. Perhaps you have heard of Kit Carson, Jim Bridger, Joe Meek, or Mike Fink. They were all mountain men at one time.

The mountain men were unable to compete successfully with the stronger Hudson's Bay Company in the Pacific Northwest. They resented the British company because of this.

16. What nationality were the owners of the Rocky Mountain Fur Company?
17. Who were the mountain men?

American Traders And The Hudson's Bay Company

The Hudson's Bay Company was powerful enough to control almost all the fur trade in Oregon Country. The mountain men were forced to work in the Rocky Mountains and the lands east of the mountains. The Hudson's Bay Company was always careful to keep out American competition.

Still, the American traders were nearly always treated well at Hudson's Bay Company posts. The story of Jedediah Smith is an interesting example.

Smith was one of the owners of the Rocky Mountain Fur Company. In 1828, he and men from his company were trapping for furs in Spanish-owned California. When the Spanish learned what Smith and his men were doing,

---

JIM BECKWOURTH: BLACK TRAPPER

Most of the fur traders were white or part white and part Indian. But there were some Black fur traders, too. The most famous Black trapper was James P. Beckwourth. Beckwourth had been an apprentice to a blacksmith in the Midwest. (An apprentice is a student who learns by working for an master worker. Blacksmiths make horseshoes, tools, etc. out of iron.) But the blacksmith was harsh with him, and Beckwourth ran away to the western wilderness. He became a mountain man for the Rocky Mountain Fur Company.

Beckwourth married a Crow Indian woman and helped the Crows fight their enemies, such as the Blackfeet. He became a respected fighter, and was made a Crow chief. But he left the tribe and headed for California. He worked as an army scout and later guided the first wagon train through the Sierra Nevada Mountains. The mountain pass he discovered, as well as a mountain and a valley, were all named for him.

---

they forced the Americans to leave. The trappers moved north to what is now the state of Oregon. There, disaster awaited them. Indians attacked and killed almost all of them.

Smith and the few survivors hurried to Fort Vancouver. Chief Factor McLoughlin welcomed them. He even bought the furs they had for a fair price. And he warned the other tribes in the area not to harm Smith's men.

Jedediah Smith was grateful for McLoughlin's help, but angry at the Hudson's Bay Company's control of the region. He decided to leave Oregon. He knew he could not compete with his powerful hosts. He went east of the Rocky Mountains to trap and trade.

Smith went away, but he didn't keep quiet. He wrote a letter to the U.S. Secretary of War, describing the British company's power and influence in the Northwest. In the years that followed, many other Americans would complain to the United States government about the company's great power.

18. Name an area of the Oregon Country where the Rocky Mountain trappers competed successfully against the Hudson's Bay Company.
19. How did McLoughlin treat the American trappers?
20. How did Jedediah Smith feel about the Hudson's Bay Company?

This photo was taken at a fourth of July festival in 1909. It was many years after the last rendezvous, but both gatherings included similar activities. The old rendezvous dances may have looked something like this.

HOW DID THE MOUNTAIN MEN LIVE?

The mountain men's lives were rough and exciting, dangerous, and lonely. The men grew used to spending long periods of time alone in the wilderness and walked as much as three or four thousand miles each year. Trapping seasons were fall and spring. During the winter they camped in crude cabins or Indian shelters. In summer, they carried their year's catch to the rendezvous.

A mountain man's life was hard and full of dangers. A man could freeze to death or starve or die of scurvy. Some men got lost in the desert and died of thirst. There were avalanches in the mountains, and rocky rivers could easily upset a boat and drown the passenger. There were grizzly bears and other killer animals, and some of the Indian tribes would attack and kill the trappers.

The men worked and walked in heavy snow and pouring rain, and they usually had no warm cabin to come home to. They had to provide all their own food, clothing, shelter, and so on. Most of the men had Indian wives who helped them provide the things they needed to stay alive.

In order to survive their life in the wilderness, the mountain men had to develop many skills. They had to be good at riding horses, shooting, and piloting boats along the river. They had to become very familiar with the land, the animals, and the Native American residents.

For example, beavers are intelligent animals, with an excellent sense of smell. Trappers had to wade through streams as they set their beaver traps, to be sure that no human smell would remain. They studied the beavers' habits as carefully as scientists, and knew where to find them and just where to set their traps.

The mountain men also studied carefully the dif-ferent Native American tribes. They learned many survival skills from the Indians. And they learned which tribes to beware of and how each tribe fought.

They knew how to build shelters, repair their clothing, and make a cache that no animal could smell and nobody else could see. (A cache — pronounced "cash" — is a hole, lined with wood or leaves to keep out wetness, where furs or supplies were stored until needed.) The mountain men also knew the geography of the West better than any other non-Indians.

As a result, mountain men were the best guides in the West. Wagon trains, survey teams, railroad companies, and the army all relied on mountain men for leadership and advice.

The mountain men did their trading at a yearly rendezvous (pronounced ron-day-voo). The rendezvous was part business and part pleasure. Sometimes as many as 2,000 people showed up, most of them Native Americans.

The business end of a rendezvous was the trading of furs for supplies. Mountain men and Indian trappers would bring all the furs they had trapped or traded over the year. The company brought supplies and trade goods in by canoe from St. Louis. Flour, sugar, coffee, alcohol, guns, ammunition, and tools were some of the things that were traded for furs at the rendezvous.

Trading was just one part of the rendezvous, however. The whole event was more a carnival than a business meeting. There were games, races, feasts, dancing, and gambling. Indians and traders all participated together. Sometimes a trader would spend his whole year's earnings in the brief excitement of the rendezvous.

JEDEDIAH SMITH

Jedediah Smith was an intelligent and religious man. Religion was rare among the mountain men, and Smith earned the nickname "the Praying Trapper."

Smith was respected both as a skilled trapper and also as a leader and explorer. He kept careful journals and added much to the geographic knowledge of his time.

Jedediah Smith came close to death many times during his adventurous life. During the trip to California, he almost died of thirst many times in the desert. Some of his men did die. Smith barely missed being killed by Indians in Oregon.

Still, he was quite young — just 31 — when he died. He and his men were in the desert again, and he was out searching for water when Comanche Indians shot him. His body was never found.

What Happened To Other American Businessmen?

Some other Americans tried to start businesses in Oregon Country at this time. None of them was very successful. Three of the best known American "failures" at this time were Nathaniel Wyeth, Hall Jackson Kelley, and Benjamin Bonneville.

Wyeth was a businessman from Massachusetts. In the early 1830's, he tried to start a northwest company that would sell salted salmon and furs. He had lots of bad luck. His first supply ship sank, and a second one was badly damaged. Also, Wyeth did not have enough experience to compete with the older company.

Neither did Captain Benjamin Bonneville. Bonneville spent a lot of money trying to start a fur trading business in Oregon Country, but he was not able to make much money. He blamed the Hudson's Bay Company for his failures.

Bonneville became famous when his story was written up by Washington Irving, the most popular American writer of his day. Irving's book, *Astoria,* is a highly romantic (and not quite realistic) history of fur trading in the American West.

Benjamin Bonneville has two other claims to fame. He was the first person to bring wagons through the South Pass in the Rocky Mountains. And the great Bonneville hydroelectric dam was named after him.

Hall Jackson Kelley was inspired by the writings of Lewis and Clark and other people who had visited the Northwest. He devoted his life to encouraging other Americans to settle there. He believed that Oregon Country should belong to the United States, not England. He strongly criticized the Hudson's Bay Company. He wrote about Oregon, and he gave many speeches.

Kelley's activities were mostly unsuccessful. In his lifetime, few Americans moved to the Pacific Northwest.

21. Who were Nathaniel Wyeth and Benjamin Bonneville? Why did their Northwest businesses fail?
22. What are Captain Bonneville's claims to fame?
23. What did Hall Jackson Kelley devote his life to?

How Did Fur Trade Contribute To Settlement?

Good fur trade requires lots of undeveloped, unpopulated land. Fur trading is a wilderness business. Trapping and settling do not go together well. Settlers start farms and towns and cities. They clear the land of trees and develop it. They chase the animals away. The coming of settlers was always a sign that the end of big fur profits was near.

Yet the fur companies themselves were responsible in many ways for bringing settlers to Oregon. For example, the Hudson's Bay Company proved how good the land was for farming and ranching. They showed that money could be made from the salmon and lumber resources of the area. The pleasant life at the forts was proof that the land was good for settlement. Many Hudson's Bay Company employees actually did settle near the forts after they retired from the fur business. John McLoughlin seemed to know all along that settlers would come no matter what he did. He made sure that by the time many American settlers came to Oregon, the Hudson's Bay Company had already taken most of the area's furs.

Fur traders also discovered some important passes through the mountains. For example, Robert Stuart and a group of Astorians once became lost in the Rockies and accidentally discovered the South Pass. Jedediah Smith and Captain Bonneville later proved that wagons could be brought through this pass. This meant that settlers would be able to use this route to get to Oregon Country. And they soon did.

24. Why does settlement bring an end to big fur profits?
25. How did fur traders help make settlement of Oregon Territory attractive?

SECTION 3: THE FIRST MISSIONARIES

Why Did Some Northwest Indians Go To St. Louis?

In 1831, four members of the Nez Perce and Flathead tribes went to St. Louis to talk to Captain William Clark, of the Lewis and Clark expedition. They explained that their tribes wanted to learn about the white people's religion.

Native Americans believed that a person's power and possessions were gifts from spirits. White explorers had powerful tools and weapons, such as guns and metal knives. Therefore, the tribes assumed that powerful spirits must have given the explorers these things. They wanted to learn about the white people's way of dealing with spirits.

An Indian agent named William Walker heard about the Native Americans' visit. He was deeply impressed. Walker described their visit in a letter which he wrote to a Protestant religious magazine. Oregon Indians were anxious for religious instruction, Walker said. He urged the church to send missionaries.

The article created a great response. Since the early 1800's, some American churches had been interested in sending missionaries to the West. Several missionary societies had been formed. Missionaries had been in Hawaii since 1819. Walker's article convinced people that Oregon would be a good location for missions.

26. Why did Native Americans want to learn about the explorers' religion?
27. How did the Protestant churches become interested in sending missionaries to the Northwest?

A Great Misunderstanding

Most missionaries did not understand the Native American culture. Many missionaries believed that if people became Christians they would change their values, customs, and beliefs. They assumed that Native Americans wanted to change their culture, as well as their religion. Of course, this was not true. They failed to understand why Native Americans wanted to learn about Christianity. Neither group understood what the other group wanted or expected.

28. What did most missionaries believe people would do when they became Christians?

The Lees Come to Oregon

Two men volunteered to go to Oregon as missionaries. They were Jason Lee and his nephew, Daniel Lee. Both were Methodist ministers.

The missionaries were supposed to go to the plateau land of the Nez Perce and Flathead — the people who had requested teachers. But the Methodists settled in the Willamette Valley. They wanted to be close to Fort Vancouver for supplies and protection, and they wanted good farm land. They planned to use the Willamette location as a base for other missions. The Lee's first mission was located 10 miles north of the present site of Salem, Oregon.

The Native American population in the Willamette Valley was small. But the land was fertile and good for settlement. Several former Hudson's Bay Company employees had settled there already.

29. Where did the Lees build their mission?

Daniel Lee was one of the first missionaries in Oregon Country. How did the Native Americans and the missionaries misunderstand each other?

Reinforcements. . . And A Replacement

The missionaries had plenty of work to do. They built a house, started a garden and a school, began holding religious services, and adjusted to the new environment. Soon they asked the Methodist church to send more help. The men especially wanted some women to come. The churches agreed that the men should be married. Then they could start a community of Christian families.

In 1837, Dr. Elijah White and his family, a carpenter, a blacksmith and his family, and three young single women joined the mission. The women were all soon married to the single men at the mission.

Still the mission wanted more people and support. Jason Lee decided to go east to talk to church leaders. He also carried a message to Congress, asking the United States government to claim Oregon.

Lee returned with 52 people, including farmers, mechanics, teachers, a doctor and more missionaries. They opened new missions, both north and south of the Columbia River. This group is sometimes called the "great reinforcement."

By now, the Lees had a large garden, herds of horses and cattle, and a congregation of twenty-five adults. Jason Lee seemed to be more interested in white settlement than in converting or teaching the tribal people. He was not successful in his missionary work. Few Native Americans became interested in Christianity. Fewer and fewer Native American students were coming to his school. Finally, the Religious Board of the Methodist Church decided to replace Lee. They sent another missionary named George Gary to take Lee's place in Oregon.

30. What was the "great reinforcement?"
31. Why was Lee "fired?"

SPOKANE GARRY

Some of the most successful missionaries were Native Americans who had been educated at Christian schools. The most famous of these was Spokane Garry.

In 1825, George Simpson picked two Indian boys to go to the school at Red River. (This is the present location of Winnipeg, Manitoba, in Canada.) The boys were both sons of chiefs. One was from the Spokane tribe, the other was a Kootenai. Simpson named them Spokane Garry and Kootenai Pelly.

At the school, they studied reading, writing, English, history, geography, farming, and the Christian religion. Their teachers were Episcopal priests.

Four years later, they returned to their people. Little is known about Kootenai Pelly. But Garry became an important tribal leader. He lectured and preached about Christianity to several tribes. He taught his followers to say prayers in the morning and before meals and to obey the Ten Commandments. Unlike the white missionaries, Garry never forced his people to give up their traditional way of life. His simple style of Christianity was popular.

But then the Walkers and the Eells set up the Tshimikain mission nearby. They criticized Garry's kind of Christianity. The missionaries started religious arguments that divided the tribe. Garry and others grew angry as a result.

Garry helped lead his people in difficult years while American settlers were taking over their land and killing many of their people. Garry's own land was stolen by a white farmer. He died four years after this happened. He was over 80 years old.

SECTION 4: CATHOLIC MISSIONS

A Request For Black Robes

The Lees served as ministers to the Protestants who lived in the Willamette Valley. But there were French Canadian Catholics in the area who had come west to work for the Hudson's Bay Company. The French Canadians wanted Catholic priests to come to Oregon also. They asked McLoughlin to request that priests be sent.

This request presented the company with a problem. The company did not want any "black robes" to settle near the Lees' mission. (Catholic priests wore long, black garments, so "black robes" was the name that Native Americans used to identify them.) The two different religions would probably compete with each other for Native American members. Each religion would criticize the other, and the Indians might become angry with both kinds of missionaries.

32. Who first requested that Catholic priests be sent to the Northwest?
33. Why didn't the Hudson's Bay Company want any "black robes" to come?

Bishops And Missionaries

The Hudson's Bay Company finally allowed some priests to come to Oregon. The British government required them to do this. The first to arrive were French Canadians — Father Francois Blanchet and his assistant, Father Modeste Demers. They built their first mission on the Cowlitz River in 1838. It was called St. Francis. Blanchet and Demers were not very involved in teaching the Indians. Instead, they served the French Canadian Catholics who already lived in the area. Both men were later made bishops.

Most Catholic missionary work was done among the Plateau tribes. The most famous missionary was Peter John de Smet. He was a Jesuit priest from Belgium. De Smet had lived and worked among the Native Americans in Iowa before he came west. He was trusted and respected by the Native Americans.

De Smet became known as a peacemaker. He helped create friendlier relations between the Blackfeet and their traditional enemies, the Flathead and the Nez Perce. He also helped keep peace between Native Americans and the new settlers.

34. Who were the first Catholic priests in the Pacific Northwest?
35. Who was Peter John de Smet? Why was he important?

How Were Protestants And Catholic Missionaries Different?

Protestant missionaries disapproved of many parts of the Native American culture. They believed the Indians could not become Christians unless they gave up their traditions. Many Protestant missionaries demanded that Indians give up their old religious beliefs and that they live and dress and worship like whites. Protestant missionaries would not accept Indians into the church unless they made great changes in their lifestyle.

Catholic priests were less demanding. They would baptize large groups of Native Americans into the Catholic faith. They were more willing to accept some tribal traditions. Also, Catholic missionaries did not anger the Native Americans by trying to bring more settlers onto tribal lands. They were often better accepted by Indian communities.

Neither the Protestants nor the Catholics were very successful. They were not able to convert large numbers of Native Americans to Christianity.

36. Why did Catholic missionaries often have better relations with Native Americans than the Protestants did?

A restoration of a Catholic mission at Cashmere, Washington.

Protestants And Catholics

The Hudson's Bay Company always felt that problems would arise from having Catholic and Protestant missionaries in the same area. They were right. Both groups tried to convince the Native Americans that the other was wrong. Sometimes the situation was similar to a political campaign, each side strongly criticizing the other. The Native Americans were caught in the middle. They were confused, and they resented it. As a result, many of them grew to distrust all missionaries, or did not take them seriously.

There were conflicts among the settlers, too. Catholic and Protestant settlers competed with each other for control of the settlements for many years.

37. *What problems were caused by competition between Catholics and Protestants?*

The Coeur d'Alene Mission was one of the first Catholic missions in the Northwest.

MOTHER JOSEPH

Today, a skilled, intelligent woman may pursue almost any career she wishes. But in 1843, there were few challenging job opportunities for talented women. Esther Pariseau was a young French Canadian woman with just this problem. At age 20 she was a skilled carpenter and woodcarver. Her father, a carriage-maker, had taught her; and he praised her abilities.

But no one would hire a woman carpenter in those days. No one, that is, except the church. Esther Pariseau decided to become a nun. After careful consideration, she chose the Daughters of Charity as the order she would join. They were located in Montreal, Quebec — not far from her home.

At the Daughters of Charity Convent, Esther Pariseau had many duties. She helped supervise the kitchen, garden, shoe shop, chicken yard, and laundry, as well as the weaving and dyeing of cloth and the making of soap. She also managed the candle-making business there. Soon she added responsibilities in nursing, sewing, and accounting.

In 1856, she was sent to Vancouver, Washington Territory. Here, she was known as Mother Joseph. (The title "Mother" shows that she was director of the Order's activities in this area.) During her 46-year stay in the Northwest, Mother Joseph accomplished an amazing amount. She established eleven hospitals, five Indian schools, seven academies, and two orphanages.

Best-known of the buildings was Providence Academy in Vancouver. It was begun in 1873, and was used as a school until 1966. The building is still standing and is now occupied by offices and shops. Mother Joseph participated personally in the construction of this building — as she did in other projects. She carved most of the woodwork in the chapel, for example.

Mother Joseph could often be seen on the building site of her projects. She might be testing the strength of a beam, checking the foundation, laying bricks, or doing carpentry. She kept doing this kind of work until she was almost 80.

Mother Joseph was also responsible for raising the money to fund her projects. There were few people in the Northwest then, and she often had to travel great distances on horseback. She and a small group of nuns travelled with a guide to the gold fields of Idaho, Colorado, and British Columbia. They visited the young Northwest settlements, too, begging for money for their charity projects. Most of the land was wild and unsettled, and they spent the nights in a tent, far from any other humans.

All in all, Mother Joseph's life was full of adventure, sacrifice, hard work, and responsibilities that were rare for a woman of her time — rare, in fact, for almost anyone.

In 1977, the Washington State Legislature voted to place Mother Joseph's statue in The United States Capitol Building in Washington, D.C. Each state is allowed only two statues in this collection. The other Washington State representative in the Capitol Building is Dr. Marcus Whitman.

SECTION 5: THE AMERICAN BOARD MISSIONS

The Whitmans Become Missionaries

A second group of Protestant missionaries came to Oregon Country in 1836. This group was sponsored by the American Board of Commissioners of Foreign Missions, which represented the Presbyterian, Congregational, and Dutch Reformed Churches. The American Board group was not much more successful at converting the Native Americans than the Lees. However, they were more successful at helping to bring American settlers to the Northwest.

The best-known of the American Board missionaries were Marcus and Narcissa Whitman. Like many missionary couples, the Whitmans were married just before they were hired. The trip to Oregon was their honeymoon.

Some people believe that the man who recruited the Whitmans also played as matchmaker. This man was Reverend Samuel Parker. When he met Marcus Whitman and Narcissa Prentiss, they were living in different towns. They both wanted to be missionaries to Oregon. But the American Board would only consider married couples. Some people believe that Parker suggested to Marcus that he go meet Narcissa. He did, and she agreed to marry him. They were both hired by the American Board.

38. Who hired the Whitmans as missionaries to Oregon?

What Were Marcus And Narcissa Whitman Like?

Narcissa Prentiss had turned down more than one offer of marriage before she agreed to marry Marcus Whitman. She was an extraordinary woman. She was well-educated, intelligent, and attractive. She had an excellent singing voice, she spoke well, and she enjoyed being at the center of a group.

Unfortunately, these qualities did not prepare her well for the job she chose. Narcissa Whitman was also proud and intolerant. She never got along well with Native Americans at the mission. She had a strong sense of duty and always worked hard, but she longed for "polite socie-ty." The lonely mission life made her unhappy, nervous, and ill.

Her husband, Marcus, was vigorous, energetic, strong, and fearless. He was a skilled and dedicated doctor. Sometimes he would ride a hundred miles through winter snows to visit a patient.

Yet Marcus Whitman was also badly suited for his job in some ways. He was serious, stubborn, and sometimes rude. He also seemed to be more interested in white settlement than in Native Americans, at least after 1843. Another missionary, Reverend Perkins, said that Whitman ". . . looked upon (the Native Americans) as an inferior race. . . doomed. . . to give place to a settlement of enterprising Americans." Dr. Whitman himself admitted in 1843 that, "I have no doubt our greatest work is to be able to aid the white settlement of this country."

39. What personal qualities of Marcus and Narcissa Whitman made them well-suited for their jobs?
40. What qualities made them poorly suited for their jobs?

Travelling To The Rendezvous

In 1835, Marcus Whitman and Samuel Parker travelled with fur traders to Oregon. They planned to find out whether any tribes really wanted missionaries. If so, the two men would choose locations for missions.

At first, the fur traders were suspicious and unfriendly toward the ministers. They were afraid that these people would demand annoying changes in their lifestyles, such as making them stop travelling on Sundays. On one occasion, the traders even threw rotten eggs at them.

But Whitman soon won their respect. He did

PROTESTANT MISSION •
CATHOLIC MISSION +

more than his share of heavy work. He cared for the men who became ill along the way. His skill and strength impressed the traders.

When they arrived at the traders' rendezvous, Whitman and Parker talked with the Native Americans there. A group of Nez Perce spoke to them through interpreters. They said they wanted doctors and missionaries. It seemed that Dr. Whitman had a place to go.

Reverend Parker agreed to go on ahead and choose mission sites. Dr. Whitman would go east to bring the other missionaries. They would all meet at the rendezvous the following year.

41. How did Dr. Whitman win the fur traders' respect?
42. Which tribe requested missionaries?
43. What did Parker and Whitman agree to do?

The Whitmans And Spaldings Make The Long Trip

Another missionary couple joined the Whitmans. They were Henry and Eliza Spalding. Surprisingly, Henry Spalding was one of the men that Narcissa had refused to marry. Spalding had known Narcissa since childhood, and at one point he had asked her to marry him. Her rejection caused bad feelings between them that lasted many years.

Despite these feelings, all four people agreed that they should go to Oregon together. They

This is Henry Spalding. He and his wife, Eliza, came West with the Whitmans. No photos were ever taken of Narcissa or Marcus Whitman.

A LONG HARD TRAIL

The missionary party had plenty of problems on their trip west. Rev. Spalding was kicked by a mule, and once he was knocked out of a ferry boat. He ended up in the water, along with a cow. One night the tent and blankets were blown away in a heavy storm.

Eliza Spalding was sick during most of the trip. Also, there were many quarrels between the missionaries.

Near the rendezvous, a messenger went ahead with the news that two white women were on their way. Joe Meek led a welcome party of trappers and Indians, to greet the travellers. They came galloping and yelling down from the hills and nearly gave the missionaries a big scare.

---

started out in the spring of 1836. They were accompanied by William H. Gray, a mechanic for the mission.

Dr. Whitman was determined to take wagons along on the trip. He wanted to prove that wagons could be brought through the mountains. A successful crossing would encourage settlers to move to Oregon.

The trip was difficult. One wagon was left behind along the way. The other had to be made into a two-wheeled cart. They took it as far as Fort Boise. Narcissa Whitman recommended that future travellers "not bring any baggage whatever, only what was necessary to use on the way." Many supplies could be purchased at Fort Vancouver, and other belongings could be sent around South America by ship.

Narcissa Whitman and Eliza Spalding were the first white women to make the long, rough, overland trip. They created quite a sensation at the rendezvous. And they inspired other American women to make the trip later.

44. Why did Dr. Whitman want to take wagons along on the trip west?
45. Why was the journey of Eliza Spalding and Narcissa Whitman especially significant?

How Did McLoughlin Help?

Reverend Parker failed to meet the other missionaries at the rendezvous. He had taken a ship and gone home. The Whitmans and Spaldings would have to choose their own mission sites. First, they would travel to Fort Vancouver and talk to John McLoughlin.

It must have been quite a relief to arrive at Fort Vancouver. At last the tired travellers could

This model represents the arrival of the American Board missionaries at Fort Vancouver. Can you pick out John McLoughlin? Who else was here at this event?

eat good meals and sleep in a warm house. Once again the Chief Factor gave his American guests a warm welcome. He even invited the women to stay at the fort while their husbands chose the mission locations. Later, McLoughlin gave them many supplies to help get the missions started.

46. How did McLoughlin help the missionaries?

Where Did They Settle?

Marcus Whitman chose a place on the Walla Walla River, 25 miles east of Fort Walla Walla. It was called Waiilatpu, which means "place of the rye grass" in the Cayuse language.

Waiilatpu was near the intersection of the main trails into Oregon Country. It was good farming land. But it was not a good place for a mission. The Cayuse people who lived in this area were proud and aggressive. They were friendly at first but grew to resent the missionaries.

Henry Spalding chose a location on the Clearwater River in the Nez Perce country. It was called Lapwai, meaning "place of the butterflies." It was close to the present site of Lewiston, Idaho.

The Nez Perce people were unhappy that Whitman chose a location in Cayuse country.

They wanted both missionaries on Nez Perce land. They warned the Whitmans that the Cayuse were an unfriendly people.

47. What locations did Whitman and Spalding choose for their missions?
48. What were the advantages and disadvantages of Waiilatpu?

What Did The Missionaries Do?

The Whitmans and the Spaldings had plenty of work to do. Like all pioneers, they had to build their houses and other buildings and furniture. They planted crops, raised animals, chopped firewood, and did many other daily chores.

As soon as they could, they began their missionary duties. They held religious services and started schools. Dr. Whitman also spent as much time as possible treating the sick.

The Whitmans built a sawmill and a flour mill. Henry Spalding translated and printed books in the Nez Perce language.

The missionaries soon had children to take care of, too. Both couples had their first children — both daughters — in 1837. Unfortunately, the Whitmans' daughter, Alice Clarissa, drowned when she was two years old.

49. What were some of the missionaries' daily activities?

MISSIONARY DIARIES

Some of the best descriptions of the missionaries' life came from the writings of Narcissa Whitman and Mary Walker. Narcissa kept a diary along the trail that is full of daily details like these:

Our cattle endure the journey remarkably well. They are a source of great comfort to us in this land of scarcity. They supply us with sufficient milk for our tea and coffee which is indeed a luxury. . . We have plenty of dry Buffalo meat which we purchased from the Indians and dry it is for me. I can scarcely eat it, it appears so filthy, but it will keep us alive and we ought to be thankful for it. . . [1]

Mary Richardson Walker also had stories about their trip to Oregon country.

"In the forenoon rode 10 miles. . . Got my horse in the mire; not hurt any. Felt well: picked gooseberries at noon. In the afternoon, rode 35 miles without stopping. Pretty well tired out, all of us. Stood it pretty well myself. But come to get off my horse (I) almost fainted. Laid as still as I could till after tea; then felt revived. Washed my dishes, made my bed, and rested well.

". . . we heard crackling in the willow bushes. I looked and saw something black. The hunters sprang from their horses, drew their guns from their cases, and aimed them at the willow swamp. They watched till they saw the bushes stir, then fired, then waited till they stirred again, then fired. After 5 or 6 shots, one of the bears was wounded, and ran out to escape. . . The firing continued, and soon we heard a growling. After a few more charges the other bear was routed, and attempted to escape; but just as he had proceeded up the hill far enough to give a fair view, a hunter lodged a bullet in his neck. He stopped instantly, turned a fine summersault, and lay still for a while. They fired again. After struggling a while he crawled back to a bunch of willows and died.[2]

[1]Allen, Harriet Day, comp., *A Pioneer Honeymoon: Selections from the Diary of Narcissa Prentiss Whitman,* 1808-1848, New York: Board of National Missions, 1946, p. 6.

[2]Phillips, Paul C., ed., *Historical Reprints,* Missoula: University of Montana, 1931, pp.7-8.

Who Helped Build The Missions?

The Whitmans were helped at Waiilatpu by a Black trapper named John Hinds. He stayed at the mission after helping to build it, and he died there in 1836.

The Nez Perce were very helpful to the Spaldings at Lapwai. They helped the missionaries move their belongings. The Native Americans also helped them build a traditional shelter of buffalo robes for the first winter. Henry Spalding gratefully wrote about the Nez Perce in his diary: "They took entire direction of everything, pitched. . .our tent, saddled our horses, and gladly would have put victuals (food) to our mouths, had we wished it." The Spaldings paid them for their help with tobacco and other goods.

50. Who was John Hinds?
51. How did the Nez Perce help the missionaries?

New Recruits

In 1837, William Gray went east to bring back more people for the missions. He was married while he was away. He and his wife returned in 1838 with a man named Cornelius Rogers and three missionary couples. They were: Mary and Elkanah Walker, Reverend and Mrs. Cushing Eells, and Mr. and Mrs. A. B. Smith.

Gray also brought back some cattle. Reverend Spalding was worried that all the buffalo would soon be gone. This would leave the tribe without an important source of food. Spalding encouraged the Nez Perce to raise herds of cattle, so that they would always have meat. The Nez Perce soon became skilled ranchers.

The Smiths stayed at Waiilatpu, and the other two couples started a new mission at Tshimikain. Tshimikain was located in the land of the Spokane tribe, northwest of present-day Spokane.

52. Who did Gray bring from the east?
53. Why did the missionaries encourage Native Americans to raise cattle?

Tshimikain Mission

Personality Problems

The American Board missionaries often quarrelled among themselves. Henry Spalding was still jealous of Marcus Whitman because he had managed to marry Narcissa. And the two men disagreed about how to run the missions. No one got along with William Gray, who could be quite unpleasant. Fortunately, the Walkers and the Eells got along quite well together. But quarrels between the other missionaries continued. They wrote several letters to the American Board, criticizing each other.

Finally, the Grays and the Smiths left the missions. The Whitmans and Spaldings worked out an agreement and seemed to be at peace with each other. They wrote another letter to the American Board and promised that the quarrels were over.

54. Give some examples of disagreements or bad feelings between the American Board missionaries.

What Was Dr. White's Bad News?

Waiilatpu was soon receiving American visitors. A small group of settlers arrived in 1840, on their way to the coast. Another group passed through in 1841. And in 1842, 114 new settlers arrived with a small wagon train.

The 1842 group was led by Dr. Elijah White who earlier worked at the Lees' mission. White carried shocking news from the East. He had a letter from the American Board which ordered the closing of Lapwai and Waiilatpu. The Grays, the Smiths, and the Spaldings were to return to the East. The Whitmans were told to move to Tshimikain. The Board had heard too many complaints from the Oregon missions.

The missionaries were horrified! Whitman refused to leave Waiilatpu. He wanted to stay where he could help new settlers.

It was late in the year, but Marcus Whitman decided to make the dangerous trip across the mountains. He had to talk to the Board members and make them change their minds.

He was successful. He returned the following year with permission to keep all the missions open.

55. When did groups of settlers begin passing through Waiilatpu on their way to the coast?
56. What bad news did Elijah White bring from the American Board?
57. Why did Marcus Whitman go east?

This painting shows the Waiilatpu Mission as it might have looked after the wagon trains began to arrive. Why was Dr. Whitman pleased with Waiilatpu's location?

The first legislature of Washington met in this small building. How do you suppose the first legislature was different from the one we have today? How would it be similar?

UNIT 5

AMERICAN GOVERNMENT COMES TO OREGON COUNTRY

Few people have the experience of starting a government where no government existed before. It's hard to imagine living somewhere with no judges, no police, no laws or elections or government services, and no taxes.

Yet the first American settlers in Oregon Country were in exactly this situation. The Native American residents had political and social customs that governed their behavior. But from the settlers' point of view, they were living in a place that was not part of any country and had no formal government at all.

If you were in the settlers' place, what do you think you'd do? What kind of government would you want? Would you want a government at all? Would you want to be part of the United States? How would you convince your neighbors to agree on the same kind of government?

Keep these questions in mind as you read this unit. There are five sections:

1. Provisional Government
2. Oregon Fever
3. Settling the Border Dispute
4. A Violent Response
5. Two Territories

SECTION 1: PROVISIONAL GOVERNMENT

How Did Early Settlers Live?

The early settlers in Oregon Country had to do without many items that they had been accustomed to. For example, their diet was quite limited, especially at first. Sugar, salt, and other basic foods were often not available, or they were too expensive. Sometimes a family lived almost entirely on deer meat for the winter. Pioneer journals are full of complaints about the boring food.

The first settlers lived in crude, tiny cabins with dirt floors. Four children and their parents might live, eat, work, and sleep together in a small two-room building. Often they had no glass for windows. Many settlers had no furniture other than the log tables and benches they made themselves.

The pioneers had to make almost everything themselves. They made their own soap and candles, for example, and many of their farm tools. Children's toys included hand-carved wooden tops and doll furniture. Pioneers made their shoes, socks, hats, and other clothing. They prepared leather from animals they killed and spun yarn from sheep they raised.

All farmwork had to be done by hand or with the help of animals. Clearing the land for the first crop was often extremely difficult. In Western Washington, the land was usually covered by thick forests. Every tree had to be chopped down and the trunks removed. After a while, the settlers were able to buy dynamite. They used it to blow up the huge tree stumps to make them easier to remove.

Then the crops had to be planted, tended, and harvested. Food had to be put away for the winter. Firewood had to be cut. Water had to be hauled from a well or stream nearby. And in Eastern Washington, the streams sometimes dried up in the summer. Everyone worked hard. Even the children worked "until they cried from weariness."

1. Name some things that early settlers had to do without.
2. Name at least five things that pioneers had to make themselves.

A settler's cabin in Oregon Country. What does this photo tell you about how the settlers lived?

Pioneer Entertainment

The pioneers had little time for entertainment, and few opportunities for it. Their "near" neighbors might live 30 miles away. There were no theaters or libraries. The few books they owned were loaned and exchanged from one family to another until they were worn out.

At Christmas parties and on other special occasions, people would bring a few musical instruments. Singing and dancing were favorite party activities.

For many Central Washington settlers, one very special event was a yearly trip to The Dalles, Oregon. This was the closest city and the only source of many goods. At The Dalles, families could buy windows, furniture, new tools, gentler hand soap, imported foods, and other items.

Some settlements soon developed into cities, such as Tacoma and Walla Walla. In these places, the pioneer period ended very quickly. But in remote areas, many settlers lived this kind of lifestyle until late in the 1800's.

3. What did pioneers do for entertainment?

Why Did The Settlers Need A Government?

Many things were missing from the early settlers' lives. Some of them were obvious and some were not so obvious.

For example, one of the things that many settlers missed very much was their American government. They missed the services, protection, and orderliness that a government offered.

The settlers believed they needed an army to protect them from possible Indian attacks. They wanted a system of police and courts to deal with criminals. More importantly, they needed some kind of government to handle such day-to-day problems as registering marriages, settling land claims, distributing the property of people who died, and printing money. Settlers also wanted schools, roads, and other government services.

4. Why did American settlers want some kind of government?

British Government Or American?

The Hudson's Bay Company had served as an informal government for British citizens in Oregon. Chief Factor McLoughlin acted as govern-

ing official.

But the Americans refused to accept the authority of the British company. Many American settlers hoped that Congress would claim Oregon as U.S. territory. The federal government would then provide Oregon with an army, a governor, a system of money, and other services. Several settlers wrote to Congress requesting this.

5. Why did American settlers want Congress to claim Oregon as U.S. territory?

How Did Congress Act Toward Oregon?

The members of Congress didn't seem very interested in Oregon at this time, however. Senator Lewis Linn of Missouri was one exception. He tried many times to get Congress to claim Oregon for the United States. But each time, his proposals were defeated or ignored.

In 1842, it seemed that one of Linn's proposals was finally going to pass. The President even appointed an Indian agent — the first U.S. government official for Oregon. He was Dr. Elijah White, the former missionary who informed the Whitmans of the plan to close Waiilatpu.

In the end, Congress defeated Linn's proposal once again. The 1842 bill did not pass.

6. How did Congress respond to Senator Linn's proposals about Oregon?

A Wealthy Man Dies

Some settlers grew impatient with Congress' delays. They decided to get a government started themselves. The first thing to do was to get the other settlers to agree to the idea. It would be necessary to get everyone together at some kind of meeting.

The death of Ewing Young in 1841 gave the settlers a perfect opportunity for such a meeting. Ewing Young was one of the wealthiest settlers in that area. He had made a fortune by selling cattle and operating a sawmill. He had no known living relatives. Since there were no laws or judges, there was no official way to decide who should get Ewing Young's property.

Canadian and American settlers got together at the funeral and appointed a judge. This man, Ira Babcock, was authorized to settle the question of Young's property.

EWING YOUNG

Ewing Young was the American trapper who accompanied Hall Kelley on his trip north from California. The Spanish government sent word that Young was a horse thief. As a result, Lee and McLoughlin refused to help him.

Young was furious. He went into a business that both McLoughlin and Lee opposed: he began to make and sell liquor.

Lee was finally able to make Young drop his liquor manufacturing business and take up a more community-minded profession. Lee and McLoughlin organized a cattle drive from California and offered Young the chance to lead it. Settlers needed cattle badly and Young made a small fortune selling the animals.

7. How did Ewing Young's death point up the need for a government?

8. How did the settlers agree to settle the question of Young's property?

What Happened At The Meetings?

But the Americans wanted to do more than appoint a temporary judge. They wanted a more permanent form of government — a government that could deal with other problems in the future.

At Young's funeral, government supporters discussed these ideas with the other settlers. They agreed to meet again to talk about setting up a government.

At the meetings that followed, the settlers chose a sheriff and other officials. They also selected a committee to draw up a code of laws. Father Blanchet was chosen to head this committee. The settlers agreed to meet a few months later to hear the committee's report.

9. What actions were taken at the meetings following Ewing Young's death?

Why Wasn't A Government Formed?

Father Blanchet never called the committee together. He resigned his position as committee chairperson. An American settler, William Bailey, was appointed to take his place. But Bailey didn't do anything with the committee either.

Why did both men fail to work with the committee to write a code of laws? Why couldn't a government get started?

There were several reasons. First, the population was divided into several conflicting groups. The Protestants and Catholics opposed each other. The French Canadian and American settlers often opposed each other. The Americans opposed the Hudson's Bay Company. Some of the Americans resented the power of the Lees' mission. The mission itself was split by arguments. None of the groups wanted the others to get too much power. Their disagreements made it hard to work on starting a common government.

Also, Chief Factor McLoughlin opposed the formation of a government. He was a very powerful person in the Oregon Country, and it was almost impossible to start an important project without his approval.

10. What were the conflicting groups in Oregon Country?

11. Why couldn't a government get started yet?

What Were The Wolf Meetings?

In February of 1843, interested settlers had another opportunity to bring up the issue of government. The settlers were meeting to discuss a common problem: wolves and other animals were killing their cattle. The settlers needed to start a "defensive and destructive" war against the wild animals.

Altogether, three meetings were held. At the second meeting, settlers agreed to pay a bounty (reward) to anyone who killed a wolf, panther, or bear. Every cattleowner would contribute to the bounty fund. Everyone supported the idea.

But again, some people didn't want to stop after solving the problem at hand. They wanted a government. Someone proposed that another committee be appointed. This committee would consider setting up a government.

The settlers approved this proposal. They agreed to hold a third meeting to hear the committee's report.

12. What common problem led to the wolf meetings?

13. What other issue besides wild animals came up at the meetings?

What Happened At Champoeg?

On May 2, 1843, the settlers gathered at Champoeg for the third Wolf Meeting. They waited for the committee report.

The committee announced that they were in

favor of starting a government. The American settlers who wanted a government began to cheer.

There are many stories of what happened next. The settlers were supposed to vote on the committee report. But the voting was very confused. Perhaps people didn't really understand what they were voting on. Perhaps the vote was so close that nobody knew which side won.

A popular story says that the confusion was settled by Joe Meek. Supposedly, he stepped forward, drew a line in the dirt with a stick, and said, "All in favor of the report and an organization, follow me." The opposing voters then lined up on opposite sides of the line. Joe Meek's side won. The government could get started. The defeated French Canadians left the meeting. The remaining settlers elected several officials. They also appointed another committee to write up a code of laws.

14. What was decided at Champoeg?

What Was The Provisional Government?

The Champoeg committee then held public meetings at Willamette Falls. They wrote a series of laws, based on the Iowa Territory Laws and the Northwest Ordinance of 1787.

They presented these laws to the community on July 5, 1843. Each law was read, debated, and voted on by those who attended the meeting. The people then voted to approve the whole code. It was called "The Organic Act of the Provisional Government of Oregon." (The word "organic" shows that this act created a new government. The word "provisional" means temporary. American settlers believed this government would last only until Oregon became a U.S. territory.)

15. Define these terms: "organic laws," "provisional government."

What Did The Organic Laws Say?

The Organic Laws created a government with three branches, similar to the United States government. The Legislative Branch consisted of nine representatives. Legislative districts were based on population. The Judicial Branch consisted of a superior court and local justices of the peace. The Executive Branch was to be a committee of three. (Normally, the Executive is one person — a governor. But settlers from the different groups still did not trust each other. They wanted the executive power to be held by more than one person.)

The Organic Laws also set up rules for claiming land. According to the laws, each adult male could claim 640 acres (one square mile). He had to mark his boundaries and file an official claim. Then he had to build a cabin or other structure on the land.

The Organic Laws guaranteed certain rights, including the right to worship and the right to trial by jury. Cruel or unusual punishment was prohibited. Native Americans were to be treated fairly. Slavery was prohibited. And the laws urged that schools should be started as soon as possible.

One unusual part of the Organic Laws is that taxes were voluntary. They were not required. Still, most people paid, although some people paid with food instead of money.

16. What were the three branches of the Provisional Government?
17. What were the rules for claiming land?
18. What rights were guaranteed?

The settlers built blockhouses like this where they could gather for protection in case of an Indian attack. Protection for themselves and their farm animals was one government service the settlers felt was needed. What were some others?

SECTION 2: OREGON FEVER

Wanted: American Settlers

The people who wrote the Organic Laws seemed confident that the United States would one day claim the Oregon Country. Yet in the summer of 1843, there were actually very few Americans in the Pacific Northwest. Clearly, more American settlers would have to arrive before the dream of becoming a United States territory could be realized.

It was not long before the settlers came. As a matter of fact, nearly 1,000 Americans were already on their way to Oregon while the Organic Laws were being written. These people made up the first really large group of settlers to travel across the Oregon Trail. This wagon train of 1843 was called the Great Migration.

19. What was the Great Migration?

Some Great Migration Leaders

The Great Migration was organized by Peter Burnett of Missouri. For months, he had travelled around his state, talking to people about going to Oregon. Many people in Missouri signed up for the expedition. Other people came from Ohio, Illinois, Kansas, and Tennessee.

Doctor Marcus Whitman, who was returning from his trip to the eastern mission offices, also joined the wagon train. His knowledge, help, and enthusiasm were extremely important to the trip. One member of the Great Migration, named Jesse Applegate, wrote this about Whitman:

"His great experience and. . . energy were of priceless value. . . His constant advice. . . was 'travel, travel, TRAVEL — nothing else will take you to the end of your journey'." From this point on, Whitman would devote much of his time to helping white settlers in Oregon.

20. Who organized the Great Migration?
21. Where did the people in the wagon train come from?
22. What experienced Northwest settler accompanied the Great Migration?

Packing Up

The people who signed up with Peter Burnett spent the next several months planning for the trip. They had to sell their farms, purchase wagons, and decide what to take along. Eagerly, they read the writing of Lewis and Clark and Hall Kelley, and whatever other information on Oregon they could find.

Imagine trying to pack into a small wagon everything needed for a long, slow journey and a new life in the wilderness. What would you take along? One later pioneer recommended that set-

the Oregon Trail

tlers pack the lower part of the wagon with "flour, corn meal, sugar, fruit, sorghum molasses, butter, lard, and other things in jugs and jars, well-wrapped bacons and hams, some vegetables, homemade soap, stock salt for the animals, rosin and tar for greasing the wagon wheels and other uses, medicine for both man and beast, extra bedding and clothing, and other equipment." More commonly used items were then packed on top of the other goods, or they were hung from the sides of the wagon. These might include pots and kettles, a water bucket, a rifle, an axe, a shovel, rope, and a hammer. Pioneers also brought their farm animals along: milk cows and beef cattle, horses, chickens, cats, and dogs.

23. Name some food, tools, and other items that the pioneers took along.

Getting Started

In May, 1843, all the expedition members gathered near Kansas City at the little town of Independence, Missouri. For a few weeks the tiny town was bursting with people and animals and activity.

The travellers had a fairly tight schedule. They couldn't start until enough grass had grown for the animals to eat along the way. And they had to cross the mountains before heavy snow made travel too dangerous.

The whole trip took up to six months. The oxen that pulled the wagons were more powerful than horses, but they were very slow. The average speed was only 12 to 18 miles a day. The same distance on the freeway would take you less than 20 minutes today!

24. What town did the Great Migration leave from?
25. What animals pulled their wagons?
26. How long did the trip take?

Rules Of The Road

Before they left, the people elected leaders and agreed on some of the rules of the road. One common rule or procedure was that the order of the wagons changed from day to day. Each family had a turn to be at the front and to be at the rear. The rear wagons had to put up with the dust raised by the others.

It took a lot of time to herd the cattle along beside the wagon train. The animals slowed

A wagon train descends a hill.

everyone down. So the train would split into two parts, or columns. The people with animals were called the cow column. They had to travel longer hours each day in order to keep up with the faster column.

For protection against hostile Plains tribes, the two columns stayed close to each other until they got to Central Wyoming. Then they split up into smaller groups for the mountain crossings.

27. What did the travellers agree on before they left?
28. Why did the wagon train split into two columns?

What Was The Travellers' Daily Schedule?

A day of travel with the cow column started at 4:00 a.m. The animals had to be herded together, breakfast had to be eaten, and the wagons had to be loaded and ready to go by 7:00. The long, slow day of travel began.

At noon, the leader of the train selected a place to stop for lunch. After an hour's rest, the journey began again.

Toward evening, each day, the leader would look for a place to camp. The wagons were drawn into a circle and chained together for the night. The animals roamed outside. The circle of wagons provided a shelter against unwanted visitors, both human and animal.

Within the circle, campfires were built and dinners prepared. A little music or dancing and conversation might provide a brief entertainment before the travellers went to sleep.

29. What were the daily routines of life on the trail?

Hard Work, Danger, And Romance

During the day, some men would ride off on horseback to hunt animals such as deer, antelope, or buffalo for food. Children would gather firewood as the wagons moved slowly along. Sometimes on the wide, dry prairies, both firewood and water were hard to find. Some people might have to ride a long way to get them.

Every day, it seemed, there were problems or dangers as well as adventures and new things to see. New trails had to be broken when the land was too rough or when the old tracks had been worn too deep to use. Sometimes Indians scared or attacked the travellers. There were diseases and deaths and many births. Often there was romance too, and there were several marriages along the trail.

30. Name some duties and problems of wagon train travel.

The Worst Part Of The Trip

The most difficult part of the trail was the end. No one had taken such heavy wagons into the Snake River Country and across the Blue Mountains of Oregon before. The traders at Fort Hall (located in what is now Eastern Idaho) urged the travellers to leave their wagons behind. But Dr. Whitman was sure they could make it. He convinced the travellers to try it.

It wasn't easy! Sometimes there was no grass for the cattle to eat. There were trees that had to be chopped down and gullies or ditches that had to be filled.

Travelling along the Columbia was difficult, too. The wagons were loaded on barges and floated downstream. But they had to be portaged around the falls. Some of the boats were wrecked, and two people drowned.

Getting the cattle down the river was even harder. The south bank of the river was a hard route to travel. Some people tried to swim their cattle across to the north bank, but many animals drowned. After 1845, an overland route became available, and many settlers paid a toll to use it. This was known as the Barlow Road.

31. Why was the end of the trail so difficult?
32. Who talked the travellers into taking their wagons into Oregon?

Why Not Stay Home?

The trip from Independence, Missouri, to Fort Vancouver was difficult, exhausting, and often dangerous. Many people died along the way. Some drowned, some died in accidents, many died of diseases, and a few were killed by Indians.

Many animals were also lost. Cattle starved to death in the mountains and deserts, drowned in the rivers, or died from drinking polluted water.

The trip was expensive, too. The wagon and

PIONEER WOMEN DESCRIBE THE TRAIL

Thousands of women helped their families make the long and difficult trip across the Oregon Trail. Several of them kept journals of their travels. The following descriptions of life along the Oregon Trail were taken from the journals of two pioneer women:

"The night was very rainy and disagreeable. Our tent was completely drenched. . . We must make the most of it and live in the mud a day or two.

". . . I hung out what things were wet in the wagon, made griddle cakes, stewed berries, and made tea for supper. After that was over, made two loaves of bread, stewed a pan of apples, prepared potatoes and meat for breakfast and mended a pair of pants for William. Pretty tired."[1]

"A beautiful day. . . I mount a horse and help to drive the loose cattle. We do not go far until we come to a river where we stop for the balance of the day. . .

"We travel over dreadful, sandy road. The poor (cattle) did not get one bite to eat this morning. . .

"It was very cold last night. There was ice this morning on the water in the basin. The wind is blowing very hard. The dust is so thick we cannot see through it. Oh, it is horrible! We are a little bit on this side of South Pass eating dinner. I can see nothing for I have the curtain tied tight down to keep the wind and the dust out. . . Oh if we were only all the way (there). how glad I would be."[2]

[1] *Diary of Charlotte Emily Stearns Pengra*, 1853, Eugene, Oregon; Lane County Historical Society.

[2] *Diary of Helen Stewart 1853*, Lane County Pioneer Historical Society, Eugene, Oregon, 1961. (edited by Ruth Pelz)

PROFILE OF THE OREGON TRAIL

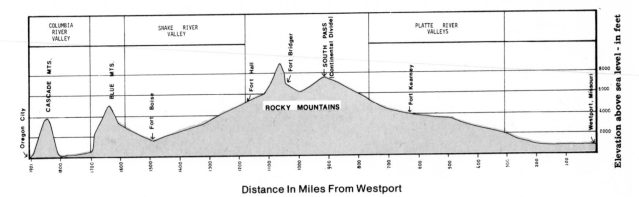

Distance In Miles From Westport

(12 Miles West Of Independence, Missouri)

other supplies cost $1,200 to $1,800 — at a time when wages averaged $1.50 a day. A family usually had to give up many things in order to come.

Why, then, did people want to come? First, there were several reasons for wanting to leave the Midwest, where most settlers had lived. There had been a depression in the mid-1840's, and money was scarce. People hoped they could make more money in Oregon. Midwestern farmers were angry at the high cost of transporting their goods to eastern cities. Farmers in Oregon could sell their crops in Asia, they believed. They would not have to compete with East Coast farmers. Also, some people were anxious to leave the states where slavery was practiced.

33. What were some dangers of the trip to Oregon?
34. Why did people want to leave the Midwest?

Why Did People Want To Go To Oregon?

In addition, the stories people heard about Oregon made it seem quite attractive. Lewis and Clark, Hall Kelley, Marcus Whitman, and others talked about the good farm lands and the healthy climate. Water, wood, fish, and other natural resources were abundant, they said.

But the main attraction of Oregon was free land. Senator Linn's bill guaranteed free land to those who would go to Oregon and claim it. This bill would give 640 acres (one square mile) to every adult male and 160 acres to each child. (The bill did not mention women.) The bill had already been passed by the Senate, and people expected the House of Representatives to pass it, too. (Actually, the bill failed to pass, but settlers

did not learn this for quite a while.)

Another attraction was the adventure of moving to the frontier. Some people wanted the chance to get ahead in politics or business. Also, many people were influenced by the belief that America should stretch from coast to coast. They believed that North America was meant to come under the democratic government of the United States. This belief was called Manifest Destiny. (Manifest means obvious, and destiny is fate or future.) Manifest Destiny was an important issue in American politics for several years.

In the years following the Great Migration, thousands of Americans went west over the Oregon Trail. About 1,500 people made the trip in 1844, about 3,000 in 1845. Excitement about Oregon seemed to be spreading faster than the common cold. It was soon given the name "Oregon Fever."

35. Why was Oregon so attractive?
36. What was Manifest Destiny?
37. What was Oregon Fever?

How Did The Newcomers Change The Provisional Government?

The new settlers were not familiar with the events that led to the forming of the Provisional Government. They didn't understand the relationships between the various non-Indian groups. As a result, they couldn't understand why the Methodist mission should have special privileges. They couldn't understand why the Hudson's Bay Company was not controlled by the Provisional Government. They disapproved of the three-person executive committee. They

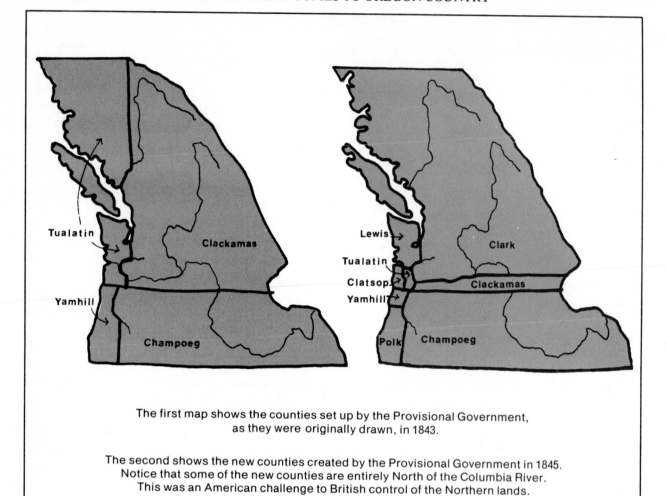

The first map shows the counties set up by the Provisional Government,
as they were originally drawn, in 1843.

The second shows the new counties created by the Provisional Government in 1845.
Notice that some of the new counties are entirely North of the Columbia River.
This was an American challenge to British control of the Northern lands.

wanted one elected governor. And they did not like the idea of voluntary taxes.

The new settlers outnumbered the old ones. In the 1844 elections, all but two of the elected legislators were newcomers.

The new legislators voted to change the government. They took away the mission's special land privileges. They organized a formal tax system. They replaced the executive council with a governor. The person elected to be the first provisional governor was George Abernethy.

Unfortunately, the new legislators also passed a law prohibiting all Blacks from moving to Oregon. Not only slaves, but even "Free Negroes" would be illegal. (Such a law was typical of the racism that existed in the United States at that time.)

38. *What aspects of the Provisional Government did new settlers disapprove of?*
39. *What new laws did the new settlers pass?*
40. *Who was George Abernethy?*

George Abernathy was elected first governor of the Provisional Government. Why did the settlers elect one governor instead of three?

SECTION 3: SETTLING THE BORDER DISPUTE

New Discussions, Old Demands

In 1841, there were only 150 American settlers in the Oregon Country. The number of British and French Canadians in Oregon was 700 to 800. By 1846, the American population had grown to five or six thousand. The Hudson's Bay Company could no longer control the area.

Clearly, it was time for England and the United States to decide who owned the Oregon Country. In 1844, the U.S. Secretary of State, John C. Calhoun, began meeting with a British official named Richard Pakenham. Their job was to agree on a boundary between American and British claims in Oregon.

Pakenham and Calhoun met several times. But they couldn't reach an agreement. The United States insisted that the border should be the 49th parallel of north latitude. But the British still insisted that the border should be the Columbia River. (See map page 92.)

One country — or both of them — would have to change its demands before the boundary could be settled.

41. Why did John C. Calhoun and Richard Pakenham meet several times?
42. What different borders in Oregon did the U.S. and Britain insist on?

Americans Settle North Of The Columbia

American claims to Oregon grew stronger every year, as more Americans settled there. British claims were strong as long as the Hudson's Bay Company was active.

The Hudson's Bay Company had been very strong ever since it came to Oregon. For years, the company controlled almost all the fur trade and most other businesses in the area. Chief Factor John McLoughlin was probably the most powerful person in the Oregon Country.

But in 1845, there were many signs that the Hudson's Bay Company was losing its power. For example, Americans started settling north of the Columbia River, where British claims were strongest.

One group of these American settlers was led by George Bush and Mike Simmons. They came almost by accident. Simmons had led a large wagon train across the Rockies that summer. The people planned to settle in the Willamette Valley. But then they heard about the new law that prohibited settlement by Negroes.

George Bush was Black. He had been a helpful and respected member of the wagon train. He had made quite a bit of money in the cattle business, and he helped pay the expenses of many of the poorer members of the train. He was familiar with the West, and his knowledge was very helpful to pioneers. Simmons and others were very angry at the law prohibiting settlement by Blacks. So the Bush family, the Simmons family, and others headed north. They wanted to settle away from the influence of the Provisional Government, in a place where Blacks might have an equal chance.

Mike Simmons founded the town of Tumwater (called New Market at first). He and Bush built a mill there. Then Bush began farming in what is now Thurston County. Bush Prairie was later named after him. George Bush's son, William Owen Bush, was later elected to the state legislature.

McLoughlin didn't want Americans to settle near Puget Sound. But once Bush and Simmons decided to do it, McLoughlin helped them, as he had helped so many of the newcomers.

43. Why were American claims to Oregon getting stronger?
44. What was one sign that the Hudson's Bay Company was losing its power?
45. Why did George Bush and his family settle north of the Columbia River?

The Hudson's Bay Company Gives In

There were other signs that the Hudson's Bay Company was losing power. One American settler actually tried to stake a claim right on Fort Vancouver land. McLoughlin ordered him to leave. The settler refused to obey. Finally, McLoughlin asked the Provisional Government for help. The government supported him. The settler left.

But this was a serious challenge to John McLoughlin's authority. A few years earlier, no

GEORGE BUSH

George Washington Bush had already had quite a full life before he started on the Oregon Trail. He was the son of a Black sailor and an Irish maid, and he grew up in the home of a wealthy Quaker ship-owner, his parents' employer. He was educated in a Quaker school. He fought in the War of 1812 and the Blackhawk Indian wars.

He married a white woman named Isabelle James who had been a nurse in the Indian wars. They had five sons. The Bushes settled in Clay County, Missouri, and made a good living selling livestock. Their neighbors respected them and asked them to join the wagon train to Oregon.

Once in Oregon, Bush became a successful farmer. He continued to help out his poorer neighbors and was considered an outstanding member of the small community. He also became friends with Chief Leschi and other Indians in the area. The Bushes named their youngest son Lewis Nisqually, in honor of their Nisqually Indian neighbors.

The Donation Land Law of 1851 did not allow Blacks to claim land. But the first Washington Territorial Legislature asked for special permission to give Bush his claim. Permission was granted.

---

one would have dared to claim company land.

The Provisional Government also acted to take away the company's power. In 1845, they declared that Fort Vancouver came under the Provisional Government's rule.

McLoughlin protested. The Provisional Government was an American government, he argued; and no American government could control British land.

But the Americans were growing stronger every year. McLoughlin could see that he would have to cooperate with the Provisional Govern-ment. He decided to participate in the government in order to have a say in its decisions. He put Fort Vancouver under Provisional Government rule.

McLoughlin's boss, George Simpson, was very angry at this. He believed that the Chief Factor was only helping to make American claims stronger. McLoughlin finally resigned as Chief Factor and became an American citizen. (He hoped, in this way, to protect his personal property.)

Simpson and the Chief Factor had many disagreements over the years concerning treatment of American trappers and settlers. Simpson always believed that the Chief Factor was too kind and helpful to the Americans. In the end, McLoughlin's kindness was not repaid. The American government took McLoughlin's land away from him and used it to build a university. McLoughlin protested, but the government paid no money for the land until after the Chief Factor was dead. His sons finally did receive some of the land in return for a large payment to the university.

46. Why did McLoughlin allow Fort Vancouver to come under the Provisional Government's rule?

Fifty-four Forty Or Fight

Meanwhile, Oregon was becoming a big issue in United States politics. Some Americans wanted the U.S. to claim all of the Oregon Country — all the way to 54°40' north latitude. This was the old border of the Russian-American Convention. These people believed

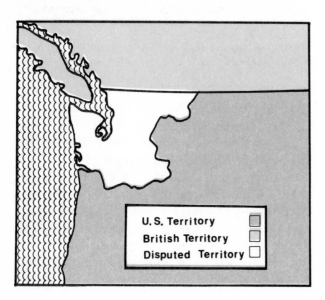

U.S. Territory ☐
British Territory ☐
Disputed Territory ☐

THE HUDSON'S BAY COMPANY: FRIEND OR ENEMY?

A great many of the American settlers had been kept alive by the Hudson's Bay Company. Without the company's supply of food and seeds, many arriving Americans would have starved. McLoughlin and the other company officials had been gracious and generous to many Americans, even though the company president disapproved.

But the American settlers — especially the newer ones — didn't like the Hudson's Bay Company. Why? First, because the company was British, not American. Also, they believed the company favored the Catholics. The Americans were Protestants. Others were jealous; they just wanted the company lands.

that America must expand its territory. They were called expansionists.

In 1844, one candidate picked a campaign slogan that had great appeal for expansionists. The slogan was "fifty-four forty or fight." In other words, the United States should get all of the old Oregon Territory. The candidate was James K. Polk. He won the election. He became president in 1845.

47. What was an expansionist?
48. Explain the slogan, "fifty-four forty or fight."

Would There Be War?

President Polk wanted to end the joint occupation agreement with England. It would be the first step toward claiming the Oregon Country. Congress agreed. They voted not to extend the joint occupation. It would end in 1848, as originally agreed.

What if the United States and England failed to sign a new treaty before the year was up? Would the two countries go to war? Everyone wondered what would happen.

Fortunately, neither country wanted to fight.

The British government was ready to give in to the old American demands. Lord Aberdeen of England made the following proposal to the U.S.: ". . .the line of boundary between the territories of the United States and (Canada) shall be continued westward along the forty-ninth parallel of north latitude to the middle of the channel that separates the continent from Vancouver's Island. . ." All of Vancouver Island would belong to Canada.

Polk asked Congress to decide if this was a good enough solution to the Oregon border dispute. Congress voted "yes." Polk signed the treaty on August 5, 1846. The United States now stretched from the Atlantic to the Pacific.

Later, the United States agreed to pay the Hudson's Bay Company for its Oregon property. This included: $450,000 for Fort Vancouver, and $200,000 for the Puget Sound Agricultural Company.

49. What did Congress vote to do after one year had passed?
50. What country gave in to the other's old demands?
51. What border did the U.S. and England agree on?

Fort Vancouver is now a museum. Why did the British agree to give up this land?

THE TREATY OF 1846

This treaty is especially important to the history of Washington State since it marks the date that Washington's land became part of the United States. The borders described by the treaty were not all clear, however. It still was not clear who owned the San Juan Islands. Where, exactly, is "the main channel between the continent and Vancouver Island?" This issue would have to be settled later. (See Unit 7, Section 1.)

The treaty of 1846 included some other agreements, too. It protected the rights of Hudson's Bay Company employees and other British citizens who lived in the territory. It gave English ships the right to use the Columbia River and Puget Sound. And the Puget Sound Agricultural Company would still own its lands, until the U.S. needed to buy them.

Why Did England Give In?

Why did England give in? Why were the British willing to give up their claims to the land north of the Columbia River? There were several reasons.

The leaders of British government were anxious to avoid war. They wanted to maintain good trade relations with the United States. President Polk had convinced Britain that the U.S. might be willing to fight to win the land around Puget Sound. (At that time, the U.S. had no good ports on the Pacific Coast. They wanted to own the good harbors of Puget Sound. And many Americans resented the British. They wanted the Northwest lands to be governed by a democracy, not a king. So the Americans supported Polk's statements that the U.S. should get these lands.)

Britain also wanted ports in the Northwest. Earlier, the British had believed that the Columbia River would be the main trade route in this area. This was a key reason for claiming the land north of the Columbia. But travel on the river was dangerous and blocked by rapids at many points. The Strait of Juan de Fuca offered a much better ship passage to the Northwest coast. The new boundary would give Britain several good ports — on Vancouver Island and at what is now the city of Vancouver, British Columbia. So the British government was willing to accept this boundary.

Also the Columbia and Snake River areas were no longer producing as many furs as they once did. There were too many American set-

tlers in the area; they were chasing away the animals. And the Hudson's Bay Company had moved its main headquarters from Fort Vancouver to Fort Victoria.

The British did not want the land for settlement. They were more interested in the fur trade. So when the furs were gone, the land was no longer such a good investment. England would have liked to keep the ports on Puget Sound. But Polk threatened that the American people were angry and anxious to expand, and the British finally gave in.

52. Why was England ready to give up the land north of the Columbia?

Why Did Congress Delay?

It was six months later before the people in Oregon heard about the Treaty of 1846. The American settlers were pleased to hear about it. They believed that the United States government would soon make Oregon an official U.S. territory. That would bring many benefits including: U.S. Army protection against possible Indian attacks; federal money for public buildings, for government services, and for officials' salaries; guaranteed land claims; and a representative in Congress.

The settlers waited for news from Washington, D.C. They waited a whole year. Nothing happened. Why was Congress ignoring them? The settlers appointed a young lawyer named J. Quinn Thornton to go to Congress to find out.

Thornton learned that there were two reasons for the delay. First, Congress was busy with the war against Mexico. This war was not ended until 1848. Second, and more important, was the issue of slavery. Already, the country was seriously divided about whether or not to allow slavery in the territories. The Provisional Government of Oregon had voted against allowing slavery. Southern representatives in Congress did not want any more free (non-slave) states or territories to join the U.S. So they blocked all attempts to make Oregon an official United States territory.

53. What were the benefits of becoming a United States territory?
54. Why did Congress delay making Oregon a United States territory?

SECTION 4: A VIOLENT RESPONSE

What About The Native Americans?

Only British and American leaders were involved in the treaty discussions of 1846. What happened to the original owners of Oregon Country — the Native Americans? How did they react to the great numbers of new settlers?

Tribal cultures had begun to change in many ways since people of other cultures had come to Oregon. Native Americans had become dependent on metal tools and other non-Indian trade goods. Some Native Americans had learned farming, and they began to raise crops and farm animals. Tribal beliefs and customs changed as more Native Americans became interested in the Christian religion. Many of these changes were welcomed by the Native Americans.

However, non-Indian settlement was also harmful to Native Americans in many ways. Many American settlers had little respect for Native Americans' rights and cultures. Protestant missionaries taught that many of the tribal values, customs, and beliefs were wrong. They tried to get the Native Americans to change. Settlers did not respect the Native Americans' possession of their traditional land. The settlers took more and more of the land, usually without paying for it. This was not too great a problem when there were very few settlers. But more wagon trains kept coming, and the Native Americans could see that there would soon be no land left.

55. What important group was left out of the 1846 treaty discussions?
56. Name some ways that tribal cultures changed after people of other cultures came.

Deadly Diseases

One very serious problem of settlement was disease. The newcomers brought diseases such as measles and smallpox, which were new to Native Americans.

The settlers were familiar with these illnesses. They knew how to cure them, and their bodies had developed immunity (natural protection against the disease). But Native Americans did not have immunity, and they had no knowledge of cures for the strange new diseases.

As a result, thousands of American Indians got sick and died. Sometimes whole villages were wiped out.

Native Americans watched the newcomers survive these diseases, while their own friends and relatives died in great numbers. Native Americans believed that illness could be caused by an enemy with strong spirit power. So they logically assumed that some non-Indians were using their power to cause the killing diseases. Many people grew angry and afraid.

57. Name some new diseases that the settlers brought.
58. Why did Native Americans die from these diseases while others survived?
59. Why did Native Americans believe that non-Indians were causing the tribal people's deaths?

How Did The Tribes Respond?

Different tribes reacted differently to the settlement problem. Many tribal leaders advised their people to remain peaceful and friendly toward the settlers.

Clothing styles were one example of the blending of Indian and non-Indian traditions by Washington tribes. In this photo, which pieces of clothing are traditional to the tribes and which were introduced by non-Indians?

But the Cayuse near Waiilatpu reacted with anger. They were a proud and warlike people, and they resented the missionaries for many reasons. They were angry because the Whitmans never paid them for the land they took, even though they knew the whites believed in buying land. They thought the Whitmans were proud, critical, and unfriendly. The missionaries never seemed to be satisfied. For example, the Cayuse considered themselves Christians before the missionaries arrived. They had learned Christian prayers and beliefs from a tribal member called Cayuse Halket. (Halket had studied at an Episcopal school for two years, and then he returned to teach his people.) The tribe worshipped twice a day. But the Whitmans were not satisfied with the Christianity of Cayuse Halket. They refused to baptize any tribal members.

Some of the Cayuse tribe became more interested in the Catholic religion. Catholic priests were more accepting. The Native Americans asked some priests to start a Catholic mission near Waiilatpu. But the Protestant missionaries criticized the Catholics. The tribe became divided, and many people grew angry.

60. How did many tribal leaders respond to the non-Indian problem?

61. Name some reasons why the Cayuse people were angry with the missionaries.

A Warning

In 1840, some members of the Cayuse tribe destroyed some irrigation ditches at the mission. They also let horses into the grain fields to destroy the grain. While Dr. Whitman was back East, they burned some grain and destroyed the mission's mill. At this time Narcissa Whitman decided to leave Waiilatpu. She spent several months at The Dalles with the Methodist missionaries until Dr. Whitman returned.

Hudson's Bay Company officials and other missionaries advised the Whitmans to leave Waiilatpu. The damage to the mission was a warning, they said.

But Marcus Whitman was stubborn. He refused to abandon (leave) the mission site. He did not want to quit.

62. Why did some people advise the Whitmans to abandon Waiilatpu?

The Tension Continues To Grow

In the next few years, Dr. Whitman spent more and more time helping the wagon trains into Oregon. He paid less attention to the Native

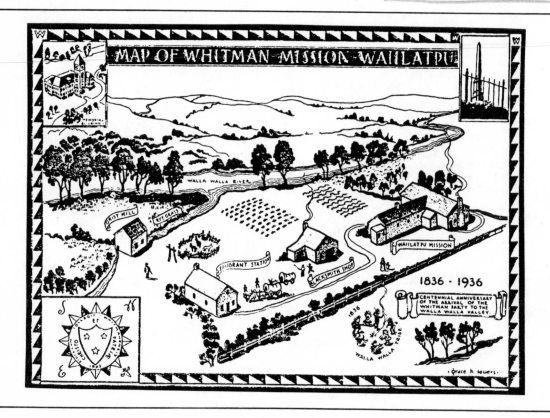

Americans. He stopped the Sunday meetings at the missions.

The Cayuse people saw thousands of arriving settlers cross their land. They thought, "If Dr. Whitman really wanted to help us, he would keep these strangers off our land. Instead he helps and encourages them." The tribe became angrier.

Two other events increased the Native Americans' anger. In 1845, an East Coast Indian named Tom Hill came to the Northwest. He told the tribal people how Americans killed thousands of Eastern Indians and had stolen their land. He told the people to kill the missionaries and take back their tribal lands before it was too late.

Then the son of Chief Peo Peo Mox Mox was killed by a white man. Dr. White, the Indian agent, had promised that all murderers would be punished. But no white man had been punished for the death of Peo Peo Mox Mox's son.

The Cayuse people were furious. They wanted to kill Dr. Whitman to "settle the score." But John McLoughlin told them not to. The tribe trusted and respected McLoughlin. They depended on him for gunpowder and other supplies. So they left Dr. Whitman alone.

63. How did each of the following cause more tension at Waiilatpu: the wagon trains, Tom Hill, Peo Peo Mox Mox's son?
64. How was McLoughlin able to prevent the killing of Dr. Whitman?

The Terrible Lie

In 1847, the crisis came. Measles struck the Cayuse village! A great number of Cayuse people lay dying or dead.

Everyone knew that Marcus Whitman was a shaman, a doctor. Many tribal members suspected that Dr. Whitman had caused the disease. Then one day, an English-speaking man named Joe Lewis had some shocking news! He claimed that he overheard Dr. Whitman say he was going to poison the Indians and take their land!

Joe Lewis was later found to be a liar. His horrible story was not true. But the Cayuse people didn't know this at the time. They thought their lives were in danger.

65. What disease killed many Cayuse people in 1847?
66. What was Joe Lewis' story?

The Council's Violent Plan

The tribal council met. They decided they would have to strike out in self-defense. A plan was made.

On November 29, 1847, Chief Tilaukait entered the mission and asked for medicine. He spoke to Dr. Whitman and accused him of poisoning the tribe. Then, another Cayuse named Tamahas, struck the doctor over the head from behind. Tilaukait struck him again. Dr. Whitman, stumbled, bleeding, out the door and died.

This was the signal for attack. Other Indian men were in the mission yard with guns hidden under their blankets.

They began to shoot. They had planned to kill only men. But they killed Narcissa Whitman too, in anger.

Altogether, 14 people were killed that week. Nearly 50 women and children were also taken prisoner. Some of the prisoners were badly mistreated and died later on. One of these was Joe Meek's daughter, Helen.

67. What happened on November 29, 1847?

This portrait of Tilaukait was painted by Paul Kane, a Canadian artist. Kane travelled the North American continent, sketching and writing about the Native Americans he saw. He visited Waiilatpu, in 1847, shortly before the Whitmans were killed.

How Did The Cayuses Try To Make Peace?

Afterward, Waiilatpu was fairly calm. The tribal council met with Father Blanchet and prepared a letter. This letter explained all the reasons why the Cayuse leaders felt it was necessary to kill the missionaries. The tribe said they wanted to make peace.

They would forget the unpaid murder of Peo Peo Mox Mox's son if the whites would forget the Waiilatpu killings. They mailed the letter to Governor Abernethy and waited for a reply.

Soon afterward, Tilaukait's son, Edward, married Mary Smith, the daughter of an American missionary. For a while, peace seemed to have come to Waiilatpu.

68. What did the Cayuse tribal council say in their letter to Governor Abernethy?

Escape

A few members of the missionary group managed to escape Waiilatpu the day of the killings. One hurried to Lapwai to warn the Spaldings.

The Cayuse wanted to kill Reverend Spalding, too, but he and his family were protected by friendly Nez Perce. The Spaldings left Lapwai soon afterward.

Another person escaped and ran to Fort Walla Walla. From there, a messenger was sent to Fort Vancouver for help. The Hudson's Bay Company sent Peter Skene Ogden out from Vancouver. Ogden arranged with tribal leaders to ransom the prisoners (pay for their release).

69. Who protected the Spaldings until they escaped to Fort Walla Walla?
70. Who arranged for the release of the prisoners?

What Was The "Cayuse War"?

The settlers in the Willamette Valley were shocked, frightened, and angered by what had happened. They feared that other Oregon tribes might join together to attack the settlements. They started immediately to put together a volunteer army. The army would go to Cayuse country and try to bring back the men responsible for the killings.

The Cayuse tribes hid in the mountains that winter to avoid the small army. Neither side really wanted to fight. But winter came, and many Cayuse people died from the cold. Finally,

five men surrendered, in order to save the tribe.

These men knew that there had been reasons for the Waiilatpu killings. They believed they would be judged not guilty and released. One of the five had not even been around on the day of the killing. However, the white jury found them all guilty, in spite of good evidence that one or all of them were innocent. The jury decided the Indians should be hanged. Many settlers believed this was unfair. They protested. But they were unable to stop the hangings.

This was called the Cayuse War, although there was really very little fighting during this time.

71. Why were the settlers afraid?
72. Why did the five Cayuse men surrender? What happened to them?

JOE MEEK

Joe Meek was a fur trapper, a settler, an officer of the Provisional Government, and later an official of Oregon Territory. Whenever there was something important going on, Meek seems to have been part of it. He had many "firsts" in the history of Oregon. Along with two other mountain men and each of their Native American wives, he brought the first wagon across the Rocky Mountains in 1840. He was the first sheriff of the Provisional Government, which he helped to start at Champoeg. He made a historic ride to Washington, D.C., to convince Congress to make Oregon a United States territory. (The President's wife was his cousin, which helped.) And he was the first marshal of the new Oregon Territory.

SECTION 5: TWO TERRITORIES

Joe Meek's Ride

The settlers' army was small and poorly outfitted. The Provisional Government didn't have the men or the money to fight a real war. Settlers believed they needed the help of the U.S. Army, in case more tribes attacked.

Someone had to go talk to Congress, the settlers decided. Joe Meek was selected. He left in March and made it to St. Louis in May — a new speed record.

Meek told officials in Washington, D.C., about the Waiilatpu incident. His story caused great interest and concern for the future of Oregon Country. President Polk urged Congress to act quickly to make Oregon a United States territory.

Senator Stephen Douglas of Illinois had already proposed that Oregon be admitted as a free territory. But Southern senators opposed this. The number of free states and territories was just equal to the number of slave states and territories. Southerners didn't want the balance to be upset.

They argued right up until the end of Congress' session. Then on the last day that Congress met that year, the proposal was passed. President Polk signed the law that created Oregon Territory on August 14, 1848. The killings at Waiilatpu had convinced Congress that they couldn't wait any longer.

73. Why did Joe Meek ride to Washington, D.C.?
74. Why did Southern senators oppose the creation of Oregon Territory?

Who Were The First Territorial Officials?

The governor, the judges, and several other officials of a territory are appointed by the president. Residents of the territory elect the territorial legislators.

President Polk selected Joe Meek to be the first territorial marshall, for example. And he chose Joseph Lane as first governor of Oregon Territory.

Meek and Lane hurried to Oregon by way of the southern route. They travelled overland through Santa Fe and Tucson to the California

When Oregon Territory was first created, it was much larger than Oregon State is today. Its borders were: the 49th parallel north latitude (except for Vancouver Island), the 42nd parallel north latitude, the Pacific Ocean, and the Continental Divide.

coast. (The northern route was too snowy and dangerous at this time of year.) Then they sailed up the Pacific Coast in a ship.

On March 3, 1849, Lane officially announced that Oregon was a United States territory.

Settlers elected Joseph Thurston as their first territorial delegate to Congress. Thurston County in Washington was later named after him.

On March 4, the day after Lane's announcement, Zachary Taylor became the new President of the United States. Taylor was not a Democrat, as Lane and Polk were. So he wanted to appoint a different governor for Oregon. He offered the job to a young man from Illinois named Abraham Lincoln. But Lincoln turned down the job offer. President Taylor chose John P. Gaines instead.

75. Who were the first governor and marshall of Oregon Territory?
76. On what date did Governor Lane officially announce that Oregon was a United States territory?
77. To whom did President Taylor offer the job as Oregon territorial governor? Who turned the offer down, and who accepted?

What Was The Donation Land Law?

Oregon Territory's delegates to Congress could not vote. But they could try to convince other representatives to pass laws that helped the territory.

Joseph Thurston helped convince Congress to pass a very important law in 1850. It was the Donation Land Law. This set up a legal system

JOSEPH LANE

Joseph Lane was an experienced pioneer. He had lived in Kentucky and then Indiana when those states were still part of the frontier. He was elected to the Indiana Territorial Legislature, but left territorial government to fight in the Mexican War.

Lane became known as a capable leader and good Democrat. After he was replaced as Oregon territorial governor, he was elected to be the territory's non-voting delegate to Congress. He held this office for 10 years. Both Lane and his Democratic party remained powerful in Oregon.

In 1860, Lane ran for a different office. He was not successful, but he did receive strong support from Oregon voters. The new office was that of vice-president. Joseph Lane and John C. Breckinridge represented the Southern (pro-slavery) Democrats in the presidential election that year. They were defeated by Abraham Lincoln.

for claiming land in Oregon.

The main part of the law described how much land a person could claim:

1. The size of the claim was 320 acres. To qualify, a person had to fill several requirements. He had to be male and either white or half-white, with one Indian parent. He had to have arrived before 1851. He had to be an American citizen or he had to apply to become a citizen. He also had to be at least 18 years old, and he had to farm his land for at least four years in a row before he could own it.

2. Another 320 acres could be claimed by the wife of a man who qualified for 320 acres. The couple had to have been married by 1851.

3. White male settlers who arrived after 1851 and before December 1, 1853, could claim 160 acres of land.

4. Wives of men who qualified for 160 acres could also claim 160 acres, if they arrived between 1851 and 1853.

78. What was the Donation Land Law?
79. What did a person have to do (or be) in order to claim land?
80. How much land could be claimed?

More People, More Marriages, More Problems

Settlers welcomed the Donation Land Law. Now their claim would be protected by law. The law inspired thousands of new settlers to move west. By 1860, the non-Indian population of Oregon Country was five times greater than it was in 1850.

The number of marriages also increased in Oregon, since a married couple could claim twice as much land. Even girls in their early teens married to take advantage of the law.

But the law caused several problems, too. The land grants were really too large. Settlers often had more land than they could take care of. Also, towns and industries were slow to develop because settlers were so far apart.

Such big land grants meant that land was taken up very quickly. All of the Willamette Valley was claimed by 1855. Some new settlers were very angry. After such a long trip, it was hard to find any good land!

81. What were some advantages and disadvantages of the Donation Land Law?

A Discriminatory Law

Today, the worst problem with the Donation Land Law seems to be its discrimination. After 1851, adult white male citizens and their wives were the only people who could claim land. Early British and French Canadian settlers could not claim land unless they became U.S. citizens. No single woman of any race or nationality could claim land. Blacks, Asians, and later mestizos were excluded. ("Mestizos" is a word of Spanish origin that means "of mixed ancestry." In this case, it refers to persons with one white parent and one Indian parent.)

Joe Meek's children were among the many people in Oregon Territory who were discriminated against because of race. Meek's wife, remember, was an Indian. Their children were mestizos.

But the worst discrimination was against the full-blooded Native Americans who lived in Oregon. The Donation Land Law in effect gave white settlers the legal right to take away tribal lands.

82. What groups were discriminated against by the Donation Land Law?

Where Did Settlers In Oregon Live?

Most of the settlers still stayed south of the Columbia River. In 1850, there were 13,000 American settlers in Oregon Territory. Only 1,000 of them lived north of the Columbia River.

However, a few little towns were beginning to grow up in the Cowlitz River Valley and around Puget Sound. These included Tumwater, Tacoma, Olympia, and Centralia. In 1851, the first families of settlers arrived at Alki Point; Port Townsend was founded in 1852.

Almost all the early Black settlers of the Northwest chose to live north of the Columbia River, away from the center of government with anti-Black laws. In 1850, there were 207 Blacks living in Oregon. Like the other early pioneers, they had a very hard life. They worked hard to build their houses, clear the land, start farms, and make almost all the things they needed for their simple lives.

But the Black pioneers had an even harder time than the whites, because they could not claim land. Sometimes a family would put years of hard work into the land only to lose it to a white family's claim. Black pioneers usually had to buy land from white pioneers.

83. How many settlers lived north of the Columbia in 1850?
84. Name some towns that were founded north of the Columbia before 1852.

A New Territory

Starting in about 1850, the more northern settlers began complaining about the Oregon territorial government. Most of the territorial lawmakers lived south of the Columbia. The northerners felt that the southern part of the territory was neglecting them and that the new capital, Salem, was too far away. They felt that Oregon Territory was just too big. It seemed fair to them that the territory could be divided into a northern part and a southern part, so that both parts would have a sea coast and both would be about the right size for a state.

The settlers held two conventions to discuss their feelings. One was held at Cowlitz Landing in 1851, and the second at Monticello (now called Longview) a year later. Both times, they prepared a memorial (a formal, written statement) to send to Congress. The memorials asked Congress to create a new territory called Columbia. The Oregon legislature supported their request.

Congress agreed to the request for a new territory. But they changed the name to Washington in order to honor the first president and to avoid confusion with the District of Columbia. The law creating Washington Territory was signed on March 2, 1853.

85. Why were northern settlers dissatisfied with the Provisional Government?
86. What happened at the conventions at Cowlitz Landing and at Monticello?
87. Why did Congress change the name of the new territory?

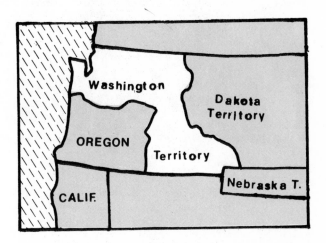

When Washington Territory was first created in 1853, it included parts of Idaho and Montana. Six years later, in 1859, Oregon became a state. The borders were changed then, and Washington became even larger.

The Native Americans in this photo were young children when the first non-Indians settled in what is now Seattle. How did their lives change in the 50 years after settlement? What changes affected the lives of other Washington Indians during this period?

UNIT 6

TREATIES AND WARS

Have you ever talked with someone from another culture? Even if you spoke the same language, you may not always have understood each other. Words, phrases, and gestures may mean something very different in different cultures. In Washington Territory, many problems were caused because Indians and non-Indians did not understand each others' culture. The early years of Washington Territory were marked by incidents of racial and cultural prejudice.

During the 1850's and 1860's, conflicts between races were often violent. In Washington Territory and other parts of the West, there was fighting between Native Americans and settlers. These fights and battles became known as the "Indian Wars." While this was going on, most of the rest of the United States was involved in the events leading to the Civil War and Reconstruction.

This unit has three sections:

1. Agreements and Misunderstandings
2. Indian Wars in Washington
3. Washington State and the Civil War

As you read, ask yourself these questions: What beliefs and prejudices caused the problems? How did the different groups try to deal with these problems? Do you think that different methods could have been used?

SECTION 1: AGREEMENTS AND MISUNDERSTANDINGS

Who Was Isaac Stevens?

The first governor of Washington Territory was Isaac Ingalls Stevens. He was appointed by President Franklin Pierce in 1853. At the same time, Stevens was appointed Secretary of Indian Affairs for the territory.

Governor Stevens was a hard-working and ambitious man. He was talented, intelligent, and also impatient. Once he decided to do something, he would put so much effort into it that he would finally succeed. For example, he decided that he was going to be first in his college class at West Point, and he was. His cousin once said that Isaac Stevens was "crazy, actually crazy or he never could work as he does."

Apparently, Stevens did not think his two new jobs would keep him busy enough. He volunteered for a third job. He would lead the survey to find the best route for a railroad to Puget Sound. Stevens was well prepared for this job. He had been working for the U.S. Coastal Survey since leaving the Army at the end of the Mexican War.

1. What three jobs did Isaac Ingalls Stevens get in 1853?

Getting Busy

Stevens had plenty of work to do. He wasted no time getting started. He travelled west with a large group of men. They surveyed the land as they went. Governor Stevens also stopped to talk with some tribal leaders along the way.

Once he arrived in Olympia, he moved quickly to start the new government. He arranged for elections, and the first legislature met just a month later. The governor and the legislators worked together to create the territory's first laws, schools, and roads. Stevens also began arrangements to buy all Hudson's Bay Company land in the territory.

2. What were some of the projects that Stevens started?

Governor Stevens

THE STEVENS' FIRST DAYS IN OLYMPIA

Isaac Stevens hurried ahead of his troops and arrived in Olympia alone. He was tired and spattered with mud from his long journey. There's a story that he went to the hotel and was not permitted to go in and eat. The people told him that they were getting ready for a big banquet, and that no one would be served until the banquet was over. But Stevens was so hungry, he asked if there wasn't anything else they could do. Finally the cook offered to take him into the kitchen and feed him some scraps.

When he came out, he overheard the people in front of the hotel. They were grumbling because the new governor was late for his banquet. Isaac Stevens stepped up and introduced himself. "I am the governor," he said. The people were embarrassed, and Governor Stevens was too full to enjoy the dinner they'd prepared.

Mrs. Stevens' welcome to Olympia was not much more cheering. Governor Stevens had returned east to bring her and the rest of their family to Washington by ship. The women had all gotten sick in Panama. And when Mrs. Stevens saw the tiny settlement that would be her new home, she said, "Below us, in a deep mud were a few low, wooden houses, at the head of Puget Sound. My heart sank. . . ."

What Was The Reservation System?

The most important duty of the Superintendent of Indian Affairs in a new territory was to make treaties with the Indian tribes. These treaties represented legal agreements between the tribe and the United States government. The treaties demanded that the tribe sell most of its land and stop any fighting against settlers or other tribes. The tribe would keep, or reserve, a part of their lands. This is called a reservation. The U.S. government promised to pay for tribal lands and to provide schools and other services on the reservation.

This system of treaties and reservations had been used by the United States government for many years. Governor Stevens planned to follow government tradition and to convince or force all Washington tribes to sign treaty agreements.

The Washington treaties were somewhat different from treaties that had been made with other tribes. In the past, the government had tried to force all tribes onto a few giant reservations. This system caused great hardships for tribal members. Most tribes were forced to leave the lands where they had always lived. These lands were sacred to the tribes, and their way of life was based on the land. In the 1830's, the United States government forced the Southeastern tribes to move west of the Mississippi River. So many Cherokee Indians died on the way to their reservation that they called this journey the "Trail of Tears."

In contrast, more Washington tribes would have reservations that were close to their traditional homes. However, some Washington tribes were still forced to move to unfamiliar lands, and all tribes had to give up most of their land.

Some other notable points of the Washington treaties were: the tribes promised to give up their slaves and to stop trading in Canada; the government promised the tribes that they could continue to hunt and fish at their traditional places. Still, the lands that most tribes received were very poor. And Native Americans got less land per person than settlers who filed land claims.

3. What were the main treaty agreements between the tribes and the U.S. government?

4. How were Pacific Northwest reservations somewhat different from earlier reservations in other parts of the country?

NATIVE AMERICANS AND THE FEDERAL GOVERNMENT

It is important to remember that the treaties with tribes were all signed by the federal government — rather than state and local governments. The federal government has continued to have special control over Native Americans. As times have changed, the government's attitudes toward Indians and reservations have changed.

The following are some of the most important changes in federal Indian policy from 1855 to the present:

1871 — Congress ruled that no more Indian treaties would be made.

1887 — The Dawes Act, also called the General Allotment Act, was passed by Congress. This law divided up reservation land among individual tribal members. Non-Indians hoped the Dawes Act would encourage tribal members to farm and to adopt non-Indian ways of life. Some tribes lost much valuable land and tribal identity because of this law.

1924 — Indians were finally allowed to become U.S. citizens.

1934 — The Indian Reorganization Act was passed. It cancelled the Dawes Act and returned some land to the tribes.

1953 — Congress voted to end reservations. (This was called termination.)

1970 — Termination ended. The government began to support the tribes' right to control programs and policy on their reservations.

Treaties With The Coastal Tribes

Only after treaties were signed would the settlers have legal claims to their land. Governor Stevens moved quickly to do this. He planned to move all the tribes onto reservations within a very short time, and was impatient with any delays.

The first treaty meeting was held near Medicine Creek in 1854. Representatives of the Puyallup, Nisqually, and other nearby tribes were there. Within a few months, Stevens had signed treaties with most of the tribes in Western Washington.

Most Coastal tribes were willing to sign the treaties peacefully. The Coastal people had been living and trading with outsiders for many years. The tribal culture had changed; people had become dependent on non-Indian goods. Also, many of the tribal people had died of diseases brought by the settlers. The Coastal tribes knew they could not resist the new settlement.

The Coastal people also knew that they could survive on a small reservation. The treaties promised that tribal members could continue to fish at their usual places. These included places both on and off the reservation. Native Americans insisted strongly on these fishing rights.

The land and waters of Western Washington were rich with food, so that a small amount of land could support a lot of people. Most Coastal tribes agreed to sign the treaties. However, some tribes never signed any treaty.

5. What happened near Medicine Creek in 1854?
6. Why were most Coastal people willing to agree to the treaties?

Who Was Leschi?

Some of the Coastal people opposed the treaties. One of these people was Chief Leschi of the Nisqually. The piece of land set aside for the Nisqually reservation was rocky and small and far from the river. Even some non-Indians were shocked that Stevens would ask the Nisqually to agree to this.

According to one witness, when Leschi heard the terms of the treaty, he said, "This means war!" Leschi's thumbprint appeared on the treaty, but Leschi later said that his signature had been forged (made by someone else). A year later, Leschi and his people did go to war against the settlers. After the fighting, the treaty was changed. The Nisqually tribe was given a larger reservation near the river.

7. Why did Chief Leschi object to the treaty?

What Happened At Walla Walla?

Governor Stevens was pleased with his quick successes with the Western Washington treaties. He expected to complete the treaties with the

DISAGREEMENT ABOUT INDIAN FISHING RIGHTS

In the treaties of 1854 and 1855, the U.S. government guaranteed to the tribes "the right of taking fish at all usual and accustomed places. . . in common with all citizens of the Territory." The traditional fishing places were not always on reservation land, but tribal people were still promised the right to fish there.

Governor Stevens knew that he had to make this agreement in order to get the Coastal tribes to sign. Salmon was the Coastal people's most important food. It was essential to their way of life.

States have the constitutional power to regulate their own resources. The new Washington State government believed it had the right to control all fishing in the state. Historically, the state has protected the interests of commercial fishing and sports fishing and has ignored the treaty rights of Native Americans. In the early 1950's, the state began to arrest Native Americans who were fishing outside of reservation lands without state licenses.

A protest was organized to call attention to the fact that the treaty was not being enforced. Native Americans staged "fish-ins" at Frank's Landing during the 1960's. There were violent conflicts between Native Americans and police.

A long legal battle has followed. Experts disagree on the meaning of the treaty phrase "in common with all citizens of the Territory." The state government believes this to mean that Native Americans must obey all state fishing laws — whenever they are off the reservation. Using this interpretation, the state claims a right to regulate all off-reservation fishing, no matter who the fisher is. But the federal court disagreed. In 1974, U.S. Judge George Boldt made a very different decision about the meaning of the treaty. He said it means that Native fishers may take 50% of the fish. Since the federal government is higher than the state, the state government must obey Judge Boldt.

This decision has angered many people. Non-Indian fishers had become accustomed to taking a large catch every year, before Indian fishing rights were enforced. Now they say they can't make a living anymore. Some have continued to fish illegally.

Sports fishers have also complained. Some Indian fishing boats and equipment have been destroyed in protest. State officials claim that they can no longer regulate the state's resources. Non-Indians point out that a large number of today's salmon come form hatcheries that are supported by state taxes. Indians on reservations do not have to pay state taxes, so they are catching fish that others have paid for, complain Boldt's opponents. But Native Americans point out that no hatcheries were needed before non-Indians overfished the rivers and caused other problems that destroyed many fish (pollution, logging, dams.) Even some judges disagree with Judge Boldt. They believe his decision is discriminatory and unfair. They also think it violates state law. Meanwhile, Native Americans complain that state and local agencies will not enforce the law. This case was appealed to the Supreme Court of the United States in 1979.

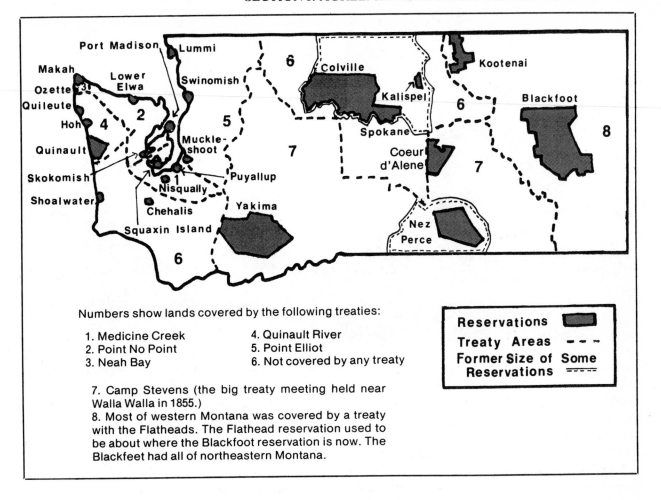

Numbers show lands covered by the following treaties:

1. Medicine Creek
2. Point No Point
3. Neah Bay

4. Quinault River
5. Point Elliot
6. Not covered by any treaty

7. Camp Stevens (the big treaty meeting held near Walla Walla in 1855.)

8. Most of western Montana was covered by a treaty with the Flatheads. The Flathead reservation used to be about where the Blackfoot reservation is now. The Blackfeet had all of northeastern Montana.

Reservations ▪
Treaty Areas - - -
Former Size of Some
Reservations =====

Plateau tribes within a few days. For this purpose, he called a meeting of various Plateau tribes near Walla Walla in 1855.

About 5,000 people arrived, including Nez Perce, Yakima, Cayuse, Walla Walla, and other bands. The huge encampment was bustling and colorful, like a festival gathering. But it was soon clear that the occasion was not a happy one. Governor Stevens' proposals made many people angry.

The Plateau peoples had very different attitudes toward reservations than the Coastal peoples had. Plateau groups were not so dependent on trade. They were hunters, and they were generally more warlike and independent than the fishing villages of the coast. Also, it was harder to make a living on the plateau. The Plateau tribes had to travel hundreds of miles every year in search of food. A small reservation might mean that many people would starve.

In addition, Stevens was talking about moving all the tribes onto one reservation. For many tribes, this would mean leaving their sacred homeland to live side by side with their traditional enemies. Peo Peo Mox Mox, Spokane Garry, and Kamiakin were among the respected tribal leaders who resisted the treaties.

Stevens was getting impatient at the delays. Finally, he offered to create separate reservations. Most of the tribal leaders agreed to sign the treaties.

8. What did Governor Stevens expect to happen at the treaty meeting near Walla Walla in 1855?
9. Why weren't the Plateau people as willing to sign the treaties as the Coastal people were?
10. How did Stevens have to change his offer in order to get the tribal leaders to sign?

Why The Treaties Did Not Bring Peace

The treaties show that they were signed or marked by both Indian and U.S. government representatives. They seem like official and binding agreements. Yet trouble started almost immediately after they were signed. There were bad feelings and even wars between Native

This unusual geological formation is know as Twin Sisters Peak. It is located in the area of the Walla Walla treaty meeting.

Americans and settlers all over the territory. It almost seemed that the treaties had caused more disagreements than they had settled. Why did this happen?

Perhaps the most important problem with the treaties was the difference in attitudes toward the land and its resources. Native American cultures taught that the earth was the source and support of all life. The earth was vital to the Native Americans' existence and to their identity. They believed that no one could own it; the earth belonged to all, and all must share it. Chief Joseph of the Nez Perce tried to explain these beliefs. He said: "When the creative power. . . made the earth, he made no marks, no lines of division or separation upon it, and said that it should be allowed to remain as then made. The earth was a person's mother. . . sacred to his affections."

Because of these beliefs, Native Americans usually did not alter (change) the physical environment very much. They used only enough resources to satisfy their needs. Their religion taught them respect for all living things, and their economy was based on this respect.

The newcomers did not have the same feelings of involvement and respect for nature. They believed that people could own the land and could change or "improve" it as they wished. Non-Indians believed that people could (and should) use the land and its resources to make money for themselves. They believed that the best use of the land was the one that made the most money. Naturally, they believed that farming, mining, lumbering, etc. were "better" uses than hunting or gathering. Because of this, they felt justified in taking the Native Americans' land.

11. What were the Native Americans' beliefs about the earth?
12. What did non-Indians believe was the best use of the land? How did this belief help justify taking tribal lands?

Communication Gaps

When you think about these different attitudes, you can probably start to guess why the treaties caused so much trouble. There was a big communication gap. The treaties simply could not mean the same thing to the Native Americans that they meant to the government officials.

The idea of buying and selling land was strange and new to Native Americans. Each family group or tribe had its own traditional fishing, hunting, and gathering grounds. These lands were used by all members of the tribe.

Other people might hunt or spend time there with permission from the local tribe. Native American culture had no concepts of trespassing or individual ownership of land. So when the tribes sold their land, they really expected that they would still be able to go back.

They expected to return to the land for two

reasons: first, to gather the food that could be found there, and second, because they loved the land and felt that it was a part of them. Their parents and grandparents were buried there. The tribal members had shared many experiences with the land, and they would always feel attached to it.

Another important communication failure had to do with tribal organization. Government officials expected the chief of the tribe to be able to represent the entire group, just as Stevens, for example, could sign a treaty as the representative of the entire United States government. But this was not how decisions were made by Native Americans. A council of elder tribal members had to talk over important decisions and arrive at an agreement they could all accept. Many tribal leaders regarded the signing of the treaties as a pledge to just go back and talk to the tribal council.

Another big problem was that Native Americans and government officials usually did not speak each other's language. Governor Stevens insisted that the treaties be translated into Chinook Jargon, which was a trade language that almost all the Indians could understand. This sounds pretty reasonable until you learn that Chinook Jargon had a fairly small number

of words and no exact grammar. It was difficult to say anything very complicated in the Jargon. Even people who spoke Chinook Jargon very well could not express complicated ideas in this language.

13. How were Native American ideas of land ownership different from the new settlers' ideas?
14. How were tribal decisions actually made? How did government officials believe tribal decisions could be made?
15. Why wasn't the Chinook Jargon a good language to use for the treaty discussions?

How Did The Government Weaken The Treaty Agreements?

Treaties and agreements between people are only valuable and meaningful if people respect them. The United States government often did not keep the promises it made in its treaties with the Indians.

For example, Stevens promised the tribes that they would not have to move until the treaties were ratified (officially approved by Congress). They were told that this process would take from several months to a few years. But settlers began moving onto the land and forcing out the Native American residents immediately after the treaties were signed. It was actually four years before Congress ratified most of the treaties. What did this mean to the tribal people? It meant they had to wait four years to begin receiving payments for land they had already lost.

Most treaties contained a section which gave the government the right to change the treaty later on (a fact that probably was not fully understood by the tribes). The government sometimes used this part of the treaty in order to take valuable reservation lands away from the tribes. For example, much of the Nez Perce reservation land was taken away when gold was discovered there.

More land was taken away from the tribes as time went on. Some reservations, such as the Puyallup, were almost all purchased or taken away. The tribal people's treaty rights to fish at traditional places has been the subject of dispute up to the present.

16. Name some ways that governments have failed to honor the treaty agreements.

CHINOOK JARGON

The tribes of the Northwest spoke many different languages. It was necessary for them to have some way to communicate with each other when they traded. The Plains Indians used sign language for this purpose. The Indians of the Pacific Northwest used Chinook Jargon.

It is not certain whether some form of the Jargon was used before the coming of non-Indians. Chinook Jargon used a combination of Chinook, Nootka, French, and English. The vocabulary was very small.

Here are some examples of Chinook Jargon words and their English meanings:

canim — canoe
chuck — water
hyak — swift, fast, hurry
lo push — mouth
la monti — mountain
mama — mother
muckamuck — food, to eat
ole man — old man, old
piupiu — to stink
tatoosh — milk
tumtum — heart
tyee — chief

SECTION 2: INDIAN WARS IN WASHINGTON

How Did Washington Indians Choose To Deal With These Conflicts?

Conflicts with non-Indians affected the lives of all Native Americans in Washington Territory. Different tribes and individuals chose different methods of dealing with these conflicts. Some realized they were powerless against the larger number of whites. They felt it was impossible to resist going to the reservations, and they went. Others chose to fight.

Chief Sealth was one of the tribal leaders who chose to go to the reservation without violence. Sealth was well known as a peacemaker and a friend of the settlers. His speech to Governor Stevens at the Point Elliot treaty meeting is a famous statement of peace. Here is part of it: "The White Chief says that Big Chief in Washington sends us greetings of friendship and good will. This is kind of him for we know he has little need of our friendship in return. His people are many. They are like the grass that covers vast prairies. My people are few. They resemble the scattering trees of a storm-swept plain. . . let us hope that hostilities between us never return. We would have everything to lose and nothing to gain. . . Your God makes your people grow strong every day. Soon they will fill all the land. Our people are ebbing away like a rapidly receding tide that will never return. . . However, your proposition seems fair, and I think that my people will accept it and will retire to the reservation you offer them. Then we will dwell apart in peace."

17. Why did Chief Sealth think his people would accept their move to the reservation?

Violence On Puget Sound

Other Native American groups around Puget Sound were not as peaceful as Chief Sealth and his people. Many were angry that their land and traditional way of life were being taken away by non-Indian settlement. They decided to fight back. During the winter of 1855 to 1856, some settlers in this area were killed by Indians.

One day, the settlers were told that several tribal groups were planning an attack on Seattle! However, a U.S. Navy warship, *The Decatur,* was anchored in Puget Sound. The ship's huge guns were fired into the forest outside the settlement. The attack was broken up.

The planned attack gave the settlers a real scare. Some people left. The United States government changed some of the treaty agreements, giving the Nisqually better land. And Governor Stevens personally saw to it that Chief Leschi, one of the tribal leaders, was punished.

Leschi was charged with the murder of a U.S. Army colonel, although there was no good evidence that Leschi was guilty. Many settlers even believed that the colonel's death was an act of war, instead of murder. The first time Leschi was brought to trial, the jury could not reach a decision. The second jury found him guilty. Leschi had many friends and supporters in the Hudson's Bay Company and the United States Army. The people tried to save him, but they were not successful. Leschi was hanged.

18. How was the planned attack on Seattle broken up?
19. Why was Leschi hanged?

What Other Battles Took Place?

There were other incidents of Indian violence in the Northwest that year. A group of Walla

A drawing of Chief Sealth

WHO WAS KAMIAKIN?

Before Kamiakin was born, an old and wise advisor to his mother's tribe predicted that he, Kamiakin, would be a great leader of his people. The old advisor also predicted that a fair-skinned people would come into the area and take the tribe's land. (This prediction was made before the tribe had met any white people.)

As a young man, Kamiakin already showed the qualities that would make him a great leader, just as the old man had said. Kamiakin was both generous and daring. He was a good judge and a good organizer. Members of other tribes began to come to him for help in settling a dispute or solving a difficult problem. Tribal villages began to recognize Kamiakin as their chief, even though he did not inherit this role.

The young Kamiakin had a peaceful nature. He criticized the killings at Waiilatpu. He asked for Catholic priests to come to his tribe.

But as he saw the tribes losing their land, and many lives, to non-Indian invaders, Kamiakin grew angry. He decided there could be no peace as long as the settlers stayed. Other chiefs sometimes wanted to compromise or make peace with the settlers and the army. But Kamiakin remained firm. He opposed Governor Stevens' treaties; he led the attack on Colonel Steptoe; he argued that the tribes should fight for their land at every opportunity.

By 1858, Kamiakin saw that he could not stop the non-Indian invasion of his people's lands. He and his family moved to Canada. By 1865, he was back in the Palouse country, where he lived for about another 10 years.

Walla Indians fought a company of volunteer soldiers in an encounter called the Battle of Frenchtown. Peo Peo Mox Mox and other tribal leaders asked for a truce. The soldiers took the tribal leaders to their camp. There are several very different stories about exactly what happened in the next few days. Two things are clear, though. Peo Peo Mox Mox was killed while he was in the camp. And the Walla Walla people were completely defeated.

During the winter of 1855, a band of Yakima, Klickitat, and Cascade Indians attacked the little settlement at the Cascades on the Columbia. They planned to sink the two steamboats that stopped there. Then they would be able to stop traffic up and down the Columbia.

However, the two ships managed to escape and go for help. The army arrived and the Native Americans retreated. One family of settlers was killed. Nine Native Americans were captured and hanged.

The leader of the Yakimas, Chief Kamiakin, was one of many Native Americans who believed the tribes should fight for their land. He believed that the only way the tribes could live

peacefully was to drive out all the newcomers. Kamiakin made agreements with some other tribal chiefs to support each other in battles against intruders.

In the 1850's, the Yakimas decided to use violence to protect their land against trespassers. At that time, miners were crossing Yakima land on their way to the gold and silver mines. The Yakima people felt this was a violation of their treaty rights. So they began to kill whites found on their land. The army responded by sending troops into Eastern Washington. Kamiakin led his people in several successful small battles against the soldiers. In these battles, the Yakimas were joined by members of other tribes. Kamiakin, in turn, fought with other tribes against the army.

The Native American leaders were not always in agreement. Some of the leaders wanted to make peace with the army before too many of their people were killed. Already many older tribal members and children had died during the retreats.

Kamiakin was one of the leaders who did not want to compromise. He believed in using every opportunity to fight for their lives and their land. Finally, though, the Yakima tribe was defeated.

20. What happened at the Cascades in the winter of 1855?
21. Why did the Yakimas kill miners who crossed their reservation?
22. In Kamiakin's opinion, what was the only way the tribes could live peacefully?

How Did The Army And The Settlers Disagree?

Governor Stevens and the settlers were anxious for the army to do whatever was necessary to stop all further attacks. But General James Wool, the commander of the Army's Pacific forces, had quite different ideas about how to deal with the conflicts.

General Wool believed that the settlers themselves were responsible for bad relations with the tribes. He believed that troubles were caused because the government did not protect the Native Americans' rights. General Wool had a different plan for preventing conflicts. In 1856, he ordered that the eastern part of Washington Territory be closed off to new settlers. Only the missionaries and Hudson's Bay Company employees would be allowed to remain. General Wool also refused to allow the settlers to form their own volunteer armies to fight the Indians.

23. Who did General Wool believe was responsible for bad relations with Indians?
24. What was General Wool's order?

What Was The Battle Of Rosalia?

In 1858, Colonel Edward Steptoe and about 160 soldiers travelled to Colville to look into some reported trouble between Native Americans and miners. At the Spokane River, the soldiers were met by about 600 members of the Spokane tribe. The Spokanes said they believed the soldiers would try to attack them. They warned Steptoe and his men not to go any farther.

A short time later, the soldiers were attacked by a group of Native Americans from different tribes. The soldiers had not expected any fighting. They had not brought much ammunition. So they tried to fight their way quickly to a safe place. They reached a hill near what is now Rosalia. Three soldiers were killed there and others wounded. Twelve Native Americans died.

Colonel Steptoe knew that he and his men couldn't stay and fight. They were weak and had no water. The soldiers left their extra horses and supplies behind on the hill and escaped in the dark that night. Friendly Nez Perce protected the soldiers and helped them get back to Fort Walla Walla.

25. Who was involved in the Battle of Rosalia?
26. How many people were killed?
27. How did Colonel Steptoe and his soldiers escape?

How Were The Tribes Defeated?

Steptoe's defeat was a shock to both the settlers and the army. The army decided to respond with force. Colonel George Wright led 700 men into Eastern Washington Territory. They attacked many villages and killed most of the hostile leaders and many other Native Americans.

Finally, Wright was able to capture 900 of the Indians' horses that were being herded away to safety. He ordered his men to kill them all. They also destroyed huge stores of food that the tribes had put away for the winter.

Leaders were dead; villages had been destroyed; there were no horses or food for the winter. The tribes all surrendered.

After they had destroyed all tribal resistance, the army reopened the area for settlement in 1859, and General Wool was fired as commander of the Army's Pacific forces.

Peo Peo Mox Mox, Walla Walla chief. He was killed at Frenchtown.

WHAT MAKES A MASSACRE?

The incident at Waiilatpu described in Unit 5 is usually called a "massacre." (A massacre is the merciless killing of a number of people.) The Cayuse killed 14 people. Colonel Wright and his men killed a great many more people — and horses — than the Cayuse did. The main cause of their killing was Steptoe's defeat, in which three men were killed. The immediate cause of the Cayuse killing was anger and fear of a disease that had already killed hundreds of tribal people. The Cayuse scalped Marcus Whitman after they killed him. Soldiers scalped Peo Peo Mox Mox after they killed him.

Do any of these events deserve to be called a massacre?

28. How did Colonel Wright force the tribes to surrender?

The Last Indian War

The last of Washington's Indian Wars was fought much later, from 1877 to 1879. This is sometimes called the Chief Joseph War.

Joseph was a chief of one of the Nez Perce bands. He is probably the best known tribal leader in Pacific Northwest history.

Joseph lived through all the tribe's important cultural changes of the nineteenth century. He was born about 1840, the son of a Nez Perce chief who was also called Joseph. As a boy, he travelled with his father and met the chiefs of the other Nez Perce bands. His tribe was strong and peaceful. They were friendly with the fur traders and missionaries, and many of the tribe

became Christians, including Joseph and his father. They signed the 1855 treaty at Walla Walla and lived peacefully for a few years.

29. Who was Chief Joseph?

Why Did The Nez Perce Lose Some Land?

The peaceful life on the Nez Perce reservation was interrupted in the early 1860's. Gold had been discovered there! Soon, hopeful miners came travelling to Joseph's people's land. The miners ignored the treaty agreements and moved onto the reservation.

The Nez Perce protested. But even President Grant was unable to keep new settlers from taking the Nez Perce land.

In 1877, the United States government decided to take away part of the Nez Perce reservation and open it up for settlement. Joseph's people would be forced to move.

30. Why were Joseph's people forced to move?

What Did The Young Men Choose?

When Joseph and his people left their home to move to the new reservation, it was spring. The rivers were flooded. Many animals drowned when they tried to cross.

The group reached the new reservation. They camped just outside it on the last night of travel. But that night, two young Nez Perce sneaked off

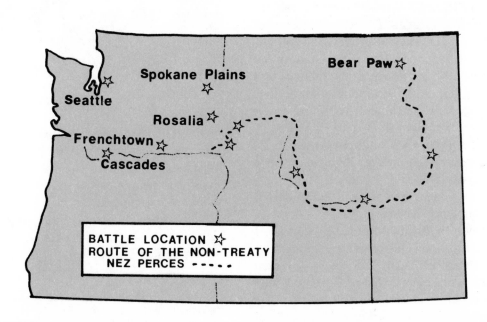

BATTLE LOCATION ☆
ROUTE OF THE NON-TREATY
NEZ PERCES - - - - -

and killed four white men who had treated them especially badly.

Joseph wanted no killing, but the young men were angry. They wanted to escape or fight, rather than move onto the new reservation. They gained support among the tribe. Joseph went along with the tribe.

Joseph's group became known as the Non-Treaties. They decided to fight their way east to the land of the Crow Indians. Most of the other Nez Perce bands stayed on the reservation. However, some individuals from other bands chose to join the Non-Treaties.

31. Who were the Non-Treaties?
32. What did the Non-Treaties decide to do?

Why Did Joseph Surrender?

Twice, the army tried to stop Joseph's band. Both times, the Non-Treaties turned them back. They reached the land of the Crows. But they discovered that the Crows were now fighting against them, together with the army. So the Non-Treaties decided to head for Canada, where they would be safe.

General Howard of the U.S. Army had taken the matter of the Nez Perce as a personal challenge, however. He didn't intend to let them get away. He and his men followed them north. Along the way, the Non-Treaties managed to make the army look pretty foolish several times, and Joseph gained a national reputation as a great military leader. (Actually, Joseph was not the tribe's military leader. The war party was led by his brother, Ollokot. But the non-Indians didn't understand that the tribes had many leaders, or chiefs, and not just one. Ollokot was better at fighting, so he led the military action. But Joseph got all the fame in the white newspapers.)

Thirty miles from the Canadian border, U.S. Army forces surprised the Nez Perce in an early morning attack. The tribe scattered. Many were killed and wounded, and Joseph surrendered. His surrender speech is now famous:

"Tell General Howard I know his heart. . . I am tired of fighting. Our chiefs are killed. . . - The old men are all dead. It is the young men who say yes or no. He who led on the young men is dead. It is cold and we have no blankets. The little children are freezing to death. My people, some of them, have run away to the hills and

Chief Joseph

have no blankets, no food; no one knows where they are — perhaps freezing to death. I want to have time to look for my children and see how many of them I can find. Maybe I shall find them among the dead.

"Hear me, my chiefs, I am tired. My heart is sick and sad. From where the sun now stands, I will fight no more forever."

33. Why did Joseph's people head for Canada, instead of staying in the land of the Crows?
34. Who was the war leader of the Non-Treaties?
35. Why did Joseph surrender?

SECTION 3: WASHINGTON STATE AND THE CIVIL WAR

How Did Slavery Issues Affect The Northwest?

While Washington officials were busy making treaties and wars with the Indians, most of the nation was concerned with another minority group — the Blacks. During the 1850's, one of the biggest issues in the eastern United States was slavery. The economy and way of life of the South were dependent on Black slave labor. Slavery was not permitted in the North. Tension between the two sides kept growing. There were angry debates in Congress and bitter feelings among different groups of American people. Finally, the Civil War broke out in 1861.

Washington Territory was far away from the debates and the battlefields. Other issues were more important to the settlers. Still, the Civil War — and the issues that caused it — affected the Northwest in several ways.

Some Northwest settlers came from slave states and some did not. Very few northwesterners had been slaveholders themselves. The Oregon settlers voted to prohibit slavery in 1844. There was little opposition to the idea. Most people felt that slavery would not fit the economy of the Northwest. There were no big plantations in the Northwest like the cotton plantations of the South.

However, the Oregon laws not only prohibited slaves, they prohibited all Blacks. Anyone who disobeyed could be fined or imprisoned. Another law said that Blacks, Mulattos, and Chinese were not allowed to vote. As a result, many Blacks chose to settle north of the Columbia River, away from the Oregon government.

When delegates wrote the Oregon State Constitution in 1857, they didn't mention slavery. Instead, they asked the voters to respond to these three questions:

1. Do you vote for the constitution?
2. Do you vote for slavery in Oregon?
3. Do you vote for free Negroes in Oregon?

The results show how strong the anti-Black feelings were at the time.

ISSUE	YES VOTES	NO VOTES
Constitution	7,195	3,125
Slavery	2,645	7,727
Free Negroes	1,081	8,640

36. How did Oregon settlers feel about slavery?
37. What group was not allowed to settle in Oregon?

Who Were Some Early Black Settlers In The Northwest?

As a result of the Oregon laws, most Black pioneers in the Northwest settled north of the

These people posed for a picture outside their South King County church in the 1890's. Why did many Blacks settle north of the Columbia River?

GEORGE WASHINGTON OF CENTRALIA

Despite their difficulties, Black settlers contributed much to the early development of what is now Washington State. One settler who especially stands out is a man named George Washington, after the first president. (He was not related to George Washington Bush who was another outstanding Black pioneer.) George Washington was born in Virginia in 1817. He was raised by a white couple, Mr. and Mrs. James C. Cochran, who were friends of his mother.

While George was young, the Cochrans moved west into the wilderness, first to Ohio, then to Missouri. George became a skilled rifleman. He learned how to knit, weave, and sew. And he taught himself reading and writing. He was six feet tall and extremely strong. He worked as a tailor and a lumberman.

After a request by Mr. and Mrs. Cochran, George was given full rights as a citizen, by a special act of the Missouri legislature. (Other Blacks in Missouri did not have such rights.) But George Washington decided to try to go to Oregon, hoping that there he might really be free and equal. The Cochrans agreed to join him.

George began to develop a piece of land near the Chehalis River. But since he was Black, he couldn't claim it himself. So the Cochrans made the claim, and he later paid them for it. He took care of the Cochrans for the rest of their lives.

On this land, George Washington planned and started the city of Centerville, later called Centralia. He was aided by his new wife, a widow named Mary Jane Cooness.

The town of Centerville began to grow, and the Washingtons helped it along. They dedicated land for a park. They helped build a church. And they found work and food for poor settlers. During the depression of 1893 especially, George Washington provided food and money for townspeople who otherwise might have starved. When he died at age 88, the residents of Centralia gave a huge funeral to honor the founder of their town.

Columbia. Here, they contributed to the growth of Washington. Several of the earliest settlers in this area were Black. They helped do the extremely difficult work of clearing land, starting farms, setting up the first industries, and starting cities. George Bush and George Washington are especially noted for their achievements during this period. (See Unit 5 for more information.)

Black people came to north Kittitas County in the late 1880's to work in the mines. They were recruited to take the place of miners on strike. The labor unions were extremely angry at the Black workers for doing this. But most Blacks had no other chances to get good jobs. They were laid off when white workers wanted the jobs.

In the following years, most of the Black workers left the mines and spread out into nearby areas. A number of Blacks homesteaded in Yakima County, for example. Few Blacks remain in the mining towns today, although the old mining town of Roslyn had a Black mayor in the 1970's.

Many of the Black settlers in Washington State found work building the railroads. A great many others worked on the ships that sailed up and down the West Coast. They served as stewards, waiters, and cabin attendants.

38. Name some jobs held by early Black settlers in Washington State.

Black Settlers Contribute To City Growth And Development

Later, other Black pioneers helped develop Washington cities. Two of the most influential Black settlers in the early years of Seattle were William Gross (sometimes spelled "Grose") and John Gayton. Gross had made money as a miner in California. He moved to Seattle and operated a hotel called "Our House" until the Seattle fire in 1889. He was known in town as "Big Bill the Cook." He became friends with Arthur Denny and Henry Yesler, and they encouraged Gross to buy a large piece of land east of downtown Seattle. (The center of his property was at 23rd and Madison streets.) In the following years, Bill Gross sold plots of his land to Black families who moved to Seattle.

John Gayton came to Washington in 1889, the year of statehood. He held several different jobs in Seattle. For example, he served as deputy sheriff, and President Franklin Roosevelt appointed him court librarian in the 1930's. Gayton became very active in Seattle's Black community. He helped establish the local Y.M.C.A. and the First African Methodist-Episcopal church.

John Gayton made sure that his children got a good education, and several members of his family became prominent in Seattle. The children and grandchildren of John Gayton included an attorney, a football star, and other outstanding figures in the community.

39. Who were John Gayton and William Gross?

How Were Northwesterners Involved In The Civil War?

In general, settlers in Washington and Oregon tried to stay out of the Civil War conflicts as much as possible. Many of them — including Joseph Lane and several other political leaders — opposed the war. These people were known as Copperheads.

However, there were some northwesterners who went east to fight in the Civil War. There was one company of Washington volunteers in the Union Army. Senator Baker of Oregon and Isaac Stevens were both killed in battle while fighting for the North. And Washington women were very active in making clothing and hospital supplies for the Civil War soldiers.

40. Explain this sentence: Joseph Lane was one of many Copperheads in the Northwest.
41. Name two Northwest leaders who were killed while fighting in the Civil War.

Civil War Military Activity And The Northwest

The only military activity of the Civil War that took place in the Northwest involved a confederate raiding ship called the *Shenendoah*. This ship cruised the Pacific Coast and attacked Yankee ships. The *Shenendoah* was so disconnected from other Civil War action that the crew refused, at first, to believe reports that the war was over. They didn't surrender until an English ship confirmed the news.

However, there were some other connections between the Civil War fighting and Washington. For one thing, several of the military leaders who became famous in the Civil War had spent

---

GEORGE B. MCCLELLAN: A DOUBLE DISAPPOINTMENT

One of the men who was involved in both Washington Territory and the Civil War was George B. McClellan. McClellan was a big disappointment to Governor Isaac Stevens and to President Lincoln. Both Stevens and Lincoln fired him.

Isaac Stevens chose McClellan to do the last part of the northern railroad survey in 1853. McClellan was supposed to explore and map the best pass across the Cascades. He never did it. Instead, he kept finding excuses why none of the passes could be used.

A few years later, Abraham Lincoln chose McClellan to be commander of the Union Forces in the Civil War. But Lincoln found his commander too timid and cautious. The Union Army was not making enough progress with McClellan in command. So Lincoln "fired" McClellan and chose Ulysses S. Grant to replace him.

---

time with the army in Washington before the war began. They included Philip Sheridan, George McClellan, George Pickett, and Ulysses S. Grant.

Also, after the Civil War started, the Army took many of its regular troops out of Washington so that they could fight in the East. Sometimes this resulted in a "wild west" kind of lawlessness in parts of the territory.

42. What was the Shenendoah?
43. Name several Civil War military leaders who spent time with the army in Washington before the war began.

How Did The Civil War Affect Northwest Governments?

While Congress was busy with slavery and war issues, they delayed action on some decisions that were important to Washington and Oregon. They did not act quickly to bring railroads to the Northwest, for example.

Disagreements about the slavery issue had also delayed Oregon's statehood during the 1850's. Congressmen from slave states did not want to admit another free state into the country. It took a long time to gather enough votes to make Oregon a state.

44. Name some important decisions that were postponed because Congress was involved with slavery issues and the Civil War.

Opening day of the first transcontinental railroad to the Pacific Northwest.

UNIT 7

THE ROAD TO STATEHOOD

The train in the photo at left was the first train to travel from Minnesota to Portland. The railroad between the Pacific Northwest and the midwestern United States had just been completed. The Northwest was finally connected to the rest of the country by rail!

This unit tells the story of how Washington Territory became Washington State. In a way, that railroad train is the story's hero.

Why? Well, before the railroads came, Washington's population grew very slowly. It was just too hard to get here. The people who already lived in Washington were anxious for their territory to win statehood. But statehood was not possible until the population was bigger. And few people wanted to come until the transportation was better.

The railroads changed all this. The trip to Washington, which used to take several months, took only a few days by train. Just six years after the first cross-country railroad came, Washington became a state.

But railroads were not the only source of drama in the years before 1889. In the 1860's, Washington Territory was the scene of a small gold rush. In the 1870's, some pigs and potatoes almost started a war. In the 1880's, some Washington cities suffered from racial violence and destructive fires. These years were also a time of tough competition between Washington settlements and the beginning of women's long struggle for legal equality here.

This unit has four sections:

1. Washington Gets Its Present Boundaries
2. Railroads and the Growth Contest
3. People From Many Countries
4. Statehood At Last

SECTION 1: WASHINGTON GETS ITS PRESENT BOUNDARIES

Why Were Roads Needed?

Throughout the Civil War period, Washington Territory continued to grow and develop. More settlers came to the area. New cities were founded, and young settlements such as Olympia, Tacoma, Seattle, and Port Townsend began to grow into towns.

Population grew slowly at first. Washington settlements were hard to get to. There was no road across the Rocky Mountains north of the Columbia River and no road across the Cascades. This meant that overland travelers usually followed the Columbia River Valley and then turned north.

The Territorial Legislature asked Congress to pay for the building of some badly needed roads. Meanwhile, Puget Sound settlers decided to build a road across the Cascades themselves. Early Northwest settlers were often too independent and too impatient to wait for the federal government to get started on a project. This road and the provisional government are two good examples of settlers taking up a project by themselves when the government refused to act— or acted too slowly.

This first wagon road crossed the Cascades at Naches Pass. The "road" was more like a trail, really. It was narrow, and extremely rough. The first wagon train to use this route was led by James Longmire in 1853. The Longmire party was close to starving and totally exhausted when they finally arrived. The road was not used very often.

1. Why did Washington's population grow slowly at first?

What Was The Mullan Road?

Soon afterward, the federal government became interested in roadbuilding, too. The army wanted to be able to move troops in and out of the territory if necessary. Congress provided money to build a road across the Rockies from the Columbia to the Missouri River.

Lieutenant John Mullan was chosen to direct the building of the road. The project was very

difficult. He and his men had to cut through 125 miles of timber, build many bridges and ferries, and carve a level path on the sides of mountains.

The 624 mile road was completed in 1860 and improved over the next two years. It was called the Mullan Road, after its builder. The road was buried in snow in the winter, and there were landslide dangers in the spring. But it was the only road there was, and people used it gratefully.

The Catholic missionary, Father Joseph Cataldo once said, "The Mullan trail wasn't much of a road. It was a big job, well done, but we used to say, 'Captain Mullan just made enough of a trail so he could get back out of here.'"

2. Why did the United States government want to build a road?
3. Why was the Mullan Road so difficult to build?

Why Did So Many People Come To Eastern Washington?

One of the first groups of people to use the Mullan Road turned out to be gold miners. Gold was first found in the eastern parts of Washington Territory shortly before the road was built. Prospectors rushed by the thousands to places that are now in Idaho, Eastern Washington, and Western Montana. By 1863, the population of this part of the territory had swelled to almost 30,000.

NORTHWEST GOLD RUSH CENTERS 1850-1900

POPULATION OF WASHINGTON CITIES IN 1880			
Walla Walla	3,588	Tacoma	1,098
Seattle	3,533	Port	
Vancouver	1,722	Townsend	917
Olympia	1,232	Spokane	350

The little settlement at Walla Walla became an outfitting center where miners could buy the supplies they needed. For a while, it was the largest settlement in Washington Territory.

4. What discovery attracted thousands of people to the eastern part of Washington Territory?

5. What Washington city was bigger than Seattle during the gold rush?

Why Was Idaho Territory Created?

Within a few years, there were far more people living in the eastern part of Washington Territory than in the western part. There was talk of moving the state capital east to Walla Walla.

This move was opposed by Western Washington and Oregon. Residents of Western Washington did not want to give up their capital to any eastern city. They did not want their government to be located near the rough, rowdy mining towns. Also, Western Washington had become mostly Republican by then, and the eastern newcomers were mostly Democrats. Republicans were afraid they might be voted out of office by

LOST TREASURE AT INGALLS CREEK

Every area seems to have some legend of buried treasure. In Washington, a mysterious legend has sent hundreds of unsuccessful prospectors into the Cascade Mountains looking for a fortune in gold.

The legend began in 1872, when Captain Ben Ingalls was accompanying a scouting party near Mount Stuart. He became separated from the rest of the party and climbed a high ridge to see where he was. From the ridge, he could see three lakes. Two of them were round and one was crescent-shaped.

Ingalls turned his horse toward the lakes and rode down to explore the valley. It was then that he made his amazing discovery. All around the crescent-shaped lake, the rock was rich with gold!

He stayed in the valley for two days and made a map, which he buried. He guessed there might be ten tons of gold in the valley. He took a few samples and rode out to find the scouting party. His first night out, Ingalls was awakened by a great rumbling. An earthquake had shaken the mountains.

When Ingalls returned, he sent the samples and news of his discovery to his friend, John Hansel. Hansel hurried out to meet him, but Captain Ingalls was shot and killed in an accident a few weeks later. The buried map was never found. Hansel took a homestead nearby and kept looking for the gold.

Over the years, many other prospectors took up the search. But the gold has never been found. Perhaps it was buried in the earthquake that night. Perhaps it is still hidden nearby. The stream that comes down from the mountains there is now called Ingalls Creek, as a reminder of the lost treasure of ten tons of gold.

Towns grew up overnight where gold was discovered. Some of the mining centers are now ghost towns; others are modern cities. Today, Helena is the capital of Montana. In 1865, it was a booming mining town.

the new residents. Washington's territorial delegate urged Congress to split Washington Territory in two. Oregon supported this idea. Oregon business people wanted to carry on their profitable trade with the eastern territories, without interference from Olympia.

President Lincoln signed the bill creating Idaho Territory in 1863. At that time, Idaho Territory included all of present day Idaho plus parts of Montana and Wyoming. Washington Territory became the same size that Washington State is today.

6. Where did some people want to make the capital of Washington Territory?
7. Why did people in Oregon and Washington support the idea of creating a new territory?

What Was The San Juan Boundary Dispute?

One part of Washington's borders still was not clearly defined. It was not certain who owned the San Juan Islands. The treaty of 1846 set the boundary between U.S. and British land at "the channel that separates the continent from Vancouver Island." The problem was that there are two channels between the island and the mainland. They are Haro Strait and Rosario Strait, and the San Juan Islands are right between them.

Which country did the San Juans belong to?

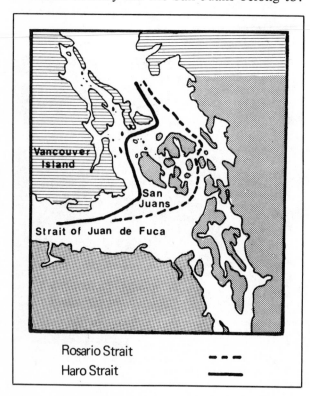

Vancouver Island

San Juans

Strait of Juan de Fuca

Rosario Strait   - - -
Haro Strait   ▬▬▬

The United States and Britain both claimed them. People from both countries settled there. Several disputes arose between them. Once the Americans tried to collect taxes from all the American and British citizens on the islands. The British citizens refused to pay. The Americans captured and sold some of the Hudson's Bay Company's sheep to pay the supposed tax bill. James Douglas, the governor of Vancouver Island, protested. Governor Stevens responded by supporting the tax collector's action. He claimed that the islands were part of Washington Territory.

The dispute was discussed by the national governments of Britain and the United States, but it was not resolved.

8. Why wasn't it clear whether the San Juan Islands belonged to the U.S. or Britain?

How Did Pigs And Potatoes Almost Start A War?

Lyman Cutler was an American farmer in the San Juans with a small, precious crop of potatoes. Charles Griffin was a Hudson's Bay Company employee who owned a pig. In the summer of 1859, Griffin's pig crawled under Cutler's fence and ate some of the potatoes. Cutler complained to Griffin to keep his pig locked up. Griffin refused. Cutler shot the pig. Griffin threatened to have Cutler arrested and sent to England for a trial.

Both countries sent troops to the islands. For a while, it seemed there might be a war. The American military commander threatened a fight. But neither country's government wanted this. After settling most of the border disputes so peacefully, the U.S. and Britain did not want to start a war over pigs and potatoes.

The two countries chose William the First, Emperor of Germany, to decide who the San Juans belonged to. The Emperor listened to both countries' claims and decided the U.S. claim was stronger, since Haro Strait is deeper than Rosario Strait. Haro Strait became the official border, and the San Juans became part of the United States.

9. How did pigs and potatoes almost start a war?
10. Who did Britain and the United States pick to settle the dispute?
11. What did William I decide?

SECTION 2: RAILROADS AND THE GROWTH CONTEST

The Growth Contest

The San Juan boundary dispute was the last act in the dramatic competition between nations for the region's land. As the island residents waited for the dispute to be settled, another drama was going on farther south.

At several locations around Puget Sound, settlements had been established. Now the people in each settlement were competing to attract more settlers, businesses, and better transportation. Each group wanted their settlement to become the largest city in Washington Territory. Single men and families had come from many parts of America to participate in the Northwest's growth contest.

They lived in small, hand-built houses on the edge of forests. But they saw a future of shops and factories, paved streets, and tall buildings. They imagined big cities bustling with people and activity. The settlers were willing to bet years of rough living and hard work on the chance that the places they picked would grow and prosper.

12. What did each group of settlers hope their own little settlement would become?

The Importance Of Natural Resources

The geography of Washington helped the early settlements grow in several ways. There were plenty of natural resources nearby, including fish, lumber, and a good climate for farming. Once the area was logged and drained, there was a lot of good farmland in Western Washington. There were coal mines near Seattle, Tacoma, and Bellingham.

Most of the lumber and coal could be sold in San Francisco. San Francisco was then the largest city on the West Coast, thanks to the California gold rush. It was easy to ship Northwest products to California, since most Washington settlements had good water transportation available. Seattle, Tacoma, Bellingham, and Port Townsend all had natural deep harbors on Puget Sound. Several other settlements were located on big rivers. Ships could easily sail in and load up with Washington resources. Then they could sail to San Francisco, Alaska, or Asia, where these resources were sold.

13. How was geography important to early Washington settlements?
14. Where were most Northwest products sold?

Steamships like this one used to be the main form of transportation on Puget Sound. They carried people and cargo between cities.

THE GROWTH CONTEST IN EASTERN WASHINGTON

The competition for railroads was intense in Eastern Washington, too. Like the towns on Puget Sound, the eastern settlements needed railroads in order to become trading centers for all the farming areas nearby.

Sometimes the competition between cities got a little out of control. Take the competition between Cheney and Spokane, for example. In 1880, both towns wanted to be county seat (the county's "capital") of Spokane County.

An election was held. The votes were counted in Spokane. Officials claimed that Spokane had won the election, but the people of Cheney complained that the election officials had lied. One night, while most Spokane settlers were at a wedding party, some Cheney settlers sneaked into Spokane. They went to the election office and kidnapped both the election official and the election records. Cheney people then claimed that they had won the election, and they moved the county government to Cheney.

Another election was held in 1886, however. This time, Spokane had a much larger population. They won the election, and the county seat was moved to Spokane, where it still is today.

Spokane was definitely the winner of the growth contest in Eastern Washington. Today, it is the trading center for the whole area known as the Inland Empire. This includes the Columbia Plateau and some surrounding areas. Spokane is the biggest city between Seattle and Minneapolis, a distance of about 1500 miles.

Railroad Magic

Water transportation from Washington Territory was fine — if you wanted to get to California or Alaska or Asia. But what about New York or Chicago? Washington settlements needed land connections with the rest of the United States. They needed railroads.

"Railroad" was a magic word to Puget Sound settlers in those days. A city with railroad connections to the East Coast would be able to attract people and money from eastern cities. The settlers would be able to sell their products to more people. The city would grow!

So each town competed for the attention of the railroad companies. Each boasted that it was the best location for railroad business in Washington Territory.

15. Why was "railroad" a magic word to the young cities?

A Winner. . . And An Angry Loser

In 1870, the Northern Pacific Railroad Company started planning a track from the American Midwest to Puget Sound. Nobody knew where on Puget Sound the tracks would go. A group of officials, including the president of the Northern Pacific Railroad Company,

This train carried coal from Black Diamond to Puget Sound. This photo was taken in Black Diamond on the day the first miners' union was formed, in 1907.

visited Tacoma, Olympia, Nisqually, Steilacoom, and Seattle. People in each place wondered if their town would be chosen for the railroad station. Excitement mounted. Had the officials made a decision? They wouldn't say.

In 1873, the company finally announced that they had picked Tacoma. Tacoma was the only town among the list that had a good harbor with plenty of flat land that the railroad company could buy cheaply. Seattle was willing to give the railroad thousands of dollars and more than 3,000 acres of land if the terminal would be built in their city. But railroad officials could acquire even more land in Tacoma. They hoped to sell this land for great profits after the railroad was completed.

That same year, Jay Cooke went bankrupt, causing the Panic of 1873. Cooke had financed the Northern Pacific, so work on the railroad was delayed for a while. The railroad workers went on strike. The line was finally completed in 1879.

The settlers at Seattle were so angry that Tacoma had been chosen that they decided to build their own railroad across the Cascades. A group of volunteers got only a short distance before their enthusiasm died out. (One historian has estimated that at the rate the volunteers were building, they would not have finished until 1970.) A Chinese American contractor named Chin Gee Hee later hired workers to complete the line to Renton.

The track was only a few miles long, but the coal business at least made money. And the settlers' determination attracted attention from other parts of the nation.

16. Which towns on Puget Sound did the Northern Pacific executives visit when they were looking for a place to build their railroad station?
17. Which town did they choose?
18. How did Seattle respond?
19. Who was Chin Gee Hee?

The Puget Sound Connection

Meanwhile, a young man named Henry Villard was busy buying up small railroad lines and steamship companies in the Northwest. In 1881, he managed to buy enough shares of Northern Pacific stock to control the company. By then, Villard controlled just about all the transportation lines in Oregon and Washington, including the steamships along the Columbia

---

A TOWN MOVES TO THE RAILROAD

The inland settlements of Eastern Washington were especially dependent on railroads because many of them had no shipping ports. Only the settlements with railroads could get their products to outside markets easily. Knowing this, early settlers tried to pick locations that would someday be near a railroad. They tried hard to get the rail companies to build their tracks through town.

The settlers at Yakima were certain they had chosen a good location. They felt sure that the Northern Pacific would build a station in their town. But then the news came. The railroad would pass through the new town of North Yakima, four miles north of the settlement.

People in Yakima were furious! Two girls in town decided to get back at the railroad with a clever prank. Behind their house, the train tracks led up a slight hill. Louise and Lily Schanno spread soft soap all over those tracks. And when the next train came, it couldn't get up the little hill. The big engine just sat there, spinning its wheels on the soapy rails. The trainmen had to get out and clean off the soap before they could move on.

Some settlers refused to move. But most people realized that businesses would have to be in North Yakima in order to survive. Some of the Yakima people put their buildings on rollers and rolled them to their new home by animal power. Stores stayed open during the entire two weeks that it took to move to their new location. Farmers tied their horses up to the outside, and the animals walked along with the moving buildings as their owners shopped. A hotel stopped every night and took in lodgers at its new locations.

Today, the new and old settlements are both part of the modern city of Yakima.

River.

Villard was determined to complete the railroad connection between the Pacific Northwest and the Eastern United States. Under his direction, the company began extending the railroad tracks in both directions. They built east from Kalama, and west from the Great Lakes. The space between the two tracks grew shorter and shorter. Finally, the two parts of the Northern Pacific Railroad met near Helena, Montana, in 1883.

There was a ceremony to celebrate the completion of the railroad. It was an important event. Settlers, supplies, and products could now go directly from the East Coast to the Pacific Northwest by train.

20. What company did Henry Villard control?
21. What happened near Helena, Montana, in 1883?

Railroads And Lumber Go Together

A railroad costs many millions of dollars to build. The United States government helped pay for the railroads by donating large amounts of land to the rail companies. After the track was laid, the company could sell the land to help pay the costs of building.

Much of the donated land was forest land. Frederick Weyerhauser was one of the first to realize how railroad companies and lumber companies could work together. The lumber company could purchase large amounts of forest land from the railroad. For a low price, the lumbermen would have a big supply of trees. The railroad company would benefit too. Soon the lumbermen would be paying the railroad to transport their new lumber.

In 1900, the Weyerhauser Company bought thousands of acres of forest land from the Northern Pacific Railroad. This made a tremendous change in Northwest logging. The small, independent sawmills had never had a sure supply of lumber. Many small mills went out of business. But a company like Weyerhauser, with its own timber supply, had much more control of its business. It was not so much at the mercy of big ups and downs in the lumber industry.

In the years that followed, Weyerhauser and the other lumber companies made other purchases of donated forest land. The purchases benefited both the lumber companies and the railroad.

22. How did the United States government help pay the high cost of building railroads?
23. How did railroad and lumber companies both benefit from big purchases of forest land?

Railroads And Growth Go Together

Railroads brought growth, and growth brought more business for the railroad. As towns got bigger and richer, the railroads got more business. More people would buy imported goods that the trains brought in, and more local products would be shipped out. What was good for the towns and settlers was usually good for the railroad. No one understood this better than James Jerome Hill. Jim Hill was president of the Great Northern Railroad. He specialized in building straight, flat rail routes that were cheap to run. And he made towns along his railroad grow!

FREDERICK WEYERHAUSER

Frederick Weyerhauser was born in Germany in 1834. His family moved to the U.S. in 1852. There he married a young German woman named Elizabeth Bloedel and began working in a lumber mill in Illinois.

Weyerhauser worked hard — 10 hours and more a day. His formula for good health and high energy was a quart of homemade buttermilk a day, plenty of fresh air and exercise, and a refusal to worry.

In a few years Weyerhauser was able to purchase the mill. He expanded his lumber business in the Midwest and began to invest in Pacific Northwest lumber. He decided to build his main Pacific Coast mill in Everett. When the mill was completed in 1903, it was the town's chief industry. Lumber and wood products are still the most important businesses in Everett.

By the time of his death, Weyerhauser's company was the biggest lumber company in the United States.

---

24. How did railroads and growth go together?
25. Who was Jim Hill?

The Empire Builder

Jim Hill built most of the Great Northern Railroad without any government land grants. Each piece of railroad had to make money to pay for itself. To make sure his trains made money, Hill did a lot of advertising. He advertised the good farmland of the Great Plains, for example. His agents recruited settlers in the U.S., Canada, and Europe. Soon there were farmers living all along the route through Minnesota and North Dakota. They grew wheat and other crops and shipped them out in Great Northern trains. Hill sold a special discount train ticket to families who would settle close to the tracks.

When the Great Northern Railroad tracks reached the Pacific Northwest, Hill began advertising Northwest lumber in the East. He charged a special low shipping rate for Northwest lumber, so that it would be cheap enough to compete with Eastern lumber.

Hill wanted his westbound trains to be full too. But there weren't very many people on the West Coast. Who could buy the eastern goods that his trains carried west? Hill decided to try to sell American goods in Asia. He developed a market in Japan and China for cotton and other products from the Eastern United States. He even built some ships to take the goods across the ocean.

Hill's advertising worked well. Soon all his trains were full. All along the Great Northern tracks, there were businesses that Jim Hill helped create. He is sometimes called "the Empire Builder" because of all the growth he helped to bring about.

26. Name some businesses that Jim Hill helped develop.
27. Why did Hill develop Asian markets for U.S. goods?

Another Railroad

Many people in Washington were glad to have the Great Northern come to the Northwest. The Great Northern charged lower shipping rates for many items, in competition with the Northern Pacific. Eastern Washington farmers were especially grateful for this. Northern Pacific's rates were so high that many farmers could barely make any money on the crops they shipped out. The Palouse area in the southeast part of the state had a national reputation as the cheapest place to grow wheat. But it also had the highest cost of transporting the wheat to market.

This had been a problem in many parts of the United States. Wherever one railroad had a monopoly, the railroad would raise its rates as high as possible. Farmers had no choice but to pay those rates.

People were eager to attract the new railroad to their cities. They were ready to do whatever Jim Hill asked. For example, the city of Spokane gave free land through town just to make sure the railroad would build there.

The people in Seattle were happy that the Great Northern chose Seattle as its terminus (end of the line). The Great Northern was completed in 1893. That year, Seattle finally got its own transcontinental railroad.

However, James Hill soon created an even more powerful monopoly than the Northern Pacific. He was able to buy the Northern Pacific in 1893. Soon, he controlled almost all rail transportation in Washington. Several of the reform laws passed in the early 1900's were designed to limit the tremendous power of James Hill and the railroad companies. (See Unit 8, Section 2.)

28. Why were Eastern Washington farmers happy to have the Great Northern come to the Northwest?
29. Why were people in Seattle happy?

Building the railroad was difficult and dangerous work. There were long hours of hard physical labor. The pay and the working conditions were usually poor. A lot of workers died of illness or accidents. Most of the workers were foreign-born. Large numbers of Chinese men were recruited to build the American railroads. Japanese and European workers helped build the railroads in the Pacific Northwest. Also, many Mormons from Idaho and Utah were hired to work on the railroads here. This photo shows Chinese and white railroad workers in the Cascade Mountains. What dangers and difficulties for the workers might be caused by the deep snow?

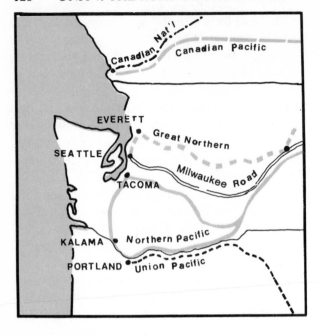

Rails Across The Mountains

The railroads were quickly extended north along Puget Sound. Short lines were built to connect the settlements in Eastern Washington. Soon almost every town had a railroad connection.

Until the late 1880's, all overland traffic to Puget Sound had to go along the Columbia River and then turn north at Portland or Kalama. But in 1888, the Northern Pacific completed the first route with a tunnel through the Cascades. A tunnel made the road less steep and kept the heavy snow off the tracks. It was called the Stampede Tunnel, since it crossed Stampede Pass.

The pass was named when work on the railroad began. The work was hard and quite dangerous, cold, and uncomfortable. The workers usually didn't last too long before they quit. They quit so fast, people said, that there seemed to be a stampede. People started calling the place Stampede Pass, and the name stuck. Many men were injured or died while working on the Stampede Tunnel.

Other transcontinental (cross-country) railroads were also completed between 1884 and 1915. In 1884, the Union Pacific (a cross-country railroad to California) built a connecting line to Portland. In 1909, the Chicago, Milwaukee, St. Paul, and Pacific Railroad completed its line across Snoqualmie Pass to Seattle. The Milwaukee Road, as this railroad was usually called, became the third line to cross the United States to Puget Sound. The trip from St. Paul, Minnesota, to Seattle took 62 hours and 30 minutes, or less than three days.

Two other railroads were built across Canada to Vancouver, British Columbia. The Canadian Pacific Railroad was completed in 1885; the Canadian National was opened in 1915. The first rail connection between Vancouver and the cities on Puget Sound was opened in 1891.

30. How did the name "Stampede Pass" originate?
31. What railroads crossed the continent to Washington State and British Columbia?

How Did Railroads Help Washington Grow?

The 1880's were a time of rapid growth in Washington Territory. Thanks to the railroad, Washington had better business connections with the Eastern American cities. Better machinery and new markets led to increased lumber production. New businesses were started in the territory and old ones expanded. The railroads also opened up new farm land, especially in the eastern part of the territory. Farming increased on both sides of the Cascades. Western Washington crops included oats, hay, hops, and vegetables. Farmers and ranchers in Eastern Washington grew more wheat, oats, and barley, and raised more sheep as the railroads made transportation easier.

The trains also brought thousands of new settlers. Cities grew with amazing speed. For several months, an average of more than 100 settlers reached Puget Sound by train every day! Compare these figures from the 1880 and 1890 census:

| City | Population | |
	1880	1890
Seattle	3,533	42,837
Tacoma	1,098	36,006
Spokane	350	19,922

Other Washington cities grew too, but not so fast.

32. How did railroads contribute to economic growth in Washington?
33. What grew with amazing speed in the 1880's?

SECTION 3: PEOPLE FROM MANY COUNTRIES

Where Did Most Settlers Come From?

The passenger trains which arrived in Washington in the 1880's and 90's carried people from many places in North America and Europe. They spoke several different languages and brought with them a variety of cultures.

The great majority of the newcomers spoke English. The largest number came from places in the United States and Canada. Many of these came from mid-western America.

There were also many large immigrant groups from non-English-speaking parts of Europe. The biggest European group arriving in Washington then were Scandinavians. Scandinavia includes the countries Sweden, Norway, and Denmark, which are fairly closely related and have similar cultures. Many of the Scandinavians who came to Washington had settled first in the American midwest, then later decided that Washington was more appealing.

The next largest European immigrant group were the people of the British Isles — England, Scotland, Ireland, and Wales. Next largest was the German-speaking group, from Germany and Austria. In addition, as the chart on page 130 shows, there were immigrants from southern and eastern European countries, as well as people of other races.

34. Which two countries contributed the largest number of Washington settlers?
35. Name the countries of Scandinavia and the British Isles which contributed many settlers to Washington.

Why Did People Move To Washington?

The newcomers had many reasons for making the trip to Washington. For example, the farming opportunities were excellent. There was still a lot of good land available at low prices — much lower than in the more settled areas of the country. Eastern Washington Territory was already becoming known for its fine wheat crops. And around Puget Sound, there was a lot of good land for dairy farms, vegetable crops, and other agriculture. The mild Washington climates were also attractive.

The rich natural resources of Washington created job opportunities. A Norwegian fisher could expect to find work in his career area here. So could a Swedish logger or a German miner. Many people came here for the opportunity to work at the jobs for which they had skills.

Some people came for the opportunities of the cities. Washington cities were growing fast, and their residents were optimistic. It seemed there were unending possibilities for success in business, politics, and city development.

Others came because they had family and friends here. For people who did not speak English, it was especially comforting to settle near people of the same culture and language.

36. Tell how each of the following helped attract settlers to Washington Territory: land prices, natural resources, climate, the cities.

How Did Advertising Help Attract Settlers?

The people in Washington Territory wanted the population to grow. They wanted to encourage settlers to come. So the territorial government printed advertisements that told about the attractions of the Pacific Northwest.

A much larger advertising campaign was started by the railroad companies. Every new settler meant more business for the railroads — more customers for imported goods and more products to ship out. The railroads also had great amounts of land to sell. So they sent out agents to tell people about the good lands along their rail routes. The Northern Pacific alone had 124 agents in Europe. They offered special low rates to families who would settle in areas near the railroad. And they paid free passage to Europe for some successful settlers who wanted to visit their homeland. These settlers would encourage their friends and family to come to the Northwest.

37. Why did the railroads want to attract new settlers?
38. What advertising techniques were used to encourage settlers to come?

Why Did Many People Want To Leave Europe?

In addition to the things that "pulled" people to Washington, there were other things that "pushed" them away from the places where

WASHINGTON POPULATION
BY RACE, IN 1890

Indian	11,181
Chinese	3,260
Black	1,602
Japanese	360
White	340,829
Total	357,232

WASHINGTON POPULATION
BY NATIONAL ORIGIN IN 1900 (whites only)*
(1890 Figures not available)

Canada:	20,284	England:	10,481
Germany:	16,686	Norway:	9,891
Sweden:	12,737	Ireland:	7,262
U.S.:	384,940	Denmark:	3,626
Scotland:	3,623	Switzerland:	1,825
Russia:	2,462	Wales:	1,509
Austria:	2,343	France:	1,065
Italy:	2,124	Other:	15,456

*These figures include people who were born in foreign countries and people whose parents were born in foreign countries. If both parents were born in Sweden, for example, the person would be counted in the Swedish national origin group. If the parents were born in two different foreign countries, the person would be counted in the national origin group of the father.

they were living. For example, many settlers came here from the American midwest because they did not like the climate. The winters were bitterly cold and the summers were very hot.

People had many reasons for wanting to leave Europe in the late 1800's. Many people were attracted to America for its freedoms. Several religious minorities were still discriminated against in some parts of Europe. And few European countries offered the opportunities for social and economic equality that could be found in America.

Some European countries had been fighting frequent wars for the last several hundred years. Some immigrants came to get away from war or to avoid having to fight. These people were attracted to America because it was at peace.

But the main reason for wanting to leave Europe was the lack of economic opportunity. In the nineteenth century, the population of Europe had tripled. The limited amount of European farmland could not support the growing population — not with the traditional farming methods being used. Few people owned land. In years of drought or depression,

thousands of people starved.

Many rural Europeans went to nearby cities to try to find work. But thousands of poor Europeans believed they would find better opportunities in America, and they were willing to risk the difficult change.

39. Give at least three reasons why a European may have wanted to come to America in the late 1800's.

The Scandinavian Experience In Washington

In 1890, a successful settler said, "My understanding is that of all the states, Washington is the one best suited to the Scandinavians." For many reasons, the Puget Sound environment was especially easy for Scandinavians to adjust to. A large number of these immigrants here had settled first in Minnesota, Wisconsin, and other midwestern states. But the special advantages of the Pacific Northwest convinced them to move.

Some Scandinavian settlers remarked that the land of Western Washington reminded them of home. The evergreen forests, mountains, long, narrow inlets, and the coastal plains could all be found in parts of Scandinavia. In addition, the main economic activities of both places were similar. Logging, fishing, and farming were all important industries in Scandinavia. This meant that the immigrants could often find a job in Washington that was similar to the job they'd had at home.

The adjustment to American life was also easy for the Scandinavians because the cultures were similar. Like the majority of American citizens, the Scandinavian immigrants were Protestant. They shared such values as hard work, education, and a belief in democracy.

Ever since their arrival, Scandinavians have been active in the fishing industry. By 1900, 32% of the fishers in Washington and Oregon were of Scandinavian background. Since the days of the Vikings, Norwegians have had a reputation as excellent sailors and boat builders. Andrew and Thea Foss, whose story appears on page 131, were among the Norwegian immigrants to Washington who made their living in the boat business. People of Scandinavian ancestry also played an important part in the development of agriculture and lumbering in Western Washington.

They have also been active in government. Several have represented Washington State in the United States Congress, including Warren G. Magnuson, Martin Smith, Mon Wallgren, Don Magnuson, and Knute Hill.

The Scandinavian influence can also be seen in the names of many Washington towns. Briedablick is from Norse mythology and means "broad view." Poulsbo was founded by Norwegian fishers and was named for a town in Norway. Hockinson, Mora, Hogdahl, and Johnsonville are among the towns that were founded and named by Swedes.

40. Name at least three career fields in which persons of Scandinavian ancestry have been successful in Washington.

This modern tug boat was named for a member of the Norwegian family who started the company.

SOME SUCCESSFUL IMMIGRANTS FROM SCANDINAVIA

Nels Peter Sorenson was born in Denmark, and he came to Minnesota with his family in 1875. He bought some farmland from the railroad there, developed it, and bought more land. He also started a coal and wood business, and he was active in local government for 20 years. Then in 1907, he sold out at a profit and moved to Western Washington. He opened a dairy in Ferndale and later became first president of the Whatcom County Dairyman's Association. He also served as director of the Meridian High School District, and was active in other community organizations.

John Nordstrom came to America from Sweden in 1887, at the age of 16. He went to work in the iron mines of Michigan, where he earned $1.60 for a ten-hour work day. He worked there for three months, until the mine closed down. After several more months of occasional work in the Midwest, he went to California and then to Washington. Altogether, he spent ten years traveling from one hard, poorly paid job to another. He worked in mines and logging camps, loaded boats and carried bricks, and worked on a farm near Arlington, Washington. Then he spent two rough and unsuccessful years in Alaska looking for gold.

On his return from Alaska, John Nordstrom decided to settle in Seattle. He went to business college, bought some land, built two houses, and married a young Swedish woman named Hilda Carlson.

He was looking for a business to invest in and decided to open a shoe store. Carl F. Wallin was his partner. When he started, Nordstrom knew nothing about shoes or selling, but he learned. The little store survived and slowly grew. For years, the Nordstroms and Wallins had lots of problems and hard work — and very little money. Finally, the store became successful and they began to open more stores. In 1929, the company was purchased by John Nordstrom's sons. Today, a chain of large department stores carries the Nordstrom name.

Andrew and Thea Foss had both come to the United States from Norway. They settled in Minnesota, but the harsh climate was hard on their health. They decided to move to Tacoma in 1888.

There, the family got a little house on the waterfront. Andrew worked as a carpenter, but he could not always find enough work to support the family. So they began to rent rowboats from their home to make a little extra money. Thea managed the boat rental business while her husband traveled to carpentry jobs around Puget Sound. Soon, Thea's boat business was bringing in more money than Andrew's carpentry.

The Foss family bought more boats and began to develop their business. In time, they owned several big steam-powered tugboats. The business grew and was passed down to later generations. Today, Foss is the major tugboat company on Puget Sound.

Other European Groups

British immigrant groups have also left their mark on Washington. Many towns were named for places in the British Isles, for example. Aberdeen and Clyde Hill got their names from towns in Scotland. Belfast is Irish; Conway is Welsh; Avon and Kent are English. British citizens have played important roles in Washington history since the days of the early explorers. The list of notable settlers from British countries includes Dr. John McLoughlin, Governor Ernest Lister, and R.H. Thomson, Seattle's famous city engineer.

German immigrants were important in the development of both Eastern and Western Washington. So many German farmers settled in Adams and Lincoln counties that German was the main language in some communities. Like the Scandinavians, many German-speaking immigrants were attracted to Washington for the opportunity to practice trades they knew. People of German and Austrian descent were early developers of several Washington industries, including breweries, banks, and lumber mills. Henry Yesler, Jacob Furth, and Bailey Gatzert were among the Washington business leaders of German origin.

A number of Russian immigrants came to Washington around the time of the Russian Revolution of 1917. The Russian community in Seattle has centered around two Russian Orthodox churches and a social hall. This is typical of many European groups. As soon as there was a community of settlers from the same cultural group, they would build a church and set up a cultural and self-help organization. These organizations provided services such as entertainment, aid for the sick, language classes, and cultural events.

The Russian culture is related to that of several other eastern European groups who all speak Slavic languages. Poles, Ukrainians, Czechs, and Croats are some of the Slavic groups who settled in Washington. Large numbers of Slavic people came to the United States between 1890-1920. They worked in Washington mills, mines, railroads, and fisheries. Aberdeen, Pe Ell, Gig Harbor, and Roslyn were some of the towns that had large Slavic populations.

Other European groups in Washington included Greeks, Swiss, French, Italians, and Gypsies and Jews from many countries.

Spokane was a rapidly growing city in the 1890's. What form of transportation helped bring about the Northwest population explosion of this period?

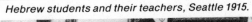
Hebrew students and their teachers, Seattle 1915.

JEWISH CONTRIBUTIONS TO WASHINGTON STATE

Among the European immigrants who came to Washington State around the turn of the century were many Jewish families. Like other European immigrants, the Jews had sailed across the Atlantic and landed in the big cities on the American East Coast. Many of them had lived in the East and Midwest before coming to the Northwest.

Most European Jews were used to living in cities. They were not interested in homesteading or farming. Many of them set up small businesses — selling furniture or fish or becoming tailors, shoemakers, or bakers.

The first Jews to arrive in the Northwest were Germans. They arrived after the 1849 gold rush in California. In the 1890's and early 1900's, Jewish settlers came here from Eastern Europe, mainly from Russia and Poland. The European Jews spoke a language called Yiddish.

Around that time, a culturally different group of Jews settled in the Northwest. These were Sephardic Jews, and they spoke Ladino, a language related to Spanish. Their ancestors had lived in Spain until they were forced to leave in 1492. They settled in Turkey and on the Greek island of Rhodes and became skilled fishers. Sephardic settlers became active in the fishing industry in the Northwest.

The Jewish immigrants were educated in their 4,000-year-old religion, and they could read Hebrew — the original language of the Bible.

As the Northwest grew, so did its Jewish population. Very often, when Jews would settle in the Northwest, their relatives soon followed. Others came to visit or work and decided to stay. In the 1930's, some of the refugees from Nazi Germany came to live in Washington State. In the 40's, some survivors of the war came from Europe. In the 50's, came Jews from the Soviet Union. They were all looking for political freedom. By the mid 1970's, the Jewish population of Washington was 15,000 One fifth of these were Sephardic Jews. (Seattle's Sephardic community is one of the largest of any United States city.)

Jews brought with them to the Northwest a tradition of community-mindedness. No sooner were the first Jewish settlers here, than they grouped together to help each other and other newcomers. By 1889, a mutual aid organization was already established. It began as Hevra Bikur Holim, a Hebrew phrase meaning society for visiting the sick. This became Bikur Holim Congregation, the oldest Jewish institution in Washington State.

Other community-minded groups were soon formed. These included the Hebrew Ladies Benevolent Society (now the Jewish Family and Child Services), the Hebrew Free Loan Society, which made interest-free loans to Jewish Americans, and Settlement House, which was founded by the local branch of the National Council of Jewish women. The American Jewish Committee was founded to fight discrimination against Jews and to protect the rights of all people.

These and other Jewish community organizations are still active. They can be found in many Washington cities, including Seattle, Tacoma, Spokane, Aberdeen, Bellingham, Olympia, and Richland.

Two Seattle public schools are named after Seattle Jewish pioneers: Bailey Gatzert Elementary School, after a Seattle mayor; and Nathan Eckstein Middle School, after a civic leader. Washington Territory once had a Jewish governor named Edward Saloman. Today, Jewish men and women are among the notable lawyers, doctors, musicians, artists, engineers, professors, and businesspeople in the state.

IMMIGRANTS NAME THEIR NEW HOMES

Several places in Washington were named by European immigrants. Many cities were named for the towns in Europe where the immigrants grew up. Some were named after the settlers themselves. Other names came from the language and culture of the countries they left. Here are some Washington cities as examples:

ODESSA — this town is in a wheat-growing area in Lincoln County. Immigrants from Russia named it after a wheat-farming area in Russia. The ancestors of these immigrants were Germans who had immigrated to Russia.

BREMERTON — named for a German immigrant, William Bremer, who is considered the town's founder.

CONWAY — named by settler Thomas P. Jones after his home in Wales.

HOCKINSON — a misspelling of the name of a Swedish settler, Ambrosius Hokanson.

KELSO — named for the founder's home town in Scotland.

LUCERNE — a settler named this town on Lake Chelan after her birthplace in Switzerland.

MILAN — named for a railroad worker's home town in Italy.

41. Many European immigrant groups established religious and cultural organizations which served the community. Give at least one example of these organizations.

42. Name at least ten countries that contributed settlers to Washington State.

Integration And Prejudice

The European immigrants' first years in America were not easy. Usually, they had to learn English and adjust to American customs. Some had to work many years at low-paying jobs. Others had the hard work of starting new farms — including clearing fields, building irrigation systems, building their house and barn, and making many of the items they needed in their daily lives.

Generally, the hard work paid off for the European immigrants. After years of effort, most of these immigrants had better lives in Washington than they would have had in Europe. The Europeans tended to be welcomed and accepted into the areas where they settled. This was especially true for immigrants from

These children came from 24 different ethnic backgrounds. The photo was taken in the early 1900's in Roslyn, Washington, a mining town in the Cascade Mountains. Why did people from all over the world want to come live in Washington State?

Northern Europe. Some of the southern and eastern Europeans had a more difficult time.

Other ethnic groups were not so easily accepted and integrated into the white American society. For example, Native Americans — who had a very different culture from the settlers — were not accepted. Native Americans were not allowed to become citizens, and they were forced to move onto reservations away from the white settlements. In the 1880's, the federal government's policy toward Native Americans was to try to make them give up their culture and adopt white American lifestyles.

In 1885 and 1886, Washington had its first serious incidents of violence against a foreign-born group of people. Those people were the Chinese.

43. Contrast the ways various ethnic groups were accepted.

Why Did Chinese Immigrants Come To Washington Territory?

The Chinese were actually the first really large group of immigrants to come to Washington from a nation outside North America. Most of the early Chinese immigrants were married men from some of the poorest parts of China. They were first attracted to America by stories of the California gold fields. Later, American businesses actively recruited Chinese men to come work in the United States. Most of these men hoped to save enough money to improve the economic condition of their families in China. Then they planned to return. Very few of them brought their wives with them.

The first Chinese immigrants came to California. They worked in the gold fields until there was not much more money to be made there. Then some of them moved on to the gold rush in Eastern Washington and British Columbia. Others opened laundries, restaurants, shops, hotels, and other small businesses in the growing Chinatown areas of California cities. A great number of them began working for the railroads throughout the American West.

Building railroads was often difficult and dangerous work. The men had no heavy machinery to help them. Often they were forced to work in terrible heat and in freezing snow. Many died.

The Chinese railroad workers made an impressive contribution to the growth of the American West. Some of the first railroad track in Washington was laid by Chinese workers.

44. What did Chinese immigrants plan to do with the money they earned in America?
45. Name some ways the first Chinese immigrants earned their living.
46. What was the Chinese immigrants' great contribution to the growth of the West?

Working For Their Families In China

After the southern railroads were completed, over half the Chinese workers returned to China. Others stayed to find other jobs here. By 1884, half the agricultural workers in California were Chinese. In Washington, many Chinese men found jobs in fish canneries, where they were noted for their skill as fish cutters. However, after 1903, machines were invented to do this work, and many men lost their cannery jobs. Chinese workers provided much of the labor for important construction projects in the Seattle area. They helped build ship canals, railroads, and office buildings. Chinese immigrants also worked in the coal mines near Lake Washington.

In 1868, the United States and China signed the Burlingame Treaty allowing free immigration of Chinese people to the United States and of Americans to China. Each country promised to protect the rights of the immigrants.

In the years that followed, many more Chinese came to the United States. The life of these immigrants was not easy. It was true that American wages were much higher than those in China. A man could send home enough money to keep his family comfortable and even relatively wealthy. But in order to do this he had to live without his family in a strange culture and work very hard for many hours each day. Usually the only positions open to Chinese immigrants were low-paying jobs that no white people wanted to do. These included jobs like cooking and laundering which were considered women's work. Chinese men were discriminated against because they looked different, wore different clothes, had a different culture, and spoke a different language.

47. Name some jobs that Chinese men found in Washington.
48. What "price" did Chinese workers have to pay for being able to make enough money to help their families in China?

An End To Chinese Immigration

The first Chinese immigrants were respected for their skills and hard work. But the attitude of white workers began to change rapidly when jobs became scarce. White workers resented Chinese competition for jobs.

Beginning in California, there were incidents of anti-Chinese prejudice and violence. Some newspapers, politicians, and labor organizations called for an end to Chinese immigration. In 1882, the United States Congress responded by passing the Chinese Exclusion Act. This law prohibited further immigration of Chinese.

49. What was the Chinese Exclusion Act?

Violence In Washington

The anti-Chinese violence that began in California was soon felt in Washington. In 1885, a group of whites tried to force Chinese workers out of a hops farm in Issaquah. The Chinese men refused to leave. The whites returned at night and fired into the workers' tents, killing three people and injuring three others.

Most of the Chinese immigrants settled in cities, and the racial problems were worse there. In September of 1885, an Anti-Chinese Congress was held in Seattle. A month later, whites in Tacoma gave their Chinese population 30 days to "get outta town or know the reason why." The threat was published in the paper. It was supported by city officials. Three hundred Tacomans escorted all the city's Chinese residents to the train, shipped them off to Portland, and burned their homes.

This newspaper advertisement from the 1880's gives an example of the anti-Chinese prejudice in this state.

THE BEST, CHEAPEST, AND MOST FASHIONABLE STOCK OF DRY GOODS AND CLOTHING ON PUGET SOUND AT THE ARCADE. BOYD, PONCIN & YOUNG, SEATTLE, W. T.

20   *DIRECTORY OF THE CITY OF SEATTLE.*

AMERICAN HOUSE,

GEO. W. WALSH, Proprietor.

MILL STREET,   SEATTLE, W. T

——

Board per day $1, Board per Week, $5, $6 & $7 according to room.   Meals, 25 cts. Beds 25 to 50 cts.

Baggage conveyed to and from the house free of chagre.

NO CHINAMEN EMPLOYED.

The situation in Seattle was not much better. Two Seattle newspapers published anti-Chinese articles which increased feelings of prejudice.

On February 7, 1886, a mob of 350 men rounded up Seattle's Chinese residents and took them to the dock. Some Chinese bought boat tickets and got on a ship to San Francisco. The others were protected by a group of volunteer Seattle citizens called the Home Guard. These citizens opposed unfair treatment of the Chinese. Many of them were businessmen who depended on Chinese workers. When fights broke out on the dock, the Home Guard helped restore order. Some of the mob members were accused of crimes, but none of them were ever sent to prison.

50. What happened to Chinese settlers in Tacoma and Seattle?

This drawing is one of a series of illustrations of the anti-Chinese riots of 1886. In this scene, Chinese shopkeepers are being told to move out. How were Chinese immigrants treated in Seattle and Tacoma that year?

SECTION 4: STATEHOOD AT LAST

State Versus Territory

There were advantages to being a United States territory, but there were disadvantages, too. The governor, judges, and other officials of a territory were appointed by the President. The residents of the territory did not elect them. Often the officials were easterners. They didn't care about the territory, and they were often absent. (Sometimes this problem got so bad that some officials had to be punished. If they were away from their jobs too long, they lost part of their salary.)

A territory could send a delegate to Congress, but this delegate could not vote. Citizens of a territory could not vote for President. Congress could veto a law passed by the Territorial Legislature.

State governments did not have these problems. Congress could not veto state laws; state residents could elect their governor and other officials. In a state, people had more control over their own government. They also had a greater voice in national government, since they voted for President, and had voting representatives in Congress.

51. What were the advantages of being a state instead of a territory?

How Does A Territory Become A State?

Almost as soon as Washington became a territory, some settlers were anxious for it to become a state. In order for this to happen, several things had to be done:

1. The Territorial Legislature had to apply to Congress to become a state.

2. Congress had to pass an enabling act. This act made the territory able to write up a state constitution.

3. The Constitution had to be approved by a majority of the voters in the territory.

4. Congress could review the proposed state constitution. Then Congress could recommend that the constitution be changed.

5. Congress had to approve the state constitution and vote to admit the territory as a state.

52. What were the responsibilities of Congress in the process of making a territory into a state?

Too Small For Statehood

In 1878, the people of Washington Territory voted in favor of becoming a state. They even wrote a state constitution. But at that time, there were only 75,000 non-Indian residents in the territory, even if the Idaho Panhandle was included.

Congress had set 125,000 as the number of people necessary for a state, although they did not always follow this rule strictly. Congress never voted on the issue of Washington statehood in the 1870's.

However, by the late 1800's the population of

LIZZIE ORDWAY: FROM MERCER GIRL

TO SCHOOL SUPERINTENDENT

In the 1860's, there were nine times more men than women in Washington Territory. Asa Mercer, the man who started the University of Washington, decided to do something about this frustrating situation. (He was one of the lonely bachelors himself.)

Mercer went back east on a recruiting tour. He stopped at churches in many states and told women about the jobs and husbands available in the Northwest. Mercer had hoped to recruit several hundred young women, but he was not successful.

The first 11 "Mercer Girls," as the women were called, sailed into Seattle in 1864. Another ship brought a second group of about 100.

Asa Mercer married one of these women. The others were soon married too — all of them but Lizzie Ordway. Ordway turned down all her offers of marriage. She had not come West to find a husband; she had come to bring New England culture to the "wilderness."

Ordway had two notable "firsts" in Washington education. She was the first teacher at Seattle's first public school building. And in 1881, she was elected the first superintendent of Kitsap County Public Schools.

Lizzie Ordway was also active in the women's suffrage movement in Washington Territory. In New England, she had studied with a noted suffragist author named Mary Hamilton Dodge. She was a good friend of Henry and Sarah Yesler and other people who were active in the suffrage movement.

Washington had greatly increased. By 1890, the population would be over 350,000. Washington citizens became confident that their territory would soon be a state.

53. What did the people of Washington vote for in 1878?
54. What was the population of Washington in 1878, when the people voted in favor of statehood? How big a population did Congress require for statehood?

Waiting For Statehood

Oregon was made a state only 11 years after it became a territory. Washington had to wait 36 years. In part, this was because Washington Territory had grown so slowly. Additional delay was caused by party politics in Congress. Washington, Montana, South Dakota, and North Dakota were all becoming ready for statehood at the same time. This would mean eight new senators and several new representatives in Congress. In the 1880's the Democrats held only a slight majority of Congress. They were afraid the new states might all elect Republicans; the Democratic majority would be lost. So the Democrats opposed statehood for the territories in the Northwest.

But in the 1888 elections, the Democrats lost their majority in Congress anyway, so there was no longer a problem. On February 22, 1889, (Washington's Birthday, of course) Congress passed an enabling act. The act described what Washington and the other three territories had to do in order to become states.

55. What four territories were becoming ready for statehood in the late 1880's?
56. What factors delayed Washington statehood?

Washington Becomes A State

The enabling act required that each territory hold a constitutional convention to write a constitution. Washington's convention started on July 5, 1889. By late August, the constitution was completed.

A special election was held on October 1, 1889, to vote on the new constitution, to elect state officials, and to choose a state capital. The constitution was passed by a vote of 40,152 to 11,879. Voters chose Olympia for the capital. (Other choices included North Yakima, Ellensburg, Centralia, Pasco, and Yakima City.) For governor, they chose Elisha P. Ferry, who had

been territorial governor from 1872 to 1880.

On November 11, 1889, Washington became a state in the United States.

57. What did the enabling act require?
58. What city was chosen for the state capital? Who was elected governor?
59. What happened on November 11, 1889?

The Constitutional Delegates Disagree

There had been disagreements between the constitutional delegates on many issues. They had argued whether to have just one group of representatives, or to split the legislature into two houses: the Senate and the House of Representatives. The two-house, or bicameral, plan won. The delegates had disagreed about how many state officials the people should elect, and how much the state should control the railroads. They also disagreed on whether the state should

---

SOME SPECIAL FEATURES OF THE WASHINGTON CONSTITUTION

Did you know that:

— When the Constitution was first written, women were allowed to vote only in school elections. They were not allowed to vote in general elections until 1910. Voters had to be male, 21 years old, and they had to prove an ability to read and write in the English language.

— The Washington State Constitution is much longer than the U.S. Constitution. It covers such areas as: taxes, corporations, tide lands, state institutions, public debt, county governments, and officials' salaries.

— The original State Constitution set these yearly salaries for state officials:
Governor - $4,000
Lieutenant Governor - $1,000
Secretary of State - $2,500
Supreme Court Judge - $4,000
Superior Court Judge - $3,000
Most other Executive Officials-$2,000
By today's standards, all these salaries are below the poverty level. Today, officials' salaries are set by the legislature and not by the constitution.

— Washington's governor can veto part of a bill. This is called an "item veto."

— In Washington, a law may cover only one subject at a time. This prevents the legislature from attaching "riders" (non-related issues) to a law that is certain to pass.

— Washington voters elect a total of nine executive officials. This is called a "divided executive." (See page 277.)

control tidelands (the lands that are uncovered at low tide.) After years of disagreement, private interests gained control of the tidelands.

There were two serious issues that the delegates could not agree on. They were: whether the sale of alcohol should be prohibited, and whether women should be allowed to vote. The delegates decided to let the voters choose. Washington voters (all male) said "no" to both questions. There would be legal drinking in the state, but there would be no women voters.

60. What two issues were Washington voters asked to decide? How did they vote?

Seattle ruins after the fire of 1889.

FIRE!

1889 was a year of excitement and celebration. It was the year Washington became a state. But it was also a year of disaster! During the summer of 1889, the downtown business areas of Seattle, Spokane, and Ellensburg were destroyed by fire. The worst fire was the one in Seattle.

It started on a hot, dry afternoon in June. A painter was heating glue in his shop at First and Marion. The pot boiled over. Some of the glue caught fire and splattered. Fire spread through the shop and the rest of the wooden building. Winds carried the flame to the next wooden building and the next. Fire-fighting equipment was rushed out, but the water pressure wasn't great enough. After a while, the water barely trickled out of the hoses.

Entire blocks were on fire now; the flames were jumping across streets. By evening, the people of Seattle knew that the entire business district had been destroyed.

Seattle's neighbors were helpful. Tacoma, Portland, Olympia, and Victoria all sent extra fire-fighting equipment. (It arrived too late, but it was a friendly offer.) Tacoma businesspeople raised $20,000 overnight for a Seattle relief fund.

You'd think those Seattle businesspeople would have been discouraged. But the boom of the 1880's was still going strong, and people were full of hope and enthusiasm. They just set up tents and shacks and ran their businesses from these temporary shelters until they could rebuild a new, brick, fireproof downtown.

Ironically, the first brick building after the fire was constructed by the Chinese labor contracting company of Chin Gee Hee. That was just three years after an angry mob had tried to chase all the Chinese out of town.

Are Women Citizens?

The issue of women's suffrage (the right for women to vote) came up many times in Washington before the state constitution was written. In fact, the first Territorial Legislature had voted on it in 1854. At that time, women's suffrage failed by only one vote!

In 1868 and 1870, the Fourteenth and Fifteenth Amendments to the United States Constitution were passed. These amendments guaranteed that all citizens could vote. Black men were allowed to vote for the first time, as a result.

Many women assumed that these amendments meant that women could vote too. Surely they were citizens, the women argued. But women were still not allowed to vote!

A Washington woman named Mary Olney Brown decided to challenge the law. She wrote articles and organized women to try to vote in 1870. Some women went to the polls (voting place), but they were turned away.

But in one town near Centralia, the women made a plan. On election day, they all took a good lunch down to the men at the polls. After everyone had eaten, the women announced, "Now we're going to vote." They did.

A visitor from another town was watching. He climbed on his horse and rode to the next town. Like Paul Revere, he galloped down the streets shouting, "They're voting! They're voting!" However, most Washington women were still not allowed to vote.

61. When was women's suffrage first voted on by the Washington legislature?
62. What was guaranteed by the 14th and 15th Amendments to the United States Constitution?

More Efforts To Win Women's Suffrage

Again and again, women's right to vote was discussed in the Washington Territorial Legislature. In 1871, two important leaders of the national women's suffrage movement spoke to the legislature in Olympia. One was Susan B. Anthony, the outstanding organizer for women's rights in the United States. The other was Abigail Scott Duniway, a feminist from Portland. Duniway published a newspaper called the *New Northwest* which covered women's rights issues. However, women's suffrage was defeated by the Territorial Legislature in 1871 and again in 1881.

In 1883, the legislature changed its decision. Washington women finally won the right to vote. But not for long. In 1887, the Territorial Court declared women's suffrage unconstitutional. (See Unit 12, Section 2 for more informa-

During the 1880's and 90's, many people campaigned to end the sale of alcohol in this state. The prohibitionist (anti-alcohol) group in this photo was called the International Order of Good Templars.

tion.) The legislature passed the law again that year, but the courts turned it down again in 1888. In 1890, women won the right to vote in school elections only. However, they would have to wait for twenty more years before they could vote in other elections.

Today, any United States citizen 18 years of age or older who lives in Washington can vote (except persons convicted of certain crimes). A voter must register 30 days before an election in order to vote in that election and in following elections.

63. Who were Susan B. Anthony and Abigail Scott Duniway?
64. Why did Washington women lose the right to vote just four years after they won it?
65. Who can vote in Washington today?

What Were The First Schools Like?

Northwest settlers were anxious for their children to get an education. The Organic Laws of the Provisional Government called for schools to be built as soon as possible. The first provisional legislature set aside land for this purpose.

The first pioneer schools were held in simple cabins. Students were charged 8 to 10 dollars a term to pay the teacher's small salary and other expenses. Often the school year was only 3 to 6 months long! The children were needed the rest of the year for work at home. Churches were usually involved in running these early schools.

Surprisingly, the city of Seattle had a university before it had its first public elementary school building. Ten acres of land in downtown Seattle were donated by Arthur Denny, Charles Terry, and Judge Edward Lander for the territorial university. The school was opened in 1861 by its only faculty member, Asa Mercer. The first qualified college students arrived in Seattle the next year, in 1862.

66. How did the Provisional Government help provide for schools?
67. What were the first schools like?

Public Education After Statehood

Public schools were opened as soon as the local government could afford it. Special taxes were raised to pay for schools. The federal government also donated a piece of land in each township. This land could be sold to get money for schools.

The Washington State Constitution guarantees a public education to every child regardless of race, color, or creed. In the first years of statehood, however, some counties did not collect enough taxes to be able to afford schools. The "Barefoot Schoolboy Law," passed in 1895, helped to change this. Under the new law, the state government provides a certain amount of money for every student. This helps to equalize (make the same) the amount of money spent on education in different parts of the state. Two years later, in 1897, school attendance became required of all children aged 8 to 15.

68. What does the State Constitution guarantee?
69. What was the Barefoot Schoolboy Law?

COLLEGES AND UNIVERSITIES

Many of the earliest settlers in Washington Territory were eager to have higher education facilites — so eager, in fact, that the territory had colleges before it had any high schools. The University of Washington was founded in Seattle in 1861, but that city's first public high school did not open until 1883.

The first private college in Washington was named for the Whitmans and opened in Walla Walla in 1865. It was started by another pioneer missionary named Cushing Eells. Today, there are four-year state universities in Pullman, Cheney, Ellensburg, Olympia, Bellingham, and Seattle; and there are over 20 community colleges in cities all over the state.

Public and private colleges and universities make many contributions to the communities where they are located. In addition to preparing young people for future careers, they may often serve as intellectual and cultural centers. Washington's universities have attracted nationally recognized artists, scientists, and writers. They have sponsored speakers and discussions on topics of importance to the state. Our colleges and universities have also served as artistic centers, with art museums and theaters for the presentation of art forms from around the world. University research in the areas of health, natural science, and the social sciences has benefited the state.

The earliest settlers realized the importance of colleges to the community, and the little settlements on Puget Sound all competed for the honor of the state university. Seattle won, and the presence of a major university has helped make Seattle the cultural center of the state.

The photos below show Seattle as it changed from a small western town to a big, modern city. Why did Seattle grow so quickly during this period?

DENNY HILL FROM FIRST AVENUE AND COLUMBIA ABOUT 1878

FROM SAME PLACE IN 1915

UNIT 8

BEGINNING THE 20th CENTURY

In the 30 years between statehood and the end of World War I, Washington went through important changes. In a very short time, Seattle and other Washington towns became modern, industrial centers. The appearance of the cities changed greatly. The downtown business districts expanded, people moved to new residential neighborhoods, and many big new buildings were constructed. Along with city growth came a changing economy. Manufacturing, shipping, and other city businesses became more important; Washington State was becoming industrialized.

Along with the big cities came big city problems, too. City services, such as water, electricity, communication, and transportation had to be expanded. Cities had to plan for the future. Industrialization created new problems for workers, and labor unions became important. During the 30 years covered in this unit, our state began to take on the appearance that we are familiar with today.

As you read, keep these questions in mind: In what way are cities still the same as they were at the turn of the century? How are they different? What needs did people in cities have then? What needs do they have today? How were those needs met at different times?

The unit has three sections:

1. Cities Grow and Build
2. The Progressive Era
3. World War I Affects Business and Labor

SECTION 1: CITIES GROW AND BUILD

Who Were The Populists?

The explosive growth of the 1880's ended with a depression that hit the entire country between 1893 and 1897. There was less money available for investment. Some businesses folded. Just about all parts of the economy suffered.

One group that was especially hard hit by the depression was the wheat farmers. The price of wheat was falling, and railroad costs were high. The farmers grew angry. They accused the railroads of monopoly and corruption. They urged the legislature to pass laws that would regulate the railroads.

The farmers felt that neither the Republicans nor the Democrats were doing enough to solve the farmers' problems. A new political party was formed by people who wanted railroad regulation and other reforms, such as income tax, women's suffrage, and secret ballots at elections. These people called themselves "Populists." The Populist Party gained many members in the southern and western United States in the 1890's.

Eight Populist legislators were elected in Washington in 1892 and twenty-three in 1894. A populist named John Rogers was elected governor in 1896. The "Barefoot Schoolboy" law was one important reform measure that Rogers helped pass. (See Unit 7, Section 4 for more information.)

The Populists did not accomplish much in the legislature. Interest in Populist reform faded out in 1897 and so did the depression. Hopes began to rise again. Gold had been discovered in Alaska.

1. What happened in the United States between 1893 and 1897?
2. What was the Populist Party?

What Was The Klondike Gold Rush?

Stories of gold discoveries in the Klondike region of Alaska were first printed in United States newspapers in 1897. That year, the ship *Portland* landed in Seattle with a ton of Alaska gold. The rush to the Klondike was on! (The Klondike region is sometimes called the Yukon since the Yukon River is the main river in this area.)

Alaska miners had fantastic stories to tell.

EARLY SCHOOLS IN COLVILLE, WASHINGTON
from Washington Schools in the Good Old Days, Superintendent of Public Instruction, Olympia: 1969

The first public school in northeast Washington was founded at Pinkney City in 1862. Pinkney City was a small place about three miles north of the present site of Colville. With its muddy streets and scattered buildings, it served as the county seat for a region of 13 eastern Washington counties, the entire state of Idaho and a portion of Wyoming.

The first teacher, a Mr. Boody, used the courtroom for his school. It was the only school in a 100 mile radius, but it began a tradition unbroken to this day.

In 1864 and 1865 Chewelah began the second school and a couple years later the third public school was established at Marcus, now under the waters of Roosevelt Lake.

By 1892 the going salary for teachers seems to have been about $50 a month, although records show some received as little as $35. Schoolhouses were made of logs, usually one room with home-made desks, two pupils to a desk. The heating plant was a pot-bellied stove in the center of the room.

The water supply was an open bucket with a common dipper. Its source was the nearest spring or stream. School buses? Whoever heard of such a thing.

Textbooks cost money and money was often too precious to be spent on such frivolities. Lunches were carried in empty tobacco boxes or lard buckets and in winter months were frozen by noon.

Each teacher was responsible for her own self-contained classroom. There was no principal. She was furnished a desk, blackboards, maps, gloves and about two textbooks per child. Children brought the rest of their books, pencils and paper from home.

For years, a rubber hose was kept on hand in Colville Elementary School to punish the misbehavors, but more often disciplinary action involved the less harsh treatment of a severe frown, a paddling on the posterior or a 5,000-word quotation to copy.

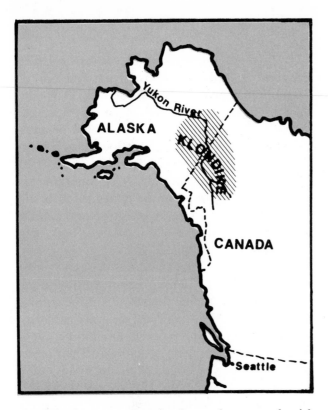

stories attracted thousands of people to the Northwest. The prospectors came here and boarded boats to Alaska.

San Francisco owed its early prosperity to the California gold rush of 1849. Port Townsend and Victoria boomed for a while when gold was discovered in 1858 on the Fraser River in British Columbia. Spokane's most important business for a while was serving nearby gold and silver miners. Seattle was to benefit in the same way from the Klondike gold rush of the late 1890's.

3. What did a ship bring to Seattle in 1897?
4. Why did thousands of people come to the Northwest in the late 1890's?

How Did Seattle Get The Klondike Business?

Puget Sound businesspeople prospered. They stocked and sold everything a hopeful prospector could need. And when the successful miners returned to the area with new fortunes, they found plenty of entertainment to spend their money on.

The competition between Puget Sound cities was on again. They all wanted to attract the gold rush business. This time, though, Seattle cornered the market. Seattle merchants were able to provide almost everything the miners would

Men had gone away broke and returned with thousands of dollars in gold. One Seattle schoolteacher went to Alaska on her vacation and made $80,000 in a month. A former slave returned with $30,000 worth of gold. These

Seattle's shipping docks were crowded during the gold rush in Alaska. Why did Seattle get so much of the Klondike business?

SEWARD'S ICE BOX

Since the seventeeth century, Russia had been interested in Alaska as a source of furs. But by the middle of the nineteenth century, the fur trading business was no longer profitable. Russia offered to sell Alaska to the United States for $7,200,000 (less than 2 cents an acre). The U.S. Secretary of State, William Seward, agreed. Alaska became a United States possession in 1867.

Many Americans disapproved of the deal. They thought Alaska was worthless. They called it "Seward's Ice Box" or "Seward's Folly" or "Seward's Polar Bear Garden."

Thirty years later, Americans found out that Seward had been right all along. Gold had been discovered! Between 1896 and 1904, more than 100 million dollars worth of gold was found in the "Polar Bear Garden." More recently, Alaska has been found to contain America's richest sources of oil.

Gold mining in Alaska made some people very rich, but it certainly wasn't easy. Many miners drowned, froze to death, or starved. The climate was cruel. During the winter of 1897-98, the temperature got down to 54 degrees below zero. Prospectors learned that they had to travel in groups and take a year's supply of clothing and food.

need. The Seattle harbor was busy with ships that would carry the miners to Alaska. And the Seattle Chamber of Commerce ran huge ads for Seattle in newspapers and magazines all over the country. They wrote letters to governors, mayors, kings, and foreign leaders everywhere, advertising Seattle as the gateway to Klondike gold. Seattle got most of the Klondike business. The other cities didn't have a chance.

5. How did Seattle business people make money from the Klondike gold rush?
6. How did Seattle get most of the Klondike business?

What Was The Alaska-Yukon-Pacific Exposition?

Seattle's publicity efforts were capped by the Alaska-Yukon-Pacific (AYP) Exposition of 1909. Four years earlier, Portland had held a big, successful fair called the Lewis and Clark Exposition. Seattle business and community leaders proposed that their city should put on a

fair, too. It would bring tourists and fame to their city.

A University of Washington professor named Edmond S. Meany proposed that the fair be built on the University's new campus. That way, the University could benefit from AYP also. At the end of the exposition, there would be additional buildings, gardens, and fountains left for the students to use and enjoy. Professor Meany's plan was adopted. The fountain you see in the background of the photo below is still part of the University of Washington campus, although some of the buildings have been torn down and replaced.

The theme of the Alaska-Yukon-Pacific Exposition was the rich future of Seattle and the Northwest. The theme slogan was, "The truth is good enough." The exhibits featured the Northwest's natural resources, including lumber, gold ore, mining equipment, agriculture. The Forestry Building was constructed of huge logs, each of which weighed about 25 tons and contained enough wood to build five houses!

Visitors were introduced to Seattle at its booming best. Altogether, more than 3,700,000 people came. President Taft was there for a visit, and James J. Hill, the railroad builder, gave the fair's opening speech.

7. What do the letters "AYP" stand for?
8. What was the purpose of the AYP?

This photo was taken on International Children's Day at the AYP in 1909. At that time, cars were beginning to be used in Washington, but other forms of transportation were still more important. Give some examples of other kinds of transportation available.

THE ALASKA-YUKON-PACIFIC EXPOSITION. The fountain in the background is still part of the University of Washington campus. Why was the exposition held?

How Did Washington Grow In The Early 20th Century?

The beginning of the twentieth century was again a period of growth for Washington. Manufacturing doubled during the period between 1900 and 1914. The lumber industry, especially, grew. Frederick Weyerhauser and David Clough opened big, modern mills in Everett in 1903. By 1905, Washington was the leading state in lumber production.

The Palouse Hills were found to be extremely good lands for growing wheat. By 1910, Whitman County had the most valuable wheat crop of any county in the nation.

THE GREAT AYP

CROSS-COUNTRY CAR RACE

AYP planners thought up a number of "publicity stunts" to help advertise the exposition. For example, the Seattle high school basketball team toured the country playing exhibition games with local teams.

One of the most unusual promotion events was a cross-country auto race. In 1909, cars were still very new, and there were few paved roads. One rule of the race was "No speed limit after Kansas."

Of the 30 cars that started the New York to Seattle race, only five finished. The winning car made it in 53 days. The trip was much longer than it is today, because the cars often had to go far out of their way to find roads.

There was an increase in private building during this period, and property values soared. City skylines changed. The Northwest got its first skyscraper; the 42 story Smith Tower was the tallest building west of the Mississippi. New houses were also built, as people moved out to what were then the outlying areas such as Seattle's Capitol Hill.

The first automobiles began to appear, followed soon after by the first speed limits. In Seattle, cars were required to stay at four miles per hour downhill and eight miles per hour when traveling uphill.

In order to meet the needs of their growing populations, the city governments had to do a lot of building, too. Electricity and water supply systems had to be bigger and more modern. New roads and bridges had to be built.

Fortunately, many of our government leaders realized that the cities should plan for future growth. For example, these leaders realized that land should be set aside for city parks before the city was fully developed. Seattle and Spokane hired a nationally famous city planning firm, the Olmstead brothers, for this job. As a result, both cities are now known for their unusually good park systems.

9. In the early 20th century, Washington led the nation in two products. What were they?
10. What projects did Washington cities have to take on in order to meet the needs of a growing population?

SECTION 2: THE PROGRESSIVE ERA

What Was The Progressive Era?

The period between 1900 and 1914 was also a time of political reform, on the national level as well as the state level. It is called "The Progressive Era."

Across the country, people were concerned about the great power of monopolies and trusts. (A trust is a group of companies which together control all, or almost all, of one industry. An example was the oil trust headed by John D. Rockefeller.) Trusts were keeping prices high and wages low. They often drove small, independent companies out of business.

Newspapers and magazines began printing stories about corruption in government and business. There was interest in protecting the rights of the public. Washington citizens shared some of the same concerns, and during this period, several important laws were passed. These laws helped guarantee good, honest government practices, and they gave citizens a more direct role in their government. Some of the most important of these laws are described below.

11. What was the Progressive Era?

HORACE CAYTON

Horace Cayton was a Seattle Black who started a weekly newspaper called the *Seattle Republican* in 1895. He married the daughter of Hiram Revels — the nation's first Black senator. The paper did well, and the Caytons were known as one of Seattle's most distinguished families.

However, Horace Cayton was a supporter of W.E.B. duBois, who was then considered a fairly radical leader in the struggle for equal rights. The paper's coverage of Black issues made it unpopular with white readers. People were especially angry at a front page story about a Black who was lynched in the South. The story came out during wartime and was considered unpatriotic. Many people canceled their subscriptions, the paper went out of business, and the Caytons were left poor.

Cayton's first son, Horace Cayton, Jr., became a noted sociologist and specialist in race relations. The younger Cayton's autobiography, called *Long Old Road* includes stories of his childhood in Seattle, a teenage adventure in Alaska, and his career as a Black professional in America.

What Were The Direct Government Reforms?

One group of Progressive Era reforms in Washington were called the "Direct Government Reforms." They were originally proposed by the Populists and included:

1. Direct Primary: The direct primary allows voters themselves to choose the one candidate who will represent each political party for state office. (See pages 275 and 276 for more information.)

2. Initiative: The initiative allows citizens to initiate (start) a law by themselves, instead of having the legislature do it. There are two kinds of initiatives. One kind is given to the legislature to vote on; the other kind is decided by the voters.

3. Referendum: The referendum allows voters a chance to approve or disapprove a law that has already been considered by the legislature. (The legislature refers a law to the voters.)

4. Recall: The recall allows voters to remove elected officials from office before their terms are up. Voters can ask for a recall election by presenting a petition stating charges against the official. Any official can be recalled, except a Supreme Court or Superior Court Judge. (These judges can be impeached by the legislature, but not recalled.)

The direct primary was adopted by the legislature in 1907. The other three direct government reforms were adopted by constitutional amendment in 1912.

12. Define the following: direct primary, initiative, referendum, recall.

How Does An Initiative, Referendum, Or Recall Work?

An initiative, referendum, or recall is started in the same way. A petition is written, stating the law to be voted on or the official to be recalled. A certain percentage of all registered voters must sign the petition. Then the issue is voted on at the next election. There are two exceptions. Constitutional amendments and some special government expenses are automatically

The owners of the Hercules mine pose, with the mine in the background. May is fourth from the left, and her husband, Al, is on the right.

MAY ARKWRIGHT HUTTON

May Arkwright Hutton was not the kind of woman to be taken lightly. For one thing she was tall, big boned, and weighed 225 pounds. For another, she and her husband had a fortune that ran up around two million dollars. They entertained some leading personalities of their time: lawyer, Clarence Darrow; labor leader, Bill Haywood; President Theodore Roosevelt; women's suffrage leaders, Carrie Chapman Catt and Susan B. Anthony; Senator Borah; Congressman Dill; and William Jennings Bryan. May wanted to be a U.S. senator herself, and she might have made it, if she'd lived a little longer.

May Arkwright had always been fat (she admitted it), but she hadn't always been rich. She came to the gold mining towns of Idaho with only a few cents in her pocket, and she got jobs doing what she knew best: running boarding houses, and most of all, cooking.

She set up a little restaurant near the planned railroad tracks in Kellogg. Soon the tracks were built and trains rolled by, and the customers came in. One of them was a quiet railroad engineer named Al Hutton. He and May got to know each other and decided to get married.

May and Al both kept working, and they invested a little money in mines from time to time. In 1897, they went in with a few other people on the "Hercules" mine near Wallace, Idaho. They worked on it as they could for four years, May and other women along with the men. Nothing too valuable turned up — until, in 1901, they struck the richest silver deposit anyone in the area had ever seen. They all became millionaires.

May said, "The Lord gave me money to serve more effectively." And she used it. The Huttons moved to Spokane in 1907 and got involved in various social projects. May became a Charities Commissioner and worked especially with orphans. She supported labor unions. She was active in the Democratic Party. In 1904, she'd been a Democratic candidate for the Idaho legislature. In 1912, she was a delegate to the national convention. Most of all, though, she worked for women's suffrage — speaking, writing articles, and organizing support in Spokane.

Whatever she was doing, people knew about it. May was never shy or subtle. She said what she meant and the newspapers printed it.

She died in 1915. The Huttons had no children of their own, and they left their money to build a huge, pleasant orphanage in Spokane.

Early twentieth century workers sort coal in a mine. What Progressive Era laws helped improve working conditions?

referred to voters. No petition is needed for these kinds of referendums.

If a majority of voters approve an initiative or referendum, it becomes a law unless it is challenged on constitutional grounds. The governor cannot veto it. A majority vote is also needed to recall an official.

The initiative and referendum have been used fairly often in Washington since 1912. Taxes, gambling, alcohol, and environmental protection have all been the subjects of initiatives and referendums in this state.

The recall is not used so often, but several Washington officials have been recalled. These included Mayors Frank Edwards (1931) and Hiram C. Gill (1911) of Seattle and Mayor A. V. Fawcett of Tacoma (also 1911). (These particular recalls were not statewide elections, of course. Only the residents of the city participate in a city official's recall.)

One more recent recall attempt was started in Seattle in 1974. Seattle Fire Department employees tried to recall Mayor Wes Uhlman because he had cut Fire Department budgets and fired the Fire Chief. A special recall election was held in 1975. Seattle voters turned down the recall. Mayor Uhlman remained in office.

13. How is an initiative, referendum, or recall started?

How Did Washington Women Finally Get The Vote?

The original Washington State Constitution said that only men could vote. A constitutional amendment was needed in order for Washington women to be able to vote, too.

The women's suffrage movement in Washington was more than fifty years old when that amendment was passed. (See pages 140 & 141 for more information.) In 1910, Washington women finally got the right to vote. Most other American women had to wait until 1920, when the United States Constitution was finally amended, too.

The constitutional amendment in Washington was the product of many years of careful organization and hard work. Leaders included the refined and educated Emma Smith DeVoe, and a big, rough, Spokane millionnaire named May Arkwright Hutton. DeVoe was president of the Washington Equal Suffrage Association. Her group included such distinguished members as Mr. and Mrs. Henry Yesler and Lizzie Ordway.

14. When did Washington women finally get the vote?
15. Who were some leaders of the women's suffrage movement in Washington?

What Progressive Era Laws Helped Workers?

Several Progressive Era laws were aimed at improving working conditions. It's hard now to imagine what people's working conditions were. Workers were often expected to put in 60 or 70 or more hours a week. Working places were often unsafe and unhealthy. There were many accidents and diseases, and health insurance as we know it today didn't exist.

Wages were low — $10 per week for many workers, $6 or less for some, especially women. Living conditions for workers were usually poor. For example, some loggers were given terrible food and crowded, uncomfortable shelters. Their mattresses were full of lice and bedbugs. They earned only $2 for a 10-hour day!

In addition, workers who tried to improve their lives were often severely punished. Strikers and union organizers often lost their jobs and were sometimes beaten and jailed.

During the Progressive Era in Washington, laws were passed that guaranteed a minimum wage for women and children. Another law said that women could not be forced to work more than eight hours a day. Another important law was the Workman's Compensation Act. This law provides financial aid to workers who are injured on the job.

16. What were some problems with working conditions in the early 20th century?
17. What Progressive Era laws helped workers?

Why Were Labor Unions Formed?

Protective laws were necessary, but they did not answer all of the workers' needs. Starting in the late 19th century, workers began joining to-gether to form labor unions. This was often very difficult and dangerous at that time. Some employers used great pressure, even violence, to prevent unions from being formed.

Workers joined labor unions to increase their power. One laborer could not change his or her working conditions alone. If one or two workers complained, the employer could just fire them. But if all the workers act together, the employer has to pay attention to their complaints. Without the workers, the employer cannot run the business.

The members of a labor union select representatives to work out agreements with management (the employers) concerning wages, hours, working conditions, and other issues. This is called collective bargaining. If the union is not satisfied with management's offer, they may choose to go on strike; that is, all union members refuse to work until an agreement has been reached.

These women are preparing strawberries in a canning factory. What were some of the problems faced by workers in the late nineteenth and early twentieth centuries?

18. Define the following: labor union, strike, collective bargaining.
19. How does a labor union increase workers' power?

What Were The Unions Like?

Some unions were formed in Washington in the 1880's. The railroad workers' union was an example. In 1894, a national railroad workers' strike stopped normal rail traffic at the Tacoma station for five days and at Spokane for ten days. This strike was organized by Eugene V. Debs, who went on to be a national labor leader and Socialist Party candidate for president. Washington State had a higher percentage of votes for Debs in the presidential election of 1912 than most states.

There were two main kinds of labor unions in Washington. The first were the craft unions. Under this system, each group of workers had their own union. For example, truckdrivers belonged to one union; carpenters had another union; salespeople would have another, etc. These separate unions were loosely organized together into a larger group called the AFL (American Federation of Labor). They cooperated with each other so they could have more power.

However, some labor organizers believed that changes were not coming fast enough through the craft unions. Some of them decided to form another union. They called a meeting in Chicago to form "One Big Union." Workers from all kinds of jobs would be able to join it. This union was called the Industrial Workers of the World. (IWW).

The IWW, or Wobblies, as they came to be called, were a radical group. They believed that "the working class and the employing class have nothing in common." They urged workers to "fight a poor day's pay with a poor day's work," to strike, and to use force when necessary.

20. What were the AFL and the IWW? How were these unions different?

How Successful Were The Labor Unions?

Many Washington loggers joined the IWW in the early 20th century. They used slowdowns, strikes, riots, and sabotage to try to win an eight-hour workday and better working conditions. But the IWW and other labor groups were not able to accomplish very much at this time. Probably the main reason was that too many people were unemployed. (In 1914, there were over 10,000 unemployed people in Seattle alone.) It was too easy for employers to find workers who would accept poor working conditions in order to have a job. The labor unions would have to wait for economic conditions to improve before they could make much progress.

21. Why were labor unions unable to accomplish much in the early 1900's?

EXPERIMENTAL COLONIES IN WASHINGTON

During the late 1800's, a few groups of people came to the Puget Sound area with plans to set up cooperative farming communities. These groups wanted to be self-supporting, and they didn't want to have much contact with other people in the state. They picked Washington because the land and climate were good for farming and because there was plenty of undeveloped land away from other settlements. In a sense, these colonies were the ancestors of modern communes.

Each community had different goals and a somewhat different organization. Some worked for social change; others tried to create an environment of freedom and self-rule, where people worked for themselves instead of wealthy bosses. The Christian Cooperative Colony at Sunnyside required that all residents be Christians and agree not to drink or gamble.

The most famous and longest lasting of Washington's experimental colonies attempted to create a tolerant community where individuals would be free to choose their own lifestyle. It was called The Mutual Home Society, or Home, and was near Tacoma. Many members of Home were anarchists; that is, they did not believe in government.

At Home, each individual could own his or her own house and household goods, but the land belonged to the community. Schools, docks, meeting halls, and other community needs were built by volunteers.

At several colonies, all work and property were shared equally among the members. Most of the experiments ended because of financial or personal difficulties or because of the hostility of people who lived nearby.

SECTION 3: WORLD WAR I AFFECTS BUSINESS AND LABOR

Washington Gets Connected

In the 1860's, it was fairly easy for Washington settlers to remain isolated from the Civil War. The battlefields at Gettysburg and Shiloh seemed very far away. By land or by ship, it took many months to travel from the East Coast to Puget Sound. Washington settlers could not get news of a Civil War battle until several months afterward.

However, by 1914, three transcontinental railroads linked Washington to the rest of the country. Coast to coast travel took only a few days. Washington had had the telegraph since 1878 and telephones since 1883. The first daily newspaper had been Olympia's *Pacific Tribune,* started in 1869. By 1914, the state had several daily papers which covered national and international news.

Washington State was no longer an island surrounded by untraveled mountains and forests. It was connected by efficient communication and transportation to other parts of the country and the world.

22. How had communication and transportation improved since the Civil War?

Foreign Trade Was Important

Better transportation meant more economic ties with other parts of the world. By the early 20th century, Washington lumber was sold in Asia, Australia, Mexico, Argentina, Europe, and Africa. Wenatchee apples were sold in New York, Boston, and other cities around the world. Wheat was shipped to Europe and Asia. Alaska was the largest buyer of Washington dairy products. Salmon, shellfish, and vegetable seeds were among the other products exported from the state.

Import businesses flourished (were successful) too. People in Washington bought imported coffee, tea, and spices, for example. They bought manufactured goods from eastern cities. Steel and other raw materials were imported for local manufacturing. In 1914, the total value of foreign trade in Seattle alone was $56,000,000.

23. Name some Washington products that were exported to other cities and continents.
24. Name some items that were imported into Washington State.

A New Shipping Route

In 1914, the Panama Canal was opened in South America. A canal across Panama had been discussed for more than 30 years. It took seven years to build. It was 4,000 miles away, but it was very important to Washington's economy.

Why was it so important? Find the canal on a world map. Look at the old shipping route from New York to Seattle, by way of Cape Horn. Compare it to the new route across Panama. The canal cuts the distance just about in half. With the canal, it was finally practical to ship things from Puget Sound to cities on the Atlantic Ocean. The ports of Seattle and Tacoma became busy with ships from all over the world.

This is a modern photo of the locks on Seattle's ship canal. Seattle's canal system was opened in 1916 to improve shipping here. What important canal was completed far away in 1914 that greatly aided Seattle shipping?

25. Why was the opening of the Panama Canal important to Washington?

How Did World War I Affect Washington's Economy?

Another distant event of 1914 had a great impact on Washington's economy. This was World War I. The battlegrounds of the war were 5,000 miles from Washington State — about twice as far as Gettysburg. Yet World War I was to have a much greater effect on this state than the Civil War.

England, France, and the other Allies, had not been prepared for war. ("Allies" was the name given to all the countries that fought against Germany in the World War. An ally is a partner or helper.) They needed supplies. As the war kept on, more and more of the people in the allied countries were busy fighting or working to support the army. There were not enough people left over to produce food and other necessities. European countries looked to America for the food, raw materials, and military supplies they needed.

In Washington State, this meant new markets for local agricultural products. (The Panama Canal helped keep transportation costs to Europe low.) More land was planted than ever before. Farmers invested in new machinery to help grow bigger crops. This mechanization of farming was an important result of the war.

The war in Europe also brought about the construction of Camp Lewis (Fort Lewis) as a permanent military post. It was named in honor of Meriwether Lewis. The building of Camp Lewis had noticeable effects on the nearby cities. Much of the material for building the barracks and mess halls came from the surrounding area. Men were needed for the construction of the camp which at this time was the largest of its kind in the United States. The soldiers stationed at Camp Lewis spent a great deal of money in nearby cities such as Tacoma and Olympia. Even today, some stores in these cities depend heavily on soldiers and their families for business.

26. How did the war help to mechanize farming?

This is how the wheat was threshed before farms were mechanized. The new machines would do the work of several people, so that each farmer could produce and harvest more crops.

How Was Manufacturing Affected?

Manufacturing was also affected by World War I. One company that benefited was the little airplane manufacturing plant just set up by William Boeing. The United States government ordered fifty of his "Model C's" for the war.

However, the most important wartime business in Washington was shipbuilding. Seattle had only one shipbuilding firm before the war started. Only 200 Seattle people worked for that industry in 1915. A year later, the number of shipbuilding employees had jumped to 6,000. By the end of the war, there were 28 shipbuilding companies in the state. Altogether, more than 50,000 people worked for them. The largest shipyards were Skinner and Eddy in Seattle and the Todd yards in Tacoma.

Lumbering increased during wartime, too. More lumber was sold in Europe. Wood was needed for shipbuilding. It was also needed to build new houses for the people who were moving to cities for wartime jobs. Spruce wood was used for airplanes because it was strong and lightweight.

27. What was Washington's most important wartime business?
28. What other Washington industries increased during World War I?

What Was The Labor Shortage?

Increased demands for Washington products meant a rapid increase in jobs. The state experienced a time of higher incomes and full employment during the war.

The United States entered World War I on April 6, 1917. Altogether, about 75,000 people left Washington State to fight in the war. A lot of working men were gone. Soon there were more jobs than workers. This is called a labor shortage.

Businesses had to compete with each other for employees. They raised wages to attract new workers. Washington factory wages were among the highest in the country. People came to the factories from other jobs, from rural parts of Washington, and from other states. The state population increased by more than 300,000 between 1910 and 1920.

29. Why did the war produce a labor shortage?
30. How did the labor shortage affect wages? How did it affect state population?

WILLIAM BOEING AND HIS AIRPLANE COMPANY

Bill Boeing's father had made a fortune in the lumber business in Minnesota. Bill lived in Seattle, where quite a few people had grown rich selling lumber. But it turned out that young Boeing would make his fame and fortune from a business that had little to do with Washington's natural resources.

It all started in 1914 when Boeing took his first airplane ride. This was just 11 years after the Wright brothers made their first successful flight. Nobody knew very much about how to build airplanes in those days. Bill Boeing looked at the plane that he had just flown in. He decided he could build a better one. Boeing, his friend Conrad Westervelt, and a pilot named Herb Munter decided to try.

In 1916, the three men produced their first plane and started their first company. About 50 years later, the Boeing Company was the largest industry in Washington.

What Were The Effects Of The Labor Shortage?

The labor shortage had some interesting side effects. For one thing, the absence of male workers opened new careers to women. For the first time, women were working as machine operators, printers, packers, and car salespeople. They even worked in lumber camps. Employers agreed (some with surprise) that women could do the jobs as well as men. Women began coming to the cities for jobs, too. Minority workers, who had been discriminated against, also had a chance to hold better jobs during the war.

Many people left farms to come to the cities. High city wages attracted them. But this meant there were fewer people left to work in agriculture. There was a labor shortage on farms, especially during harvest time.

Where could farmowners find the extra workers they needed? Some people suggested that they should import Chinese laborers for the season. The labor unions opposed this. "What if the Chinese decided to stay?" they worried. "There might not be any jobs left for local soldiers when the war is over." Finally, the communities decided to do the whole harvest themselves. Everyone with extra time worked in the fields. Children, retired people, office workers — the whole town — helped out during the busiest weeks.

31. Why were more jobs open to women during the war?
32. Why was the farm labor shortage such a problem?

How Did High Employment Affect Workers?

The labor shortage also upset the traditional relationship between workers and employers. Before, when there were more workers than jobs, the employers were in complete control. They could keep conditions bad and wages low, and still there would always be someone willing to take the job. Workers were afraid to protest bad conditions because they were sure to get fired, and jobs were hard to find. There were few unions and few laws to protect workers' rights.

The extra high employment during the war changed some things. Now there were no lines of unemployed laborers waiting to take any job they could find. As a matter of fact, there were other companies waiting to hire workers. Businesses had to try harder to make sure their employees would stay.

33. How did the labor shortage affect the relationship between employers and employees?

Labor Union Gains

Labor unions were able to make some important gains during this time. One example was the eight-hour day for loggers.

Loggers had tried before to win higher wages and shorter hours. They had been unsuccessful. By 1917, about 2,500 loggers had joined AFL unions, and 3,000 were IWW members. They all

Some early Black settlers worked on fishing boats such as this. Many more worked on the ships and steamers on Puget Sound.

REACTIONS TO THE INDUSTRIAL WORKERS OF THE WORLD (IWW)

People objected to the IWW for various reasons. The Wobblies' radical language scared them. Many disapproved of IWW methods, such as riots and sabotage.

Then the Wobblies did something that turned almost everyone against them. They opposed American involvement in World War I. This was considered a crime. In 1917, about 100 anti-war Wobblies were arrested and sentenced to long prison terms.

IWW members suffered a great deal of discrimination and violence in the early 1900's. IWW meetings were prohibited by local governments. The IWW printing press was damaged. Members were beaten up, stepped on, and jailed.

In Spokane, IWW members were arrested for speaking on street corners. The Wobblies considered this a serious violation of their civil rights. They called for volunteers from around the country to come to Spokane and participate in their "free speech movement." Volunteers stood on soapboxes and began a speech. They were quickly arrested. But new volunteers came in to take their place. The Spokane jails became crowded with free speech demonstrators. One IWW leader, Elizabeth Gurley Flynn, became famous when she chained herself to a lamppost so that she could not be jailed. Finally, the Spokane laws were relaxed and the street corner demonstrators left.

In 1916, nine sawmill workers' unions in Everett went on strike. Some IWW members from Seattle went up to participate. Everett businessmen were furious that the IWW had come. They chased the Wobblies out of town with clubs. Many of the members were badly beaten.

In revenge, 300 IWW members rented a boat and sailed to Everett for a "Sunday Picnic and free speech demonstration." They were expected. The Everett sheriff and a company of armed volunteers were waiting for them at the docks. The Wobblies were singing union songs as their boat, the *Verona,* approached.

Suddenly, the singing was interrupted by gunfire. Who started it? Each side claimed that the other did. The *Verona* was examined in Seattle, however, and no guns were found on board. When the shooting stopped, five IWW members and two Everett volunteers were dead. Fifty others were wounded.

The *Verona* was met by police in Seattle. Seventy-three Wobblies were arrested. They were all acquitted (found innocent). Not one of the Everett volunteers was ever brought to court.

On November 11, 1919, another violent incident occurred in Centralia, Washington. The town was celebrating the first anniversary of the end of World War I. There were rumors that the lumber company owners and the American Legion planned to break into IWW headquarters that day.

The American Legion had already attacked the Wobblies once that year. They hauled several of the "Wobs" off in a truck, beat them, and threatened to hang them.

On November 11, the Legion was marching in a holiday parade. When they passed the IWW office, shooting broke out. Some of the Legion members died. Again, both sides claimed the other had started it. The Legion stormed the office. IWW member Wes Everest picked up a rifle and fired into the mob. Then he dropped the rifle, grabbed a pistol, and ran into the woods. The mob of Legion members chased him. Everest made it as far as the middle of a river outside the town before the river's dangerous current stopped him. He offered to turn himself in to the police, but the mob just kept coming. He fired, killing Dale Hubbard, the nephew of one of the mob organizers.

They put Everest in jail, but that night he was kidnapped. The men dragged him behind a truck to the Chehalis River bridge, beat him, hanged him, and shot him many times.

Several IWW members spent 15 years in prison as a result of the incident. No Legion member was ever brought to trial.

decided to call a strike. Altogether, more than 40,000 workers joined the strike. They closed down 85% of the lumber mills in the state. The loggers demanded higher wages, better living conditions, and an eight-hour day. When loggers went back to work, they continued to "strike on the job." They laid down their tools and refused to work any more. They destroyed some company property.

The owners refused to give in. The situation wore on for three months. Lumber was badly needed for the war effort. Finally, the army got involved. Soldiers were sent out to the woods to replace the loggers. Logging was considered an "unskilled" job, but the inexperienced soldiers could not do the work.

Finally, the army settled the strike. The lumber company owners agreed to an eight-hour day and some improvements in the loggers' living conditions. Loggers agreed not to hurt the war effort. The agreement came far short of IWW goals, but the big issue — the eight-hour day — had been won.

34. Why did the army get involved in the loggers' strike?
35. What did the loggers and lumber company owners agree on?

What Was The Seattle General Strike?

The end of World War I in 1918 brought problems for workers in Washington State. Soldiers returned and needed to find work. At

How did the labor shortages of World War I help loggers and other workers who were trying to improve their working conditions?

NOVEMBER 11

The first World War ended November 11, 1918. On that day an "armistice," or peace agreement, was signed. November 11 was declared a national holiday, called Armistice Day. Today, most Americans know it as Veterans' Day. In Washington, it has a double importance. November 11 is also the date of Washington's statehood, so both events are celebrated at the same time.

the same time, many industrial workers were being laid off since there was no longer a demand for war goods.

The labor organizations in Seattle were quite strong. It was the only U.S. city with a daily labor newspaper and a Central Labor Council to which each union sent representatives. The council attempted to coordinate union activities in the city.

In 1919, the Seattle shipyard workers felt that the wages they were earning were not high enough, and they decided to go on strike. They asked other unions to support them by striking also. For five days, Seattle was almost completely shut down. Streetcars and taxicabs did not run. Restaurants closed down and business was at a standstill. Only very important items such as supplies for hospitals and mail service continued. This was called the Seattle General Strike. After five days, the majority of the labor unions decided to go back to work and let the shipyard union solve its own problems.

The strike was both a success and a failure. It was successful in winning the support of thousands of workers, including non-unionized workers and some union members in Renton and Tacoma. But the purpose of the general strike was unclear. No formal demands were presented. No concrete goals were achieved. Some people formed a bad impression of labor unions as a result of the General Strike.

36. What was the Seattle General Strike?
37. Which group of workers started the strike?
38. How was the General Strike a success and how was it a failure?

The newspapers in Seattle had very different attitudes toward the General Strike. These two cartoons are a good example of those differences. Look at the cartoon from the P.I. What is the artist saying? According to him, what did the strike represent? Compare his attitudes to those of the Union Record's cartoonist. Who do you suppose would agree or disagree with each newspaper's opinion of the strike?

A Washington city in 1920, the year this unit begins. Our state economy and population have changed in many ways since this was taken. Based on the photo, see if you can suggest several differences in lifestyle between this period and the present.

UNIT 9

FROM ONE WAR TO ANOTHER

This unit covers years that your grandparents, and perhaps your parents, lived through. It is about Washington State from the end of World War I to the end of World War II. It was a time of dramatic ups and downs for the economy, including a period of rapid growth and the worst depression in United States history.

This unit has three sections:

1. The 1920's in Washington
2. The Great Depression
3. World War II

As you read about these 25 years of modern Washington history, keep in mind the following questions: What key industries were started or grew stronger during this period? What things helped the state economy become more industrialized? How did the state's population change? What effects of these changes do you see in Washington today?

SECTION 1: THE 1920's IN WASHINGTON

The End Of The Boom

When World War I ended, most of the shipbuilding business ended, too. Washington companies had very few orders for ships. Most of the shipyard workers were laid off. Other Washington industries lost business, too. Lumbering was no longer as profitable as it had been before the war. There was a short recession.

This was the end of a big boom for the state. After 1923, the economy picked up again. But Washington's economy would not for many years grow as quickly as it did before and during World War I.

1. What happened to Washington's shipbuilding industry after World War I?

How Did The Labor Movement Change?

After the General Strike, the labor movement lost some of its energy and became less radical. In the decades after World War I, Washington labor unions continued to grow. In fact, Seattle became the most highly unionized city in the United States. But the labor unions became strong by cooperating with big business. One

Northwest logging had boomed during World War I. What happened to this and other Northwest industries when the war ended?

man especially was responsible for the growing strength and cooperation of Northwest unions after the war. He was a Seattle truckdriver named Dave Beck who became the leader of the Teamsters Union.

2. How did Washington's labor unions change after the war?

What Was Prohibition?

In 1916, Washington voters had passed a law to prohibit the buying or selling of alcoholic drinks. This was called "Prohibition," and it lasted in Washington until 1932. (An amendment to the U.S. Constitution outlawed liquor all over the country from 1919 to 1933.)

People had many reasons for believing that alcohol should be outlawed. Studies had linked alcohol to poverty, crime, and disease. Some religious groups believed drinking was immoral. Some feminists argued that alcohol led men to mistreat their wives. There was also evidence that liquor manufacturers had bribed lawmakers.

As soon as Prohibition started, some people went into business making and selling liquor illegally (called bootlegging). Since Washington is so close to Canada, smuggling became common.

In some United States cities, prohibition encouraged the rise of organized crime, and there were many incidents of violence. Bootlegging in the Northwest was not quite so dramatic, but it did occur. For a while, two big gangs controlled all bootlegging operations here, until a shootout between the two gangs finally weakened both of them.

Another Seattle man then stepped in to take their place. He was Roy Olmstead, a lieutenant of the Seattle Police. Olmstead was spotted one night in Everett as he supervised the unloading of a boat full of illegal Canadian whiskey. He was fired from the police force. But that didn't stop him. He went on to build an even larger bootlegging network. He was bringing in about $200,000 a month, when federal agents arrested him in 1925. He served three years at McNeil federal prison, which is located on an island in south Puget Sound.

3. What was prohibited in Washington from 1916 to 1932?
4. What was bootlegging?

Law And Order Versus Mayor Brown

Bootleggers succeeded because many people did not believe in prohibition. They didn't think the laws should be enforced. In Seattle especially, police and public officials often allowed alcohol to be sold illegally — for a price. It was said that the police collected up to $70,000 a month in bribes.

The mayor of Seattle in the early 1920's was Edwin Brown. He believed in keeping the town "open." (An "open" or "wet" town was one where liquor was sold.) While Brown was mayor, Seattle police did little to stop illegal alcohol sales. Seattle citizens who believed in "law and order," including prohibition laws, disapproved strongly of Mayor Brown's actions.

5. What role did police and public officials often play in bootlegging operations?
6. Why did law and order supporters oppose Mayor Brown?

The Law And Order Forces Win A Brief Victory

In 1924, Mayor Brown left Seattle to attend the Democratic National Convention. While he was gone, the law and order forces scored a dramatic but brief victory.

When Seattle's mayor is out of town, the President of the City Council automatically becomes acting mayor. In 1924, the City Council President was Bertha Landes, a strong supporter of law and order. When Brown left, Landes became temporary mayor; and she was determined to use her position to clean up the town.

When the Police Chief refused to cooperate, Landes fired him. Mayor Brown heard about it and hurried back to Seattle.

7. Why did Bertha Landes become temporary mayor of Seattle?
8. Why did Landes fire the Police Chief?

The First Woman Mayor

In 1926, Bertha Knight Landes decided to run for mayor herself. She won the election as the

Bertha Landes was a leading prohibitionist in Seattle in the 1920's. In 1924, she was president of the Seattle City Council. In 1926, she was elected mayor — becoming the first woman mayor of a major American city.

law and order candidate. Seattle became the first major American city to have a woman mayor.

As the elected mayor, Landes worked to "clean up" the city and to make city government work more honestly and efficiently. She supported several progressive issues, including: expanding city parks and protecting the lakes; increased support of public utilities (water, electricity, sewage); combined city and county governments; and less power for the mayor. In fact, she believed the mayor should be replaced by a city manager to be hired by the City Council. Unfortunately, Landes was not able to accomplish many of her programs. She was defeated for reelection in 1928.

9. What was Mayor Landes' special distinction?
10. What progressive issues did Mayor Landes support?

Exclusion And The Need For Workers: A Pattern Of Asian Immigration

During the 1920's there was discrimination against Japanese and Filipino immigrants in

Washington and other western states. These two Asian groups came here later than the Chinese, but their experiences were similar in many ways.

Federal laws prohibiting Chinese immigration had caused problems for many employers. Railroads, fish canneries, and other businesses had become dependent on Chinese workers. After the Chinese were excluded in 1882, these businesses had a hard time finding workers to replace the Chinese. White workers would not tolerate the same low pay and poor working conditions as the Chinese. The employers did not want to pay higher wages. So they began looking for a new source of immigrant workers.

American companies were successful in attracting many young men from Japan. Between 1898 and 1907, Japanese immigrants came to the United States in great numbers. By the time of the 1910 census, the Japanese were the largest racial minority in Washington. They filled many of the jobs that had previously been held by the Chinese.

But the Japanese ran into prejudice also. In 1924, they were excluded from immigration. Again there was a need for workers, and again the American recruiters went to Asia. This time, they found workers in the Philippines.

The Philippines had been captured by the United States in 1899, during the Spanish-American War. It became a U.S. possession.

This meant that Filipinos could not be excluded from America. After 1920, Filipinos became the fastest-growing Asian group in Washington. But the Filipinos, too, soon met with discrimination. The number of Filipinos allowed into the United States was greatly reduced after 1934.

11. Name the first three major groups of Asian immigrants in the order of their coming to the United States.
12. Why did the Chinese Exclusion Act present a problem for some American companies?

Why Did Japanese And Filipinos Come To America?

In Japan and the Philippines — as in China— only a few people were wealthy. Many people were very poor, and there were few opportunities for a poor person to make much money.

In the late 1800's, the Japanese began to hear stories of America that were very appealing. According to the stories, America was a rich land. Wages were high, and there were many jobs. A young man could go to America and earn enough money for a good life. These stories inspired many Japanese — especially young, single men— to go to America.

The Filipinos also heard stories about America. There were a large number of American teachers in the Philippines. They talked about the great opportunities of life in the United States. They encouraged their students to

Asian immigrants were hired to harvest crops in Hawaii and the west coast states. What other industries depended on Asian workers?

As the oldest Asian immigrants, the Chinese often had more wealth and power than the newcomers from other Asian countries. Many of the labor contractors, landlords, businesspeople, and leaders of the Asian community were Chinese. This photo shows a fairly well-to-do Chinese import store in the early 1900's.

go to America for an education and for the benefits of American life.

The boat trip to America was long and unpleasant. It was difficult to leave family and friends behind. But many Japanese and Filipino men decided to make the trip. They hoped to work for a while in America, make some money, and then return to build a better life at home.

13. Why were many Japanese and Filipino men willing to make the long, difficult, and unpleasant boat trip to the United States?

What Did The Immigrants Find?

When the immigrants arrived, they quickly learned that the stories they had heard about America weren't all true. It was true that wages in America were higher than those in Japan or the Philippines. But in order to earn those wages, the immigrants had to do very hard work for long hours under poor conditions.

For example, Japanese railroad workers were sometimes forced to work ten or more hours a day in the desert, with temperatures over 100 degrees F. and no protection from the sun. In 1904, Japanese railroad workers earned $1.50 for ten hours of work. The immigrants could

not afford good food and save money to take back to Japan. There were many health problems and many fatal accidents.

Most Asian immigrants found that only hard, low-paying jobs in America were open to them. Employers discriminated against the Asians because they could not speak English and because they were not white. The jobs that Japanese and Filipino immigrants found included work at the canneries, mines, lumber mills, farms, restaurants, and railroads, or as servants in private homes.

14. Which part of the stories about America was true and which part was untrue?
15. Why did the Japanese and Filipino immigrants work at the hardest and lowest-paying jobs?

How Did Asian Immigrants Contribute To Northwest Industries?

In spite of their poor working conditions and limited opportunities, Asian immigrants made several important contributions to western industries. Chinese workers were extremely important in building the western railroads, for example. The Japanese were noted for their contributions to the agriculture of the West Coast states. They were responsible for developing the rice and citrus crops of California and the strawberries in Washington. By the time of World War I, 70% of the stalls at Seattle's Public Market were run by Japanese farmers.

Interestingly, Japanese Americans were also important in developing our aquaculture (sea farming) industry. Japanese American oyster growers were the first to successfully raise Japanese oysters in Western Washington. Today, these oysters are one of the state's important food products.

Filipinos also contributed to the agricultural industry and were important in the development of the fish canning industry of the Northwest.

16. Name at least one contribution to Northwest industries by each of the following groups: Chinese, Japanese, Filipinos.

How Were Japanese Immigrants Discriminated Against?

Some of the Japanese immigrants were very skilled and educated people. Seattle became known for its large number of Japanese intellectuals. But better-paid and more highly-skilled jobs were not available to Japanese workers because of discrimination.

Still, by working extremely hard and saving as much as possible, some Japanese were able to start farms or small businesses. As farmers, many became especially successful. They managed to raise good crops even on very poor soil.

The hard work of Japanese immigrants soon began to make some of the white workers jealous and suspicious. They feared that the Japanese offered unfair competition for jobs. And white farmers became jealous of the Japanese farmers' good crops. Since the whites and the Japanese lived separately and had different languages and cultures, they never got to know each other well.

As a result, anti-Japanese prejudice grew. There were several incidents of anti-Japanese prejudice in Washington State. Some Japanese farms and barns in the Auburn area were burned in the 1920's. Some restaurants had signs that said "No Orientals." Blacks and Japanese were not allowed at Alki Beach or in good seats at the

Early Japanese American Family

SMUGGLING-IN

Many Japanese who wanted to come to the United States could not get passports. A great number of them decided to try to get into America illegally, by jumping ship. They hired on as crew members or stowed away in ships bound for the United States. When they arrived in American ports, they would wait for an opportunity to swim ashore.

This was called "smuggling in." It was very risky. The docks were heavily guarded and those who were caught were severely punished. The following is the story of a man named Kakichi Tsuboi who successfully smuggled in to Seattle in 1913.

"Mr. Shiosaka and I waited cautiously. The night before the boat was to leave we worked on the night shift. As this was the last day in port, the guards became more or less careless. During the day I had secured a rope from the stern. Eight o'clock came. Just as I was, I quietly let myself down the rope hand over hand and submerged myself in the water, followed by Mr. Shiosaka. The sea in February was ice-cold and felt as if it cut the skin. Around the piers of Smith Cove the watchmen from the boat and from the Immigration Office were keeping close guard, darting their eyes from place to place. I swam, being careful to make no sound. I don't know where we climbed out; I was in a daze. I noticed that my shoes were gone.

Probably I kicked them off when I was swimming, but I never felt a thing.

"We ran and ran at random. We ran past Main Street and at last we found one house where a single light bulb was burning in the darkness near the hill below Marine Hospital. Through the window we saw an old black woman reading a Bible. Being so cold and hungry, and with no way of knowing whether she would be friend or enemy, I knocked at the door, asking for help as if my life depended on it. Though we couldn't communicate with words, she gestured for me to come in. Since I knew that there were so many cases where, if you trust someone and enter their house, they immediately turn you in to the Immigration Office, I couldn't feel easy. But this woman and her husband, Mr. and Mrs. John Moore, provided us with hot coffee and bread and, moreover, shorts and underwear belonging to their son.

"The next morning Mr. Moore got in touch with his friend, a Japanese named Mr. Kaneko. He came to see us and soon we went to the canneries in Alaska to work. I can never in my entire life forget the warm coffee that night, and the kindness of Mr. and Mrs. Moore."*

*Ito Kazuo, *Issei: A History of Japanese Immigrants in North America,* Seattle: Japanese Community Services, 1973, pp.62-3.

movie theaters. An anti-Japanese league was founded by businesspeople who competed with Japanese businesses. In Anacortes, 200 whites asked the city council to get rid of all Japanese employees of the local cannery. In Blaine, Washington, somebody dynamited a main water pipe. The person left behind a note that said, "Put out the Japs or . . ."

17. Why did some white workers become jealous and suspicious of the Japanese?
18. Give at least three examples of anti-Japanese prejudice.

Legalized Prejudice

Like the Chinese, Japanese immigrants were not allowed to become United States citizens. (However, the immigrants' American-born children were automatically citizens.) In 1921, the Alien Land Law was passed in Washington. This law made it illegal for non-citizens to own land. Therefore, Japanese farmers could not own their farms. Many families put their property in their children's names. Others found helpful Americans who would act as legal owners.

Some political leaders, labor unions, and other groups continued to demand a total end to Japanese immigration. In 1924, these people succeeded in getting Congress to pass an Exclusion Act. This act kept out Japanese immigrants, and also Koreans, Burmese, Malayans, Polynesians, Moaris (New Zealand natives), and Tahitians.

Hawaiian sugar plantations, as well as farms and factories on the American West Coast, had depended on Japanese labor. Now they needed to find another source of workers. They began to recruit people from the Philippines. Between 1906 and 1914, 20,000 Filipinos moved to Hawaii. Many of the Filipinos later came to the United States mainland.

19. Identify the following laws: Alien Land Law, 1924 Exclusion Act.
20. Where did 20,000 Filipinos go between 1906 and 1914?

Promises And Disappointments

Since the Philippines was owned by the United States, Filipinos did not need a visa (permit) to come here. The 1924 Exclusion Act did not

WHAT WERE THE EXPERIENCES OF THE FIRST JAPANESE WOMEN?

After they saved some money, the Japanese immigrants began to think about getting married. Life without women and families was lonely and unstable.

In the early 1900's, it was still common for families in Japan to choose husbands or wives for their children. So the young single men in America naturally wrote to their families in Japan and asked them to arrange a marriage. The man sent a photograph of himself and later received a photo of the woman who was picked out for him. For this reason, the women were called "picture brides."

The life of the picture brides was not easy. Most of them had never been far from their families before. Now they had to make a long, unpleasant boat trip to live with a man they didn't know in a country they knew almost nothing about.

For most of the women life in America was full of unpleasant surprises. The women had heard about the wealth in America. By the standards of Japan, their husbands were well-off. But most picture brides discovered that their American homes would be rough shacks or crowded apartments. They would have to work very hard, side by side with their husbands.

Often, the women worked even harder than the men. For example, a farmer's wife would get up at 4:30 a.m. to do housework and to cook for all the people who worked at the farm. Then she would go work in the fields all day. She also had to take care of the children.

This first generation of Japanese immigrants are known as *Issei*. They suffered years of hard work and little money in order to try to give their children a better life. The Issei's American-born children are called *Nisei*, and the next two generations of Japanese Americans are known as *Sansei* and *Yonsei*.

apply to them. (However, Filipinos were still not allowed to become U.S. citizens.)

Like the Chinese and Japanese before them, the Filipinos came to America in hopes of earning more money than they could make in the Philippines. Like the earlier groups, they had heard wonderful stories about the opportunities in America.

However, the Filipinos were disappointed as the other Asian immigrants had been. They found that many of the labor recruiters had lied. Wages were lower and working conditions were worse than the young Filipinos had been told. Instead of finding wealth and better lives, the Filipinos found poor jobs and racial prejudice.

The Filipino immigrants often had to travel great distances, from one poorly-paid job to another, just to earn enough to stay alive. A typical year might involve a trip to Alaskan canneries for the salmon season; work on farms in Washington, Oregon, and California as the crops were ripe; and several months in a city, such as Tacoma, San Francisco, or Stockton, California. Workers were recruited for these jobs by labor contractors (many of them Chinese), who often cheated them.

As they moved, the workers often shared living quarters with other Filipino men. The Filipino population of the West Coast became a kind of extended family, whose members would often help one another. This pattern of self-help in the face of discrimination was also practiced by the earlier Asian groups.

21. Why didn't the 1924 Exclusion Act apply to Filipinos?

What Were The Sources And Results Of Anti-Filipino Prejudice?

Labor unions accused the Filipinos of working for extremely low wages and taking jobs away from white workers. The Filipino immigrants were also criticized for their lifestyle. Without permanent homes or families, many single young men turned to pool halls and gambling for entertainment. Some Filipinos married women of different racial and ethnic groups, but this only added to prejudice and anger against Filipinos. Filipinos were often criticized for their gambling, for their aggressiveness, and for their attention to white women.

As a result of prejudice, Filipinos were discriminated against in jobs, schools, restaurants, and even in churches. Some movie theatres had segregated seating for Filipinos. (Other racial minorities were seated in this same section, away from whites.)

In 1928, there were several cases of anti-Filipino violence in Washington. A mob of 150 white men stopped two busloads of Filipino farmworkers near Cashmere. The mob threatened the farmworkers and forcefully prevented them from getting to the fields where they were going to work. In Wenatchee, a group of 200 white laborers raided the camp where 22 Filipino cannery workers were staying. Police had to come and break up the mob. In following years, there were other outbreaks of anti-Filipino

violence in the towns of Sumner, Orting, and Puyallup.

22. Give at least three examples of anti-Filipino discrimination.

How Were Filipinos Excluded?

After the beginning of the Great Depression of the 1930's, jobs became extremely scarce. Unemployment was very high. Filipino workers had an especially difficult time trying to make a living. During the Depression, white workers grew even more resentful of Filipino competition for jobs. Labor unions and other groups began demanding an end to Filipino immigration.

But the Phillippines were still owned by the United States. How could this group of United States nationals be kept out of America? Congress found an answer in the McDuffie-Tydings Act of 1934. This law provided that the Philippines would become an independent country by 1946. The law declared that Filipinos were now aliens and could no longer enter the United States without permits. Only 50 permits would be granted to Filipino immigrants each year.

23. What was the McDuffie-Tydings Act?

CARLOS BULOSAN

Carlos Bulosan was a Filipino American writer and union organizer. He came to America in the 1920's. Bulosan lived and worked in many places on the West Coast, including Seattle and the Yakima Valley. His autobiography, America Is In The Heart, *is a moving account of the struggles and sufferings of a minority immigrant to the United States.*

SECTION 2: THE GREAT DEPRESSION

What Was the Great Depression?

During the late 1920's many people in the United States, as well as in the state of Washington, had been enjoying a period of prosperity. Business had grown during and after World War I. People had jobs, and they had money to spend. The United States was producing more goods than ever before. This has come to be remembered as a period of "fast" living and violence. You may have heard the term "Roaring Twenties" in the movies or on television. That is partly what the 1920's were like.

The United States had become a world leader. But many Americans wanted to forget about the war and what it had done. Then an event took place which shook the whole nation. The good times that many Americans had enjoyed came to an end with the terrible depression that began in 1929. It lasted for many years and affected nearly every family in the United States. It is still referred to as the Great Depression.

There were many reasons for the depression. Perhaps the most important was that people were buying too many stocks and bonds on credit. There was some reckless buying and selling of land. Business firms were also using a great deal of credit to expand. People began to lose faith in the stocks and bonds they had purchased. Thousands of individuals started to sell their bonds and their property. As they did, the prices dropped until their holdings had little value. Many wealthy people were now broke, and workers were out of jobs. Many banks failed and people lost all or most of their savings. The United States was in a depression that hurt nearly every section of the country, including the state of Washington. By 1933, one-third of the country's working people were out of work. People without jobs cannot buy such things as houses and cars; sometimes they cannot even buy all the food and clothing they need. So during the depression, factories had to close or slow down production.

To make things worse, there were long droughts (periods with no rain) in many parts of the country. Much of the nation's best farmland turned into a dry "dust bowl." The country was

This photo shows a Boeing airplane of the 1930's called a "Clipper." Why did Boeing and most Washington companies lose money in the 1930's?

in a very complicated economic crisis.

24. What portion of all U.S. workers were unemployed in 1933?
25. Name some factors that helped cause the Great Depression.

Breadlines And Hunger Marches

The drought in Washington was not as bad as in many places. Still, all of the state's industries were deeply affected by the depression. Lumbering, fishing, and manufacturing suffered. About 287,000 workers in the state became unemployed.

As the depression wore on, some wages fell to as little as one-half their former level. The low wages and poor working conditions led to several strikes. The dock workers, sawmill workers, and employees of the *Seattle Post-Intelligencer* were on strike for months.

Thousands of Washington families did not have enough money for food. Unemployed people organized large "hunger marches" to Olympia to ask the state government for help. Modern public assistance programs such as food stamps and social security had not started yet. Some charities offered bread and soup once a day to the unemployed. Hungry people waited in long "breadlines" for these free meals.

Some of Washington's unemployed people tried to find ways to help themselves. They organized a group called the "Unemployed Citizen's League." The League spread information about unemployment problems. League members helped each other by sharing food and trying to locate jobs.

The Communist Party had candidates running for public office during the 1930's, but they never received more than a few thousand votes. By the end of the 1930's the violence, the strikes, the unrest and unhappiness of the times were coming to an end. Some of these depression problems are now history, but others have not been solved even today.

An organization called the Washington Commonwealth Federation (WCF) played a significant role in Washington politics of this period. The Federation supported President Roosevelt's New Deal, and they campaigned for such goals as higher wages, old age pensions, public ownership of natural resources, civil liberties, and an end to the sales tax. Several candidates endorsed by WCF were elected to office in 1936. These included Lieutenant Governor Vic Meyers and Congressman John Coffee. The WCF also backed Warren Magnuson and Henry Jackson, later U.S. Senators, in their early political careers.

26. What organizations tried to help solve the hunger problems of the 1930's?

What Did The Federal Government Do?

The depression continued to grow worse, instead of better. It quickly became a greater problem than private charities or even the state government could solve. People turned to the federal government for solutions. In 1932, the voters elected Franklin D. Roosevelt to replace President Herbert Hoover. They hoped Roosevelt could find a way to get the economy back on its feet.

During the depression, many banks could not collect on loans made to businessmen, farmers, and others. In 1933, so many banks had closed because they did not have money to cover withdrawals by their depositors that President Roosevelt declared a bank holiday. During and after the bank holiday, Congress passed laws about banks and banking. One of these laws gives states the right to pass legislation allowing banks

to have branches. Washington and Oregon did pass state laws permitting state-wide branches. Since the state law of 1933, large banks in Seattle, Spokane, and Tacoma have developed branches in many parts of the state.

Roosevelt promised a "New Deal" for the American people. He was willing to experiment with new approaches to the nation's problems. Some New Deal laws helped strengthen American banks, businesses, and agriculture. These included federal insurance of bank deposits to keep banks from failing again. Other programs called for soil conservation and more scientific farming methods.

Still other New Deal laws created jobs, protected workers, helped businesses, or provided direct aid to the unemployed. Minimum wages, Social Security, and Unemployment Insurance were also started during the New Deal.

27. Why did people turn to the federal government for leadership during the Great Depression?
28. What was the New Deal?

The Government Creates Jobs

Most unemployed people did not want welfare; they wanted jobs. During the 1930's, the federal government hired thousands of jobless people to work on special projects. For example, the Civilian Conservation Corps (C.C.C.) hired people for outdoor work, such as tree planting and park improvement. Many of Washington's hiking trails were built by the C.C.C. Another program hired researchers to study such issues as flood control, sewage systems, and social problems. Artists were hired too. The mural in Seattle's University District Post Office is one product of the federal artists' project of the 1930's.

But the biggest, most important New Deal projects in Washington were the hydroelectric dams. The Bonneville Dam was approved by Congress in 1933; the Grand Coulee Dam in 1935. The Grand Coulee alone created more than 7,000 jobs. Hundreds of millions of dollars poured into Washington State, helping to soften the depression here.

29. Name some New Deal projects that created jobs in Washington State.

The Battle For The Grand Coulee Dam

There were lots of objections to the idea of building the Grand Coulee Dam. At first, people

Rally of unemployed workers in Seattle in the early 1930's. What issues and needs are mentioned in the signs?

HOOVERVILLE

During the Depression, hundreds of unemployed fishermen, seamen, miners, well-educated businessmen, and lumbermen wandered into Seattle looking for work. Instead of jobs, they found only breadlines and bare, crowded rooms to sleep in. These were independent, hardworking men, most of them, and they wanted to do something for themselves.

A few of them noticed an abandoned shipyard that was south of Dearborn Street on the Seattle waterfront. There was plenty of vacant land there and lots of scrap lumber and tin — a perfect place for a temporary "city!" A couple of men built shacks there and moved in. The idea caught on fast. Within a month, there was a neighborhood of over 100 shacks. The men called their new town "Hooverville" after President Herbert Hoover. (Many people blamed Hoover for causing or worsening the depression. There were a lot of bitter Hoover jokes during the 30's.)

Twice, Seattle Health Department officials came in and burned Hooverville down. Twice, the men rebuilt their shacks. In 1932, Seattle voters elected John Dore mayor. He was more sympathetic to Hooverville's people and he agreed to let the men stay. (No women or children were allowed in Hooverville, however.)

The men of Hooverville elected a "city council" made up of two whites, two Blacks and two Filipinos. They chose a temporary mayor, and they ran their community almost like a regular town.

Local businesses helped out the men at Hooverville with scrap building materials and extra food. The men made money however they could. Some found old boats, repaired them, and went fishing. They sold a few fish and shared with their neighbors. Other men built small carts and went into the recycling business. They gathered old cardboard and newspapers or scraps of metal, and resold them. Most of the men at Hooverville were used to hard work and rough living. They knew that somehow they would be able to survive.

said it was impossible. Later, they said that no one could afford to build it. After the federal government voted to pay for the dam, many Congresspeople and government leaders complained that it was a waste of money. And the people who owned private power companies thought it was dangerous competition.

The Grand Coulee might never have been completed without the hard work of a few people who really believed in it. One of the most important leaders of this movement was an Ephrata lawyer named James O'Sullivan. He spent 30 years giving speeches, writing articles, talking to government leaders, and working out agreements to keep the dam's opponents from stopping construction.

30. Who was James O'Sullivan?
31. Why did different groups oppose the high dam?

A Bold Plan For Eastern Washington

People had first started talking about a Grand Coulee dam in the early 1900's. Eastern Washington farmers needed irrigation so that they could take advantage of the good, but dry, soil. An irrigation system for this area would require a huge reservoir, big enough to store up water to last through the dry summer months.

Some Eastern Washington residents had a bold idea. They suggested building a very high dam on the Columbia near the Grand Coulee. Water from behind the dam could be pumped into the Grand Coulee, which was a natural place for a reservoir. From there, canals could carry the water downhill to farms.

Meanwhile, the dam could be used to control floods, to improve navigation, and most of all, to provide electricity. Sales of that electricity could help pay for all other uses of the dam.

32. Why was an irrigation reservoir needed?
33. What was the plan for the Grand Coulee Dam?

Engineering Challenges

While O'Sullivan and others were solving political problems, the engineers at the dam site had different challenges to deal with. The Grand Coulee Dam would be the largest structure people had ever built. Twenty million tons of concrete would go into the dam. That's enough to build a six-lane highway around the United States! New systems had to be designed to solve

the dam's unusual problems. At the beginning, for example, one of the river banks kept slipping and eroding away, before the dam's foundations could be built. How do you make a giant cliff of clay stand still? "Freeze it!" suggested the engineers. They ran pipes through the clay and built a giant refrigeration system. It worked! After the dam was completed, the engineers took out the pipes and thawed out the cliff again.

34. Why did engineers refrigerate the river bank?

It's All Water (And A Few Fish) Over The Dam

The dam created other problems, too. The lake that backed up behind the Grand Coulee Dam flooded ten small towns. The people and many of the buildings in those towns had to be moved. New towns had to be built to replace the old towns and to house the thousands of people who would come to work on the dam.

A more difficult problem was the effect of the dam on the salmon. Salmon are hatched in fresh water streams. When they have grown to about the size of a finger (they're called fingerlings at this stage), they swim down to the ocean. A few years later, the full grown salmon swim back upstream to the place where they were born. There they spawn (lay their eggs) and then they die.

The dam could destroy all the salmon runs in two ways. The fingerlings might be killed going over the dam and through the power generators. Or, the adult salmon would be stopped by the dam on their trip upstream. They would never reach their spawning grounds. Either way, all

The Grand Coulee Dam under construction.

the salmon could be wiped out. Commercial and sports fishers, conservationists, and Native Americans all wanted to be sure this did not happen.

35. Why did the dam pose dangers to the salmon?

How Were Salmon Protected?

Studies of the fish and plans for protecting them were begun immediately. It was found that fingerlings could pass safely over the dam. In order to allow the adult salmon to get past Bonneville dam, a "fish ladder" was built. Salmon could jump up one step of the ladder at a time and so get around the dam.

But the Grand Coulee Dam would be too high for a fish ladder. So the government began to transplant the fish! Each year for seven years, the salmon that reached the foot of the Grand Coulee were trapped. The water-filled traps were raised by elevator and the fish were carefully unloaded into special trucks. These trucks hauled the salmon to streams and tributaries down-river from the Grand Coulee. New spawning "homes" had been prepared for the fish. There, fences were built across the stream to keep the fish from escaping. The fish were forced to spawn in a new place. The next generation would return to this new home.

However, these methods could not entirely make up for damage to the salmon runs. In addition to the dams, there were problems from pollution, logging, and previous overfishing. So the government also built several fish hatcheries. Here, large numbers of salmon were hatched, and then released into streams. Still, there were problems with all these methods, and the salmon runs were smaller than they had been.

36. Name three methods that the government used to help maintain the salmon runs.

J.D. ROSS AND THE ISSUE OF PUBLIC POWER

More than half the electricity used in the Pacific Northwest comes through the federal government agency called the Bonneville Power Administration (BPA). The BPA gets its name from the Bonneville Dam, the first federal dam constructed in the region. Today, the BPA sells the electricity from over 30 dams and thermal power plants. The BPA also coordinates federal electrical production with other electric producers in the region. And it manages a system of power lines that carry electricity to many areas of the western states.

The first director of the Bonneville Power Administration (BPA) was a man who had spent most of his life in the public power business. He was J.D. Ross — the former head of Seattle City Light and the person that Ross Dam was named after.

Ross believed that industries would go where there was cheap electricity. He worked for many years to make sure that Seattle City Light could supply large amounts of cheap power. He believed that this would make Seattle grow. As head of BPA, Ross worked to develop low cost electricity for the whole Northwest.

This was not always easy. There was a lot of powerful opposition to the idea of government-owned power, both in the Northwest and around the country. The leaders of the opposition were the private power companies. They argued that the government should not compete with private companies in the power business. They said that public power was un-American because it went against the idea of free enterprise.

Those who supported government-owned power had many criticisms of private power companies. They argued that private companies often bribed government officials, did nothing to help the area grow, and charged extremely high rates so they could make bigger profits.

The public power companies in Tacoma (started in 1893) and Seattle (started in 1906) had shown that public power could indeed cost less than private power. For example, Seattle residents paid less than half the national average rate for electricity in 1930.

Yet opponents were able for many years to keep public power from expanding. During the 1920's, an association of private power companies spent almost one million dollars to defeat all public power laws. (Some of the money was used to pay people to steal or destroy public power supporters' petitions.)

J.D. Ross became a powerful figure in Seattle politics. He was able to get what he wanted for City Light most of the time. He was responsible for starting the dam system on the Skagit River, which now produces most of the city's electricity.

In 1931, Seattle Mayor Frank Edwards made the mistake of trying to fire the City Light director. Ross supporters around the city were outraged! They held a recall election and succeeded in removing the mayor himself from office instead. The new mayor rehired Ross.

The Grand Coulee Dam was the largest concrete structure yet built. Why was it so important to the Northwest economy?

Many Hydroelectric Dams

The big generators at Bonneville Dam started rolling in 1938; the Grand Coulee Dam began producing electricity three years later. The Northwest's hydroelectric power was vital to the country's war efforts. In 1943, 90 percent of the dams' electricity was being used for war-related purposes.

Today, there are about 15 federal dams on the Snake and Columbia Rivers. This system of dams is run by the Bonneville Power Administration. It makes up the biggest electric company in the world. Many more hydroelectric dams have been built by governments and private power companies around the state.

Today, hydroelectric power is one of the state's most important natural resources. Several industries have moved to Washington State because of the large amounts of cheap electricity available here. The aluminum industry is a good example. Washington's hydroelectric power is also "exported" to California and other western states.

37. What valuable resource comes from Washington's dams?

How Was Northwest Art Boosted During The Thirties?

While the Grand Coulee Dam was transforming the land and economy of Eastern Washington, a handful of people in Western Washington were beginning to transform Northwest art. The 1930's marked some important milestones in the development of the arts in Washington.

The Seattle Art Museum — the largest art collection in the state — was opened in 1933. It was donated to the city by Richard Fuller and his mother, Margaret E. Fuller. Along with the building, they also donated a fine collection of Asian art.

Also during the 1930's, a group of Northwest painters were emerging, who would win national recognition as originators of a "northwest style." The earliest and best known of these painters was Mark Tobey. Tobey first settled in Seattle in 1923, and lived here on and off for many years. He came to this Northwest city — as did many nationally-known artists — to teach at the Cornish School of Art. He had a great influence on younger painters in the Northwest.

In 1934, Tobey travelled to Asia, where he studied calligraphy (elegant writing) and brushwork. He developed a style known as white writing, which suggested Asian art and also the electric lights of American cities at night.

Mark Tobey was one of many artists to participate in a New Deal program that was created to employ artists during the difficult depression years. This program funded writers and performing artists as well as visual artists. Among

Asian art forms influenced many Northwest artists. This photo shows a Japanese dance festival called Bon Odori. This photo was taken in Seattle in 1935. The festival is still celebrated here every year.

other important Northwest painters employed by this New Deal program were Kenneth Callahan and Morris Graves. They were paid by the government to paint murals in public buildings. Like Tobey, Graves was deeply influenced by Asian art and religions. His paintings of birds and animals have been shown in America's most important art museums.

Kenneth Callahan was born in Spokane and later settled in Long Beach. He and Graves both spent part of their school years in Seattle. Callahan's paintings have been shown in the major art museums of the country, and some of his work can be seen at the Seattle Playhouse, the Washington State Library in Olympia, and at several post offices in the state.

Nellie Cornish — a pianist — established an art school in Seattle which gained a national reputation. The school featured a program of integrated arts education, including music, dance, and visual arts. Since its founding, the Cornish School has attracted many well-known artists to its faculty, including dancers Martha Graham, Merce Cunningham, and Robert Joffrey.

38. Read the boxes on this page to help you name three women who were important in some way to the arts in Seattle, and identify the contribution of each.
39. Name three important Northwest painters.

GREAT PHOTOGRAPHERS FROM WASHINGTON STATE

In the days when few people owned cameras, and all photographers had to develop their own film, Washington State produced four important photographic artists. The first was Edward Curtis. Curtis came to Seattle with his family in 1888. As a young man, he opened a studio there, taking portrait photos in order to raise money for his real interest. He wanted to photograph American Indians before their traditional ways of life disappeared.

Curtis' interest in photographing Indians became a passion. For 30 years, he traveled around the western United States, taking photographs, learning and writing about 800 tribes. He saw his family only rarely.

Curtis had already spent $40,000 of his own money on the project when he was able to convince millionaire J.P. Morgan to sponsor it. The result of the many years of extremely hard work was a set of 20 volumes of photographs and text. Curtis made use of the best paper and printing methods available. The foreword was written by President Theodore Roosevelt. The volumes were an immediate success in 1928, and remain a unique and important historic and artistic work.

Two of Edward Curtis' early assistants later became important photographers themselves. One was his brother, Asahel Curtis, who is noted for his photos of Northwest scenes. Asahel started his career as a photographer in Alaska during the gold rush of 1897. He later worked for Seattle newspapers and set up his own photo studio in 1905. The same year, he helped found the Mountaineers Club. (Imagine climbing mountains with the heavy cameras and poor hiking equipment of 1907!)

Asahel served as chairperson of the Mount Rainier National Park Advisory Board for 25 years. He was active in other civic affairs too, unlike his brother Edward.

In the early 1900's, a young Seattle woman came to work at Edward Curtis' studio. She was Imogen Cunningham. As a teenager, Cunningham had been inspired by the work of a photographer named Gertrude Kasabian. Cunningham decided to order a camera, and she built a darkroom in her family's woodshed. There, she taught herself how to develop pictures.

After working for Curtis, Imogen Cunningham went to Dresden, Germany, on a scholarship and studied photographic chemistry. She developed a new method of coating photographic paper. Cunningham's career as a photographer lasted more than 75 years. She knew and worked with many famous American photographers and has influenced the course of photographic art in this country.

A fourth Washington photographer — whose work has recently been rediscovered — was Darius Kinsey. Kinsey ran a small portrait studio in his home. But, he is best known for his photographs of the state's loggers and lumber industry. Kinsey carried his camera into the many forests of Washington, sending the plates home to his wife for developing. His work provides unique insights into an important period in Washington history. Photos by Kinsey and both the Curtis brothers appear in this book.

SECTION 3: WORLD WAR II

When Did The Depression End?

Federal programs certainly helped bring more money and higher employment to Washington during the 1930's. But Roosevelt's New Deal was not able to solve all the problems of the nation's economy. Unemployment was still very high in 1940, especially among minority groups, as the U.S. census showed:

Percentage of unemployment in 1940

White	9.8%
Black	21.5%
Other races	11.1%

The Great Depression did not really end until the beginning of World War II. The United States began selling war supplies as soon as the war began in Europe, and the American economy began to improve. 1941 is the year the United States entered the war. Americans' incomes increased rapidly after that.

40. What 1941 event marked the end of the Great Depression?

How Did World War II End The Depression?

Since the late 1930's Germany, Italy, and Japan had been invading and conquering countries near them. World War II had begun in Europe and Asia, but the United States was not yet involved.

Then on December 7, 1941, Japanese bombers made a surprise attack on Hawaii and destroyed the United States air and navy bases at Pearl Harbor. The attack seriously damaged military defenses in the Pacific. The next day, the United States declared war on Japan.

The war created sudden new demands for workers and goods of all kinds. The United States and our allies needed weapons, transportation equipment, and military supplies. They needed clothing, medical supplies, and food in large quantities.

Farmers who had been unable to sell their crops during the depression were now asked to grow more. Factories that had nearly closed down during the 1930's were busy again, and new factories were started.

The United States armed forces needed

This graph represents the average individual income in America between 1929 and 1945. How long did it take the annual earnings to reach their 1929 levels again after the crash? What caused the big increase in earnings after 1941?

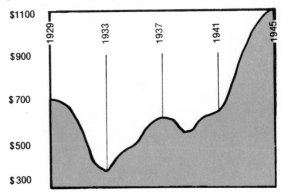

millions of young men and women to fight in the war. The farms and factories at home needed millions more workers. The result was a labor shortage. There were jobs for everyone. Even older people, mothers of young children and others who might not normally have looked for jobs — even these people were needed.

The unemployment problems of the 1930's were over. The country was busy again. People were working, and they had money to spend. This is how World War II brought an end to the Great Depression.

41. Give some examples of goods and workers that were needed during the war.
42. Why did people have more money to spend during the war than during the Depression?

How Did Wartime Employment Affect Women And Minorities?

The labor shortage of wartime meant job opportunities for many people who had not been able to find good jobs before. This was especially true for women and minorities.

While most Washington men were away fighting in the war, many jobs were filled by women. Just as in World War I, thousands of women were able to work at jobs that had always been "for men only." For example, only about one out of 40 employees in aircraft manufacture were women in 1940. By 1944 about half of Boeing's employees were women, and they were doing many kinds of work.

Today the aerospace industry employs many women in a variety of jobs. What 1940's event opened many industrial jobs to women and minorities for the first time?

Since women workers were badly needed for the war effort, the federal government helped pay for day care centers. This allowed more women with young children to work.

Wartime employment also had a great impact on minorities. Because of the labor shortage and because of efforts by Black organizations and the federal government, many minority people had their first opportunity to get good jobs. This was true for Blacks in the Pacific Northwest. Thousands of Blacks came to the state to work in war industries. Boeing, for example, recruited and hired many Black workers during World War II.

In 1940, Blacks in Washington were greatly outnumbered by Native Americans and Japanese. By 1950, the Black population was four times as large. There were about as many Blacks in the state as all other minority races combined, according to the United States Census.

Most of the Black newcomers were from the American South. The southern Blacks had a different culture from the Northwesterners. They tended to have less education and different religious traditions, for example. But all Blacks had to live in the same parts of town because most housing in Seattle was segregated. (The federal government's public housing project was an exception. Seattle had the only integrated public housing in the country.) These areas quickly became crowded, and there were some conflicts. Some of the earlier Black residents blamed the newcomers for growing anti-Black prejudice in Washington State.

PUBLIC SCHOOLS DURING WARTIME

World War II had a great impact on Washington public schools. The rapid increase in population brought a serious problem of overcrowding. There were not enough classrooms for all the new students, and there was a wartime shortage of materials to build new schools. As a result, some classes met in hallways and basements; some students went to school only half day so that another set of students could use the school part time.

There were not enough teachers in wartime, either. Many teachers had joined the military or had taken higher-paying jobs in wartime industries. School districts were forced to take on retired teachers and underqualified people. An interesting result of the teaching shortage was that married women were also given the opportunity to teach. For many years, married women had been prohibited from teaching school. The Seattle School District also hired its first Black teachers during the war.

Throughout the state, school bus routes were changed during wartime because of a shortage of buses, gasoline, mechanics, and parts. Many students were asked to walk much farther to their bus stops, and some school buses were used to take workers to factories. Field trips and bus rides to athletic events were canceled.

Students in Washington schools were asked to participate in the war effort in several ways. War industries created part time jobs for students, and sometimes the school schedule was changed to allow students the time to work. This was true in farming areas, where all people participated in harvesting and other duties. Students also helped gather scrap metal for re-use by the United States armed forces.

In addition, the schools began offering vocational education classes to train workers for war industries. Aircraft construction, shipbuilding, and other technical classes were offered.

The State Superintendent of Public Instruction at this time was Pearl Wanamaker. Mrs. Wanamaker helped guide Washington schools through the rapid changes required by the war. She also fought for higher salaries and better training for teachers and helped reorganize the state's school districts.

WASHINGTON POPULATION, BY RACE, 1890-1970

	White	Black	Native American	Japanese	Chinese	Filipino	Spanish Language
1890	340,829	1,602	11,181	360	3,260	0	
1900	496,304	2,514	10,039	5,617	3,629	0	
1910	1,109,111	6,058	10,997	12,929	2,709	17	
1920	1,319,777	6,883	9,061	17,387	2,363	958	
1930	1,521,661	6,840	11,253	17,837	2,195	3,480	
1940	1,698,147	7,424	11,394	14,565	2,345	2,222	
1950	2,316,496	30,691	13,816	9,694	3,408	4,274	
1960	2,751,675	48,738	21,076	16,652	5,491	7,110	
1970	3,251,055	71,308	33,386	20,335	9,201	11,462	70,734*

HOW ACCURATE IS THE CENSUS?

Although census-takers try to be as accurate as possible, the census figures are never quite perfect. Minority groups often complain that the census does not give the true size of their group. Their complaints are often justified. There are several reasons why the census may give an inaccurate count of American minorities.

One problem is that the census is taken only once every ten years. The population of a minority group may change greatly in ten years. For example, the rapid increase in Filipino immigration since 1970 is not reflected in the figures above. Another important problem in counting minority groups is that it is not always easy to decide who belongs in what group. The following are some examples of the problems faced by census-takers:

1. Like many people from Argentina, Mr. "A" has a German name. He comes to the U.S. and marries a Chicano woman and they have three children. Spanish is the language spoken at home. Yet the whole family has a German last name. They may not be counted as Hispanic people.
2. The members of family "B" are all Filipino. But like many Filipinos, their last name is of Spanish origin. They may be counted as Hispanic people instead of Filipinos.
3. The "C" family are migrant farmworkers. They were traveling so often in the year of the census, that no census interviewer ever saw them. They were not counted.
4. Suppose the husband and wife are of two different races. How should the children be counted?
5. Should a person with one Asian grandparent, for example, and three white grandparents be counted as Asian? What factors should be considered?

The census bureau is always testing new methods to try to get a more accurate count. Can you suggest some specific questions or methods that might help? If you were taking the census, how would you do it?

* There have been people of Spanish names and language in this state since the 1890's, but the census did not count them as a separate group until 1970.

43. *Why were women able to get jobs in wartime that they had never been able to get before?*
44. *Over 20,000 Blacks came to Washington during the war. Where did they come from and why did they come here?*

How Did The War Affect Washington's Population?

Thousands of men and women of many races came to Washington during World War II. In fact, the war was responsible for the state's biggest population boom ever. The population here increased by 500,000 between 1940 and 1943. That's almost 500 people a day!

Thousands of people came to Washington on jobs that were related to the war. They worked at Hanford and at the many military bases around the state. Even more people came to find high-paying jobs with Washington's wartime industries. Most of these people settled in the big cities of Western Washington.

The sudden increase in population caused many problems. One of the biggest problems was a shortage in housing. A temporary answer to this problem was the building of housing projects. Schools also had a building shortage. To meet this problem, portables were added to many schools. Roads, sewers, electricity, food, clothing, and hundreds of other items had to be provided for the newcomers.

45. Why did so many people come to Washington during World War II?

How Did World War II Affect Washington Industries?

A huge amount of money was spent on weapons and war equipment in the United States. The United States government needed large numbers of ships, airplanes, trucks, tankers, guns, and other supplies. The factories that produced these and other war products made a lot of money during the war. Washington industries did especially well. This state ranked among the top two in the nation in the value of government war contracts per capita. ("Per capita" refers to the amount of money divided by the number of people in the state.)

Shipbuilding boomed. Ten times as much

These men are on the repair ship Houston, one of many U.S. naval ships that docked in Puget Sound during World War II. What other defense activities were located in the Puget Sound area?

money was spent on shipbuilding in 1942 as in 1939. There were 88 shipyards in the state during the war, giving jobs to about 150,000 workers. Some of the largest were the Todd Shipyard at Seattle and the Kaiser Shipyard at Vancouver. They built destroyers, small aircraft carriers, landing craft, cargo ships, and other vessels. At the time, 30,000 people worked at the Puget Sound Naval Shipyard at Bremerton. Ships were built and repaired there.

Another Washington industry that grew during the war was aluminum refining. No aluminum was produced in the state in 1940. But by 1942, one-third of all the aluminum produced in the United States was produced here. One aluminum plant alone was producing enough of this metal for 30,000 fighter planes a year.

Other industries also boomed. The Pacific Car and Foundry Company in Seattle built Sherman tanks, tractors, and trucks. The lumber industry in the state was important. Minerals such as lead, copper, and zinc were mined. Tacoma produced about one-tenth of the nation's copper and many chemicals needed during the war. The aircraft industry led the state with more than a billion dollars in contracts by 1942. In eastern Washington, farm production was at an all-time high.

46. Name at least four state industries that boomed during World War II.

RATIONING AND CONSERVATION DURING WORLD WAR II

During World War II, so many of our natural resources were being used for the war that there were shortages of many items. Most of our gasoline had to be used by the military, for example. There was not enough gas left for private citizens. As a result, the U.S. government began to ration gasoline. This means that each person was allowed only a limited number of gallons of gas. After their gas ration was used up, people were not allowed to buy any more until the next ration was issued. Sugar and meat were also rationed. Recycling was another wartime method of conserving resources. This photo was taken in wartime in downtown Seattle. People donated unused metal items, and the government recycled them for making military equipment. You can see from the large quantity of metal items that a great many people participated in this wartime recycling program. What items are being recycled in your community today?

What Did Boeing Do?

The Washington company that grew the most during the war was Boeing. Like many manufacturers, Boeing had boomed briefly during World War I, then struggled to survive through the 1930's. Due to military contracts, Boeing expanded greatly during the war. In 1940, the company had 4,000 workers. By 1944, the number had jumped to more than 45,000. Aircraft manufacturing has remained one of the state's biggest and most important industries.

During the difficult years of the Depression, Boeing had begun work on a bomber. They called it the B-17, or Flying Fortress. At the beginning of the war, Boeing was building nearly sixty B-17's a month; by December, 1943, this figure had almost doubled.

But the U.S. Air Force needed a bigger, longer-range plane. They needed a bomber that could fly at high speeds over long distances. In 1942, the Air Force awarded a contract to Boeing to build that new superbomber. This plane, the B-29, became an important part of the U.S. military activity in the Pacific.

Boeing planes played a major part in defeating Germany and Japan. More than one-half of all bombs dropped on Germany fell from Boeing bombers. Ninety percent of the bombs that were dropped on Japan were carried by B-29's, including the atomic bombs.

47. What two Boeing planes were used for most of the bombing in World War II?

A Secret In The Desert

Part of the research that went into developing the atomic bomb also went on in Washington, although hardly anyone knew it at the time. The location was the Hanford Atomic Works, in the Tri-Cities (Pasco, Richland, and Kennewick) area. In 1940, this area was a thinly populated desert. Only about 400 people lived in Richland at the time.

Now if you were the army, and you wanted to hide 51,000 people and a number of top secret buildings, where would you put them? Not in downtown Seattle, certainly. A desert was the obvious answer. And suppose you also needed large amounts of electricity. What desert would you pick?

The Army Corps of Engineers had exactly this problem in 1942. They needed a place to build a top secret atomic fuel factory for the war. They looked around the country for a location and settled on this part of Eastern Washington. It was perfect. There was rail transportation, power from both the Grand Coulee and Bonneville Dams, and no neighbors. The army bought more than 200,000 acres of desert property.

48. Why was the Tri-Cities area a perfect location for a top secret atomic fuel factory?

What Was The Mystery City?

Almost overnight, a "mystery city" sprang up. There were housing, mess halls, and work areas for 51,000 employees. Nearby, the tiny town of Richland (1940 population — 200) was undergoing a big change. A completely planned city was being built for 15,000 people to live in. This would be the administration center for the Hanford project.

Hanford employees were working on a project so secret that almost no one knew what anyone else was doing. Hanford's neighbors had some guesses. During election year, they joked that it was a factory to turn out Roosevelt's campaign buttons. Other people guessed that it was an expensive hideaway for high government officials. Almost no one knew the truth until after the war. Then it was announced that the Hanford Works had been part of the developing of the atomic bomb. The whole program included two other top secret bases and was known as the "Manhattan Project."

Today, Hanford is used for other purposes. There are research laboratories there and an atomic reactor which is used to generate electricity.

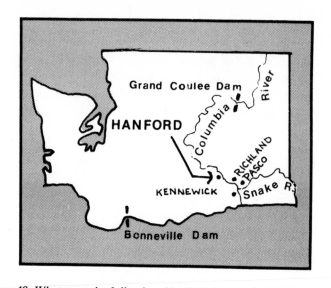

49. What were the following: Hanford Works, the Manhattan Project, the "Mystery City"?
50. How as Hanford used during the war? How is it used today?

Special Precautions

Because Washington is on the West Coast — relatively close to Japan — and because Boeing and other key defense sites are located here, some special precautions were taken during World War II.

The Boeing plant was hidden by camouflage. Using cardboard, paint, wire, and other materials, people built an elaborate disguise for the buildings. From the air, the plant looked like a residential neighborhood complete with cars, garages, fences, and other features.

In addition, many people were stationed at military bases all over the state. Some new bases were opened. There were more than 10 military posts in the Puget Sound area alone.

The bombing of Pearl Harbor had taken the country by surprise. There was widespread fear that Japan would attack the American West Coast. Because of this, many Americans felt that it wasn't enough to protect the area from attacks by the Japanese armed forces. These people believed that any person of Japanese ancestry might be dangerous. They believed that all Japanese people should be removed from the West. They even wanted to remove those people who had been living and working in the United States for many years, and even their children, who were born here and were American citizens.

51. What unusual precautions were taken in Washington during World War II?

BOEING'S BIG COVER UP IN WORLD WAR II
This peaceful looking neighborhood, photographed from the air, is not at all what it seems. No one lives in those tidy houses, no one drives down the streets or plays on the sidewalks. In fact, it's not a neighborhood at all! It's a Boeing plant under its wartime camouflage! Examine the photo to see if you can pick out the factory buildings.

How Did American Responses Change?

Actually, Japanese Americans were active and law-abiding members of the community. They were the largest racial minority in Washington State. The Japanese American Citizens' League (JACL) had held its first convention in Seattle in 1930. This group had been working to improve the welfare of Japanese Americans and to promote good citizenship.

The majority of the Japanese in this country considered themselves loyal Americans, even though the law prevented them from becoming citizens. Like all Americans, Japanese Americans were shocked by the bombing of Pearl Harbor.

After the bombing, Japanese American leaders denounced the government of Japan and declared their support of the United States. Around the country, many leaders praised all Americans of Japanese descent. They reminded the country that Japanese Americans were loyal and should not be mistreated because of their origins. Several of our highest ranking military leaders argued that the West Coast Japanese could not endanger the war effort.

Yet just two months after Pearl Harbor, President Franklin Roosevelt ordered the building of several internment camps in isolated areas. A month later the order came. All people in the western states with as little as one-eighth Japanese ancestry would be evacuated (removed). They would be forced to go to the camps. About 13,400 persons were evacuated from Washington State.

52. Outline some good arguments against suspicions of the Japanese Americans.

How Did Japanese Americans React?

The first families to be evacuated were those on Bainbridge Island. They were given only eight days to sell or store all their possessions, to arrange for someone to take care of their homes and farms, and to pack what little they would be able to take along. None of the Japanese American families on the coast were given enough time to prepare. Many of them had to sell their belongings for much less than they were worth. No one knew how their land and houses would be when they returned.

However, most Japanese residents of the American West Coast decided to obey the relocation orders peacefully. The Japanese American Citizens' League encouraged its members to cooperate with the government. They felt this would prove that they were loyal and law-abiding Americans.

Jimmy Sakamoto, a JACL leader and newspaper publisher, shared this attitude. "I stand to lose my living," he said. "I have a wife and two children to support and I also support my aged parents. I don't know what kind of work I can do in the interior. However, this is war. I'm a good American citizen and if I've got to go, I've got to go, that's all."

A few Japanese Americans actively protested the evacuation. One of them was Gordon Hirabayashi, a University of Washington student. Hirabayashi was a Quaker, (the Quakers are a religious group that does not believe in war) he already opposed the war on religious grounds. He refused to fight. He also refused to obey the special laws for Japanese Americans. He violated the special curfew and refused to register for the evacuation and was arrested, convicted, and sent to jail. He appealed his case to the United States Supreme Court, but the Supreme Court did not free him. Hirabayashi spent two years in jail for his protest.

In spite of the way they were treated by the United States government, many Japanese

Americans volunteered to serve in the United States armed forces. Over 20,000 Japanese Americans served in World War II, including an especially large number of Japanese Americans from Hawaii. (The people of Japanese ancestry who lived in Hawaii were never forced to go to internment camps. Japanese Americans made up quite a large percentage of the Hawaiian population, and they were needed to fill jobs during the war.)

An all-Japanese unit — the 442nd Infantry — served in Italy and France. The 442nd became

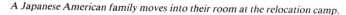
A Japanese American family moves into their room at the relocation camp.

WHAT WERE THE RELOCATION CAMPS LIKE?

The Japanese internment camps were like prisons in several ways. There were barbed-wire fences and armed guards. People were not allowed to leave.

They lived in barracks which had been quickly built. Some were not even finished at first and had no running water. Each family shared one room.

Many other factors made life in the camps unpleasant. They were located in deserts, where the temperatures were extreme and winds blew dust everywhere. The land was bare and unfriendly. There was not much to do. People grew bored and frustrated.

There was little privacy. Traditional family roles were broken down. For example, every-one ate together, so there was no opportunity for the family to be alone at meals.

On the other hand, the camps offered some people the first chance to really use their skills. Except for a few white directors, everyone who helped run the camps was Japanese American. There were Japanese American doctors, nurses, teachers, and supervisors. For many, it was the first time they were able to use their talents and gain confidence and pride in highly skilled jobs.

After a short time, some people in the camps were released to work on nearby farms. Others were able to get jobs in the Midwest and Eastern United States.

famous for their many heroic acts. They broke military records for the number of medals earned. Daniel Inouye of Hawaii, who later became a U.S. Senator, was one of many Japanese American soldiers who was injured while fighting for the United States. Other Japanese Americans served in military intelligence units in the Pacific battle zones.

53. Why did most Japanese Americans go along peacefully with the evacuation orders?

Internment Comes To An End

Some other Americans actively opposed the internment camps. These included the Council of Churches, the American Civil Liberties Union, and Washington Congressman John Coffee. Representative Coffee called the evacuation "a mockery of the Bill of Rights." But the United States Supreme Court refused to declare the evacuation an unconstitutional act.

In 1945, the Supreme Court ruled that the camps had to be closed. By then the war was almost over, and the Japanese Americans had already begun returning home. The administration had already decided that internment should be ended and that people should be released.

But each family was given only $25 and the price of their tickets home. Many returned to find their houses and property stolen or gone. They had a hard time finding jobs.

A large number of Japanese Americans decided not to return to the West Coast at all. Some of them stayed where they had been sent to work during the war. Others moved to eastern and midwestern cities. Between 1940 and 1950, Washington's Japanese population dropped from 14,565 to 9,964.

ANTI-JAPANESE PREJUDICE
IN OTHER COUNTRIES

The United States was not the only country to pass laws that discriminated against Japanese immigrants. Canada and Mexico both passed exclusion acts in the 1920's. There was an anti-Japanese riot in Vancouver, British Columbia. Mobs broke all the windows in Japanese-owned buildings. British Columbia also forced its Japanese residents into wartime relocation camps in 1942.

---

54. When and why were the relocation camps ended?
55. What happened to Japanese Americans after they were released from the camps?
56. What was the 442nd Infantry?

What Problem Was Caused By The Wartime Boom?

The manufacturing industries of Washington boomed during wartime. Wages in the factories were high. From around the country, people came to Seattle and other Washington cities to look for jobs. Many people left the rural areas of Washington to come to the cities for work.

At the same time, the agriculture industry was becoming increasingly important. Food was badly needed by the United States and its allies. Washington farmers could sell all the crops they could possibly produce.

However, the farmers had a problem. Many people had left farming areas to join the armed forces or to work in the cities. There was a farm labor shortage, just as there had been in World War I. Children, old people, and office workers in rural areas all helped with the work, but more people were still needed.

57. Why were farmworkers badly needed during World War II?

Where Did the Wartime Farmworkers Come From?

The United States government made several arrangements to provide workers for Northwest farms. There was a prisoner-of-war camp for captured German soldiers located in the Yakima Valley. These prisoners worked in the fields.

In addition, some of the Japanese American men in the internment camps were released to do farmwork. The farm wages were very low, but they were higher than the wages that could be earned in the camps. Farmers appreciated the Japanese American workers because they did such a good job. Even though their families were locked in internment camps, these Japanese Americans made an important contribution to the war effort. They helped save some of America's badly needed crops.

However, there were not enough Japanese Americans or German prisoners to fill the needs of all the farms around the country that needed help. A larger group of farmworkers was needed. The United States and Mexican governments worked out an agreement for Mexican workers to come work on American farms. The workers would be guaranteed housing and health insurance and a minimum wage. They would not be allowed to replace American workers. The United States promised that farmers would not discriminate against the Mexican workers. The workers would return to Mexico after the harvest was over.

This was called the bracero program. ("Bracero" is a Spanish word that comes from "brazo," which means "arm." The meaning of bracero is similar to the English expression "hired hand.")

The first braceros came to the United States in 1942. Thousands of workers came to Washington in the years that followed. The braceros were responsible for saving important crops all over the country.

58. Name three groups of people who worked on Washington farms during the war years.
59. What was the bracero program?

When Did The First Mexicans Come To Washington State?

The braceros were not the first people of Mexican background to come to Washington State. People of Mexican background had been coming to the Yakima Valley since the 1890's. But most of them had worked here only a short time. They returned to their homes in Mexico or in the area sometimes called Aztlan. In the early 1900's, some Mexican citizens came north to work in the canneries in Alaska. Then they returned to Mexico.

In the 1930's, Chicanos, who are American citizens of Hispanic background, moved here from Wyoming, Colorado, Montana, and Texas. They had been working on farms in these states, but after the Depression started, there were very few jobs. Many Chicano farmworkers became unemployed. Some of them moved to farmland areas of the Yakima Valley to try to find work. Chicano communities began to grow in several towns of Eastern Washington.

60. When did the first people of Mexican background come to Washington?
61. Why did many Chicanos come to Washington during the 1930's?

SOME PROGRESS BY CHICANOS

Some of the Chicanos and Mexican Americans from Washington opened restaurants and small businesses. Some went to the cities to work in wartime industries. By the end of the war, several Washington towns and cities had permanent Chicano communities.

Many Chicanos from Washington and around the country joined the United States armed forces. The 88th Division was made up mostly of Mexican Americans. Many members of the 88th and other Mexican Americans won medals for their bravery during the war. One American soldier, José Lopez, received the highest medal of the United States and also the highest medal of Mexico.

After the war, many Chicanos took advantage of their veterans' benefits and went to college. Partly as a result of the veterans' programs, there are now Chicano professionals in all fields, including education, government, law, business, and entertainment.

What Problems Did Chicanos And Braceros Face?

Unfortunately, braceros experienced racial prejudice in Washington State, as in the rest of the country. Chicanos also experienced prejudice. For example, Chicanos and braceros were not allowed in Yakima area taverns or theaters in the 1940's. Chicanos were prevented from getting good, high-paying jobs. Many bracero and Chicano farmworkers were forced to live in poor, unsanitary housing. Employers were supposed to provide food for the braceros, but often this food was as cheap and poor as possible.

Further problems were caused after the war was over. The bracero program was supposed to be a wartime program, designed to take care of a wartime labor shortage. After the war, there were more people in the Yakima Valley and fewer jobs. There were plenty of American workers of Chicano and other racial backgrounds who needed work.

But growers liked the braceros because they were a cheap, dependable labor supply who left town after the harvest. They asked the government not to stop the bracero program. Senator Warren Magnuson and other United States legislators from Washington supported a continued bracero program for the Northwest. They were successful. The bracero program was kept going until 1964.

WHO ARE THE MEXICAN AMERICANS?

Centuries before Columbus came, the land we now call Mexico was the home of several great civilizations. There were busy cities, built around huge stone temples. There were experts in astronomy, mathematics, and other studies who developed a very accurate calendar and wrote many books. There were artists and architects who created beautiful works of art. The people of these highly developed cultures were Native Americans. They were the early ancestors of today's Mexicans and Mexican Americans.

Cortes and other Spaniards conquered many of the Native American civilizations of Mexico. The Spanish destroyed most of the great stone temples and built Catholic churches instead. They killed many people. They destroyed the books and much of the art. The King of Spain gave away land to Spaniards without paying attention to Indian claims. Spanish priests opened missions among the Indians. Here, Indian workers ran the farms and mission businesses, and the priests taught the Catholic religion. The Spaniards and their descendants became the upper classes and the landowners, while the Indians worked for them and became the poor classes.

People in the Spanish settlements adopted the Catholic religion and the Spanish language. But there were few Spaniards and many Indians. Most of the Spanish settlers were men. They married Indian women. Over the years, a race and a culture developed that was a blend of Spanish and Indian background. The mestizos became the biggest racial group. ("Mestizo" is a Spanish word which means "of mixed race.")

In 1810, Mexico became independent from Spain. Soon afterward, American settlers began moving into Mexican territory — into lands now the southwestern United States. The Americans wanted the land and felt they ought to have it. They refused to obey Mexican laws. The American population in Texas and California became quite large.

In 1836, Texas declared its independence from Mexico. (Calfornia declared its independence a few years later.) The Mexican Army tried to stop the secession of Texas, but it was unsuccessful. In 1845, the United States annexed Texas (made it part of the U.S.). Mexico considered this an act of war.

In 1846, war broke out. The United States Army invaded Mexico. Despite some brave attempts to

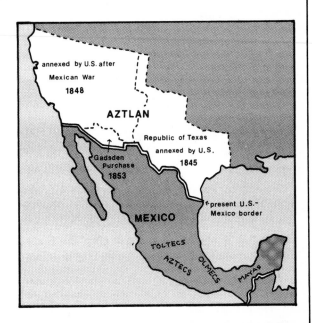

resist, Mexico was forced to surrender. In 1848, a peace agreement was signed in the village of Guadalupe Hidalgo. In this treaty, the United States paid 15 million dollars and received about half of the territory of Mexico. This area is sometimes called "Aztlan." The United States promised certain rights to the 80,000 Mexicans who lived in this area. They were promised the right to keep their lands and to become American citizens. In 1853, the United States purchased another piece of land from Mexico, called the Gadsden Purchase.

Some provisions of the treaty of Guadalupe Hidalgo were not honored. Many natives of this area had their land taken away. This ethnic group has suffered discrimination because they speak Spanish and have a different culture.

In the twentieth century, thousands of Mexicans have come to the United States legally or illegally. Some of them worked here for a while and then returned to Mexico. Others stayed, and the Mexican American population grew and spread to different parts of the United States.

Today, the term Mexican American is used to describe people who were born in the modern country of Mexico and who later moved to the United States. The people of Aztlan are often called Chicanos.

Meanwhile, wages and working conditions for both braceros and American farmworkers remained poor. Chicanos in Washington State and around the country became involved in efforts to try to improve their working conditions. Chicanos have been among the earliest organizers for agricultural workers' rights. In Washington, for example, Chicanos were among the workers who tried to go on strike against the hops farmers in 1933. The strike was organized by the IWW. (See Unit 8 for more information on this union.) It was unsuccessful. Some strikers were beaten and jailed. In recent years, Chicano farmworkers have been more successful at organizing unions to raise wages and improve working conditions. (For more information, see pages 214-5.)

62. List some problems of braceros in Washington.
63. Why was the bracero program continued after the war?

How Did World War II Affect Filipinos In Washington?

Japanese planes bombed the Philippines on the same day as they bombed Pearl Harbor. A few days later, Japanese forces invaded and conquered the Philippines.

Many Filipinos living in America rushed to enlist in the U.S. armed forces. They were anxious to help defend both their native land and the nation where they had made their new home. Again, the Filipinos encountered discrimination. They were refused admission to the armed forces. Finally, President Roosevelt issued special permission for Filipino soldiers. Two all-Filipino combat units were formed. They won many medals during the war.

Combined U.S. and Filipino forces drove the Japanese out of the Philippines in 1945. The next year, the country became independent as planned.

THE END OF GALLOPING GERTIE
Tacoma citizens were proud of the modern new bridge across the Tacoma Narrows. It opened on July 1, 1940. But their pride turned first to surprise, then to horror: the bridge wouldn't stay still. The engineers had not accounted for the winds that blow across the Narrows. Not too long after it was finished, the bridge began to move. Like a giant concrete snake, it lifted and fell in graceful waves. Residents nicknamed the bridge, "Galloping Gertie." During a severe windstorm on November 7, it collapsed. Fortunately, no one was killed. Another bridge was built and still stands today.

The Filipino soldiers' bravery helped change popular American attitudes toward this Asian group. After the war, Filipino veterans were allowed to become American citizens.

During and after the war, many single Filipino men had a chance to return to the islands

Washington's Asian populations have continued to grow. How did World War II effect the Japanese and Filipino American population of our state?

WASHINGTON'S GROWING ASIAN POPULATIONS

Name of Group	Chinese	Filipinos	Japanese	Korean	Vietnamese
number of immigrants arriving in 1970	299	877	figures not available	228	
1971 immigrants	251	750	figures not available	327	
1972 immigrants	360	662	figures not available	339	
1973 immigrants	285	759	figures not available	468	
1974 immigrants	324	738	131	721	
1975 immigrants	407	820	figures not available	771	4,283

These figures are courtesy of the Asian American Demonstration Project.

and marry. Since they were citizens, the men could bring their wives to the United States with them. The Filipino population of Washington increased. This is sometimes called the "second wave" of Filipino immigration.

64. Why did Filipinos here want to join the U.S. armed forces during World War II?

65. Name at least two important effects of Filipino participation in World War II.

This irrigation canal brings water to farms in the Yakima Valley.

Compare this photo of Seattle taken in 1975 to some of the earlier Seattle photos in this book. What are some of the most important changes? In what important ways have the lives of the people in Washington changed in the last few decades? How is your life different from your parents' lives?

UNIT 10

THE MODERN PERIOD

It's hard to imagine life without television, yet Washington had no TV stations until 1948. Most people are now accustomed to freeways for long-distance auto trips, yet Washington's interstate freeways only opened in the 1960's. It's hard to imagine Seattle, Spokane, and other big cities without their surrounding ring of suburbs. Yet the rapid growth of suburbs is also a recent development.

Many things which we now take for granted have only been commonplace since World War II. The War marked a key turning point in the state's population, in the state economy, and in the lifestyles of most people who lived here.

As you read this unit, pay attention to the ways that our recent past has affected the present. Ask yourself how Washington is changing now. How can this understanding of the past and present help us make better plans for the future?

The unit has two sections:

1. Economic Ups and Downs
2. Working for Equal Rights

SECTION 1: ECONOMIC UPS AND DOWNS

The End Of World War II

In April, 1945, President Roosevelt died and Vice-President Harry S. Truman became President. In May, 1945, the war in Europe ended, but the Japanese still had to be defeated. Allied military leaders believed that the Japanese home islands would have to be invaded. In August, 1945, events took place which made this invasion unnecessary. The first atomic bomb was dropped from a Boeing B-29 on August 6. It destroyed the Japanese city of Hiroshima. Three days later, a second bomb was dropped on the city of Nagasaki. After these two bombings, Japan surrendered. There was no need to invade the Japanese home islands.

Members of the American armed forces started coming home from the war. Almost 500,000 of them came first to the military bases in Washington State. Some of the war veterans decided to stay here. Other people who had come here earlier to work in the state's wartime industries also stayed. The new residents were attracted by the pleasant environment and the high standard of living which Washington offered. By 1950, the state population had grown to almost 2.4 million.

1. Why did many military personnel and wartime workers choose to stay in Washington after the war?

Women sail out to welcome returning soldiers at the end of World War II. What changes had taken place in Washington while the soldiers were gone?

Adjusting To A Peacetime Economy

Washington industries lost much of their wartime business after World War II. The shipbuilding and airplane and other defense industries could not use as many workers. There was a short recession. Up to 120,000 people were unemployed, including laid-off workers and returning veterans.

During this time, industries were switching over to a peacetime economy. Factories that had made weapons got ready to make trucks, home appliances, and consumer goods instead. The Boeing Company offers a good example of this process. In the late 1940's , Boeing continued to develop new bombers and was able to sell some to the United States military. But the demand for bombers was much lower than it had been during the war. In order to develop a new source of income, the company decided to invest most of its money in the development of a new passenger plane. The result was the Boeing 707, the first passenger jet. It was ready for production in 1954, and became one of the best-selling airplanes ever built. Because of the 707 and other successful passenger jets, Boeing was able to expand rapidly in the 1950's and 1960's.

Other Washington companies were able to make successful changes, too. More jobs were created in peacetime industries. By the early 1950's, Washington State and the rest of the country had entered a time of growth and prosperity.

2. Why was there a short recession after World War II?
3. What new products helped Boeing expand rapidly in the years after World War II?

Prosperity

In the middle of the 20th Century, industrial growth and personal prosperity went hand-in-hand. Average family incomes climbed steadily during this period. The median income in Washington increased from $3,523 a year in 1950 to $10,407 in 1970 — nearly three times as high. This meant that people had more money to spend. They were able to buy more products. So local businesses were able to produce and sell more goods.

Growing businesses meant more jobs. These jobs attracted more people to the state. Washington's population continued to grow faster than that of most states, and the larger popula-

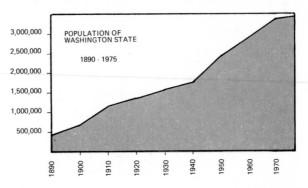

By 1978, the state population was 3,774,300 — an increase of more than 300,000 since the 1970 level of 3,409,169.

tion created an even bigger local market for goods. The economy was booming, and unemployment decreased, reaching a low of 3.5% in 1968.

4. Explain how industrial growth and personal prosperity went hand-in-hand.

How Did Lifestyles Change?

Growing prosperity, along with technological developments, brought several changes in lifestyles. People were able to buy more time-saving machines, such as cars and dishwashers. They had more leisure time and more money to spend on entertainment.

More people went to college, too. Many veterans had had their education interrupted by the war. They had given service to their country, and now the government repaid them in part by paying for their college education. Universities in this state grew as more and more veterans took advantage of this opportunity. Colleges continued to grow as the children of these veterans reached college age. The state legislature created several new community colleges in 1965, and the state's four-year colleges expanded.

Another government program helped veterans buy houses. Because of this assistance program and the higher income levels of this period, large numbers of young families were able to buy their own homes. The construction industry boomed as thousands of new houses were built. A large number of these new houses were built in the suburbs of big cities, such as Seattle and Spokane. The growing size of the suburbs was another important trend of the post-war years.

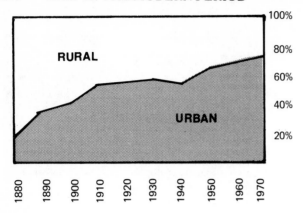

5. Name some lifestyle changes that resulted from economic prosperity.

Why Did The Suburbs Grow?

The post-war decades brought building booms to cities around the state. Big new commercial and industrial buildings were going up in Spokane, Seattle, and other large urban centers. The smaller cities were growing, too. New industries were locating in the cities, creating more jobs, and attracting people from rural areas.

MC CARTHYISM IN WASHINGTON STATE

One of the most powerful issues of postwar America was anti-communism. The Soviet Union had fought together with the United States against Germany during World War II. But soon afterward, the United States and the Soviet Union became suspicious and distrustful of each other. Russian control and influence were spreading rapidly in Europe, and many Americans believed that the Soviets wanted to dominate the world. They believed that there were many spies, communists, and sympathizers who were helping Russia to overthrow the United States government.

A kind of national panic, or hysteria, resulted. Both the United States Congress and the Washington State Legislature formed committees to investigate "un-American activities."

Although these investigations were conducted by elected representatives, their methods were obviously unconstitutional. People accused of being pro-Russian or communist were assumed guilty until they could prove their own innocence. They often were not given a chance to defend themselves. They did not have the right to a trial. The Constitution guarantees freedom of speech and freedom of the press. But those who were accused often lost their jobs. Hundreds of writers and actors in the film industry and more than 1,500 federal government employees lost their jobs as a result of the investigations. Many were unable to find other employment in their career area. Several committed suicide.

Unfortunately, several politicians made use of the committee investigations to advance their personal careers. The best known of these politicians was Senator Joseph McCarthy. From 1950 to 1954, he led a powerful Senate committee which attacked the Army, the State Department, the CIA and other government agencies. McCarthy claimed that many employees of these agencies were working to weaken or overthrow the United States government. Although he had little or no evidence for these claims, McCarthy attracted a great deal of publicity and public support. He became one of the most powerful politicians in the country. Today, the word McCarthyism is used to describe this style of public accusation without clear evidence. Other public officials became very critical of McCarthy, and in 1954, the Senate voted to censure (publicly criticize) him.

The Washington State Legislature created its own Committee on Un-American Affairs in 1947. Its chairman was State Representative Albert F. Canwell of Spokane. Several notable Washington State citizens were accused before the Canwell Committee. Some of these people lost their jobs, others suffered for years from public hostility. None of them were tried in court and allowed to defend themselves. Chairman Canwell even ordered some of the defendants' lawyers out of the room. (A defendent is the person who has been accused.)

The story of Melvin Rader is a good example. Rader was a philosophy professor at the University of Washington. He had been active in liberal and humanitarian issues, but he had never joined the Communist Party. However, an informer named George Hewitt testifed that Rader had attended a secret school for high-level communist leaders.

Rader chose to fight the charge. (Other accused professors refused to say anything at all to the committee.) He gathered the evidence to prove his innocence. But he was not allowed to present it for more than a year. Finally, a series of articles by *Seattle Times* reporter Edwin Guthman publicly cleared Melvin Rader. He was awarded a Pulitzer Prize for his articles.

The Canwell Committee hearings were discontinued in 1948. Representative Canwell was not reelected, but he continued to accuse Rader and others of "un-American" activities.

The McCarthy period was an example of the loss of some people's constitutional rights. But it was not the first time it had happened. During other critical times in our history, such as the Civil War and World Wars I and II, some constitutional rights have been suspended. The World War II internment of Japanese Americans (Unit 9, Section 3) and the "Red Scares" after World War I (Unit 8, Section 3) are examples. As you will see in Unit 12, citizen involvement is always necessary to help protect our constitutional rights.

This photo shows two symbols of postwar prosperity for many Americans: a car and a new house. Why were so many families moving to the suburbs?

The population of Washington was becoming increasingly urbanized.

Yet during this period of urbanization, some of the cities themselves began to lose population. Where did the people go? More and more of them were moving to the suburbs. By 1975, the fourth largest and fastest-growing city in the state was Bellevue, a suburb of Seattle.

The cities were becoming noisy and crowded. The suburbs offered bigger houses and yards, more open space, and newer, quieter neighborhoods.

Thousands of newcomers to the state, as well as Washington residents, moved to the suburbs. To support this growing population, a great deal of new construction was required. Schools, libraries, hospitals, roads, and sewage systems had to be built. (Tax money paid for most of these, as well as police and fire protection and other government services.) In addition, shopping centers, restaurants, gas stations, and many other businesses were built in the suburban areas. By the 1970's, the east side of Puget Sound was beginning to look like a "megalopolis" — a totally developed urban area, with unbroken suburbs between the urban centers.

Serving the new communities, and the state as a whole, were thousands of miles of new roads. During the 1960's, the state's major interstate freeway building took place. I-5, the new Lake Washington floating bridge, the Hood Canal floating bridge, and most of I-90 were built at this time.

6. Why did many people move to the suburbs?
7. What is a megalopolis?

How Did Washington Industries Change?

World War II brought many changes in the state population. It also marked an important turning point for Washington industries. Before the war, the state economy had depended mainly on raw materials such as logs and lumber, fish and wheat. Since the mid-20th Century, however, many more finished products are being made in this state. For example, more logs are now made into plywood, insulation board, chipboard, paper, plastics, doors, and wall panels; and they are sold as finished products rather than raw lumber. Potatoes are turned into french fries, instant mashed potatoes, and other products. Fruits, vegetables, and meats are canned and frozen. Aluminum is used to make window frames, doors, campers, and trailers, as well as airplanes.

Different parts of the state have worked hard to attract new factories. Spokane, Tacoma, Pasco, and other cities have developed industrial parks. At these locations, there is land to build factories on, available power, and transportation facilities. Bellingham worked hard to get its new aluminum plant. Richland and Kennewick are working now to attract more projects into the Hanford Atomic works.

It is good for the entire state that different kinds of industries are growing. This kind of diversification makes the state economy stronger. With many industries and many different products, the state can still prosper, even if there is a drop in the demand for one product.

8. What basic change in Washington industries took place after World War II?
9. How does diversification make the economy stronger?

How Did Agriculture Change?

Non-manufacturing industries have also undergone important changes since World War II. Agriculture is an example. In 1952, the irrigation system of the Grand Coulee project was put into operation. (This part of the project had been delayed by the war.) Water from Lake Roosevelt, behind Grand Coulee Dam, was delivered to the dry lands of Eastern Washington with huge pumps and a system of canals and reservoirs. Over one million acres were irrigated.

The population of this entire Central Washington area has more than doubled since 1950. The towns of Moses Lake, Othello, and Quincy more than tripled in population between 1950 and 1960. Because the land is able to support many more farmers, there is a need for machinery suppliers and all the businesses that make up a modern farming community.

The Columbia Basin project is not yet complete. More land will be brought under irrigation in the next decades. The growth of this region will continue to provide more jobs in the area, and more products that will be sold throughout Washington, the United States, and in foreign countries.

Some of the crops produced in this state have also changed. Improved varieties of wheat are being grown in the dryland areas. Irrigated lands are now producing sugar beets, potatoes, grapes, and other newly important crops.

By the 1970's, Washington State led the United States in producing apples, hops, and spearmint. Washington was also among the top five states in the production of grapes, peppermint, strawberries, pears, sweet cherries, sweet corn, alfalfa, asparagus, peas, potatoes, and winter wheat.

While the value and number of crops increased, the number of farmers was decreasing. New farming methods depended on big investments in expensive machinery. Only a very large farm could use these machines efficiently. Many small farms went out of business. Agriculture was becoming big business, sometimes called "agribusiness."

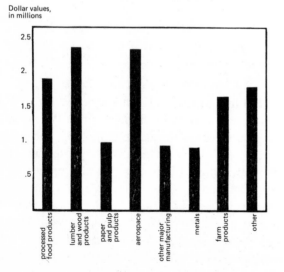

VALUE OF WASHINGTON INDUSTRIES, 1973

Dollar values, in millions

2.5

2.

1.5

1.

.5

processed food products | lumber and wood products | paper and pulp products | aerospace | other major manufacturing | metals | farm products | other

10. What important engineering project was completed in 1952?

11. Washington is among the top five states in the production of several crops. What are they?

12. Why did the number of farms decrease?

What Other Industries Were Growing?

Other industries changed and developed in the post-war decades. The growth of foreign trade was especially rapid. In 1960, the total value of exports and imports from Washington State was somewhat more than one billion dollars. By 1968, the value of the state's foreign trade had doubled. By 1971, it had doubled again, to more than four billion dollars. In the next three years, the value of imports and exports doubled still again — to eight billion dollars in 1974. (These figures do not include Vancouver and other Washington port cities in the Portland trade area.)

Transportation to and from Washington State has continued to improve. The Seattle-Tacoma Airport was opened in 1949 and now ranks third in the nation in the number of overseas passengers. More flights are made to Alaska from Sea-Tac than from all other airports in the world combined. In the 1970's, Sea-Tac was remodeled, and a new terminal was completed at the Spokane International Airport.

New building has also improved shipping in the state. Many ports are now equipped to handle containerized cargo. Dams and locks on the Snake and Columbia Rivers have made it possible to take barges as far as Pasco, Washington; and, in season, as far as Lewiston, Idaho. Ocean-going vessels can travel as far up the Columbia as Portland and Vancouver. (For more information, see Unit 11, Section 5.)

Transcontinental railroads plus some shorter railroads also serve the state. Some of these railroads connect with railroads in Canada. Trucking companies provide service throughout the state and to the rest of the country.

Washington's defense industries have also grown. Since 1950, the United States had been almost continually involved in military conflict somewhere. The Korean War lasted from 1950 to 1953. In 1954, the country started to become involved in the longest war in its history: the war in Vietnam. The United States did not pull its troops out of Vietnam until 1974. Washington's military bases were busy, as thousands of ships and soldiers came through. Also, many companies here produced weapons and war supplies. In 1970, Washington ranked fifth in the amount of federal defense money coming into the state.

Reduction in the federal government's defense spending is felt immediately in Washington because it means fewer job opportunities.

13. Mention at least two building projects that contributed to the increased value of trade.

WHAT WERE SOME KEY ECONOMIC EVENTS?

1949 — SEA-TAC AIRPORT WAS OPENED. The coast-to-coast trip that once took six months or more could now be made in a few hours. Businesses benefited from improved transportation.

1950-3 — THE UNITED STATES was involved in the war in Korea. This was followed by involvement in the Vietnamese War, until 1974. Both brought business for Washington's weapons manufacturers and other industries.

1952 — THE GRAND COULEE IRRIGATION SYSTEM BEGAN DELIVERING WATER TO FARMS IN EASTERN WASHINGTON. Crop production boomed on irrigated land. Much new land was opened for farming.

1953 — A SUGAR REFINERY WAS BUILT AT MOSES LAKE. Sugar beets had become an important crop in Washington. The Moses Lake factory became the largest beet sugar refinery in the Americas. Other food processing plants were also being opened in Eastern Washington.

1954 — THE FIRST OIL REFINERY WAS BUILT AT FERNDALE. There are other refineries at Anacortes.

1955 — BOEING PRODUCED THE 707. Boeing planes had started carrying passengers in the 1930's. Back then, the passenger company was known as Boeing Air Transport. It later became United Air Lines — the nation's largest airline. The 707 was Boeing's first passenger jet (as opposed to the older, slower propeller models). Boeing sold a lot of 707's and went on to build even larger jets. The 747 superjet was first flown in 1969.

1956 — NATURAL GAS BEGAN COMING TO THE STATE THROUGH PIPELINES FROM CANADA AND THE SOUTHWESTERN UNITED STATES. A new fuel was available to homes and businesses.

1962 — THE SEATTLE WORLD'S FAIR WAS HELD. Century 21 boosted tourism, retail sales, and other industries.

1964 — FOUR PRIVATE COMPANIES MOVED INTO THE HANFORD WORKS. Each company agreed to bring other businesses into the Tri-Cities area.

1966 — THE SIXTH ALUMINUM PLANT IS BUILT IN THE STATE. This plant at Ferndale became the largest aluminum plant in the world.

1968 — BOATS WERE ABLE TO TRAVEL UP THE COLUMBIA AS FAR AS THE TRI-CITIES. The Army Corps of Engineers had been dredging (digging) and improving the river channel for many years. Cities on the river benefited from improved transportation.

1968 — OIL COMPANIES DECIDED TO BEGIN DEVELOPING THE OILFIELDS AT PRUDHOE BAY, IN ALASKA. Many individuals and businesses sold supplies to the pipeline builders. Many workers and goods passed through the ports in this state.

1969 — BOEING LOSES BUSINESS AND BEGINS LAYING OFF WORKERS. Eventually, more than 50,000 aerospace workers in the state lost their jobs.

1973-4 — ENERGY SHORTAGES AFFECTED NORTHWEST BUSINESSES AND CONSUMERS. There was a national shortage of gas and oil, and droughts led to a shortage of hydroelectric power in the state. Droughts also hurt wheat and other crops.

1974 — SPOKANE HOLDS A WORLD'S FAIR. Expo '74 brought increases in tourism and other businesses and left the city with a new cultural center.

THE IMPORTANCE OF RESEARCH

Many of the new manufactured products are the result of recent research and technological development. Governments, universities, and large industries all employ researchers to develop new methods and products. There are also some private research companies in the state, including Battelle Memorial Institute, which has offices in Seattle and Hanford.

There are many research projects currently underway including the following: The federal government has built test windmills near the Columbia River to study the possibility of wind-generated electricity in the Northwest. Researchers at the Lummi Indian Aquaculture project are studying nutrition of salmon raised in saltwater pools. The Weyerhauser Company has chemists, computer programmers, soil and forest scientists, geneticists, and other experts working to grow healthier, better trees in a shorter time. Students and faculty at the University of Washington medical school are looking for new cures for diseases.

14. Why is federal defense spending important to Washington?

Seattle Puts On A Fair And Invites The World To Come

Although Washington is distant from most world population centers, tourism has recently become one of our most important industries. This industry received a tremendous boost in 1962. That year, Seattle put on a world's fair, called Century 21. The fair succeeded in attracting people from all over the world. By the end of the year, the city had a wide reputation as a center for tourism.

Century 21 featured exhibits from countries in Europe, Asia, Africa, and North and South America. Several American businesses had exhibits, too. There were restaurants serving food from many countries. And there were all kinds

The Pacific Science Center is one of the outstanding buildings left over from the Century 21 Fair. It was designed by Seattle architect Minoru Yamasaki. Yamasaki's work is now well-known around the country. What other buildings from the fair are still being used?

of entertainment, including roller coasters, movies, performances, and technological displays.

Architectural highlights of the fair included the country's first monorail, the Pacific Science Center, and, of course, the Space Needle.

Century 21 made a profit and brought great amounts of trade and tourism to the city in 1962. It also left the city with a large public park, convention center, and entertainment center. The fairgrounds are now called the Seattle Center and include an opera house, a playhouse, an arena, a coliseum, several large meeting rooms, and a branch of the Seattle Art Museum.

15. What was Century 21?
16. What Century 21 buildings are still used by Seattle?
17. What important industry was boosted by the World's Fair?

This photo shows the inside of a Boeing airplane plant. The company had come a long way since Bill Boeing built his first tiny factory on the shores of Lake Union. The Everett plant alone covered 63 acres! It was in Everett's giant ten-story building that the first 747 superjet was built.

The Boeing Boom

Many state businesses boomed in the 1960's. But one company "outboomed" them all. That company was Boeing. Boeing engineers had been full of confidence from the successes of their World War II bomber designs. They went on to design a series of faster and more modern planes. The B-47 "stratojet" bomber was perfected in 1947. In 1952, Boeing produced an updated jet bomber called the B-52. In addition to the 707, there were the 727, the 737, and finally the giant 747 superjet. Other Boeing designs of those years included rockets, helicopters, and plans for the fastest aircraft yet— the supersonic transport (SST).

From around the world, the orders came pouring in. The armed forces and airline companies from this country and many others were buying Boeing planes. Boeing stepped up production and hiring and by 1968 employed 101,500 people. That accounted for more than half the manufacturing jobs in the state!

18. What is the largest manufacturing industry in Washington?

Over-Dependence On One Industry

Meanwhile, some people were beginning to worry that too many people — in Seattle especially — had become dependent on Boeing for their income.

Years earlier, Seattle had been dependent on lumber in much the same way that it was now dependent on the aerospace industry. Back then, when the demand for lumber went down, the city suffered a recession. By the 1960's, economists worried that the same thing could happen again. If Boeing lost business, the results might be disastrous. A healthy economy is a diversified economy, they said. (A diversified economy is one that is based on several important industries.) But Boeing had plenty of business then, and economic disaster seemed a long time away.

It wasn't. In 1969, Boeing lost some federal contracts, and commercial airlines stopped ordering so many new planes. Boeing began laying people off. By 1973, the company had fewer than one half of the 1968 number of employees. Meanwhile, Seattle's unemployment skyrocketed. Fifteen percent of the city's labor force was on the unemployment lists in 1971 — one of the highest levels in the country! Somebody put up a billboard out by Sea-Tac airport saying, "Will the last person leaving Seattle please turn out the lights."

Not only Boeing employees lost their jobs. Thousands of other people whose jobs depended on business from Boeing and its employees were also out of work. The fruit and wheat production in Washington was down in 1968 and 1969, too. This added to the statewide recession.

19. Why were some people worried that Seattle had become too dependent on one industry?
20. What effects did the decline in Boeing's work force have on the Seattle area?

Handling The Hunger Problem

As the layoffs continued, more and more people ran out of money. They had spent their savings and used up their unemployment insurance payments. Hunger became a real problem.

The economic crisis in Seattle was unusual because of the kinds of people affected by it. Normally, a recession hits hardest at unskilled or non-unionized workers and minorities. However, the long lines of people at Seattle's unemployment office included a high number of skilled workers and professionals. In this sense, Seattle's crisis resembled the Great Depression of the 1930's.

The state and federal programs did not help all hungry people in Seattle. So local churches, synagogues, and private individuals organized a service called "Neighbors in Need." Neighbors in Need set up 34 "food banks" to provide free food for the hungry. They made 300,000 donations in the first year alone and stayed in operation for more than five years.

21. What was Neighbors in Need?
22. Why was Seattle's recession unusual?

Economic Problems

The hardships of unemployed Washington workers were made even worse by inflation. Across the country, prices were rising rapidly. Even workers who had not lost their jobs were having financial problems. They found that their paychecks just did not go as far as they used to.

As the level of inflation kept growing, so did the level of unemployment. Millions of Americans were laid off their jobs. By 1974, the unemployment level in many U.S. cities was as high or higher than it was in Seattle.

It is unusual to have such high inflation and high unemployment both at the same time. Inflation has usually occurred in this country during times of economic growth and prosperity. American economists could not agree on what had caused the economic problems of the 1970's. They also could not agree on how to solve the problems. In 1971, President Nixon

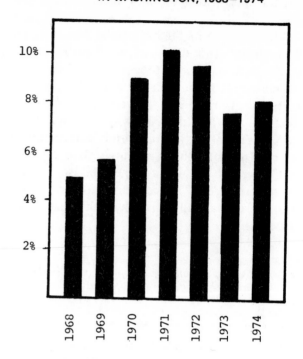

PERCENT OF UNEMPLOYMENT IN WASHINGTON, 1968–1974

called for a national wage and price freeze. He declared that no prices or wages could be raised for three months. During the following year, increases would be regulated by the government. These policies helped hold down prices for a while, but they failed to solve the underlying economic problems. Economists still could not agree about what to do.

The inflation of the 1970's had an effect on lifestyles. Food and fuel especially became so expensive that many people changed their eating and driving habits. For example, the average price of beef rose from 80 cents a pound in 1967 to $1.15 a pound in 1972 — almost a 50% increase in five years. Magazines and newspapers were full of suggestions for less expensive meals.

Gasoline prices almost doubled in 1973 and 1974, a time of a serious fuel shortage. There were long lines at gas stations, and a shortage of heating fuels. The heat was turned down in schools, homes, stores, and workplaces; and people tried to drive their cars less. That summer, fewer people drove long distances on summer vacations. In 1979, there was another gasoline shortage, with similar effects.

23. Why was the economic situation of the 1970's unusual?
24. Why did many people change their eating habits?
25. What were some effects of the fuel shortage of 1973-74?

How Did Low Rainfall Cause Other Fuel Shortages?

The Northwest suffered from another kind of fuel shortage in 1973: a shortage of electricity. The winter and spring of that year had been unusually dry. The rivers and lakes behind the hydroelectric dams were at their lowest level in 30 years. Less water going over the dams meant that less power could be produced.

Experts warned that another dry winter could cause a serious loss of electricity. Washington's governor, Dan Evans, urged businesses to turn off their electric signs and to turn off their lights at night. Individuals were asked to cut down on their use of electricity, too.

Fortunately, the autumn rains and snowfall of 1973 were quite heavy. The worst of the electric shortage never came. But people here learned that the weather might have a serious effect on their energy resources.

The winter of 1976-7 brought another serious drought to the Northwest. Governor Dixy Lee Ray again asked the people of the state to conserve electricity. Very little snow fell in the mountains that winter. Ski resorts were unable to open, and they lost a lot of money. Farmers in Eastern Washington worried that there would not be enough irrigation water for next year's crops. They were in danger of losing large amounts of money, too. Fortunately, 1977 was a wet year. The crops survived, and losses were much lower than expected.

26. What caused an electricity shortage in the Northwest in 1973 and again in 1976?
27. Why weren't the shortages as bad as they could have been?

A Pipeline

One result of the national fuel shortage was the decision to build the Trans-Alaska pipeline system. Ever since the 1920's, American companies had known of rich oil deposits in northern Alaska. But at that time, there was no efficient way to get the oil out.

In 1968, the oil companies decided to begin developing the North Alaskan oil fields. But first, they would need a way to transport the oil. They proposed a pipeline — either across Alaska to a shipping harbor, or across Canada to the United States. The Alaska pipeline was preferred, but there was strong opposition to both

The dam at Snoqualmie Falls generates electricity. How might low rainfall reduce the amount of electricity that could be produced here?

plans. Environmental groups warned that the pipeline could easily destroy the ecological balance of the Alaska wilderness. They took the issue to court. In 1969, the court ordered that pipeline work be stopped for environmental reasons.

However, the fuel shortage of 1973 convinced many Americans that Alaskan oil was needed. The pipeline construction was started.

A lot of people and equipment for the Alaska pipeline left from Seattle. Washington businesses and individual investors profited from the Alaska business. Washington companies made tools, equipment, housing, and other supplies for the pipeline camps. Shipping companies here were hired to transport the goods to Alaska. Other people made money by investing in Alaska real estate.

28. How did the fuel shortage affect the Alaska pipeline?

Economic Recovery

Supplying the pipeline was not the only new source of jobs in Western Washington. Lumber industries, shipbuilding, and trade were expanding. There were more service jobs and more government jobs available. Slowly, Washington's economy was recovering.

The highest level of unemployment was reached in 1971. After that, Washington began adding new jobs at a rate nearly twice as high as the United States as a whole.

In the Seattle area, the rate of growth was even higher. Electronics, truck and railroad equipment, and machinery manufacturing were among the expanding industries. Job opportunities in trade and manufacturing were expanding still more rapidly.

Since the recession of 1970, Seattle has been working hard to enlarge its economic base. The efforts have been fairly successful. By 1975, only 12.5% of the jobs in the Seattle area were with the aerospace industry. Seattle's unemployment rate had dropped to about 8%. In the middle 1970's, this was actually lower than the unemployment levels in many American cities. However, 8% is considered a high level of unemployment in this country.

Economic recovery was more complete in Eastern Washington, which had not been hit so hard by the 1970 layoffs. The eastern cities such as Spokane did not experience such big booms as Seattle, but they didn't experience the dramatic economic downturn either.

The economic base of Eastern Washington had been growing. Electric power from the dams provided power for aluminum plants and other industries. The Tri-Cities area had benefited from ship transportation on the Columbia River and from new industries at Hanford. New mineral refineries were built near Spokane. Food processing plants were built near areas where crops were grown.

In 1978, 26,000 industrial jobs and 75,000 jobs in trade and services were added to the state's employment pool — more new jobs than in any one year before, except 1966.

29. What new industries helped make the economic base of Eastern Washington grow stronger?

If Seattle Can Do It, Why Not Spokane?

For a few years in the 1800's, Walla Walla was the biggest city in Washington, and the eastern part of Washington Territory had a bigger population than the western part. (For more information, see the description of Washington's gold rushes, on pages 120-1.) But ever

---

NUCLEAR POWER COMES TO CENTRAL WASHINGTON

The nuclear industry first came to Washington State in 1942. That was the year the government began building the Hanford project. More than 50,000 workers began manufacturing plutonium—the fuel for the atomic bomb.

In 1952, President Dwight Eisenhower announced the beginning of U.S. government support for ''peaceful uses'' of nuclear power. Since then, the federal government has spent billions of dollars on nuclear research and aid to private industries involved with nuclear power.

A lot of this money has come into Washington State. Hanford was one of the first nuclear-powered electric generating plants. It has been a central storage area for the radioactive waste materials produced by nuclear plants around the country.

There have been some problems associated with Hanford. Some of the poisonous waste stored there has leaked out. A portion of it got into the Columbia River. And some researchers believe that radiation from the plants has caused high cancer rates among workers.

But the Hanford site is important to the Tri-Cities economy. It was sold in 1964 to four private companies and now brings private, as well as government funds into the area. It provides many jobs. Because of Hanford's economic importance, it has received the support of elected officials in Central Washington.

CHANGING EMPLOYMENT PATTERNS 1968 - 1974

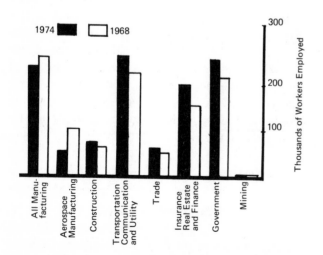

1974 ■ □ 1968

Thousands of Workers Employed

300

200

100

All Manufacturing | Aerospace Manufacturing | Construction | Transportation Communication and Utility | Trade | Insurance Real Estate and Finance | Government | Mining

since statehood, Western Washington has had most of the state's population.

People in Eastern Washington often complain of neglect. They say that the political power of the state is all on the west side of the mountains. The big western cities always get their way, they feel. Once in 1909, the Spokane Chamber of Commerce had even asked that Eastern Washington be made into a separate state. The Columbia River would be the border between a smaller state of Washington and a new state, called Whitman or Lincoln. This idea did not gather enough support, and it was abandoned. However, some feelings of resentment still remain.

Residents of Spokane believed their city deserved better treatment. They boasted that Spokane was the biggest city between Seattle and Minneapolis. Spokane was the capital of the "Inland Empire," the rich farmland of the Columbia Plateau. People in Spokane were proud of their city and believed it deserved recognition.

Business leaders of Spokane got together and decided to try to win that recognition in a big way. They decided to put on a world's fair. If Seattle can do it, so can Spokane, they believed. A world's fair would bring in enough money to fix up part of the city, and afterwards Spokane could have a cultural and entertainment center like Seattle's. Tourism and other Spokane businesses would benefit. A world's fair would really put Spokane on the map.

The area around this clock tower in Spokane used to be run-down and unattractive. It was rebuilt as part of Expo '74.

30. Why do people in Eastern Washington often complain about the western half of the state?
31. What are Spokane's special "claims to fame" as a city?
32. How could Spokane benefit from a world's fair?

Doing The Impossible

Fair planners chose ecology as the theme of Spokane's Expo. They called it "Celebrating Man's Fresh, New Environment." Such a current popular topic would help attract both exhibits and visitors. But there was one embarrassing problem. The location selected for this ecology-minded fair was an island in the Spokane River in a run-down section of downtown Spokane. The river was polluted. So was the air.

Fair planners and Spokane officials decided that this was a perfect opportunity to improve Spokane's environment. A river clean-up was organized, involving governments in Washington and Idaho. The run-down buildings were torn down; grass and trees were planted. At the end of the fair, Spokane had a clean river, an attractive downtown park, and a civic and cultural center which the city can keep on using.

Many people believed that a city as small as Spokane could never put together a world's fair. Most people had never heard of Spokane, critics argued. And when they did hear of it, they pronounced it wrong, saying "Spokain." But Spokane was able to do the impossible. Expo '74 won national and international attention. The United States government chose Expo '74 as the kick-off event for the nation's bicentennial celebrations. Many foreign nations set up exhibits at the fair, and visitors came from around the world.

33. What was Spokane's embarrassing problem? How was it solved?
34. What special recognition did Expo '74 receive from the United States government?

SECTION 2: WORKING FOR EQUAL RIGHTS

What Factors Helped Create A Sense Of Unity?

World War II had been an important common experience for all groups of Americans. Whites, Blacks, Asians, and Native Americans, foreign-born and American-born citizens had all worked together to help win the war. Women and men, people of all ages, had shared in a common effort under their common government.

After the war, modern technology brought other kinds of shared experiences. Thanks to better transportation and greater mobility, more Americans were moving and traveling. They had a chance to become acquainted with other American lifestyles. Television, radio, and other modern communication systems brought the same information to every home.

A wheat farmer in Whitman County and a factory worker in Tacoma might have very different jobs, income levels, and lifestyles. But they could learn the same news and watch the same people on television each evening. They could learn about and buy the same products. Their homes might even look very similar.

The federal government was also responsible for growing similarities in the lives of Americans. Since the Great Depression of the 1930's, the role of the federal government had been growing. People of all lifestyles in all parts of the country were affected by federal government assistance and regulations.

35. How did each of the following bring Americans closer together and give them more shared experiences: World War II, television, the federal government?

The Response To Inequality

Many factors of the postwar period allowed Americans of all groups to have more shared experiences. At the same time, however, some groups were realizing that they were not free to share all the benefits of American life. Black soldiers had fought as hard as whites during the war. Women and men workers had contributed equally to the war effort. Yet when the war was over, a great number of women workers and minorities were laid off. Salaries for most women and minorities remained low in spite of the postwar boom. (See the graph below.)

One of the most important historical trends of the postwar period involved the efforts of women and minority groups to achieve true equality in America. Washington State groups participated in each of the national movements. The largest struggle for equality was the Civil Rights Movement of American Blacks.

World War II had marked an important turning point in Black attitudes. America and its allies were fighting Germany. Germany's terrible discrimination against its minorities was one of the main issues of the war. (The German government murdered six million Jews and hundreds of thousands of other minorities.) Many Blacks complained that America opposed dis-

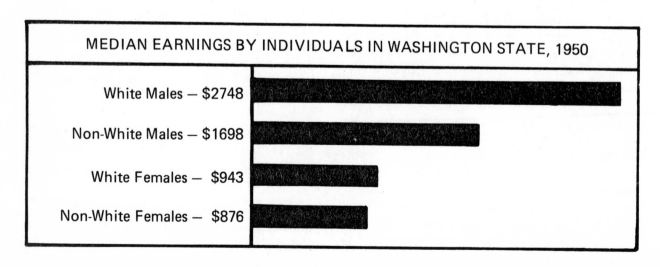

MEDIAN EARNINGS BY INDIVIDUALS IN WASHINGTON STATE, 1950

White Males — $2748

Non-White Males — $1698

White Females — $943

Non-White Females — $876

crimination in Europe but practiced it at home. Some defense industries refused to hire Blacks. In the Army, they were assigned to segregated units. In the other services they were allowed to serve in only a few jobs.

American Blacks were angry. They joined to demand an end to this discrimination. A Black leader named A. Phillip Randolph organized 50,000 Blacks to march on Washington, D.C., in May, 1941. (Randolph had earlier organized a union of railroad porters.) President Roosevelt tried to talk Randolph out of holding the march, but he stood firm. Finally, the President gave in. He ordered an end to racial discrimination in war industries, and he set up a committee to enforce this rule. After the President took these actions, Randolph called off the march.

In Washington State, Blacks were protesting discrimination in some industries. The President's order opened more Washington jobs to Black workers.

36. What were many American Blacks angry about during World War II?
37. Why did A. Phillip Randolph organize a march on Washington and why did he call it off?

What Was The Civil Rights Movement?

Blacks around the country continued to protest discrimination. Then in 1955, a southern minister, Martin Luther King, Jr., organized a boycott of the Montgomery, Alabama, buses. Before this time Blacks on these buses had been forced to give up their seats to whites. Now they refused to use the buses until this policy was changed. (This is a boycott.) They were successful.

In the years that followed, Blacks in Washington and around the country used boycotts, demonstrations, and other methods to fight discrimination. This became known as the Civil Rights Movement, and Reverend King became its outstanding leader.

The year earlier, 1954, was an important one for Blacks. That year, the United States Supreme Court ruled that segregation of schools on the basis of race was unconstitutional. This ruling led to busing and other desegregation methods.

38. Name two events of the 1950's that greatly affected American Blacks.

WHAT GROUPS WORKED FOR RACIAL EQUALITY BEFORE WORLD WAR II?

There was some progress in the area of minority rights before the war. The NAACP (National Association for the Advancement of Colored People) had been formed in 1905 by W.E.B. duBois and others. The NAACP and the Urban League — both organized and staffed by Blacks — helped Black Americans obtain better housing, education, and other services. The NAACP focused on legal issues affecting Blacks. By 1930, both these organizations had branches in Seattle.

Christian Friends for Racial Equality was a multiracial group founded in the 1940's to combat discrimination. It was headed by Edith Steinmetz and concentrated on issues that most directly affected people such as discrimination in jobs, restaurants, and theaters. Seattle had an anti-discrimination group in the 1940's called the Civic Unity Committee.

Some New Deal programs had helped Blacks, and President Roosevelt prohibited racial discrimination in war industries. He also hired several Black Americans for high-level positions in the government — such as Mary McLeod Bethune, a respected educator who became director of the Office of Minority Affairs. The federal government sponsored a Seattle Negro Repertory Theater in Seattle during the 1930's. This theater company included as many as 90 people. For most of the company, this was their first opportunity to be professional actors. They were directed by Florence and Burton James of the University of Washington, and they performed several plays by Black writers.

After the Congress of Industrial Organizations (CIO) was formed in 1935, some labor unions began recruiting Black members. CIO unions were open to all workers in an industry. For example, everyone in the steel industry from janitors to welders could join the same CIO union. This was unlike the AFL unions which were open only to workers with the same skill (truckdriving, cabinetmaking, etc.) . AFL unions usually did not allow minorities to join at that time.

Winning More Rights

A very important issue of the Civil Rights Movement was voting rights. The fourteenth and fifteenth amendments to the United States Constitution guaranteed that all U.S. citizens could vote. These amendments were passed in 1868 and 1870. But more than 80 years later, in 1960, large numbers of Black citizens could not vote. Southern states used many methods to keep Blacks from registering and voting. Without the vote, Blacks had no political power. They could not influence government decisions. They could not enjoy the same rights and freedoms as other American citizens.

Another key problem was segregation. In Washington and other states, most Blacks could find housing only in certain, older areas of the cities. Property owners and real estate agents would not rent or sell housing in other areas to Blacks. These segregated areas tended to be more run-down and crowded than other areas. Black families who tried to rent or buy homes outside the segregated areas were usually turned away or told that the house was no longer available. This was true in Seattle, Spokane, and other cities all over the country. The Bremerton Navy base had one living area for whites and another for Blacks. The Hanford works had segregated living areas, too.

In addition, Blacks were not allowed in many restaurants or theaters. Most high-paying jobs were not open to Blacks. Other minority races suffered the same problems in many parts of the country.

39. Name two key issues of the Civil Rights Movement.

EDWIN PRATT

The 1960's were often viewed as a decade of violence, because of the several tragic assassinations of those years. In addition to the Kennedys and Dr. Martin Luther King, Jr., several other civil rights leaders were killed. One of them was Edwin Pratt, executive director of the Seattle Urban League. Pratt realized that his life might be in danger, but he continued with his efforts to integrate Black Americans into Washington State communities. He became a respected civil leader.

One evening in 1969, he heard a noise at the door. Someone had thrown a rock at the house. Pratt opened the door to investigate. Mrs. Pratt was standing by the window in the next room and she saw a man outside with a gun. She tried to warn her husband not to open the door, but it was too late. The shot struck Edwin Pratt, and he died instantly. The murderers escaped and were never identified.

Pratt's murder attracted national attention. He was honored by a city-wide day of mourning in Seattle, and a "freedom mural" at Seattle University was dedicated to him. There is also an Edwin T. Pratt Memorial Scholarship Fund, which provides tuition grants to non-white students. The fund is supported by contributions from individuals and organizations and is administered by the Seattle Urban League.

What Civil Rights Laws Were Passed?

Around the country, people of all races were working to stop segregation and to win equal rights for all citizens. A key event in this effort was the Civil Rights March of 1963. This was the biggest protest march ever to take place in Washington, D.C. One of the march's chief organizers was Dr. Martin Luther King, Jr.

Black and white civil rights supporters in Washington State participated by staging a march in Seattle on the same day as the Washington, D.C., demonstration. There were civil rights protests in Kennewick and other Washington cities in 1963, too. Both Martin Luther King and his wife, Coretta, visited Seattle in the 1960's.

The tremendous efforts of Civil Rights supporters led to two important federal laws. One law prohibited discrimination and segregation in jobs and public places. The other law prohibited discrimination in voting. They were passed in 1964 and 1965.

40. Name three important events of the Civil Rights Movement from the years 1963-65.

From Outside The System To Inside

Some people, both Black and white, had died in the Civil Rights struggle. And it was not over. Blacks and other American minorities have continued to work and organize to win equal rights and opportunities.

After 1966, the minority rights movement in Washington — as in other states — became more radical. "Black Power" replaced "civil rights" as the name of the movement. Black Power leader Stokely Carmichael spoke in Seattle in 1967. Soon, Washington State had a Black Panther Party.

During this same period, Black Washingtonians were becoming more active in all levels of state government. In the 1960's, several Blacks were elected to public office. For example, Charles M. Stokes, Sam Smith, and George Fleming were all elected to the state legislature from Seattle. Stokes later became a judge of the Seattle District Court, and Sam Smith became president of the Seattle City Council. In 1970, Peggy Maxie became the first Black woman elected to the legislature here.

There were several outstanding Black lawyers in Washington in the 1960's. For example, a

Peggy Maxie

victed in 1964. In 1966, Smith became the state's first Black superior court judge. Later, he became assistant dean of the University of Washington Law School.

Most of Washington's Black population live in the big western cities. However, Eastern Washington was the home of one of the state's best known Blacks of the post-war period. He was Arthur Fletcher of Pasco. Fletcher served on the Pasco City Council, and was a candidate for lieutenant governor of Washington in 1968. In 1969, President Nixon appointed him Assistant Secretary of Labor.

41. Identify the following: Sam Smith, Charles Z. Smith, Peggy Maxie, George Fleming, Arthur Fletcher.

Black attorney, Charles Z. Smith, was recognized for his leadership in the case against Dave Beck. Smith's work on the Beck case impressed Attorney General Robert Kennedy, who hired him to lead the government case against another Teamster leader, James Hoffa. Hoffa was con-

Citizen Organizations Protest The War In Vietnam

Citizen organizations were active in the 1960's in other fields besides civil rights. The war in Vietnam, especially, sparked years of protest activity in Washington State — as it did in the rest of the country. There were major demonstrations in Washington, D.C. almost every year until the Vietnam conflict finally ended in 1975.

Seattle and other Northwest cities usually had local demonstrations in support of the larger

Washington citizens organized large marches to protest the war in Vietnam. What other methods did they use?

marches in Washington, D.C. In addition, there were many local protest rallies, especially at the universities. Thousands of Washington voters wrote letters to government leaders protesting the United States role in Vietnam. Many young men here and in other states refused to go into the army after they were drafted. Some of them went to jail rather than fight in Southeast Asia. There were speakers, discussions, and anti-war protests of all kinds.

The most dramatic anti-war protests — both here and around the United States — were those of 1970. That spring, President Nixon ordered American troops to invade the country of Cambodia, as well as Vietnam. The President's action brought protests in cities and college campuses throughout the country. Some of the demonstrations were violent, and at Kent State University in Ohio, National Guardsmen fired guns at demonstrators, killing five of them.

The Kent State killings led to even stronger protests. In Seattle, for example, there was a whole week of demonstrations. Thousands of students at the University went on strike, and the campus was closed down for one day of mourning. There were marches on the University of Washington campus, in the downtown business district, and even on the I-5 freeway. One downtown march attracted more than 10,000 people.

42. What events caused the dramatic anti-war protests of 1970?

43. How did people in Washington State participate in national anti-war protests?

What Else Were Citizens Groups Doing?

Other causes were also gathering energy during the 1960's. The environmental movement was becoming increasingly important, and there were some important successes. The Seattle area won national attention for its success at cleaning up the water of Lake Washington. These clean-up efforts were started by citizen activist groups. (More information on Lake Washington will be found on page 290.)

Other citizen groups in Seattle organized to plan for the area's future. One group wanted local governments to build adequate road and sewage systems, and they wanted to set aside open land for parks and recreation. They realized that this had to be done before it was too late — before all the land was used up by suburban developments. The group proposed a number of projects, and called their plan "Forward Thrust."

The Forward Thrust programs were voted on in 1968. Several of the programs were approved by voters, including over 300 million dollars' worth of improvements. The Waterfront Park in Seattle was a Forward Thrust project, as were millions of dollars of sewer improvements. Other projects were turned down. One of these was a rapid transit system that would have carried area commuters to downtown Seattle by rail.

The Waterfront Park in Seattle. How were citizen groups involved in the development of this park?

In the 1970's, public and private groups worked to preserve or improve the quality of cities around the state. Some important urban preservation and development programs included the Public Market in Seattle and the Havermale Island area in Spokane (which was the site for Expo '74). Both of these projects won broad community support.

44. Name some areas of citizen activist concern in the 1960's.

What Issues Did Native American Groups Work On?

The oldest minority group in Washington, and the first to protest their treatment by the white majority, were Native Americans. The Indian rights struggle that began with Leschi, Kamiakin, Peo Peo Mox Mox and other tribal leaders had not died. After World War II, Native Americans in this state were actively working to restore their treaty rights and to improve their living conditions.

The treaties were official agreements — somewhat like laws — between the United States government and the tribes. But the government broke their treaty promises many times.

Two main controversies involving the broken treaties came up in Washington in the 1970's. One debate involved the fishing rights which were legally guaranteed by the treaties but not enforced. (General background on this issue is given in Unit 6, Section 1.)

The other important treaty issue was tribal land. The treaties had guaranteed certain pieces of land to the tribes as reservations. In the years since the treaties were signed, the government had taken away much of this land. For example, the army had illegally taken 300 acres from the Nisqually reservation. This land was added to Fort Lewis, and the Indian residents were forced to move to land that was not part of any reservation. Other reservation land was taken by private investors, who acquired it at prices below its true value.

A large number of Native American protests in Washington in modern times have centered on these two issues. The box on this page gives some examples.

Daybreak Star Arts Center

NATIVE AMERICAN EFFORTS TO REGAIN LAND

Many of the Native American protests of the 1960's and 1970's were attempts to regain land. This was true in Washington State and in other parts of the country as well.

In 1970, a group called United Indians of All Tribes invaded and claimed Fort Lawton in Seattle. At that time, the army was using only a small portion of the old Fort. The rest of the land was not being used. The Indian group, led by Bernie Whitebear, demanded that Fort Lawton be turned into an Indian education center.

The city at first refused. They wanted the land for a park. Talks continued for a year between United Indians and the government. Finally, a settlement was reached. United Indians of All Tribes Foundation got 20 acres; the rest of the Fort would become a city park. The 20 acres were dedicated in 1974 by a Sioux religious leader named Lame Deer. Today, this is the location of a multi-purpose Indian cultural center called "Daybreak Star."

At about the same time, other Native American land claims were being made in Tacoma by the Puyallups. The Puyallup reservation had once included some of the most valuable land in this city. The total reservation was 18,000 acres. By the 1880's, the city had grown to the reservation's edge. Businessmen wanted the Puyallups' land for railroads, for its timber, and for development. They lobbied Congress for permission to buy the land. Over the years, whites managed to buy most of the reservation land. By 1970, only 20 acres remained in tribal ownership.

As the Puyallups lost their land, they also lost educational and medical services. These services are only provided to Indians who live on reservations. Tribal chairwoman, Ramona Bennett, led the Puyallups in a number of protests. Sit-ins, demonstrations, and court action were used to try to regain lost land. The Puyallups also worked to set up special health and educational facilities for the tribe.

Other Native American groups around the state were also taking the government to court over broken treaties. For example, the Colville and Spokane tribes were still trying to get payment for tribal losses due to the Columbia River dams.

45. Name two ways that the U.S. government had broken the treaties of 1854 and 1855.

On And Off The Reservations

In the twentieth century, a large part of Washington's Native American population chose to move away from the reservations. Cities offered more job opportunities and a chance to get away from federal control. However, Native Americans who lived off reservations had many disadvantages. They were not eligible for some government programs. Reservation tribes received medical, economic, and educational assistance from the federal government. And reservations helped preserve tribal identity, tribal culture, and an Indian way of life.

Also, some reservation tribes were able to develop their own businesses. For example, the Lummi tribe was developing a profitable "aquaculture" business. (Aquaculture is the business of growing seafood in a controlled environment. It is like farming the sea.) The Lummis built saltwater ponds where they now raise salmon and other seafoods. These foods are sold in North America and Europe. The Swinomish tribe operates a fish-processing plant. The Quinaults are also in the fish-processing business. These businesses have meant more jobs, higher incomes, and greater independence for tribal members.

46. What are some advantages of life on a reservation?
47. Describe the Lummi tribe's aquaculture business.

What Services Did Indian Groups Provide?

Meanwhile, other Indian groups were trying to find ways to meet the many needs of urban Indians in Washington State. One of these groups was the Indian Women's Service League which was started in 1958 by Pearl Warren. The service and social activities programs started by Ms. Warren's group are now housed in the Seattle Indian Center in downtown Seattle. The center's programs include counseling, emergency food and clothing, legal services, and job referrals, as well as recreation. The center also runs a shop where American Indian crafts are sold.

Elizabeth Morris attracted national attention for her work as director of the center in the 1970's. In 1974— her last year with the center —

Respect for tribal customs is an important part of modern Native American activities. Many traditions are being revived. Canoe races such as this are a part of yearly Indian festivals in the Pacific Northwest today.

she was selected for a Woman of the Year Award by the Seattle chapter of Women in Communications.

Institutions such as hospitals and schools have often discriminated against Indians and have failed to meet their special needs. Better health care and education services have been especially needed. Some reservation and urban Indian groups have begun to set up their own clinics and schools. For example, Bernie Whitebear and United Indians helped set up an Indian clinic in Seattle. A noted speaker and Indian activist named Janet McCloud set up one of the first Indian Heritage schools for Nisqually children. The Colville and Yakima tribes are developing special cultural and educational programs on their reservations.

48. Identify the following: Pearl Warren, Elizabeth Morris, Janet McCloud, Seattle Indian Center.
49. Why have Indian groups set up their own clinics and schools?

What Asian Americans Were Elected to Office?

Just 20 years after the Japanese were ordered to report to relocation camps, the first Asian American was elected to the Seattle City Council. He was a Chinese American named Wing Luke. Luke was the first American of Asian background to win any major election outside of Hawaii. In his short career as a councilman, Luke worked hard for progressive issues such as open housing, human rights, Indian fishing

Wing Luke

rights, and the protection of Seattle's historic districts. Unfortunately, Wing Luke was killed in a plane crash in 1965. He is remembered by several memorials; an elementary school, an Asian art museum, a scholarship, and a youth award have all been named for him.

In the years after Luke's death, several other Chinese Americans were elected to public office in the Seattle area. Liem Tuai became president of the Seattle City Council; John Eng became a state representative from Seattle; Ruby Chow was elected to the King County Council; and Warren Chan became the first Superior Court judge of Asian descent on the West Coast.

50. Identify the following: Wing Luke, Liem Tuai, John Eng, Warren Chan, Ruby Chow.

What Groups Make Up The Asian American Population?

The major Asian American groups in this state continue to be Japanese, Chinese, and Filipinos. (For the histories of these ethnic groups in the state, see Unit 7, Section 2 and Unit 9, Section 1.)

There are also several other smaller Asian groups in this state, including people of Korean, Samoan, and Southeast Asian origins. After World War II, the Korean War, and the war in Vietnam, many American soldiers returned with Asian wives. Thousands of other people have immigrated from Asian countries.

The most recent Asian group to arrive in Washington are the Vietnamese. After U.S. troops were pulled out of Vietnam in 1974, many Vietnamese families chose to move to the United States. They lived in refugee camps on the West Coast until American families or citizen groups volunteered to "sponsor" them. A sponsor would support and help the family until they had learned English, found jobs, and adjusted to American life.

51. Name some different origins of the Asian Americans who live here.

A Story The Census Didn't Tell

The 1970 census showed the Japanese Americans and Chinese Americans in this state had attained high average educational levels and high average incomes compared to other racial groups, including whites. Americans of Japanese, Filipino, Chinese, and Korean backgrounds had made contributions to the state in

---

SOME IMPORTANT DATES IN ASIAN AMERICAN HISTORY OF THE 1950's TO 1970's

1952	— People of Japanese origin became eligible for U.S. citizenship.
1962	— Wing Luke became the first Asian American outside Hawaii to be elected to a major political post. He became a Seattle city councilman.
1965	— Immigration laws revised. Discriminations against Asian people were finally taken out of the laws. The immigration of Asian women and Filipino immigration have increased rapidly as a result.
1966	— The Alien Land Law — which had been used to prevent Asian Americans from owning land — was finally repealed.
1974-75	— Vietnamese immigrants were arriving in the United States after the end of United States involvement in the war in Vietnam.

the arts, the sciences, business, and government.

Yet a 1973 study in Seattle by the Asian American Advisory Council showed that Asian Americans were still discriminated against. For example, jobs in health professions, news media, education, the construction industry, and some public services were not usually open to Asian Americans. Many Asian professionals had lower salaries than other people with the same education. And Asian Americans were still the subject of racial stereotyping in books, television, and other media.

One racial stereotype of Asian Americans has been the belief that they are passive and quiet. Actually, Asians have been active union organizers during most of their history in America. Asian workers helped organize the first cannery workers' unions in the Northwest, for example. Filipino Americans have been active in organizing agricultural workers and fish cannery workers on the West Coast. The earliest Japanese workers acted together to demand better working and living conditions on work crews for the railroads and mines. These last groups

A demonstration by Asian Americans in Seattle's International District.

were not formal labor unions, but they served the same purpose quite effectively.

Today, Asian Americans are actively working for many community goals. They have been working to establish special schools, clinics, and community centers. There are now a Filipino center, a Japanese center, a Chinese center, and a Korean center in Seattle. Social services, recreational activities, and ethnic studies are available through the centers. Bilingual programs have been started in Seattle, Tacoma, and other Washington school districts.

52. What problems were Asian American leaders trying to solve in the 1960's and 1970's?

What Non-Minority Was Discriminated Against?

One group that worked for equal rights in the 1970's was not a minority. In fact, they numbered about 53% of the country's population. Yet statistics showed they earned much less on the average than the rest of the population. They were discriminated against in jobs, finance, marriage laws, and other areas. What was this group? Women!

Women of all races had lower average earnings than men (see graph on p. 214). In Spokane, for example, about 25% of the male workers earned over $10,000 a year, but only 3% of the working women earned this much. Around the state, most working women held low-paying clerical or service jobs. Only 11% belonged to unions.

Women usually had trouble getting loans, and married women could not enter some kinds of business and financial contracts without their husband's permission. A number of state laws discriminated against women in other ways.

The words "feminism" or "women's liberation" were used to describe the movement to change the laws, economic practices, and public attitudes which discriminated against women.

53. Name some ways that women have been discriminated against.
54. What is feminism?

What Was The E.R.A.?

In order to change the state's discriminatory laws, a constitutional amendment was proposed. It was called The Equal Rights Amend-

WASHINGTON WOMEN IN GOVERNMENT

State Representatives Phyllis K. Erickson of Parkland and Frances North of North Bend.

Women in Washington began winning elective offices before most American women were allowed to vote. Clara McCarty and Lizzie Ordway were two of several women who were elected county school superintendents while Washington was still a territory. Bertha Landes of Seattle was the first woman mayor of a large American city. Several women have served on the Seattle City Council. Belle Reeves was secretary of state in the 1940's. By the 1970's, Washington had women judges, senators, representatives, council members, mayors, county commissioners, and even a sheriff.

For many years, two women represented Washington voters in the United States Congress. They were Julia Butler Hansen and Catherine May. Catherine May was the first elected, in 1958. She was a Republican from the Yakima area and served until her defeat in 1970. President Nixon later named her to the railroad board.

Julia Butler Hansen was first elected in 1960. She rose to the powerful position of chairperson of the House subcommittee in charge of appropriating money for parks, hydroelectric dams, Indian reservations and related programs. She retired in 1974.

Hansen had spent almost all her life in the small town of Cathlamet, Washington, where her parents had been active in politics before her. Her father had been sheriff, and her mother served as superintendent of schools. Julia Butler Hansen's own career included work as a secretary, author, swim instructor, dietician, company manager, and Washington State representative. She was also the first woman elected to the Cathlamet City Council, in 1937.

---

ment (ERA) and it read: "Rights and responsibilities under the law shall not be denied or abridged because of sex." ("Abridged" means limited, or cut short.) The state ERA was passed by the state legislature in the winter of 1972. The state amendment was then submitted to state voters as a referendum in November. (All amendments to the state constitution must be approved by both the legislature and the voters.)

A statewide campaign committee was formed to distribute information on the ERA before the November election. Women's groups from around the state participated, including the League of Women Voters, NOW (National Organization for Women), the Feminist Coordinating Council, and Washington Women Lawyers. One of the lawyers served as co-chairperson of the campaign. She was Betty Fletcher, President of the King County Bar Association.

The ERA passed, although the vote was so close that final results were not announced until

three weeks after the election. Some of the effects of the ERA are discussed on pages 280-81.

55. What was the ERA?

What Else Did Women's Groups Do?

The ERA was one of the first issues supported by the newly formed Washington State Women's Political Caucus. This group, founded by Black, White, and Chicana women of the state, has also supported the campaigns of women candidates.

At the same time, women's groups have been working in other areas, too. Several court cases were started against employers who illegally discriminated against women. NOW and other groups continued to protest discrimination against women on the part of television and other public media. Feminists, educators, and the American Civil Liberties Union worked to-

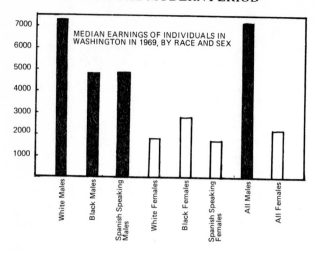

Women, as well as minorities, have been discriminated against by several labor unions. Recently, though, women workers are beginning to get jobs in almost every field.

gether to pass laws that prevent discrimination in public education. Student groups worked to increase the number of women students in professional schools and the number of highly-paid women faculty members. Women's groups set up programs in job counseling, health care, women's studies, self-defense, and other areas.

Individual Washington women have been successful in many fields. For example, Dorothy Stimson Bullitt, an outstanding businesswoman and community leader, started the state's first television station and directed it for many years. She was honored as the state's "first citizen" in 1959. Dixy Lee Ray was director of the Pacific Science Center in Seattle and was selected to direct the nation's Atomic Energy Commission. In 1976, she was elected Washington State Governor. Author Betty McDonald gained national fame for her book, *The Egg and I*. Other Washington women have become leaders in such fields as education, politics, arts, and entertainment.

56. What issues did women's groups take up in the 1970's? Name at least two Washington women of national fame. What were their accomplishments?

Labor Activity

During the 1960's and 1970's, some minority groups were working through labor unions to try to improve their wages and working conditions. The 1964 Civil Rights Act prohibited racial discrimination by all unions in the country. However, integration did not come quickly to all trades. In the past, many employers had hired minority workers to break strikes and weaken white unions. Some unions still resented this and refused to accept minorities. The con-

struction unions, still refused to accept minority members. The United Construction Workers, an organization of minority workers, closed down construction at the University of Washington and Seattle-Tacoma Airport in 1969. The group was drawing attention to lack of minority construction workers on these jobs.

By the late 1970's, minorities and women were making significant progress in getting union jobs.

57. What law prohibited racial discrimination by labor unions?

Why Was A Farmworkers' Union Needed?

Another labor activity involving large numbers of minority people was the effort to organize farmworkers. Farmworkers include the people with the most tedious jobs in agriculture. They trim, thin, and harvest the crops. This often requires stooping and bending for long hours each day. The work is hard and the wages are low. The temporary camps that farmworkers live in may not have adequate water or waste disposal systems. Bad living and working conditions can lead to diseases, back trouble, and pesticide poisoning.

Also, the work on each crop only lasts a few weeks every year. In order to keep working, farmworkers usually must travel from one crop to another. (People who do this are called migrant workers.) Migrant workers have had special problems because they are not permanent residents of any city or state. They have not been able to qualify for many state services, including welfare and health programs. Migrant children must change schools often, and they often miss the chance to finish high school. Until recently, migrants were not able to vote. As non-voters, migrant workers had no political power. Voters used to have to live in Washington for a whole year before they could vote here. Now qualified voters may register as soon as they arrive.

It has also been very difficult to organize farmworkers into labor unions, since the workers don't stay in one place very long. Early attempts to organize the farmworkers were usually unsuccessful. An effective union was badly needed, so that farmworkers could improve their working conditions.

Cesar Chavez, the head of the United Farm Workers Organizing Committee based in California, visited Washington State in 1969, and his brother came in 1978 to help in starting a farmworkers' union here. Since Chavez' first visit, the union has had some successes in this state. In 1970, a Supreme Court decision guaranteed organizers the right to meet with farmworkers. The unions have been working since then to expand their membership.

58. *Describe the work done by farmworkers.*
59. *What special problems have been caused because migrant workers have to travel so often?*

What Other Goals Did Chicano Groups Work Toward?

Chicanos have led the farmworkers' movement, and they have been working toward other

One of the main techniques of the farmworkers union was the "boycott." (To boycott is to refuse to buy, sell, or use something.) Grape pickers were among the many farmworkers who were not receiving a decent wage for their work. So the UFW called on people around the country to boycott, or refuse to buy, grapes. This would put pressure on farm owners to recognize the unions. Here, Chicanos hold a rally in Seattle to support a UFW boycott.

WASHINGTON'S SPANISH-SPEAKING PEOPLE

Most people of Spanish language in Washington can trace their family origins to ancient Mexico. Several words are sometimes used to describe people in this group. The word "Mexican" describes a person who is a citizen of Mexico. "Mexican American" is one word for an American citizen of Mexican background. "Chicano" refers to natives of the American Southwest — which used to be part of Mexico. Today, the word Chicano is used by Mexican Americans who are working for equal rights as Americans and who take pride in "La Raza" — the Mexican race.

Some of the Spanish-speaking people in Washington have come from Cuba, Puerto Rico, and other Latin American countries besides Mexico. Some are from Spain. The word "Hispanic" is sometimes used to describe the entire Spanish-speaking ethnic group. ("Hispanic" means of Spanish or Portuguese origin.)

The Hispanic peoples of Washington make up one of the largest ethnic groups in the state. The 1970 census showed about the same number of Black and Spanish-speaking people in Washington.

goals in this state, too. The "Año del Mexicano" project (the year of the Mexican) of 1970, represented the Chicanos' struggle to preserve their language and culture. Chicano educators were starting bilingual education programs. In 1967, Tomás Villanueva, a Chicano who was active in the union, opened a cooperative grocery store for UFWOC members in Toppenish. Prices were lower here than at regular grocery stores, and the co-op carried many ethnic foods. Villanueva also helped start special medical services for the farmworkers, and he helped start Northwest Rural Opportunities (NWRO). NWRO sponsored such programs as child care services and Chicano-owned farms.

The federal and state governments have started some programs for migrant workers in Eastern Washington. The Migrant Family Health Center was opened in 1970. A travelling clinic brings medical workers to the camps at farms in Yakima, Chelan, Douglas, and Okanagan counties.

A key issue for Chicanos in Eastern Washington in the 1960's and 1970's was voting rights. Before the 1970's, Washington citizens had to prove they could read English before they were allowed to vote. No Spanish speaking people were hired to register voters. The Mexican American Federation claimed this was unconstitutional discrimination. They took this issue to court and won. Eastern Washington government officials were ordered to allow and assist Mexican American citizens to register.

Voter registration is still an important part of Chicano political activities in Washington and around the country. More registered Chicano voters means greater political power and the possibility of electing Chicano officials. This is important in Washington towns such as Mabton, Sunnyside, Toppenish, and Wapato, where Chicanos are becoming the majority ethnic group.

60. Identify the following: Tomás Villanueva, NWRO, Migrant Family Health Center.

European Ethnic Groups And Institutions

The Chicanos are only one of a number of ethnic groups in Washington State. As the chart on page 217 illustrates, our state's population includes people from quite a few European countries. Among this group are people who are bilingual and bicultural; the European culture of their ancestors still plays an important role in their lives. There are people in the state who consider themselves Swedish Americans, Italian Americans, Polish Americans, et. al., and they take pride in both their cultures. In every part of the state are communities of people who are drawn together through their shared European cultural origins.

In these ethnic communities, there are several institutions which help keep the traditional culture alive. Several ethnic communities revolve around the local church or temple. For example, the Greek Orthodox Church in Seattle serves as a social and cultural — as well as a religious — center for the Greek American community of that city. The town of Wilkeson, near Mount Rainier, was once the home of many Slovakian and Ukrainian miners. Today, the Holy Trinity Russian Orthodox Church is still attended by families of Eastern European origin. Synagogues are centers for the many Jewish groups of our state.

In addition to the religious institutions there are various clubs, halls, and community centers. These used to play a much more important role in the ethnic communities than they do today, but many organizations are still active. Some examples include the American Croation Club of Anacortes and the Swedish Club of Seattle.

Several newspapers around the country are published in European languages other than English. The "Bulletin of the Russian Colony" is a Northwest example.

61. Give at least one example of each of the following institutions of Washington's European ethnic groups: church, club, native language newspaper.

European Folk Arts In Washington

Each European immigrant group brought with it a rich tradition of folk arts, including music, dance, and visual arts. Some of these traditions are several centuries old, and many are still practiced by skilled members of these ethnic groups.

Interest in European dance traditions is shared by numerous groups around the state. The dances of nearly every European culture are represented. Some examples include the Polish group, Polonie; the Ukranian women's group called Honei Viter; the English dance exhibition group, Leafield, and the dancers of the American Croatian Club. There are classes and performances of dances from Greece, Scotland, Germany, Latvia, and Scandinavia, for example. Some groups, such as the Latvian and Ukrainian are made up of natives or descendants of that culture. Other groups are open to participants of all backgrounds, and many groups learn dances from several different cultures. A good example are the Silver Spurs dancers from Spokane. This group is made up mostly of high school students. They have toured the United States, performing dances of many countries.

62. Name at least three folk dance groups in Washington.

What Other Folk Arts Are Practiced?

Along with the dances, there are many groups who play traditional European music. For example, there are groups, such as the Keith Band, who play Scottish highland bagpipe music. The Junior Tambouritzans and the Balalaika Trio are two of the Eastern European musical groups. Scandinavian music is promoted by the Scandia organization in Seattle. Connected with

ETHNIC ORIGINS OF WASHINGTON'S POPULATION: 1970

Country of Origin	Number of Foreign Born	Number With Foreign or Mixed Parentage	Total	Country of Origin	Number of Foreign Born	Number With Foreign or Mixed Parentage	Total
Canada	35,977	100,569	136,546	Switzerland	1,686	5,989	7,675
Germany	14,096	57,257	71,353	Yugoslavia	1,857	5,723	7,580
United Kingdom	16,085	44,437	60,522	France	1,473	4,672	6,145
Norway	11,657	48,770	60,427	Czechoslovakia	1,198	4,939	6,137
Sweden	7,420	37,831	45,251	Hungary	1,352	2,917	4,269
U.S.S.R.	4,256	19,210	23,466	Greece	1,406	2,655	4,061
Italy	4,347	17,075	21,422	Western Asia	1,226	2,185	3,411
Mexico	4,424	13,468	17,892	Lithuania	238	1,198	1,436
Japan	5,257	10,520	15,777	Cuba	369	201	570
Denmark	2,372	12,050	14,422	Other Europe	6,424	18,483	24,907
Netherlands	3,911	9,386	13,297	Other Asia	9,717	8,984	17,701
Ireland	1,841	11,425	13,266	Other American	2,099	3,074	5,173
Austria	2,074	8,258	10,332	All other	2,161	3,575	5,736
Poland	1,930	7,891	9,821	Not reported	5,154	14,750	19,904

(To get this information, the census forms asked the following questions:
Where was this person born?
What country was his father born in?
What country was his mother born in?
For more information on how the census is taken, see the tables on page 179).

SOURCE: U.S. Bureau of the Census, 1970 Census of Population, *General Social and Economic Characteristics, Washington.*

Scandia are Scandinavian fiddlers, quartets, and string ensembles, as well as folk dancers.

Several visual arts and crafts from European cultures are also practiced. There are experts at Norwegian folk painting called Rosemaling, at Scandinavian embroidery, and at bobbin lace. Washington has artists who create delicate paper cut designs in the Polish tradition and Ukrainian painted eggs.

In many of the local historical museums around the state, you will find examples of European folk arts — pieces that were brought here by immigrants many years ago. And modern folk arts of all kinds can be seen at the annual Folk Life Festival in Seattle. This festival is held at Seattle Center on Memorial Day weekend.

63. Name at least two styles of European folk music played in Washington.
64. Name at least two European folk crafts practiced in the state.

A Multi-Ethnic State

The many ethnic groups represented in Washington State add great cultural richness. People in this state — especially in the big cities — have opportunities to experience cultural traditions from all over the world.

Each year, there are many ethnic festivals and holidays that all people can participate in. The St. Patrick's Day celebrations of the Irish community are well known. There are many others. Special events among the Asian communities include the Chinese New Year, the Bon Odori dance festival of the Japanese, and Jose Rizal Day (in honor of the national hero of the Philippines). Several Washington towns have festivals that celebrate the European origins of its settlers. The Norwegian-founded town of Poulsbo has a Viking Fest every year, and Odessa has a Deutsches Fest, in honor of the German settlers there.

Each of these festivals offers a chance for members of the state's ethnic communities to celebrate and share their special cultures. Between holiday times, there are other opportunities to share and learn about the many ethnic cultures of our state. In the cities there are restaurants with food from many different countries and shops that sell imported food, clothing, and other items.

A Native American woodcarver practices his art at the University District Street Fair in Seattle.

In addition, there are some excellent museums in Washington which feature the art and artifacts of our ethnic cultures. The Seattle Art Museum has an outstanding collection of Asian art. Other Asian art and artifacts can be seen in Seattle at the Wing Luke Museum and at the Burke Museum of the University of Washington. The Burke Museum also has an excellent collection of Pacific Northwest Indian art. Native American art can be seen at the Cheney Cowles Museum in Spokane and at many smaller museums around the state, too. The Maryhill Museum was dedicated by Queen Marie of Romania, and it houses objects from European royalty. Almost every city has its historical museum with objects saved from the early periods of settlement. Among these objects, there are often reminders of the ethnic origins of the settlers.

Like all U.S. states, Washington is multi-ethnic. Through festivals, shows, restaurants, and historical displays, we all have a chance to appreciate and enjoy the many cultures of our state.

65. Name at least four holidays or festivals with ethnic origins. Tell which country each festival comes from.
66. Name at least four museums in Washington that have ethnic art collections of some kind.

The Arts In Washington State

Arts of all kinds have been booming in Washington in recent years. Thanks to Expo '74, Spokane has an excellent performing arts center. The opera house is used by the Spokane symphony and other local and visiting groups.

There are several art museums and performing centers in other cities of the state. Tacoma has a sizable art museum. Fort Warden State Park near Port Townsend hosts art classes and performances of all kinds. Many of our smaller urban centers, such as Walla Walla and the Tri-Cities, have semi-professional orchestras, theater groups, or dance companies.

The Washington State Arts Commission and other government agencies help bring art exhibits, performances, and art classes to all parts of the state. For example, the Artists in the Schools program has offered students the chance to learn from poets, actors, painters, photographers, and dancers. This program has helped bring the arts to rural areas of the state which have no permanent arts facilities.

Naturally, there are more arts activities in the state's largest city, including the Seattle Symphony, Seattle Opera, Pacific Northwest Dance, Seattle Repertory and ACT Theaters. Seattle is also the home of several other performing arts groups and a wide variety of galleries and museums. During the 1970's, Seattle gained national recognition for its commitment to the arts. In the years following Century 21, Seattle's art scene was expanding rapidly and receiving growing government support. The Seattle city government now helps sponsor free public arts festivals, art classes and performances in the Seattle parks, and original art in public buildings— as well as providing financial support to individual artists and arts organizations.

> **WHAT NATIONALLY RECOGNIZED AUTHORS HAVE LIVED IN WASHINGTON**
>
> In recent times, a few nationally recognized poets and fiction writers have made their homes in Washington. For example, the Pulitzer Prize-winning poet, Theodore Roethke, taught at the University of Washington in the 1960's. One of the country's best-known science fiction writers, Frank Herbert, lives in Port Townsend. Nard Jones and Archie Binns are known for both novels and historical works.
>
> Gary Snyder is a nationally recognized poet who has lived in and written about the Pacific Northwest. Betty McDonald and Tom Robbins have won a national audience for their comic novels with Northwest settings.
>
> There have also been several notable writers of non-fiction. These have included Edmund S. Meany, a distinguished early historian of Washington State, and Vernon L. Parrington, who won the Pulitzer Prize for his work, *Main Currents in American Thought*. Both these men were professors for many years at the University of Washington. William O. Douglas, who was best known as a justice of the United States Supreme Court, was also a distinguished writer. Some of his books recount Douglas' experiences growing up in Eastern Washington.

67. Name at least two of each of the following in Washington State: art museums, symphonies, theater groups, dance companies.

The Maryhill Museum is located in Klickitat County. It was built by railroad developer, Samuel Hill, and named after his wife, Mary.

What natural resources are shown or indicated by this photo? Can you think of some way that a different culture has used the same resources in a different way?

UNIT 11

RESOURCES AND INDUSTRIES

This book began with a description of the geography of Washington State — its location, climate, land and water forms, and natural resources. These aspects of the physical environment have affected every group of people who have lived here. Washington's geography still determines the way that many people make their living. Many of the state's major industries depend on natural resources, including lumbering, fishing, agriculture, and tourism.

Natural resources are central to Washington's economy. Many jobs depend on them. So it is important that we protect those natural resources and use them wisely.

Different groups may choose to use the same resource in different ways. Sometimes this leads to conflicts. The government passes laws to help determine how resources are used. Cultural values, economic needs, and environmental concerns may all affect the way we use natural resources.

In this unit, you will learn about the natural resources and industries of great economic importance in this state. There is a short history of each and a discussion of its role in the economy today. Some key environmental issues are also discussed.

The unit has six sections:

1. Natural Beauty is a Resource
2. Using Our Forests
3. Food and Jobs From the Sea
4. Agricultural Resources
5. The Regional Economy
6. Energy Needs and Resources

As you read this unit, keep the following questions in mind: What are Washington's major industries and products? What kinds of jobs are available here? What factors have affected the way natural resources are used? What are the main environmental problems concerning our natural resources?

SECTION 1: NATURAL BEAUTY IS A RESOURCE

What Recreational Opportunities Are Available?

Washington ranks high among the fifty states in the variety of natural environments here. There are snow-capped mountains and grassy, rolling hills. There are dense rainforests and treeless semi-deserts. There are flat, fertile river valleys and sandy beaches. Few states offer as great a variety of landscapes.

Large areas of the land in Washington are undeveloped. More than a million acres have been preserved as national wilderness areas. Millions more acres are part of the national parks and forests. Altogether, the federal government owns or controls about one-third of the land in the state; and much of it is undeveloped land, available for public use. The state government also owns much undeveloped land.

All this publicly-owned land adds up to a great variety of recreational opportunities in the state. There are places to go hiking, skiing, camping, fishing, hunting, bicycling, and sightseeing. There are opportunities for water sports and outdoor recreation of all kinds. Washington's great beautiful out-of-doors has something to attract just about all people, whatever their recreational tastes.

1. Give several examples of different natural environments found in Washington.
2. About how much land in Washington State is owned by the federal government?

Enjoying The Great ''North Wet''

Washington has 2,000 miles of saltwater shoreline, so many lakes that some of them don't even have names, the third-largest river in the country, and more boats per person than any other place in the United States. This is a state with plenty of water in every form and almost every water sport you can think of. There are

The Columbia River is a source of electricity, irrigation water, and transportation. The river also offers recreation opportunities. There are places along the river for boating, swimming, and just enjoying the view.

swift and icy mountain streams, big rivers, saltwater bays, and clean, quiet lakes. (Most parts of Western Washington also have plenty of water in the air — as well as on the ground — during most of the year.) This water provides hydroelectricity, irrigation, and transportation. It supports fish and other seafood. It is also one of the state's main recreational resources and an important tourist attraction.

Somewhere in, on, or near the water in Washington, there's a sport for everyone. There are plenty of low-lying lakes and streams to swim in. Those people who don't mind the chill can swim in Puget Sound or some of the many lakes in the mountains. Along the saltwater beaches, there are opportunities for clam digging and shell hunting, picnics, and hiking. The national seashore on the Olympic Peninsula offers u-nique wilderness hikes along the ocean. The hikes lead through dense rainforests down to rocky, undeveloped beaches where there are places to camp. At low tide, visitors can explore the beautiful and unusual marine life of tidal pools.

3. Name some uses of Washington's water resources.

More Sports For Water Enthusiasts

Boats of every kind can be found on Washington waters. There are sailboats, motorboats, canoes, and kayaks. Some people choose to ride the rivers on rafts or inner tubes. Others ride behind their boats on water skis. There are boat races throughout the year: sailing races, canoe races, hydroplane races, even a race of boats made out of empty milk cartons. The hydroplane races in Seattle and the Tri-Cities are among the major boat races in the country each year.

Another popular water sport is fishing. There is good fishing in almost every part of the state, from high mountain streams, to large, low-lying lakes, to the saltwaters of Puget Sound and the Pacific Ocean. Some fishing requires a boat, some requires long hikes into the wilderness; some fish can be caught from the end of a city dock. Guests can even fish from the windows of a modern motel in Seattle! The most important sport fish are salmon and trout, especially the steelhead.

4. Name some water sports available to people in Washington.

These people have found a rather unusual way to enjoy Washington's water resources. What are some others?

Up Into The Mountains

Even people who never go for a swim can get a lot of pleasure from Washington's lakes, streams, and saltwater. The water adds a special beauty to cities and countryside.

So do the mountains — whenever they aren't hidden by the clouds. The chief mountain ranges of Washington are the Olympics and the Cascades. There are also the Blue Mountains in Southeastern Washington, and the Selkirk Range of the Rocky Mountains system. The Selkirks touch the northeastern corner of this state.

The mountains are dotted with lakes and streams. There are forests at lower altitudes. Higher up, there are alpine meadows which are full of flowers during summer months. The highest peaks are snow-covered all year round.

The Cascades and the Olympics are both quite "young" compared to most mountain ranges. Because of this, they are unusually rocky and rugged. A hike into Washington's mountains can be a visit to some of the most beautiful scenery in the world.

Every year, thousands of people go into these mountains for a closer look. They go to the mountains to hike, climb, ski, camp, picnic, and fish.

5. What mountain ranges are in Washington State?
6. What are some popular mountain sports?

Mountain climbing has been a sport in Washington since the late 1800's. These early twentieth century climbers had none of the specialized clothing and equipment of climbers today.

Exploring The National Forests

Large parts of the state's mountain ranges are still available for public use. Many thousands of acres of mountain lands are part of the nine national forests in Washington State. They are called Gifford Pinchot, Mt. Baker, Snoqualmie, Wenatchee, Colville, Olympic, Okanogan, Kaniksu, and Umatilla. Parts of the national forests are open for summer and winter activities, such as hiking, climbing, snowshoeing, horseback riding, cross-country skiing, and snowmobiling. The longest trail through the state is the Cascade Crest Trail. It is part of a trail system that stretches from Canada all the way to Mexico.

National forests are managed by the United States Department of Agriculture. Logging still goes on in these areas, and some people live on national forest land. Other federally-owned lands are maintained as "wilderness areas." These lands remain in a natural state. Wilderness areas give us a taste of what the Pacific Northwest was like before non-Indians began to develop it.

7. Name some of the national forests in Washington.
8. What is a wilderness area?

What Are The National Parks?

There are three national parks in Washington. These parks include some of the most beautiful and unusual mountain lands in the state.

Olympic National Park is the fifth-largest na-

A campsite on the Olympic Peninsula in the early twentieth century. The tent was made of silk.

tional park in the country. It includes mountains, forests, lakes, glaciers, wildlife, beaches, and unusual rain forests.

Mount Rainier National Park includes the state's highest mountain and thousands of acres of land around it. The park offers every kind of hike, from easy afternoon strolls to dangerous and difficult technical climbing. Mount Rainier is often used as a training area for mountaineers who wish to climb more difficult peaks. For example, the first American team to climb Mount Everest — the world's highest mountain — practiced here. One of the team members, Jim Whittaker, lives in Seattle. He has climbed Mount Rainier more often than many people in the city have walked up the steep hill from Seattle's waterfront. Whittaker's wife, Diane Roberts, is a mountain climber and also an outdoor photographer. In 1978, she and her husband were members of the first American team to climb K-2, another of the world's highest and most difficult mountains.

North Cascades National Park includes wilderness areas, developed park areas, and a scenic highway. Visitors can enjoy activities from an afternoon drive to a long backpacking trip. There are forests, streams, snowy peaks, and beautiful views.

9. What national parks are located in Washington? Name some attractions of each park.

Caves, Islands, And Forts
(Among Other Attractions)

There are over 100 state parks and heritage sites in Washington. (A heritage site is a place of special historic, geological, archaeological, or architectural importance that has been preserved

Hurricane Ridge in the Olympic National Park is a popular drive for tourists. How is natural beauty an important economic resource?

Speed boating on the Sun Lakes in Eastern Washington.

as a state park area.) State parks include some of the most unusual land formations in the state. For example, the main attraction of Crawford State Park in Northeastern Washington is a huge limestone cave. This cave is over 1000 feet long and includes several natural stone "sculptures." Sun Lakes State Park near Grand Coulee Dam includes interesting geological formations and several lakes. There are opportunities for camping, hiking, swimming, boating, fishing, horseback riding, and golf. Other state parks and heritage sites are centers for the arts. Fort Flagler has an annual music camp for students each summer. Fort Worden is the location of varied art classes and performances. Nineteen state parks can only be reached by boat; they are all islands in Puget Sound.

State heritage sites include Chief Sealth's grave, Saint Paul's Mission, and the site of our constitutional convention. A heritage site near Walla Walla is dedicated to Sacajawea, the young Shoshone Indian woman who helped guide Lewis and Clark.

10. Identify the following: *Crawford State Park, Fort Flagler, Sacajawea.*

Wildlife To Watch Or Hunt

There are opportunities for sport hunting in most parts of the state during some seasons of

The cities attract tourists too. This is the site of Spokane's Expo— the 1974 World's Fair.
The volcano-shaped American pavilion is reflected in the windows of another fairground building.
What structures from Expo '74 are still used?

the year. Deer are the most important game animals. There are also elk, bears, cougars, bobcats, coyotes, foxes, raccoons, and badgers. Some animals may be trapped for their furs, including: beaver, muskrat, river otter, and fox. Bird hunters will find pheasants, partridges, quail, grouse, ducks, geese, and other game birds.

Other people prefer to enjoy the wildlife rather than to hunt it. There is plenty to enjoy. Deer and rodents such as chipmunks, marmots and pikas are abundant in the mountains. Lucky hikers may also see mountain goats, bighorn sheep, moose or caribou, which are more rare. (Unlucky hikers may run into bears.) Other native animals include skunks, weasels, and porcupines. Some animals are protected by law and may never be hunted. Wolverines, eagles, hawks, and owls are among them.

On Washington's saltwater beaches, a different kind of wildlife can be found. Ocean tidepools are full of anemones, crabs, snails, and other small, colorful animals. In the offshore waters, otter, seals, and even whales can sometimes be seen.

11. Name several animals in each category:
*   a. game animals*
*   b. animals that are trapped for fur*
*   c. protected animals*

A proud family shows off a great day's catch. What are the most popular sport fish of the Pacific Northwest?

Tourism Is Big Business

All of this outdoor sports activity creates hundreds of jobs for the people in Washington State. Workers are needed to run hotels, resorts, restaurants, and ski lifts and to make and sell recreational equipment — from boats to backpacks. There are jobs for park rangers, ski instructors, motel managers, tour guides, boat skippers, and snowmobile mechanics. According to some calculations, tourism is the third largest industry in the state.

Among the most valuable recreational businesses are boating and downhill skiing. Washington's ski slopes attract an average of more than a million people each season. Recreational equipment is a booming business. Some of the nation's largest and best known manufacturers are located in Washington. And sport fishing accounts for close to one-third the value of fisheries here.

Our state's natural beauty is one of its valuable natural resources. Preserving a part of the land in a natural state is necessary for economic reasons as well as for the protection of wildlife, soil, and clean water, for the opportunity to enjoy and learn from nature.

12. Name at least five jobs related to the tourist industry in Washington State.
13. Why is it important to preserve a part of the land in a natural state?

How Are Land-Use Decisions Made?

Of course, public recreation is not the only use for which our wilderness lands may be used. A mountain wilderness region may have forests that lumber companies want to harvest or minerals that some mining company wants to develop. Beach property may be in demand for oyster farms, pulp mills, and private resorts, as well as for public enjoyment. One kind of use often makes other uses impossible. As a result, the competition between different groups for the same area of land may be intense.

Our federal, state, and local governments have many ways to influence or control the way land is used. For example, local governments pass zoning laws. Zoning laws govern the use of land within a city or county. They specify which lots or areas may be used for single family dwellings (houses), for multiple unit housing (du-plexes, apartments, etc.), for shopping centers, and for industry and other uses. The state and federal governments determine how to use the land in their ownership, and they also have some control over other lands in the state. For example, the United States Forest Service is responsible for distributing national forest lands among lumbering, grazing, recreation, and other uses. Congress can vote to add new lands to the na-

---

WORKING OUT A COMPROMISE ON THE
ALPINE LAKES REGION: A CASE STUDY

About 75 miles east of Seattle, in the central Cascades, lies one of the most beautiful regions of Washington State. It is called the Alpine Lakes Region. In this part of the Cascade Mountains, there are almost 700 lakes. In the lowlands, there are large lakes surrounded by forests. Higher up in the rocks and alpine meadows are many smaller lakes. The Alpine Lakes Region also includes river valleys and rugged mountains.

The area offers opportunities for many kinds of recreation, including hiking, climbing, camping, fishing, picnicking, hunting, and boating. Three major highways connect this region to the big cities on Puget Sound. Each year, thousands of people take advantage of the region's attractions. In 1972, for example, 930,000 people visited the Alpine Lakes Region. They spent about $23 million dollars on food, lodging, transportation, and other items.

Clearly, the region is an important state resource. However, different people in the state had very different ideas about how this resource should be used. Environmentalists believed that as much land as possible should be left as it was, in order to protect the area's natural beauty and its wildlife. On the other hand, the lumber companies believed they ought to be able to harvest all the valuable lumber from the area. Some developers wanted to build large resorts in the Alpine Lakes Region. And some companies wanted to start mining in the area.

In the early 1970's, the environmentalists formed a group called the Alpine Lakes Protection Society, or ALPS. ALPS members, together with the Sierra Club, began working to convince Congress to create a National Wilderness Area in the Alpine Lakes Region. This would mean that part of the region would be permanently off-limits to logging, building, motor vehicles, and any kind of major development.

At the same time, lumber company representatives tried to convince Congress not to create a wilderness area, or at least to keep it very small and away from the good timber lands. They were supported by lumber workers' unions. The lumber companies and other businesses claimed that a great number of workers would be laid off if the wilderness area was created. They said that the state economy would be hurt by the loss of valuable trees and minerals. Environmental groups argued that the wilderness area's impact on the economy would be very small.

Both ALPS and the lumber companies had many supporters. A number of government officials and private citizens became involved in the issue. Several of these different groups began discussions and debates to try to work out a compromise plan for the region. During this time, each group tried to win good publicity and strong public support for their point of view.

ALPS held meetings and demonstrations. They printed bumper stickers and sent speakers to talk to interested citizen groups. They urged people to write letters to their congressional representatives. The lumber companies lobbied Congress and local officials. They spread news stories about the jobs and profits which they believed that ALPS would destroy.

The discussions went on for five years. The final result was that Congress passed a bill creating 393,000 acres of wilderness area. The wilderness would be surrounded by over 500,000 acres of land under federal control. These 500,000 acres could be used for both recreation and logging. The wilderness area was smaller than environmentalists wanted, but larger than the lumbermen felt was necessary. It was a compromise for both groups. President Ford did not approve of the bill. He felt the wilderness area was too large and too expensive. But some of Washington's representatives had sponsored the bill. They and Governor Evans strongly urged the President to sign it. Ford signed the bill. The Alpine Lakes Recreation Area was officially created in 1976.

tional parks and wilderness areas. (The North Cascades National Park was created by Congress in 1967, and the Olympic National Park was expanded in 1977.)

The government's land-use decisions may be very important to large numbers of people. So every time an important decision is made, a number of groups and individuals will be working to convince the government to decide in their favor. The case study of the Alpine Lakes region, on page 228, gives a good idea of how these governmental decisions are made and of how people may influence the decisions.

14. Give an example of a type of land-use decision that the state and federal governments make.

How Does Government Help Control Air Pollution?

Land-use decisions are only one way in which our governments are involved in protecting the quality of our environment. Each level of government has become involved in many other kinds of environmental issues.

For example, an important aspect of environmental quality is clean air. Air pollution can damage the recreational value of an area, it can damage wildlife and crops, and it can cause illness in humans. Our federal, state, and local governments have all passed laws to protect the quality of the air we breathe. The federal government requires that all new cars have pollution-control devices. Since 1970, there have been federal standards for air quality. State and local governments have set up programs to test and regulate the amount of pollution in the air.

The Washington State Air Pollution Control Board set up the first statewide air quality standards in 1968. Since then, industries can be fined if they fail to meet these standards. Some businesses have made great progress toward stopping the harmful air pollution that they were producing. A good example is the Bethlehem Steel plant in Seattle. Clouds of thick, ugly smoke used to pour from the factory. Today, the sky above the steel plant is clear.

Most of our air pollution comes from auto and truck exhaust. Local governments are trying to keep down the number of cars on the road by encouraging people to ride in carpools and buses. King County has tried several techniques to encourage this. Several parking spaces are reserved for carpools only. Metro Transit offers parking lots near suburban bus stops and free bus service in downtown Seattle. These services help discourage people from bringing their cars downtown. The government offers free help in matching up people who can carpool together, and it pays for public education on the issue.

15. Name some harmful effects of air pollution.
16. What do governments do to help stop air pollution?

What Pollution Problems Still Exist?

In spite of the laws and efforts of government, many air pollution problems still exist. Despite government efforts to encourage bus and carpool use, there are just too many cars on the road in our big cities. As long as so many people are driving so many cars, there is always the danger of high levels of air pollution. Many people believe that the most important step to ending air pollution is the creation of better public transportation systems.

Sometimes weather conditions lead to extra pollution problems. Seattle, Tacoma, and Spokane are all partly surrounded by mountains. These mountains restrict the flow of air out of the cities. Sometimes the dirty city air becomes trapped in the lowlands, and pollution builds up to unhealthy levels. The air in Western Washington is frequently cleaned out by rain. But during the dry season, the air above Seattle and Tacoma sometimes reaches dangerous levels of pollution.

Still other problems seem to be caused because of conflict between environmental concerns and economic concerns. For example, the ASARCO copper smelter in Tacoma has been violating air quality standards since they were first imposed. But the smelter employed about 1000 people. Company owners said they would have to close down the plant and lay off all the workers if they were forced to install the equipment to cut down on pollution. The Air Pollution Control Agency postponed enforcement of air standards at the plant until 1980.

17. How do the following contribute to continued air pollution problems: weather conditions, lack of good public transportation systems, the need for jobs?

SECTION 2: USING OUR FORESTS

What Is Washington's Most Valuable Industry?

Forest resources have always been important to the economy of the Pacific Northwest. The Coastal Indians used wood — especially cedar — to make their houses, canoes, utensils, furnishings, and even clothing. They were skilled woodcarvers, and examples of their work are now displayed at many art museums. In addition, the forest environment sheltered plants and animals that Coastal and Plateau tribes depended on for food.

The first Europeans in the Northwest were impressed by the huge, thick forests that covered most of the coastline. The explorers realized that Northwest lumber could be valuable if it could be exported.

The explorers were right. Since the middle 1800's, forest products have made up the state's most valuable industry.

18. What natural resource has accounted for the state's most valuable industry since the middle 1800's?

A forest of Douglas fir, the state's most important commercial tree.

forests of our state. However, some of our forests are not natural. They were planted like a crop. These planted forests, called tree farms, are made up of all Douglas fir trees.

19. What is the most commercially valuable kind of tree in Washington?
20. What tree is noted for its ability to last a long time in the rain?
21. Why do trees grow so well in Western Washington?

What Are The Western Washington Forests Like?

The richest forest resources of our state are located in Western Washington. The mild, rainy climate is excellent for trees, and they grow quickly here. Douglas firs — the state's most commercially important type of tree — grows very well in Western Washington. The Douglas fir is valuable because it grows especially tall and straight. This makes it good for telephone poles, dock pilings, and lumber. Douglas fir is also the main tree used in making plywood here.

Another important tree of the Western Washington forests is the western red cedar. Cedar can be split easily and it lasts a long time in the rain. Native American cedar totem poles are still standing after surviving more than 100 years. The water-resistant quality of cedar makes it an important roofing and siding material today.

Other commercial trees of Western Washington include the Sitka spruce, the western hemlock, and western white pine. Many varieties of trees usually grow together in the natural

What Are Eastern Washington Forests Like?

Eastern Washington forests look very different from the wetter forests on the west side of the Cascades. The western forests are thick and dark. Little light reaches the forest floor, which is covered with mosses, ferns, and other plants. The rainforests of the Olympic Peninsula grow very thick. The dry eastern forests are fairly open and sunny and have very little undergrowth.

The Eastern Washington forests do not grow as fast or as thick as those of Western Washington. The eastern climate is dryer, and there are greater extremes of hot and cold temperatures. Therefore, logging is not as important to the Eastern Washington economy as it is in the west.

Trees cannot grow in very dry climates. There are no natural forests in the lowland areas of Eastern Washington where yearly rainfall is very low. But some of the hilly or mountainous areas are forested.

The most valuable tree of Eastern Washington is the ponderosa pine. This tree grows tall and straight. The wood of the ponderosa pine is very soft and it does not split when nailed. It is used for making paneling, plywood, and crates.

22. What is the most commercially important tree of Eastern Washington?
23. How are the forests different in the eastern and western parts of our state?

What Was The Early Logging Industry Like?

The forests of Western Washington were the first to be commercially developed. The Hudson's Bay Company built the first sawmill in the Pacific Northwest at Fort Vancouver. By the 1830's, the company was already shipping large amounts of lumber to China and Hawaii each year. By 1860, there were 32 sawmills in Washington Territory. Most of the early mills were small, independently-owned businesses like Henry Yesler's sawmill in Seattle. Soon private individuals and companies from the eastern United States began investing in Pacific Northwest lumber. Some companies built whole towns, including the lumber mill and homes for workers. Port Gamble was an example of a company town, and investors were responsible for much of the early development of both Everett and Tacoma.

The first commercial loggers cut down trees with axes and giant handsaws. They transported all logs to the sawmills by water. This meant that they could only harvest trees that were near to saltwater, streams, or rivers.

The first addition to people-power in the forests was the ox team. The oxen would haul logs to streams, allowing loggers to cut trees located farther from the water. A "skid road" of split and oiled logs made pulling easier for the animals. (See the photo below.) Later, steam locomotives were used, or steam-powered engines dragged the logs on overhead wires.

Logging was a common job for newly-arrived immigrants. Whole crews might be made up of Swedes, Poles, or Japanese. Most of these log-

Before trucks were introduced, logs were hauled out of the forest by teams of oxen. Notice that log sections have been laid across the trail at regular intervals. They were greased with dogfish oil. This helped the freshly-cut logs slip along more smoothly. Such trails were called "skid roads."

gers were single men who might work at a job only a week or two, then move along.

24. *Who started the Northwest's first sawmill?*
25. *Name two of the Washington towns that were developed by wealthy investors in the lumber industry.*
26. *Tell how each of these was used in the development of the logging industry: steam power, ox power, people power.*

An Exhaustible Resource

Until the early 1900's, most lumber companies practiced a policy of "cut and run." They did not own the forest lands, and they did not think of trees as a resource that might one day be exhausted. So they raced through the forests and harvested the trees they wanted, carelessly wasting the rest. The sawmills were wasteful, too. Many parts of the tree were not used.

The lumber business was booming, and many companies were competing for a share of the profits. Loggers were rushing to harvest as much as they could as fast as they could. In the process, the Northwest lumber industry was using up forests much faster than they could grow. And the forests were not being replanted.

This attitude toward the forests was not a new one in America. In previous years, the industry had logged off millions of acres of forest. Most of the harvestable lumber was already gone from the eastern and midwestern United States.

Farmers approved of the lumbering activity. To farmers, trees were a nuisance. They had to be removed before plowing could begin.

27. *What was the policy of "cut and run"? Why was it popular?*
28. *Why did farmers support the logging of millions of acres of forests?*

Why Did Attitudes Toward The Forests Change?

Several things happened in the early 1900's to help change the way our forests were treated. First, the federal government began regulating our forest resources. People had talked about forest regulation before. But it was not until the Theodore Roosevelt administration of the early 1900's that some effective laws were passed. At that time, the national forest system was established. The federal government now controls how much of these forests can be harvested each year. (See the information on Gifford Pin-

chot on this page for more background.) Also at this time, lumber companies began to buy up huge quantities of forest land. Weyerhauser's purchase of railroad land in 1900 had started a new tradition. Once the companies owned their land, they could become more committed to caring for it.

Also in the early 1900's, the economics of Northwest logging began to change. In 1906, the city of San Francisco was almost destroyed by an earthquake and fire. This created a big new demand for lumber to rebuild the city. It was the peak of the Northwest lumber boom. Companies raced to cut more and more trees to fill the new demands. They cut much more than could be used. When San Francisco stopped needing great amounts of lumber, the Northwest companies began losing money. Then, to make things worse, wood began to lose favor as a building material. It was being replaced by brick and cement. The lumber companies were left with stockpiles of lumber they couldn't sell.

The effect on the overall economy of Washington State was very serious. Since the first settlements, the lumber industry had been

---

WHO WAS GIFFORD PINCHOT?

One of the national forests in Washington State was named for the man Gifford Pinchot. Pinchot was a pioneer in scientific forestry in America. That is, he was one of the first to study how our nation's forest resources could be protected and preserved.

Before Pinchot's time, Americans too often acted as if the forests would last forever. As a result, many of the best forests in the country were logged off. This caused other problems. Without trees, the soil eroded more quickly, streams became unhealthy for fish, and wild animals died.

Gifford Pinchot loved the out-of-doors, and he decided to study the science of forestry. He studied in France because in the 1880's there were no forestry schools in the United States. Later, Pinchot went to work for the federal government, where he became head of the United States Forest Service. Pinchot was trusted and respected by his friend, President Theodore Roosevelt. Together, they helped give the American government and the American people an awareness of the need to conserve our natural resources.

Pinchot believed that our forests should be efficiently managed. He wanted to end waste and make sure there would always be trees for logging. He did not believe in ending logging. Pinchot's policy is known as "conservation for use."

the largest employer — especially in Western Washington. When the demand for lumber went down, many people lost their jobs, and several towns lost their only big industry. Washington's economic growth slowed down and never really picked up again until World War II.

29. How did each of the following help preserve Washington's forests: the federal government, lumber company-owned forests, declining demand for lumber?
30. Why did the declining demand for lumber have a serious effect on Washington's economy in the early 1900's?

How Has Technology Changed The Forest Products Industry?

Forest products still make up the state's biggest industry, according to some figures. But the industry is different today than it was a century ago. For example, the technology is very different. Today, loggers use trucks, tractors, and heavy machinery. The machine in the photo below can both cut and lift a tree. One operator can now do the work that it took several men and animals to do before.

Other technological changes have improved the machinery at sawmills. Saw operating used to be hard and dangerous work. Today's machines are safer and faster, and they also use much more of the tree. In modern mills, the log first passes through streams of water under great pressure. This removes the bark. One set of saws cuts the log into chunks, then another set cuts the chunks into strips, automatically saving as much of the lumber as possible. Other saws cut the chunks into raw timber. Bark, chips, and sawdust are all saved to make wood pulp and other products.

The development of new products is perhaps the most remarkable advance in the forest industry. In the 1800's, most lumber exports consisted of raw logs and timbers. Today, much of the value of the lumber industry comes from manufactured products, such as plywood, paper, chipboard (made from compressed wood chips), cardboard, and plastics. This variety of products helps keep the industry more stable. Even when the demand for raw lumber goes down, the other products continue to bring income into the state.

Other technological changes involve the growing of the trees themselves. Researchers are working to develop better soils and pesticides and better forest fire-fighting methods. Many trees are now raised on special farms, like other agricultural crops.

31. Give an example of a technological change in each of the following areas: logging machinery, sawmill machinery, lumber products, growing of trees.

How Is The Government Involved In Forestry?

Today, government is involved with our forests in many ways. The government helps pay for forest fire fighting and for research into better ways to grow trees. The state and federal

Giant new machines make logging much easier. Technology has also affected the type of wood products sold. What important wood products have been made possible?

government own much of the forest land in this state, and government has the power to control these forests. It decides how to distribute public forest land among the various needs for forest use. Part of the forest is harvested for lumber; part is saved for recreation; some forest lands are allotted for mining or other uses.

The companies that harvest government-owned forests must obey government rules. The state Forest Practices Act of 1945 requires logging companies to get a permit before they can log an area. In the application for a permit, the company must show how it will take conservation into account in its work. If a company fails to obey the laws, it can be forced to pay the costs of replanting the area. The state and federal government cooperate on management and re-planting as well as fire-fighting in publicly-owned forests.

32. Who owns much of the forest land in Washington?
33. How does the state Forest Practices Act help regulate the forests?

What Controversies Are Involved In Forest Use Decisions?

The government must balance many demands in its decisions about how the forests will be used. One of the important forest controversies of the present is the issue of clearcutting. Clearcutting is the practice of harvesting all the trees in an area. In another method, called selective harvesting, only some of the trees are cut and the others are left to grow. Clearcutting is much cheaper than selective harvesting. Roads can be cut into the forests and large machines brought in. The remaining trees can then be cut down more quickly and easily.

The lumber companies point out that clearcutting has other advantages. Young Douglas firs need lots of light. But little sunlight gets to the floor of the thick western forests. New trees cannot start growing in an old forest; they need clear land. Other plants and bushes also grow in a clearcut area, and these plants provide food and shelter for deer, mice, and other animals.

However, environmentalists point out many drawbacks of clearcutting. It is ugly, especially when very large areas are cleared of all trees. Clearcutting on steep slopes and poor soils can have many harmful results. Once the trees are gone, the soil may wash away. It may be im-

possible for a new forest to grow in its place. Washed-out soil may clog up the streams, killing fish, and creating floods. Many people argue that clearcutting must be carefully regulated. They suggest that thin strips of clearcutting be alternated with strips of uncut trees. This would help protect the beauty and the soil of the forest, and it would help guarantee that the forest would continue to grow.

At present, 70% of the national forest lands are reserved for logging. Some people think this is too much. But loggers feel they would be unable to find work if any less land were allotted.

Government decision-makers have a responsibility to take all these factors into account when they make a decision about how to use a particular forest.

34. Give at least two reasons for clearcutting and two reasons against.

What Natural Dangers Do Forests Face?

Even if trees are not cut down by lumber companies, the forests face several natural dangers. Deer, elk, or other animals may eat the young trees. Mice and squirrels eat the seeds which might have started new trees. Bears sometime peel the bark off trees in order to eat the sweet layer below it. This can kill the tree. Several kinds of insects and diseases can attack the trees. And forest fires can destroy thousands of acres in a short time.

1902 was an especially bad year for forest fires in Washington. There were a total of 110 fires, one of which destroyed 239,000 acres of Western Washington forest. This huge fire was called the "Yacolt Burn." The blaze wiped out several towns and killed about 50 people. The smoke was so thick that it was dark in daytime. Even more than 50 miles away, in Seattle, the streetlights had to be turned on in the middle of the day.

After this catastrophe, the state government created its first programs for forest fire control. Today's forest fighters use airplanes, parachuting "smoke-jumpers," chemicals, and other advanced methods to try to control forest fire damage.

35. How can bears and mice endanger a forest?
36. What was the Yacolt Burn?

These big machines are part of a pulp mill. What products are made from wood pulp?

WOOD CELLULOSE WORLD

The Puget Sound country is in part a wood cellulose country. For example, it is due to the Puget country primarily that our state is second in the production of woodpulp in the nation. That means we are one of the great world producers, as well.

As the Number 2 producers of woodpulp in the nation, it has always seemed to me that not enough of us Puget Sounders know about the fascinating world of wood cellulose.

Take any scrap of paper, tear it and hold one of the torn edges up to the light. Along that edge will appear a slight fuzz. Here and there tiny strands will appear separately, like fine hairs.

Those tiny strands are cellulose fibers. Paper is made by floating millions of such fibers suspended in water on moving screens. As the water is drained through the screen these fibers form a thin mat which, squeezed and dried, becomes paper.

And most of the fibers used for paper today are wood cellulose fibers. Hundreds of tons of them are produced in the Puget country every day in the form of woodpulp, raw material for paper and other products. Glued together by a substance called lignin, these tiny fibers constitute about half the bulk of an average Puget country tree.

Few Puget Sounders notice the fibers in a piece of torn paper. Tiny as they are, they mean much to the economy of the region, create thousands of jobs, and as many thousands of products necessary to every day living.

The paper in your book, your newspaper, the facial tissue you keep handy, are products of woodpulp and in all probability of woodpulp made in the Puget country. So are school books, wrapping paper, paper bags and shipping sacks, paper milk containers, drinking cups, building paper, and a list in addition that would take days to recite.

And by chemical miracles this woodpulp is changed into rayon, cellophane, explosives, photographic film, plastics in a multitude of forms, from a thing like the base of your telephone, or the case of a radio, to pipe which carries crude petroleum from the oil fields. Not to mention hundreds of new papers and plastics for special use in the fields of electronics and outer space.

At least 20 million tons of woodpulp for these vital purposes are used each year in the United States alone, and much of it comes from the Puget country.

I am not one to discount the aesthetic beauties of our forests, but from what I have said you can see that much more goes on there than meets the casual eye. Each quiet tree — each quiet tree is a most complex factory powered by the rain and the sun. A tree builds itself by growing successive layers of cells, and each species of tree grows fibers uniquely its own.

And it was discovered, some thirty years ago, that the wood cellulose of the Puget country is especially adapted to woodpulp — and twenty years ago we began a system of tree farms and forest renewal which permits us to grow and harvest trees perpetually for this purpose. So wood cellulose and all its wonders are among the things which make unusual this land where you and I live.

From: "Puget Sound Profiles" by Nard Jones, Puget Sound Power & Light Company

SECTION 3: FOOD AND JOBS FROM THE SEA

Why Is The Pacific Northwest Such A Good Fishing Area?

Off the coast of Washington, Alaska, and British Columbia lies one of the richest fishing grounds of the world. This is one of the few areas in the world's oceans where cold water rises from the ocean bottom. As it rises, this water carries up important minerals. These minerals provide nutrition for billions of microscopic plants and animals, called plankton. The plankton, in turn, provides food for larger sea life — from tiny fish and shellfish to giant whales.

This abundant sea life has always been important to the people of the Pacific Northwest. In ancient times, there were even greater numbers of fish, otters, and other animals that can be eaten. The sea was a rich and dependable food source for the Native American cultures of the Pacific Northwest Coast. Today, seafood is not so central to our economy, but it still provides jobs and income for a significant number of people.

What Is The Life Cycle Of Salmon?

The most important product of the sea — for the Native Americans as well as for Washington State today — is salmon. In 1974, salmon made up nearly half the total value of processed sea food products from the state.

Salmon are unusual among sea animals in that they spend part of their lives in freshwater and part in saltwater. They hatch in gravel beds in small streams, live in the streams from two months to a year (depending on the species, or type, of salmon). Then they swim downstream to the ocean where they live and grow for two to six years.

When the salmon have matured, they return to the same stream bed where they were born. This is a long and difficult process. The fish must travel upstream, jumping over rocks and rapids. Often they are badly injured and exhausted by the time they arrive at the end of their journey. Here in the stream bed, the female prepares a nest in the gravel and lays her eggs in it. The male swims over the nest and fertilizes the eggs. Both parents die soon afterward.

37. *Explain how the following things contribute to the richness of sea life in the Pacific Northwest: (1) cold water rising to the surface from the ocean bottom, (2) plankton.*

38. *What is the most valuable seafood product of Washington?*

39. *Briefly describe the life cycle of salmon.*

TYPES OF NORTHWEST SALMON			
Names of Type	Average Adult Weight	Special Characteristics	Spawning Season
Chinook, king, tyee	10-50 Pounds 4-23 Kilograms	Largest Pacific salmon, commercially important, good sport fish	Spring to early autumn
Chum, dog, fall	8-18 Pounds 4-18 Kilograms	Dark-colored bars on sides, spawning male has large teeth	Autumn (the latest spawner)
Sockeye, red	5- 7 Pounds 2- 3 Kilograms	Dark red meat	Summer to early autumn
Pink, humpy, humpback	3- 5 Pounds 1- 2 Kilograms	Smallest Pacific salmon, heavily spotted, hump behind head	September to early November
Coho, silver, hook-nose, blue-back	6-12 Pounds 3- 5 Kilograms	Bright silver, sharp teeth	Autumn

Native Americans And Salmon

The Native American salmon fishing technology was based on a familiarity with the behavior of the fish. They knew that great numbers of salmon would start their upstream run at the same time every year. During these times, the people would travel to a traditional fishing spot along the river to catch the salmon that were swimming upstream.

In those days, there were many more salmon in the yearly runs. So many fish filled the streams that the water appeared silver. Fishers could dip nets into the rivers, and in a few weeks they could pull out enough fish to feed the entire village for a year. (See Unit 2, Section 2 for more information.)

Since salmon were the Coastal peoples' main food, they caught and ate a great number of them every year. But there were few people in the region then. They did not need all the fish, and they allowed a large number of salmon to complete their journey upstream to the spawning grounds. Each year, enough new salmon were hatched to make up for those that had been caught.

40. Why did salmon survive and reproduce in large numbers, even though Native Americans ate a great many of the fish every year?

How Did New Technology Endanger The Salmon?

After Europeans and Americans arrived, the number of salmon began to go down. The non-Indians became interested in catching large amounts of salmon to sell. The Hudson's Bay Company and, later, American businessmen such as Nathaniel Wyeth tried to start a business selling the fish overseas. They salted the fish and packed them in barrels. This packing method was not very effective. Often the salmon would spoil before they reached the buyers. Then in 1866, the first salmon cannery was built in the Pacific Northwest, at Eagle Cliff, Washington, on the Columbia River. Canned salmon could be stored and preserved for long periods of time. This meant that people could make a lot of money by catching and canning the fish and selling them around the world. Many people got involved in the Northwest salmon business.

More people were fishing in the rivers, and they were taking more fish. They developed

Many Filipinos worked in Northwest fish canneries, and they helped organize the first labor unions in this industry. What other Northwest industries employed many Filipino immigrants?

machines that could capture large numbers of salmon. One method, called the salmon wheel, scooped up all the salmon in a river as they swam upstream. Very few fish escaped and arrived at their spawning grounds. Traps were built across some streams with the same effect. The number of salmon dropped off sharply. In some areas, they were almost totally wiped out.

Other technological developments have also endangered Northwest salmon. Dams have blocked rivers, making it impossible for salmon to pass. Logging and farming have led to soil erosion; mud has been washed into streams, and spawning beds have been destroyed. City and factory wastes have polluted the water, killing more fish. The first gasoline-powered boat engine appeared here in 1903. With a faster engine, people could gather fish farther from shore. Refrigeration has made long boat trips possible, and has provided another way to ship and sell salmon.

All these developments have helped reduce the number of salmon in Northwest waters. It has been necessary for the government to regulate our fish resources, so that they are not forever destroyed.

41. How did each of the following contribute to the decline in salmon: fish canneries, salmon wheel and traps, pollution?

Scandinavian immigrants helped develop the fishing industry in Washington. Many of them worked on boats like this.

How Does The Government Regulate Our Salmon Resources?

There have been some laws to regulate salmon fishing since 1890. But in the past, the laws were not strong enough, and they were not enforced. Today, many government laws and programs help protect salmon and other sea resources. Some laws limit the amount of fish that may be caught. These laws prohibit certain fishing methods, and they limit fishing to certain places and certain times of year. Other laws control water pollution of different kinds.

Care is taken to protect salmon when dams are built. Often a fish ladder is built beside a dam so that salmon can get over the dam in small steps. The government also runs several salmon hatcheries, where millions of tiny salmon are raised and later released into streams.

42. Describe at least four ways the government helps protect salmon.

What Other Fish Are Valuable?

Another commercially important fish is the halibut. Halibut are one of several kinds of fish that live near the ocean bottom. They are large,

flat fish, and their coloring blends in with their environment. Adult halibut may weigh more than two hundred pounds.

In the early 1900's, American and Canadian fishers began intensive halibut fishing in the Pacific Northwest. In 1915, the harvest reached a record peak of 63 million pounds of halibut in one year. Afterwards, the size of the catch declined. People had taken too many of the fish. Halibut would have to be protected, or they would be wiped out. Regulation of halibut fishing involved two countries, Canada and the United States. So an international commission was formed. Since 1924, this commission has regulated the times and areas where halibut fishing may take place and the number of fish that may be caught. As a result, the catch has more than doubled since 1930.

Pacific Northwest fishers harvest other kinds of bottom fish, too, including flounder, sole, rock fish, and cod. These smaller bottom fish are usually harvested by trawling. A trawl is a large net with weights at the bottom. It is hauled along the ocean bottom behind a boat, then raised to remove the fish. Halibut are caught with long lines, stretched far beneath the water surface with smaller hooked lines off the big one. The fishers can pull these short lines to the surface to remove the fish. Then they place a small fish on the hook as bait and lower the line again.

Other valuable fish include smelt, herring, and albacore. (The albacore is a small tuna which usually weighs from 9-25 pounds.)

43. What is the largest and most valuable bottom fish?
44. Name at least five other fish of commercial importance in Washington.

How Are Oysters Raised?

After salmon, the most valuable seafood product of Washington is the oyster. Oysters will grow in shallow, protected saltwater bays or inlets, where the tides sweep in and out to bring the oysters food. These conditions exist in a few places in Washington. Willapa Bay is the main oyster farming region of the state. Other oyster beds are located in Hood Canal, Grays Harbor, and Puget Sound.

Oysters are raised in shallow waters near the shore. Old oyster shells are usually strung on wires, and these wires are hung on underwater fences. The baby oysters, called "spat," must attach themselves to old oyster shells in order to grow. When the oysters are mature, the wires are hauled in for the harvest.

The main variety of oysters raised in Washington is the Pacific oyster. It was first imported from Japan in 1902. By that time, most of the native Northwest oysters had been destroyed by pollution and over-harvesting. Large numbers of the tiny spat are imported from Japan each year. Today, some oyster seed is raised in special laboratories here in Washington. The Lummi tribe is developing its own seed cultivation, for example.

45. What kind of environment do oysters need to grow in?
46. What country do Pacific oysters come from?

What Other Shellfish Are Harvested And Sold?

Several varieties of clams and crabs are harvested by professionals for sale and by amateurs for their own use. The most important commercial crab in Washington is the Dungeness. Only mature males, with shells at least six inches across, may be taken. Another less important variety are the red crabs — sometimes called cancer crabs — which are smaller than Dungeness.

Crabs are commonly caught in baited traps, called crab pots. These are placed on the ocean bottom and marked with a buoy. They are hauled up into boats to remove the crabs that have become trapped inside.

Several varieties of clams are also harvested in Washington. The largest is the king clam, or geoduck (pronounced gooey-duck), which has a long, fat neck. Most geoducks are harvested underwater, though a few may be dug up at extremely low tides.

Many varieties of clams live in the intertidal zone (the area that is underwater at high tide and uncovered at low tide). They may be dug up or raked out of the sand at low tide.

The most highly prized variety is the razor clam. Razor clams can burrow quickly down into the sand and are a challenge to clam-hunters. They are dug up with shovels or with metal tubes called clam guns.

Butter clams and little neck clams are among the other shellfish harvested in Washington. Some shrimp and abalone are also caught and sold.

47. Name the following kinds of Washington shellfish: the largest clam, the most important crab, the most highly prized of the smaller clams.

Sport Fisheries

Each year, thousands of Washington residents gather varieties of fish and other seafoods for their personal use. In season, park beaches are full of clamdiggers. Many people own their own crab pots. And fishing is a popular recreational activity. The silver salmon is a favorite sport fish, for example, because it puts up a good fight.

One of the most highly prized sport fish is the steelhead. (A 1933 state law said that steelhead could only be taken by sport fishers.) Like salmon, steelhead hatch in fresh water and then go to the ocean. They return to their breeding grounds in yearly runs. But, unlike the salmon, they may spawn and return to saltwater many times.

Sport fishers gather many other kinds of fish, too, in both salt and fresh water. Probably the most popular freshwater fish are trout. They are found in mountain streams in several areas of the state. Saltwater fish such as smelt, cod, and flounder are also caught for personal use.

48. How are steelhead like salmon? How are they different?

Fishing boats and pleasure boats at the docks at Neah Bay. Many of the Makah Indians here, as well as Native Americans around the state, still make their living as fishers. Which tribes own their own aquaculture business?

SECTION 4: AGRICULTURAL RESOURCES

What Natural Factors Contribute To Agriculture?

Washington has several natural resources which help create good conditions for agriculture in different areas of the state. The deep volcanic soil of the Palouse Hills is excellent for growing wheat. Many of the river valleys in Western Washington have rich soils, as a result of repeated river floods long ago. The Skagit Valley soils are especially good; a large variety of crops are grown in the Skagit area.

Available water resources are quite different in different parts of the state. Most of Western Washington gets plenty of rain. But it rains very little in the summer, so some crops require irrigation. Water for irrigation is usually available from the many rivers and streams flowing down out of the mountains.

In Eastern Washington, irrigation water is more badly needed and more expensive. The climate is very dry, and there are few rivers. Getting water to the crops requires huge, expensive irrigation systems, like the one at Grand Coulee. But once irrigated, the Columbia Plateau provides hundreds of thousands of acres of rich farmland.

The mild temperatures of the Pacific Northwest are good for many crops. The growing season, or time between frosts, is quite long. In some parts of Western Washington the growing season is more than 300 days a year. Some vegetables can be grown and harvested in the winter. Climate, water, and soil all contribute to agriculture in Washington.

49. What natural resources help create good conditions for farming in Washington State?
50. What is a growing season?

What Was The Early History Of Agriculture In Washington?

The history of agriculture in Washington goes back to the time of the first non-Indian settlers. Farming was introduced to the Northwest by fur traders. At first, the traders planted gardens at the forts to raise food for their own use. These gardens were so successful that the Hudson's Bay Company set up a separate agricultural company. This company operated three big farms, where grains, fruits, vegetables, and farm animals were raised and exported.

When the missionaries arrived, they tried to interest the Indians in farming. (Although other Native American groups had traditionally practiced farming, the Northwest groups had not.) As a result of the missionaries' teaching, some tribes began planting crops. The Yakimas built one of Washington's earliest irrigation systems. And the Nez Perces — who had been skilled horse breeders — raised cattle.

These circular fields in the Columbia Basin are 135 acres each. They are irrigated by electrically-powered moving sprinklers.

The Seattle Public Market opened in 1907, the year this photo was taken. The market provided the chance for owners of small farms to sell directly to their customers. At that time, most of the open fruit and vegetable stands shown here were run by Italian and Japanese immigrants.

As settlers arrived on the Oregon Trail, they began farming, too. There were few stores in the region then, and people had to grow or gather their own food. The most popular area for early farm settlement was the Willamette Valley. By the 1850's, some settlers had planted large orchards and gardens in these areas, and they were already exporting food to California.

51. Who were the earliest farmers in Washington?
52. What did missionaries want the Indians to do?
53. To what area did the early Willamette Valley settlers export their extra crops?

What Farming Methods Have Been Used On The Columbia Plateau?

Farming on the Columbia Plateau developed more slowly. The plateau lands seemed too dry for crops. But people soon discovered by experimentation that the land could be very fertile. Settlers developed two methods for farming on the Columbia Plateau.

The first method, called "dry farming," is used for raising grains and seed peas. In many areas of Eastern Washington, the soil is very

deep. The top layer of soil may dry out, but the deeper layers can store moisture for many years. Farmers allow the land to absorb rainfall for a year or more before they plant a crop. Then the long roots of wheat and some other crops can reach down and use the moisture that has been stored in the soil. This method is still used by some Washington farmers.

Other crops need irrigation. The early farmers had to dig deep wells for water or build canals to carry river water to their fields. Often, this was very expensive. Most settlers could not afford to build their own irrigation system. As early as 1867, some private irrigation companies were formed. But many of these went bankrupt in the panic of 1893.

In order to solve these financial problems, the state and federal governments began passing laws to help start irrigation projects. The state allowed landowners in an area to get together and set up irrigation districts. Each landowner could be taxed to help pay irrigation costs. The federal government has also built many large-scale irrigation projects of its own over the

HOW IS WHEAT GROWN?

"Wheat is planted from seed — usually in the fall, in land which has been previously prepared. It starts sprouting in the fall and becomes dormant during the cold winter. As spring comes, the wheat plants start to grow and become a rolling green carpet. Gradually as spring turns to summer, the green fields turn to amber gold. When this golden field of grain is relatively hard and dry it is ready for harvest. The big machines called combines now roll into the fields to cut this grain. The kernels of wheat are separated from the straw and these kernels fall through a screen into a tank on the combine. The straw is blown out behind.

Trucks carry the grain from the field to storage facilities on the farm, or to local elevators where it is stored for later sale. At the elevator, wheat is sorted according to kind and quality and is kept in prime condition for shipment to market."

Washington Wheat Commission

years. Today over 1.5 million acres of Washington croplands are irrigated.

54. *What is dry farming?*
55. *Why have the state and federal government helped finance irrigation projects?*

Cowboys On The Old Snoqualmie Trail

There is another important agricultural use for the dry lands of the plateau: ranching. Back in the 1860's and '70's, the Yakima and Kittitas Valleys were called "cattleman's paradise." There were miles and miles of open green pasture, with shade along the creeks. It was an ideal location for cattle grazing. For several years, cowboys and their cattle herds roamed the hills of East-Central Washington.

Some of the cattle ranchers became quite wealthy. Ben Snipes is a good example. He came to the California gold fields in 1852, then went

Cattle ranching on the Columbia Plateau. How is cattle raising different in Washington today than it was in the middle 1800's?

north to look for gold along the Fraser River in British Columbia. While he was there, he realized that selling beef cattle to miners could be a good business. While still a teenager, he purchased his first cattle and began ranching. Twenty years later, he owned several ranches and up to 125,000 cattle!

All this took place before the railroads were built. There was only one method for getting the cattle from their pastures to the people who wanted beef. Cowboys had to round up the herds and walk them to market. The cattle route to Seattle lay along the Snoqualmie Trail. The trip took six days. Roadhouses, taverns, and corrals were soon built along the way, where the cowboys could spend the night.

But cowboy days did not last long in Washington. Ranchers tried to raise too many cattle on the land, and the animals ate too much of the grass. An extremely cold and snowy winter in 1880-81 killed thousands of cattle. But settlement was the main reason for the end of this kind of ranching. Settlers claimed land and put up fences, and the cattle could not roam freely over the hills any more. Settlers and ranchers often became very angry with each other.

Ranching is still an important business in Washington, but today's ranches have fenced pastures. And the animals eat special feed grains and grasses in addition to, or instead of, the wild plants of the open field. Thanks to new transportation and refrigeration methods, the animals can be easily shipped to nearby packing plants. Here the meat is frozen or canned and prepared for sale.

The most valuable range animals are cattle.

RODEOS

One modern reminder of the cattle ranching tradition of Washington is the rodeo — an event that takes place each year in several cities. The first rodeos were informal competitions between cowboys at the yearly cattle round-up. Cowboys of different races participated. Here in the Northwest, some of the best cowboys were Indians!

Over the years, rodeos have become professional sporting and entertainment events. Each year, thousands of fans attend the big rodeos at Ellensburg, and Toppenish, Washington, Pendleton, Oregon, and other Northwest cities.

THE LONELY LIFE OF A SHEEPHERDER

In the 1870's, cowboys drove their cattle across the open pastures of the Kittitas Valley. At the same time, a very different kind of ranching was going on in Eastern Washington: sheepherding. Each spring, the shepherd would accompany his flock to grazing areas in the mountains. There, he lived alone in a little covered wagon. In the wagon were books, a bunk, and often a musical instrument to help pass the lonely days. A shepherd might go for months without seeing a single other human being.

Most of Washington's early sheepherders were of English, Scottish, or Basque origin. (The Basque country is a part of Spain, but the people there have their own language and culture. There are still several Basque sheepherders in the Rocky Mountains of the Pacific Northwest.)

They graze on lowland grasses in the spring. Then they are moved up to mountain pastures in the summer, after the lowland grasses have turned brown. In autumn, rains restore the lowland grasses, and the cattle are returned. They pass the winter at the ranch, eating hay that was harvested the year before.

Some of the summer rangeland is in national forests. The national government owns other rangelands, too, and leases pastures to cattle-owners.

Sheep are raised in Washington by the same methods. Some graze on open pastures, and others are raised on farms. Sheep are hardy animals and can survive in steep, dry mountainous areas. Most Washington sheep are raised east of the Cascades. They are raised both for their meat and for their wool.

56. What factors brought an end to the old days of cowboys and cattle drives in Washington?
57. How is modern ranching different from ranching in the 1870's?

What Are Western Washington Farms Like?

There are farms of some kind in every county of Washington. In the river valleys of Western Washington, dairy farms are most important. The wet, cool climates and grassy fields of this area make it an ideal place to raise dairy cows. Other important farm products of Western

Washington include chickens, vegetables, and berries of every kind. Several specialty crops are grown in some western areas; for example, flower bulbs are an important product of the Skagit Valley.

In Western Washington, small family farms are most common. These are sometimes called truck farms, since the owners may truck their own crops to local markets. The Pike Place Market in Seattle is one of several places where farmers can sell their crops.

Past floods have deposited many layers of good soil in the flat river valleys of Western Washington. But these same lands are often in great demand by businesses, since the land is easy to build on. Much of the state's best farmland has been lost to urban development.

58. Why is Western Washington well-suited to dairy farming?
59. Why has much of Western Washington's best farmland been lost?

Technology On Eastern Washington Farms

Most Eastern Washington farms look different from the small farms of Western Washington. The eastern farms tend to be very large and highly specialized. On the Columbia Plateau, it is common to see thousands of acres planted in the same crop.

These huge farms are highly technological. They use large, expensive machines to plow, plant, thin, and harvest the crops. Specially developed seeds and fertilizers are often used. The crops are sprayed with chemicals to fight insects and diseases. Growing conditions are scientifically tested throughout the year.

Technology is also responsible for new irrigation systems. More and more farms use an electrically-powered sprinkler system, with a huge sprinkler pipe up to 1/4 mile long. This pipe is mounted on wheels. It turns around a central point, creating a giant circle of irrigated land, 135 acres large.

These big, technological farms are run very differently from traditional family farms. They are very expensive to start and are often owned by big businesses. (A lot of Eastern Washington farmland is now owned by oil companies, sugar companies, and national grocery store chains.) Since machines do most of the work, there are few permanent jobs on these farms. Instead, the owners hire a few specially-trained managers and machine operators. Then at harvest season and other busy times, they hire migrant laborers, who work for a while and then move on to other areas and other farms.

60. Give at least three examples of highly-developed technology on giant Eastern Washington farms.
61. What kind of workers are needed on these farms?

What Are The Main Crops Of Eastern Washington?

Of course the major crops of Eastern Washington are also different from those of Western Washington. This is natural, since the geography is so different. Wheat is well adapted to the dry climate and is the most important crop. Peas are also grown through the dry farming method and are often alternated with wheat. Some of the peas are frozen and canned to sell as vegetables. Others are dried and can be used for making soup or animal feed. Part of the pea crop is sold as seed.

Idaho leads the country in the production of potatoes, and Washington ranks second in this crop. Potatoes need irrigation, and the main potato-growing areas of Washington are in the central part of the state, in counties near the Grand Coulee project. Another very valuable

VALUE OF FARM PRODUCTION

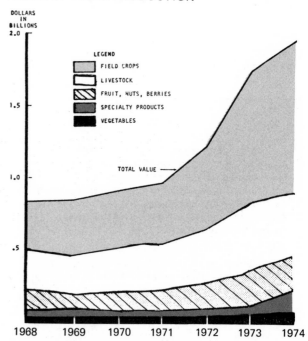

DOLLARS IN BILLIONS

LEGEND
FIELD CROPS
LIVESTOCK
FRUIT, NUTS, BERRIES
SPECIALTY PRODUCTS
VEGETABLES

TOTAL VALUE

2.0

1.5

1.0

.5

1968   1969   1970   1971   1972   1973   1974

COMBINES HARVESTING WHEAT
*In 1918 it took twenty-four horses to pull the combine and five men to operate it. Then the sacks of
wheat still had to be picked up from the field later and hauled to the warehouse. Now one man
operates a modern combine and the bulk wheat is put directly from the combine
into a truck and hauled away.*

WHEAT — WASHINGTON'S NO. 1 CROP

Few people in Washington are farmers — only about 1% of the state's population in 1972. But five times that many people depend on agriculture for their jobs. A great number of these jobs are located in the cities. For example, wheat — the state's most valuable crop — supports thousands of jobs in flour mills, bakeries, transportation, printing, insurance, farm machinery, fuels, fertilizers, and so on. In 1972, for example, the state's wheat crop sold for $256.4 million. But a Washington State University economist estimated that it was actually worth about $460 million in jobs and income.

Almost every part of the state economy benefits from the agricultural industry. The largest share of the money generated by the wheat crop goes to the farmers themselves. The next largest share flows directly from one household to another, without passing through any business establishment. This share includes rent paid by farmworkers, for example. This share came to $133 million. The next largest part included all sales directly or indirectly related to wheat. Wages and profits from these sales together totaled $85 million.

Other parts of the economy received more than $10 million each. They were:

Services	$46 million
Insurance and real estate	$29 million
Communication and utilities	$22 million
Transportation services	$18 million
Chemical and petroleum manufacturing	$11 million

Receiving more than $1 million were:

Printing and publishing	$ 5 million
Paper products	$ 4 million
Beverages and other foods	$ 4 million
Meat and dairy	$ 4 million
Livestock and products	$ 3 million
Vegetables and fruits	$ 2 million
Construction	$ 2 million
Canning and preserving	$ 1 million

Receiving more than $500,000 benefits were: forestry, fishing, and mining; fabricated metals; other transportation; other vegetable crops; other agriculture; textiles and apparel; lumber and wood; and machinery.

The flat, fertile river valleys of Western Washington are excellent land for several crops. These areas still support many small family farms.

Several of these crops — grapes, hops, and mint, for example — are grown almost exclusively in the dry and sunny Yakima Valley. Before irrigation, this area was nearly a desert. Now it is one of the best farming areas in the state.

Another crop that deserves mention is hay. In 1974, hay ranked sixth in value among all the state's agricultural products. Hay is unique in that it is raised in quantity in every subregion of the state.

63. *Name at least five specialty crops of which Washington is among the top producers.*
64. *Name at least two specialty crops of the Yakima Valley.*

product of Washington's irrigated farmland has been the sugar beet.

After wheat, the most valuable crop of Eastern Washington is the apple crop. Apples and other fruits are the main products of the eastern slopes of the Cascades. These fruit-growing areas make up a farming region that is quite different from the wheat and grain lands in the southeast quarter of the state. The fruit orchards are not as large as the wheat farms. They are very carefully tended and intensively farmed. Washington State is the leading producer of apples, and Wenatchee calls itself the apple capital of the world.

Other important fruit crops of this area are pears (which ranked as the state's tenth most valuable crop in 1974), peaches, plums, cherries, and apricots.

62. *What are the first and second most valuable crops of Eastern Washington?*

Other Important Crops

In addition to the major crops already discussed, Washington ranks among the top five states in many specialty crops, including grapes, peppermint, strawberries, sweet corn, alfalfa, and asparagus. Washington is first in the production of hops (used in making beer) and spearmint.

The Importance Of Food Processing

The agricultural products of the Pacific Northwest help support another of the region's biggest industries: food processing. Many raw food products are processed in some way before they are exported. Meats and seafoods, fruits and vegetables are usually canned or frozen. Much of the wheat is ground into flour, and some of it is made into bread and other baked goods. Other products of the food processing industry include beverages, dairy products, and sugar.

The dairy industry is a good example of the food processing industry in Washington. Creameries in the state process whole milk into cream, butter, cottage cheese, and other prod-

PRINCIPAL FARM COMMODITIES
Listed in Rank Order of Total Crop Value

1976 COMMODITY	VALUE (THOUSANDS)	1977 COMMODITY	VALUE (THOUSANDS)
WHEAT	394,697	WHEAT	268,458
MILK	244,014	MILK	244,690
APPLES	191,250	APPLES	189,000
CATTLE & CALVES	180,206	CATTLE & CALVES	183,810
HAY	161,436	POTATOES	138,752
POTATOES	139,500	HAY	133,760
BARLEY	48,859	EGGS	44,115
EGGS	47,435	SUGAR BEETS	33,642
HOPS	34,039	HOPS	32,522
SUGAR BEETS	33,516	MINT OIL	29,808

SOURCE: WASHINGTON STATE DEPARTMENT OF AGRICULTURE

These Klondike gold miners were independent adventurers. Today, most mining goes on in large machine-equipped mines owned by big companies.

MINERALS AND MINING: ANOTHER NATURAL

RESOURCE INDUSTRY

At times in Washington's history, mineral resources have been very important to the economy here. In the second half of the nineteenth century, coal was one of the state's most important exports. In the 1850's and '60's, thousands of people came to Washington to look for gold. But the gold rush lasted only a short time. Coal mining is no longer as important since coal is not such a common heating fuel, and Washington's coal is fairly expensive to mine.

Minerals are not as valuable to the state economy as they once were, but some mining still goes on. There is an electrical generating plant in Centralia that is powered by Washington coal. Some gold, silver, copper, lead and other metals are mined in the Cascades and the Okanogan Highlands. There are some important uranium deposits in the northeastern corner of the state.

The minerals of greatest economic value here are not metals but building materials: limestone, sand, gravel, clay, and stone. These materials are known as industrial minerals and are found at many locations throughout the state.

Washington exports a lot of copper and aluminum. But these metals are not mined here; they are refined here. One of the world's largest copper smelters is located in Tacoma. Copper and other metals are usually not found in a pure state in the earth. Instead, they are mixed with other kinds of rock. This mineral-bearing rock is called ore. The Tacoma smelter receives tons of ore and processes it, in order to separate out the copper. Aluminum is another important metal refining industry of the Northwest.

ucts. Probably the first was the Martin and Hubbard Creamery, established in Cheney in 1880. The first evaporated milk was produced in Kent in the 1890's. This Kent creamery was the beginning of the Carnation Company, now the largest producer of evaporated milk in the United States.

Today's typical dairy farmer stores the day's milk in refrigerated holding tanks, where it is picked up regularly by refrigerated trucks from the creamery or dairy plant. At the creamery, the milk is sterilized and bottled for sale or made into the many dairy products we're familiar with: butter, cheeses, ice cream, yogurt, etc.

In 1970, there were over 90 licensed dairy plants in Washington, including 21 that manufactured ice cream, 13 that made butter, and 12 that made cottage cheese. All milk and dairy products we buy have been processed in some way.

65. Name at least three food processing industries.

APPLES

Andy Gossman had a good life in Iowa; he was a pharmacist and a teacher. But he wasn't satisfied. Andy dreamed of growing apples; he wanted to develop new and better apple trees. He was inspired by the story of Johnny Appleseed, who had planted apple trees all over the Midwest.

Andy Gossman finally realized his dream in Central Washington. Here, he found excellent conditions for raising apples: thick volcanic soil, sunny days, and plenty of irrigation water from the streams that flowed down the Cascades. In 1906, he established the Columbia and Okanogan nurseries. In the following years, he developed 14 new varieties of fruit trees and won many awards.

Andy Gossman and other Washington orchardists and scientists have made apples one of the state's most important crops. Today, one fifth of the United States apple crop is grown in Washington. Because of new packing and storage methods, Washington apples can now be kept for up to 10 months and shipped all over the country.

The most popular varieties are the red and golden delicious apples. They are harvested in September, then individually wrapped and stored in special low-temperature, low-oxygen warehouses. Refrigerated trucks and railroad cars keep the apples fresh on their journey to distant markets. The first apple seeds took six months or more to get to the Northwest by ship or covered wagon. Today's apples can be shipped to East Coast markets in a couple of days.

Workers sort apples for sale. The food processing industry provides thousands of jobs for people in Washington.

SECTION 5: THE REGIONAL ECONOMY

What Are Primary And Secondary Industries?

The natural resource industries are sometimes called primary industries. Farming, logging, and mining are all examples of primary industries. The products of primary industries — such as fruits, wheat, minerals, and lumber — support other businesses, called secondary industries. These include all kinds of processing and manufacturing. For example, plywood manufacturing is a secondary industry that depends on logging. Bakeries depend on wheat. Copper smelting depends on raw copper ore.

Before statehood, Washington's economy was based almost entirely on primary industries, especially logging. In the twentieth century, secondary industries have become increasingly important. This section will pay special attention to the roles of manufacturing and trade in the state economy.

66. *Define primary and secondary industries and give an example of each.*

Aluminum refining became an important industry here during World War II. Today, many aluminum products are manufactured in this state.

the Northwest economy since World War II. The increase is partly due to the huge amounts of cheap electricity from Northwest dams. Improved transportation and new technology have also contributed to growth.

67. *Which manufacturing industry was most important during World War I? During World War II?*
68. *Name at least two things that have contributed to the increased importance of manufacturing in Washington.*

What Has Been The History Of Manufacturing In Washington?

The earliest manufacturing industries in Washington had to do with the processing of local resources. Some examples included the milling and making of wood products, the grinding of wheat, and the salting and preserving of fish. In the larger settlements, there soon began a number of small businesses that manufactured items for local use. These included printed materials, clothing, leather products, and tools.

Manufacturing grew steadily, but somewhat slowly, in importance until the early 1900's. World War I caused a great, temporary increase in manufacturing here. At that time, shipbuilding was the leading industry.

World War II brought a bigger and longer-lasting boom for Northwest factories. It was during this war that airplane manufacturing emerged as a major state industry. In fact, the war marked an important turning point for the state economy. Manufacturing of many kinds has become an increasingly important part of

What Are The Important Manufacturing Industries?

The most valuable manufacturing industry and the largest single employer in the region is the aerospace industry. Boeing, the largest company in this field, has been producing helicopters, missiles, boats, and parts for nuclear reactors in addition to airplanes. They have also been developing satellites to capture solar energy. One non-aerospace product that has captured international attention is the Boeing hydrofoil. These fast passenger boats are being used in Hong Kong and Japan and tested on Puget Sound.

Other large Washington companies also make transportation equipment, including ships, trucks, and railcars. Several additional local firms provide parts and services for these companies. For example, there are companies that make machine parts and electronic equipment for Boeing and for Washington shipbuilders.

A number of manufacturing businesses are tied to the key natural resource industries of the state. Food processing is an important example. So are our many wood and paper products. Today, every part of the tree is used to make a wide variety of products. Paper, plastics, rayon, plywood, and furniture are among the many wood products manufactured here.

The number of manufactured products from Washington has been continually expanding. Some manufacturing businesses that have recently been added or expanded include sporting goods, electronic instruments, clothing, plastics, printing, and publishing.

69. What is the most valuable manufacturing industry and the largest single employer in the state?
70. Name at least ten of Washington's important manufactured products.

The Importance Of Trade

The primary industries and manufacturing of Washington help support another very important economic activity. That activity is trade.

The Pacific Northwest is rich in resources that are lacking in other parts of the world. On the other hand, many important resources and manufactured goods are not available here. Our economy — like that of most world regions — depends on trade, on the export of local products and the import of items from other regions. For example, Northwest wheat growers sell about 85% of their crop to other countries. The aluminum industry here is entirely dependent on foreign sources of aluminum-bearing ore, called bauxite.

Because of its geographic location, Washington's main trading partners are the countries of the Pacific Rim. (See Unit One, Section 2.) Washington is the closest state to such key cities as Yokohama, Japan, and Vancouver, British Columbia. Because of location, and because Washington has many excellent ports, our state has become an important center of trans-Pacific trade. Products from the 48 contiguous states are shipped out of Washington ports to Asia, Australia, Canada, and Alaska. Similarly, products from Pacific Rim countries arrive at Washington ports for distribution to other parts of the United States.

71. Why has Washington become a center of trans-Pacific trade?

What Is The History Of Washington's Trade?

Trans-Pacific shipping has been central to the Northwest economy ever since the first traders arrived. In those days, furs were the most important export. They were traded for blankets, tools, and other imported items from Atlantic coastal cities. Furs were shipped to Asia, Europe, and the eastern United States.

Over the years, the main imports and exports have changed — and so have the forms of transportation. In the 1860's and 1870's, the main Northwest exports were lumber and coal, and San Francisco was the most important market.

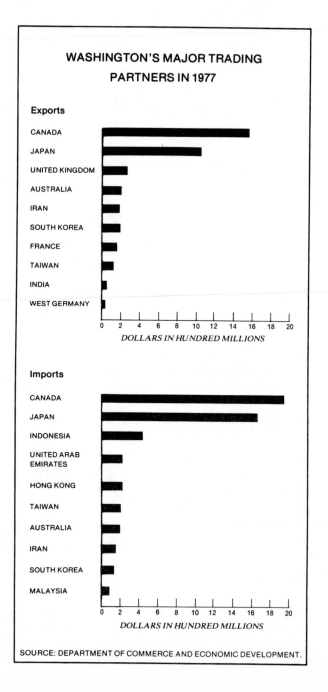

WASHINGTON'S MAJOR TRADING PARTNERS IN 1977

Exports

CANADA, JAPAN, UNITED KINGDOM, AUSTRALIA, IRAN, SOUTH KOREA, FRANCE, TAIWAN, INDIA, WEST GERMANY

0 2 4 6 8 10 12 14 16 18 20
DOLLARS IN HUNDRED MILLIONS

Imports

CANADA, JAPAN, INDONESIA, UNITED ARAB EMIRATES, HONG KONG, TAIWAN, AUSTRALIA, IRAN, SOUTH KOREA, MALAYSIA

0 2 4 6 8 10 12 14 16 18 20
DOLLARS IN HUNDRED MILLIONS

SOURCE: DEPARTMENT OF COMMERCE AND ECONOMIC DEVELOPMENT.

Steamships were the main transportation, and overland travel was still very difficult.

Then in the 1880's, the first cross-country railroads came to the Pacific Northwest and brought great changes in trading patterns. Now Northwest businesses were better able to sell their products in other parts of the United States. And Washington became a gateway for trade between all parts of the United States and Asia. Lumber, Washington's most important export, was carried by both the ships and the railroads.

Many other historic events have affected Washington trade. For example, the Klondike Gold Rush of 1897 brought a boom in shipping between Alaska and the Washington ports — especially Seattle. The opening of the Panama Canal in 1915 gave Washington cities much better access to Atlantic markets. World Wars I and II brought great increases in shipbuilding, international trade, and military use of some port facilities.

72. Name the most important exports in the following historical periods:
  a. fur trading period.
  b. the 1860's and 1870's.
73. Name at least three events that affected Washington trade and tell why each was important.

How Has Changing Technology Affected Trade?

Technological developments and building programs have also contributed to trade. For example, the Columbia River has been greatly improved as a shipping route. Long ago, the river was swift and dangerous. Big ships could not travel far upriver, and even the best canoes could not navigate some parts of the Columbia. In this century, a number of dams have been built across the river. These have raised the water level and slowed the river down. A series of locks allow ships to pass by these dams, and it is now possible to travel as far as Lewiston, Idaho. In 1962, Congress approved funds to dig a deeper channel in the Columbia so that even larger ships could sail up the river.

Individual cities have built new piers, warehouses and other facilities to improve their ports. In order to accomplish this, some cities have voted to set up a public port district — a separate government unit that can manage and maintain the port. Tacoma established its public port in 1910 and Seattle in 1911, for example. Now there are 71 port districts in the state.

New technology has required remodeling of the ports. Most of today's ocean cargo is "containerized." It is shipped in huge steel boxes that

Washington's harbors are busy 24 hours a day with ships from all over the world. This Japanese ship is loaded with "containerized" cargo. The containers can be lifted directly onto trucks or trains so that no goods have to be unpacked and repacked.

Due to dams and river development, some of our important port cities are located in Eastern Washington, along the Snake and Columbia Rivers.

COLUMBIA RIVER

This photo shows some of the docks of the Port of Pasco. Many of the agricultural products that pass through Eastern Washington ports are shipped to foreign countries. For example, Saudi Arabia purchased 9-10 million dollars worth of Washington apples in 1977, making it the world's largest importer of apples from our state. (The Saudis then distributed them throughout the Persian gulf, to Kuwait, Oman, and South Yemen.) Other major apple importers include Hong Kong, Great Britain, Mexico, and Singapore.

About 80% of the wheat grown in Washington is exported. Much of it goes to Asian countries, including Japan, Taiwan, South Korea, and the Philippines.

The Port of Pasco is equipped to handle containerized cargo. Products such as hay, soybeans, and cattle hides are loaded into large containers. These containers can then be hauled by barges, trucks, or ocean-going ships. At the Port of Pasco, containers full of Eastern Washington agricultural products are loaded on barges. These barges are hauled to Portland where the containers are lifted onto ships from all over the world.

Richland, Kennewick, and other Eastern Washington cities also have busy ports.

can be lifted — by special cranes — directly from ships onto rail cars or trucks. Changes in technology have also brought changes in the products we trade. Today, airplanes are one of the state's most important exports, and we import large numbers of automobiles, television sets, and cameras. Of course, all these items were unknown when the first trade ships sailed into Puget Sound more than a century ago.

74. What developments helped open the Columbia River for ship travel?

75. Define the following: public port district, containerized cargo.

How Does Trade Affect The State Economy?

All this trade activity has a significant impact on the state economy. State government studies in 1972 estimated that 10.1% of all jobs in

Washington are directly or indirectly related to international trade. This includes dockworkers, truck drivers, and workers in industries that export most of their products.

While other Washington industries may suffer great variations in employment and income, the shipping industry has been steadily growing. It has helped to stabilize our state's economy. Even during the economic recession of the early 1970's, the value of trade increased dramatically. (See Unit 10, Section 1.)

76. How has trade helped make our economy more stable?

What Do We Trade? Who Do We Trade With?

Washington's major exports are aircraft, logs and lumber, pulp and paper products, fish and wheat. Our major imports are oil, natural gas,

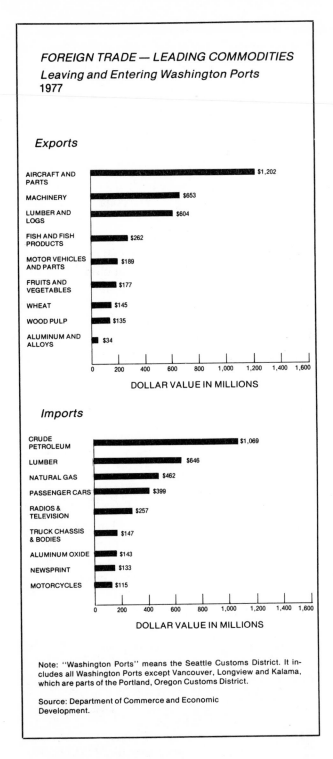

FOREIGN TRADE — LEADING COMMODITIES
Leaving and Entering Washington Ports
1977

Exports

AIRCRAFT AND PARTS	$1,202
MACHINERY	$653
LUMBER AND LOGS	$604
FISH AND FISH PRODUCTS	$262
MOTOR VEHICLES AND PARTS	$189
FRUITS AND VEGETABLES	$177
WHEAT	$145
WOOD PULP	$135
ALUMINUM AND ALLOYS	$34

DOLLAR VALUE IN MILLIONS

Imports

CRUDE PETROLEUM	$1,069
LUMBER	$646
NATURAL GAS	$462
PASSENGER CARS	$399
RADIOS & TELEVISION	$257
TRUCK CHASSIS & BODIES	$147
ALUMINUM OXIDE	$143
NEWSPRINT	$133
MOTORCYCLES	$115

DOLLAR VALUE IN MILLIONS

Note: "Washington Ports" means the Seattle Customs District. It includes all Washington Ports except Vancouver, Longview and Kalama, which are parts of the Portland, Oregon Customs District.

Source: Department of Commerce and Economic Development.

From 1970-76, Canada accounted for 37% of all foreign trade passing through Washington ports. Second in volume of trade is Japan, with 23% of all import and export value. Canada and Japan are the major markets for Washington products and also the major sources of our imports. Other important trading partners include Australia and countries of Eastern Asia and Western Europe.

77. List at least three of each of the following for Washington State:
a. major exports.
b. major imports.
c. main trading partners.

What Kinds Of Jobs Do Major Industries Provide?

The major industries provide jobs for many of the people in our state. In the lumber industry, for example, there are jobs for loggers, sawyers, mill workers, tree planters, forest rangers, and fire fighters. A great many other jobs exist to provide services to these workers. Every logging town needs teachers, health care workers, salespeople, mechanics, and other workers.

The chart on page 202 shows the biggest employers in Washington. Notice that the largest numbers of people are in manufacturing, trade, and government careers. (In this case, trade includes all stores as well as larger sales operations.)

Within each category, there is a great variety of careers and employment opportunities. Let's look, for example, at the Boeing company, which is the largest single employer in the state. In March, 1978, the company's job openings included the following: bookkeepers, secretaries, clerks, accountants, buyers, testers, estimators, analysts, technicians, illustrators, designers, metal workers, electricians, repairpersons, computer programmers, engineers, planners, coordinators, personnel workers, managers, and others.

78. Name at least five jobs that are directly connected with the lumber industry and five jobs connected to the aerospace industry.

Canadian lumber, and the mineral bauxite (from which aluminum is refined). This state has also become an important receiving center for electrical equipment and for automobiles and car parts — primarily from Japan, Italy, and Germany.

Washington's main trading partners are still the countries of the Pacific Rim. Canada, our neighbor, is our most important trading partner.

AGRICULTURAL EMPLOYMENT

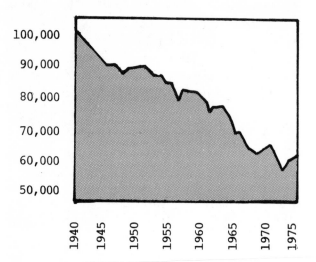

Bigger industries do not always mean more jobs. Recently, machines have taken over much of the work that people used to have to do. This means that production may stay high while the number of jobs goes down. The effects of technology have been especially notable in agriculture. The value of farm products had risen quite steadily. From 1940 to 1944, the average value was 355.6 million dollars. In 1974, farm products were valued at nearly two billion dollars. But during the same period, the number of agricultural jobs dropped to almost half the 1940 levels.

How Are Jobs And The Economy Related?

Changes in Washington's economy mean changes in the kinds of jobs available here. For example, when coal mining became less important, many miners lost their jobs. Other workers were affected, too. Some of the people who made their living by cooking for miners or selling goods to them or renting them rooms also lost their jobs. These people had to find new ways to earn a living. Some of them moved to the big cities to look for work with new manufacturing companies. Some of them had to learn new job skills.

When a new industry comes to a region, jobs are created. When an industry prospers, the number of jobs in that industry often goes up. When the industry loses business, many of the workers lose their jobs. Understanding the state economy can help people here to make better choices about what kinds of job skills to learn. It can help people prepare for jobs that will probably last a long time.

79. What happened to coal miners when coal became less important?
80. Explain at least one way that jobs and the economy are related.

How Are Job Opportunities Changing?

Blue-collar workers include skilled and unskilled laborers, from plumbers and carpenters to machine operators to truck loaders. In the past, most people in Washington have worked at "blue-collar" jobs. However, since World War II, the number of "white-collar" jobs has been growing fast. White-collar workers include professionals, managers, clerical and technical workers, and salespeople. By 1970, there were about 200,000 more white-collar than blue-collar workers in the state.

The fastest-growing employment group has been the professional group. This means that there has been a rapid rise in the number of doctors, engineers, designers, administrators, and other professionals. There has also been a notable increase in the number of service jobs. Recently, more and more people here have found work in such fields as health, food, and clothing services.

81. Define the following: white-collar workers, blue-collar workers.
82. What employment groups are growing rapidly?

Where Can People In Washington Learn Job Skills?

Almost all the jobs just mentioned require some kind of special education after high school. Most of those on the list require degrees or certificates that can be obtained at the many community colleges in Washington. Almost every major city in the state has a community college. The courses offered at some of these

A white-collar worker in a Washington industry.

schools include: arts and science, welding, printing, accounting, data processing, electronics, agricultural management, forest technology, drafting, dental hygiene, law enforcement, advertising art, design, secretarial science, and appliance repair. Most programs take one or two years to complete. Some courses are also available at public and private technical schools.

Most professional and technical fields require longer courses of study. There are about 20 colleges and universities in Washington that offer B.A., M.A., or Ph.D. degrees. The largest is the University of Washington in Seattle, which had over 33,000 students in 1970.

Job training is also available through several government programs. The federal, state, and county governments all help sponsor job services, such as training programs, career counseling, job referral, and job preparation workshops. The main government agency in charge of these programs is the Washington State Department of Employment Security. This agency has job centers in big cities around the state where people can come for free assistance in finding jobs.

83. Name some courses of study available at Washington's community colleges.
84. What is the state's largest university?

How Does Washington Compare With The Rest Of The Country?

In general, people in Washington State have more education and higher incomes than the national average. The 1970 census showed that Washington ranked twelfth among the states in median income level. Half of Washington's families made more than $10,404 and half made less. (This is the median level.)

Educational levels in the state also tend to be high. In 1972, Washington ranked second in the country in the median level of education. Whites had a median of 12.4 years of schooling and non-whites had a median of 12.1 years in school.

About 8% of the state's families had incomes below the national poverty level. As a result, Washington ranked 28th among the states in the percentage of extreme poverty.

In 1977, 8.6% of the state's population was unemployed. During the recession of the early 1970's, Washington unemployment levels were much higher than the national average. As the

The photo above shows Clara McCarty, first graduate of the University of Washington. She was the only graduate out of a class of 17. Today, there are more than 30,000 students at the University.

1970's came to a close, however, unemployment in this state was close to the national average.

In education, as in other areas, there are differences between the various racial and ethnic groups of the state. The chart on the next page gives some basic statistics on these different groups.

85. How did Washington rank among the 50 states in the following categories: median income level, median educational level?
86. Use the chart to find the group which fits each of the following descriptions: (a) greatest percentage of poverty, (b) highest percentage of college graduates, (c) highest average income.

What Is A Regional Economy?

When we talk about Washington's economy, we are referring to all the sources and the distribution of products and services in this state. Employment, growth, and the success of local industries are all important factors of the state economy.

We can also talk about the regional economy of the Pacific Northwest. The Pacific Northwest is an economic region, as well as a geographic region. The states of the Pacific Northwest share many of the same industries and products. Lumbering, fishing, wheat and potato farming, cattle ranching, and dairying are among the industries that are important in other Northwest states.

87. Define the term "economy" as used above.
88. Name some industries shared by other Northwest states in addition to Washington.

AN ECONOMIC PROFILE OF RACIAL AND ETHNIC GROUPS IN WASHINGTON STATE IN 1970

	White	Black	Native American	Japanese American	Chinese American	Filipino American	Spanish Speaking
Median Income of Families	10,467	8,188	6,818	12,455	10,845	8,791	8,330
% of Population Below Poverty Level	7.2%	16.8%	25.5%	7.9%	6.9%	12.5%	17.6%
% of Population who are High School Graduates	63.9%	48.6%	37.3%	74.9%	57.1%	50.4%	49.8%
% of College Graduates	12.8%	5.6%	2.9%	17.8%	23.9%	17.7%	9.4%
% of Population in "White-collar" jobs*	51.2%	35.3%	27.1%	52.0%	51.6%	35.0%	37.3%
% in "Blue-collar jobs*	32.8%	36.8%	46.6%	27.6%	20.8%	35.5%	34.9%
% in Service jobs*	12.6%	26.8%	19.6%	15.5%	27.2%	23.9%	12.5%
% of Farmers and farmworkers	3.4%	1.0%	6.7%	4.9%	0.4%	5.6%	15.2%

* "White-collar" workers include professionals, salespeople and office workers. "Blue-collar" jobs include industrial and construction jobs; service jobs might include cooking, cleaning, etc.

Economic Interdependence

The states of the Pacific Northwest are economically interdependent in several ways. Several industries in one part of the region depend on the products of another part of the region. For example, the smelter in Tacoma gets much of its raw copper ore from Montana. The bakeries in Seattle use wheat from the Palouse country of Washington, Oregon, and Idaho. Houses and factories on the Columbia Plateau may be built of lumber from Western Washington and Oregon. The ships that leave Portland, Seattle, and other Northwest ports carry products from all over the region.

The entire Pacific Northwest region often shares similar economic problems. A drought may easily affect farmers all over the region. A drop in the demand for lumber may cause a loss of income in each Northwest state. When unemployment is high in one area, and people have less money to spend, many industries around the region may lose money in sales.

Similarly, a boom in one industry may bring greater profits to another. When the Boeing Company was expanding rapidly in the 1960's, thousands of people moved to Seattle from other areas. New housing was needed. This brought a boom in the construction business and new demands for Northwest lumber. More aluminum was needed from the refineries around the region. And the new residents bought more products from all over the region.

The various governments of the Pacific Northwest cooperate in several ways to promote the regional economy. Keeping the Columbia River clean requires the cooperation of all the states, for example. And the water and power from the federal Columbia Basin project must be distributed among all areas of the region, as well as other western states. The governors of the Northwest states sometimes meet together to coordinate state policies on certain issues. And many federal government agencies have a central headquarters in Seattle that serves all of Washington, Oregon, and Idaho.

89. Give an example of an economic problem that could affect all parts of the Pacific Northwest region.
90. Give an example of a product from the Columbia Plateau that is needed by an industry in Western Washington or Oregon, and give an example of a western product that is needed on the Plateau.

SECTION 6: ENERGY NEEDS AND RESOURCES

Energy And The Economy

In the early days of settlement, Washington industries relied on people-power and animals to do much of the work. Trees were cut down with handsaws and hauled by ox teams. Oxen or horses pulled the plows, and much farming was done by hand.

As our industries have become more mechanized, they have come to depend on other sources of energy. Today's industries consume great amounts of oil, gas, and electricity every year. We also consume more and more of these energy resources in our personal lives, too — for heat, light, transportation, and home appliances. Our economy and our way of life depend on our energy supplies.

Energy is important to the state economy in several ways. Energy supplies make up a large part of the value of our foreign trade. Oil is by far our biggest import. In 1976, well over a billion dollars worth of crude oil came through Washington ports from foreign countries. Natural gas was second in import value, at 354 million dollars in 1976.

Many people in Washington make their living in the production and distribution of energy supplies. There are jobs at the oil refineries on Puget Sound, at dams and power plants, at gas stations, and at electric companies. Energy supplies make up an industry itself, and they are needed by all of our other industries. Without enough energy supplies, many of our industries would have to cut back or stop production. Many jobs would be lost. The impact on our economy would be very serious.

91. What three kinds of energy sources are consumed in great amounts by industries and individuals in this state?
92. Name some jobs in the production and distribution of energy supplies.
93. What are our two most valuable imports?

Energy And The Environment

Energy is necessary for our way of life, but it is also the source of many problems. Some of our most serious environmental problems involve the ways we produce and transport energy.

Consider Alaskan oil, for example. The ecology of inland Alaska is very fragile. Plants and animals have a hard time surviving in the cold, arctic climate. The activity of building the oil pipeline has disturbed this delicate environment.

Once the oil reaches the end of the pipeline, it must be loaded onto ships and carried to the other 49 states. Shipping the oil poses more environmental problems. In the last several years, there have been many accidents involving oil tankers around the world. Millions of gallons of oil have spilled into the oceans as a result. This oil has killed birds, fish, and other marine animals. It has washed ashore, temporarily ruining beaches. Fisheries and tourist industries have suffered losses. Because of the risk of accidents, many people have opposed the building of new oil tanker ports in their community.

Big aluminum plants such as this one located at Trentwood near Spokane (too large to fit in one photo) use nearly a third of the state's electricity. Where else does the state's electricity go?

Every kind of energy we use has certain environmental problems associated with it. These environmental issues will have to be considered along with the economic issues as we plan how to fill our energy needs in the future.

94. What environmental problems are associated with the development and transportation of Alaskan oil?
95. What two kinds of issues must be considered as we plan how to fill our energy needs in the future?

Why Will We Need More Power?

Planning for future energy supplies is very important. We depend on energy and we are going to need even more energy in the future.

There are several reasons why our energy needs are growing. First, our population is growing: Washington's population increased almost 20% between 1965 and 1970. And the other western states — which also use electricity from Washington — were growing even faster. Some experts predicted that Washington's population alone would be half again as large by the year 2000. If all these people continue to use energy at the rate we use it now, we will need more power each year.

Actually, it is possible that each person will use even more electricity in the future. Individual energy use has been growing steadily since World War II. Since the war, more electric appliances have become common in homes.

Businesses and industries are also using more power than they used to. Many jobs that used to be done by people are now done by machines. Most of the new machines require electricity. If our rate of electricity use continues to rise as it has, we will need even more electricity in the future.

We may have sufficient electrical power in the Northwest now. But at the present rate of growth, we will soon have less than we need. Something will have to be done. There are two important questions before us now. The first question is whether our need for electricity must continue to grow. Is it possible to reduce our needs? Secondly, if we need more power, where will we get it? How can we get the most possible electrical power at the lowest possible prices while doing the least possible damage to the environment?

96. Give three reasons why our need for electricity is growing.

97. Why may we need new sources of power?

Where Do We Get Our Energy Now?

Before we look at future energy supplies, let's examine how the state has been meeting its energy needs. In the 1970's, most of the state's natural gas came from Canada. Most our oil and oil products (including gasoline) were also imported from foreign countries. However, Alaska was becoming an increasingly important source of these fossil fuels. Our coal was mined locally, in Washington and Montana. However, very little coal was being used in Washington at this time.

Electricity must be generated by another power source. Most of our electricity is produced by giant machines, called generators. These generators are usually set in motion by the power of flowing water or steam. In the 1970's, about ¾ of our electricity was produced at hydroelectric dams. Generators are located inside these dams, and they are turned by water flowing through them. The next most common source of electrical power was fossil fuel — especially diesel and coal. These fuels are generally burned to heat up water until it turns to steam, and this steam is used to turn generators.

Less than 1/10 of the state's electricity was produced at nuclear plants. In these plants, uranium undergoes an atomic reaction. The re-

---

WHAT IS A FOSSIL FUEL?

In Unit 1, Section 1, you learned that coal was formed long ago when plants decayed in water and then were covered by rock. Slowly, over many thousands of years, the decayed materials were compressed and became coal. Oil and natural gas were also formed very slowly from once-living materials that became buried under rock.

Gas, coal, and oil can all be burned as fuels. Since they are all evidence of ancient life, they are called fossil fuels. (A fossil is any evidence of life that has been preserved in rock.)

There are limited amounts of fossil fuels in the world. Since they take so many thousands of years to form, they are not replaceable. Once we burn our fossil fuel resources, they are gone forever. The time is approaching when there will be no more gas, coal, or oil. This is why we must conserve the fossil fuels we now have and also develop new sources of energy for the future.

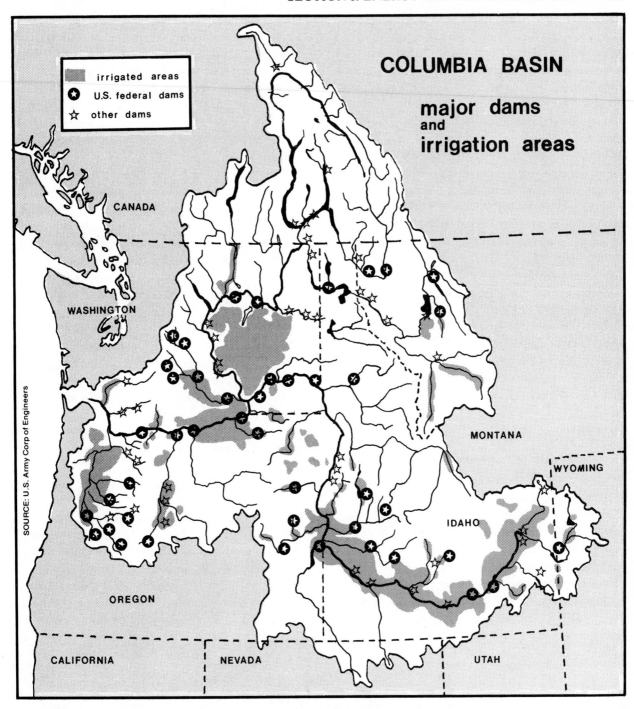

COLUMBIA BASIN

major dams
and
irrigation areas

- irrigated areas
- U.S. federal dams
- ☆ other dams

CANADA

WASHINGTON

MONTANA

WYOMING

IDAHO

OREGON

CALIFORNIA   NEVADA   UTAH

SOURCE: U.S. Army Corp of Engineers

action releases huge amounts of heat. Some of this heat is captured to boil water, and the steam is used to turn generators. Fossil fuel and nuclear plants are both examples of thermal electricity. ("Thermal" means having to do with heat.)

The fossil fuels and electric generation methods we use now are just a few of the energy sources available to us. The following pages discuss several ways that we might get more energy in the future. As you read, pay attention to the advantages and disadvantages of each method.

98. Name three fossil fuels used in Washington and give at least one source of each.
99. Briefly describe how each of the following energy sources is used to make electricity: fossil fuels, atomic reactions, falling water.

Can We Make More Hydroelectric Power?
Washington State is fortunate to have so many good locations for hydroelectric dams.

These dams are expensive to build, but they are cheap to operate. Hydroelectric dams require no expensive fuels. They run on falling water—basically a free source of power. Thanks to our hydroelectric resources, Washington has some of the lowest electric rates in the country.

Hydroelectric generation has a few problems. The dams cause some disruption of the river environment. And in years of drought, there may not be enough water to turn the generators.

However, these problems are small compared to most other energy sources. Falling water is non-polluting and can be regulated to meet varying needs. And the dams have the added benefits of reducing floods, improving navigation, and aiding irrigation.

With so many advantages, why don't we meet all our future energy needs with hydroelectricity? Unfortunately, there are few remaining places where dams can be built. Most of the rivers in our state have been fully developed. A few more dams are planned, but then we must look for other energy sources.

100. What are the special advantages and disadvantages of hydroelectricity?
101. Why can't hydroelectricity meet all our energy needs?

Conservation As A New Energy Source

The first place to look for new sources of energy is the energy we already have. In other words, how can we use our present energy supplies more efficiently? How much energy is now wasted but could be saved?

Many people believe that we could meet almost all our growing energy needs through conservation. They believe that we do not have to build any more power plants than those already planned. Conservation, these people suggest, offers a plentiful new supply of energy. Conservation does not have to mean total sacrifice — such as no heat — but it does mean making the most efficient use of the heat we have by means such as good building design and effective insulation.

How much energy do Americans waste? The American Physical Society estimates that our energy production is only 10-15% efficient. In other words, 85 to 90% of the possible energy supply is lost. This loss includes heat that escapes through poorly insulated buildings. It includes energy wasted by inefficient cars and appliances. We waste energy when we use unneeded lights or throw away aluminum cans instead of recycling them. When energy is changed from one form to another, some energy is wasted, too. When oil is burned to make steam that turns generators to make electricity, energy is lost in each step. If the electricity is then changed to heat energy (as in an electric stove), some energy is lost again. These and other kinds of energy waste could be reduced by more careful use of our resources.

In 1976, the city of Seattle made a study of its energy needs for the year 1990. This study predicted that conservation could save about 25% of the energy used in homes, 30% of the energy used in commercial places, and almost 32% of the energy used by industry.

Studies have shown that conservation methods cost much less than building new power plants. And many new jobs could be created in

Coal used to be a major fuel and a major export in the Pacific Northwest. These early twentieth century workers are waiting to start their shift in the mines. Today, much less coal is used and produced in the state. Why may coal become a more important fuel again in the future?

remodeling or adapting buildings for better energy use.

Conservation requires some lifestyle changes, such as turning down the heat a few degrees and turning off unneeded lights. But of all possible energy sources, conservation does the least damage to the environment.

102. According to a city of Seattle survey, how much energy could be saved through conservation in homes, industries, and commercial places?
103. Name at least four ways we waste energy.
104. Name at least three advantages of conservation as an energy source.

Should We Build More Coal-Fired Plants?

Even with conservation, we will probably need some new sources of power before the end of this century. Let's look at the possibility of building more coal and nuclear plants and then examine some other energy sources.

The main advantages of coal-fired plants are that the fuel and the technology are both available here. There is one coal-fired plant in Washington already, near Centralia. A great deal of coal can be mined in the Pacific Northwest, especially in Montana.

The main problems with coal plants involve pollution. The burning of coal can cause serious air pollution. And the mining of coal also causes problems. Much Northwest coal is strip-mined. This means that the surface layer of earth is taken away, and coal is mined from a big open pit. In this open type of mine, pollution-causing minerals may be washed into streams. Vegetation and wildlife may be destroyed, and the open pit is ugly. (Strip mines can be refilled and replanted, and the land can restore itself. But few mining companies do this.)

Coal is quite a bit more expensive than hydroelectric power or conservation. But when cheaper sources are no longer available, coal may be a practical fuel.

105. Give at least one advantage and one disadvantage of coal-fired plants.

How Expensive Is Nuclear Power?

Several utility companies would like to build more nuclear power plants in Washington State. Supporters say that nuclear power can answer our future needs for electricity without causing pollution. Since no burning takes place in a nuclear plant, there is no air pollution — as there is at coal and diesel plants. Uranium (nuclear fuel) has also been a cheaper fuel than diesel and coal. Some nuclear plants require large amounts of water, and there is plenty of water available here. For these reasons, many scientists and businesspeople believe that nuclear power might provide the cheapest new source of electricity for the Pacific Northwest. Governor Ray has been an outspoken supporter of nuclear power.

However, by the late 1970's, it was becoming apparent that electricity from nuclear plants was very expensive. There were several reasons for this. The cost of uranium fuel was rising very rapidly and so was the cost of building nuclear plants. Uranium cost more than seven times as much in 1976 as in 1973. And the estimated cost of a nuclear plant in Grays Harbor County rose more than one billion dollars in one year. Storing nuclear wastes was also proving very expensive.

In addition, nuclear plants were less efficient than expected. In the middle 1970's, U.S. nuclear plants were working at an average of only 50-60% of their capacity. They were often closed down over long periods for expensive repairs. In one year, the Trojan nuclear plant in Oregon produced only 28% of the electricity it was built to produce.

Nuclear plants also pose serious health and environmental problems. Workers at nuclear plants are exposed to very low levels of radiation for long periods of time. Many scientists believe this exposure can cause cancer. One study showed a "significant increase" in cancer cases among workers at Hanford.

Each year, a large nuclear plant produces 25 tons of waste materials that must be disposed of somehow. These wastes are radioactive and extremely poisonous. No adequate system for storing nuclear wastes for such long periods has yet been developed. This is evident at Hanford, where several major leaks of nuclear waste have been discovered. A single leak in the 1960's released over 100,000 gallons of radioactive waste.

A serious accidental breakdown in a nuclear plant itself could cause thousands of deaths and billions of dollars of damage, according to estimates by the Environmental Protection Agency. Around the country, many scientists and

HOW CAN SOLAR ENERGY BE USED?

Understanding hydroelectric dams and nuclear power plants can take a great deal of scientific training. But many principles of solar energy are simple facts that we deal with in everyday life. If you've ever worn black clothes on a hot sunny day, you've experienced solar heating. Black gets hotter than other colors, because it absorbs more of the sun's heat energy. If you've stood inside by a window on a sunny but cold day, you've experienced another principle of solar heating. Glass lets a lot of sun energy (heat and light) in, but does not let it all back out.

A basic solar heating unit is a flat box, painted black on the inside, with a glass cover. When the box is exposed to the sun, it collects heat. Air or water can be circulated through this box (called a solar collector) and then used to heat a building or a tank of hot water. Since solar energy is available everywhere on the earth, this kind of heating system can be installed on individual buildings. Houses and commercial buildings can be equipped with their own free energy supply. It is efficient because energy does not have to be changed from one form to another.

Other ways of heating with solar energy require no special equipment to move the heat around. They are called passive solar systems. If you insulate your house and draw insulated curtains over windows when the sun is not coming in, then you are using passive solar heating.

Some new buildings have lots of windows on the sunny south side and no windows on the chilly north side. This is another passive solar heating technique. A United States government survey es-timated that Northwest homes could save up to 60% of their heating costs through passive solar heating.

Some other possible uses of solar energy are more complicated. There is some research into the possibility of using solar energy to generate electricity. One method uses solar power to heat water up until it turns to steam. The steam can then be used to run generators.

It is also possible to change sunlight directly into electricity in special solar cells. These cells use chemicals that are light sensitive. When sunlight hits them, a flow of electricity is started. Some scientists are researching the possibility of launching a satellite covered with solar cells. In space, the cells can work much more efficiently than on earth. The satellite would change the electricity to microwaves and beam it to earth, where it would be changed back into electricity. Boeing is one of several U.S. companies investigating such solar methods of generating electricity.

Unlike direct solar heating, these methods are highly technical and very costly. There are some environmental problems, too. A lot of space is needed. A solar steam plant could need several square miles of reflecting mirrors. A satellite would require a huge receiving antenna and open area many miles square. It is possible that the microwaves could cause damage.

These and other solar technologies are being studied. Many experts have predicted that solar power will be filling many of our energy needs by the 1990's.

engineers are working to try to make nuclear plants safer. Some experts are convinced that such a major accident will never happen, but other experts disagree.

This bank in Spokane is designed to get much of its heating energy from the sun. U.S. government studies predicted that solar energy could provide about 60% of the heat for buildings in the Pacific Northwest.

106. Give at least three reasons why Governor Ray and others believe nuclear power could be a good new source of electric power in the Pacific Northwest.
107. Give at least three dangers or disadvantages of nuclear power.

Can Solar Power Help Meet Our Energy Needs?

Probably the most promising source of extra energy is the sun. Huge amounts of solar (sun) energy reach the earth every day. The amount of solar energy that falls on the United States each year is equal to the energy from 22.4 billion gallons of oil. This is almost four times the amount of oil we use in a year. It is not now known how much of this solar energy we could capture and use.

Some of the advantages and problems of solar energy are quite obvious. Solar power is non-polluting, and it will never run out. It is free. And it is available everywhere; it does not need to be transported great distances. The obvious disadvantage is that solar energy is not consistent. Some days are cloudy and cool. The sunlight is more direct and intense in summer than in winter. And there is no sunshine at all at night.

Other problems of solar power involve learning how to take advantage of it. So far, we have not developed a solar technology to equal our fossil fuel technology. One result of this is that solar equipment is fairly expensive now.

Most experts now believe that solar power can fill many of our energy needs. Even in cloudy Western Washington, it is estimated that solar energy can provide 40% or more of the heat for our homes and buildings.

In the 1970's, scientists and inventors around the country were working on more efficient ways to use direct solar heating. Other researchers were examining more complicated ways to tap the energy of the sun. Boeing was one of the companies studying solar energy satellites, for example.

108. Give the main advantages and disadvantages of solar power.

What Other Energy Possibilities Are Being Studied?

Our governments are also studying several new ways of generating electrical energy. The federal government is studying wind power, for example. They will build an experimental windmill generator in a windy area of the Cascades. Small windmills have been used to generate electricity for individual farms for a long time. Perhaps one day they will provide non-polluting power to supplement our hydroelectric dams.

Government researchers are also studying geothermal energy. This is heat energy from the earth. ("Geo" means earth.) The inside core of the earth is always very hot. In some places, cracks in the earth's crust allow this heat to come closer to the earth's surface. There are several places like this in Washington. Perhaps the earth's heat could be used to make steam for turning generators. (Geothermal energy is already being used in several places around the world.) However, there are some serious problems that have not been solved. It is possible that the drilling of geothermal wells may lead to earthquakes. Also, the hot underground water may have many minerals dissolved in it. These minerals can pollute the air and water on the

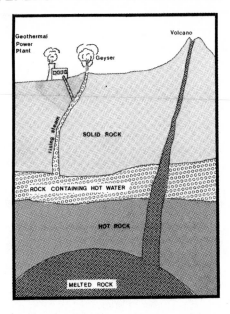

surface of the earth. Geothermal power plants would not require any expensive fuels. But the plants may be very expensive to build.

Other studies involved new sources of burnable fuels. For example, it may be possible to burn garbage for fuel. In the late 1970's, the city of Seattle was running out of places to dump its garbage. So the city government began to study how garbage could be recycled. Some of the plants being studied would use all burnable trash to generate power. (A similar study in Montana showed that garbage could produce about ⅔ the heat value of coal.)

Another possible fuel from garbage is methane gas. Methane is produced when plant and animal wastes decay in an environment without air. It can be burned like natural gas for fuel. A Seattle-based group called Ecotope operated a small methane-generating plant in Monroe, Washington, in the 1970's.

The state government was studying how to use wood slash for fuel. Wood slash includes all the parts of trees that loggers leave behind. It has not been used in the past because of the transportation problems involved, but it may be possible to use wood slash as fuel in the future.

None of these new fuels would produce enough power for a city to live on. But together, they could contribute the extra energy that a growing population needs. And they could also help solve our growing waste-disposal problems.

109. Name at least five energy sources that were being studied in Washington in the 1970's.

Does government affect our daily lives? A look in your wallet will probably convince you that it does. Government agencies print your money, issue licenses, sponsor social security and other public assistance programs, and pay for community services. Every time you drive on a highway, go to school, or pay sales tax, you are coming into contact with government. What level of government — federal, state or local — is responsible for each of the items below?

UNIT 12

GOVERNMENT
IN WASHINGTON

People in Washington are affected by several different levels of government, including federal, state, and local governments. Washington voters elect some of the officials of each level of government, and they also pay taxes to each government unit that affects them. In return, each level of government makes certain laws and regulations and offers certain services to the people who live in that governmental area.

All residents of Washington are affected by each level of government. And we can all participate. All people who are citizens of the United States have certain rights and responsibilities in their state, local, and federal governments. In order to make use of those rights and responsibilities, it is necessary to understand how our governments work.

This unit is an introduction to the various levels of government that operate in this state. As you read, think about the following questions: How is each level of government organized? How can citizens participate in government?

The unit has three sections:

1. Federal Government in Washington
2. Washington State Government
3. Local Governments

SECTION 1: FEDERAL GOVERNMENT IN WASHINGTON

Why Do We Need A Government?

One person living completely alone on an island would not need a government or laws. A small, isolated group of people may not need a formal government. They may have no legislature or judges. But they need certain common agreements about how people will interact with each other.

A large group of people usually needs to draw up a set of rules to regulate behavior. Clarence Darrow, a famous American lawyer, expressed it this way: ''A great many people in this world, unless they act with a certain kind of organiza-tion, are apt to bump into each other.'' A government keeps this ''bumping'' under control by passing laws. Laws tell us what kind of behavior is expected in certain situations.

Governments can also offer services that one or two people could not afford alone. By collecting some money from everyone — through taxes — a government can pay for schools, roads, and other necessary but expensive services. With tax money, the government can pay for an army when defense is needed. It can hire judges to resolve conflicts between people. It can provide services — such as medical care, parks, and

One of the main reasons the early settlers wanted a government was to provide schools for their children. What other services does a government provide?

pollution control — which improve the quality of our lives.

The writers of the United States Constitution listed these reasons for establishing a government:
— establish justice
— insure domestic tranquility (peaceful interactions within the country)
— provide for the common defense
— promote the general welfare
— secure the blessings of liberty

1. Give at least two important purposes of government.

What Rights Does The Constitution Guarantee?

The writers of the United States Constitution intended for citizens to become involved in their country's government. One of the main reasons that the colonies declared their independence from England was that the people in the colonies lacked control over the national government. The colonists believed strongly that they should be able to elect the officials who made and enforced the laws.

The key to participation in government is the right to vote. By voting, citizens can take an active part in deciding who will make the laws and how they will be carried out. The right to vote actually gives citizens a voice in government all year round, not just at election. Elected officials owe their jobs to the voters, so they must always pay attention to the voters' opinions. If an official does not please the voters, he or she may lose the next election. So when citizens express their opinions to officials — especially if a large group of citizens share the same opinion — the elected officials usually pay attention.

The right to vote is important only if it is used. If an individual or group of people cannot vote or do not vote, government officials may ignore them. The group's needs may not be met. The Constitution provides a framework for citizens to help make sure that the government is meeting their needs. But it is up to the citizens to make this system work.

2. What are some of the rights of citizens?
3. What is the key to citizen participation in government?

CAN I VOTE? HOW DO I DO IT?

If you are an American citizen, you may vote as soon as you reach your eighteenth birthday. You must register at least 30 days before an election in order to be able to vote in that election.

Most public buildings have a place where voters may register. Usually any library, public high school, fire department, or government office building will have an employee who is authorized to register new voters.

Registering is a simple, short process. You will be asked to give such basic information as your address and birthdate and then to sign some cards. Within a few weeks, you should receive a voter registration card in the mail. This card will tell you your precinct number. If you are not sure where to go to vote (it should be the same place for other voters in your house or neighborhood) simply call the county Board of Elections. Give them your precinct number and they will tell you where your "polling place" (voting place) is. It's usually located in a nearby church, school, or public building.

If you are registered, your name will be on a list at your polling place. Election officials will check off your name, ask you to sign a list, and explain how to use the voting machines.

Why Are Active Citizens Important?

In order to work well, our government needs active citizen participation. Our government is somewhat like a club in this sense. As long as a club has many active members, it will remain strong; but if most members stop participating, the club may die. Or the few members who remain active may always get their way, and none of the other members' needs will be met. Good, active members keep the club alive and responsive to members' needs. In a similar way, active citizens keep our government strong and responsive, as the writers of the Constitution intended it to be. There are many ways for Americans to become active in government. All of them are examples of good citizenship. Good citizenship really includes everything we do to fulfill our responsibilities toward, and to help improve our government, community, state, and nation.

Thoughtful voting is an example. Here in Washington State, citizens have a chance to vote on many issues — such as school levies, initiatives, and referendums — in addition to voting for candidates. Good citizens are active voters, and they are informed voters. They study the issues and form educated opinions about how the government should be run. They learn about the candidates and form thoughtful opinions about who will do the best job. Then they voice these opinions by voting at every election.

Good citizenship includes expressing our opinions between elections, too. Even if you are not yet old enough to vote, you can write to your elected officials to express your opinions on an issue. You should study the issues and become informed. By sharing your opinions, you will help your representatives do their job better.

Citizens can also become involved in pre-election campaigns. They may help start or work on an initiative measure. They may organize support for the candidate they feel will do the best job.

4. What is good citizenship?
5. Give at least four ways that good citizens can particpate in elections.

Women in this country worked hard to win the right to vote. Many minority groups have also had to struggle to gain and protect their voting rights. Because of these efforts, the right to vote has been extended steadily over the years. The most recent group to win the vote were 18-year olds, in 1972.

How Can Citizens Help Improve Their Government?

Good citizenship means working to make our government better, to make it work smoothly, and to make it more responsive to the needs of every group of people who live in America. There are many things citizens can do, from obeying traffic laws, to working with community groups, to asking their senators to provide more programs for senior citizens.

In this book there are many examples of this kind of good citizenship. One example is Jim Ellis, the lawyer who led the effort to organize Metro and Forward Thrust in King County. Some other examples include Emma Smith DeVoe and those who helped win equal voting rights for women, Wing Luke and others who worked for minority involvement in government, and the people like Joe Meek who helped form the first governments here.

These people, like other good citizens, were thoughtful about their government. They took time to think about why a government was needed and how it could best serve the people who were governed by it. All of them contributed their own energy and experience to make the government work a little better in some way.

6. Each of the following good citizens helped improve our government in some way. Identify at least one contribution

of each: Jim Ellis, Emma Smith DeVoe, Wing Luke, Joe Meek.

Good Citizens In The Community

Good citizenship is not limited to involvement with government directly. It can mean involvement with your community in a larger sense. Many everyday activities are examples of good citizenship; for example, picking up litter, helping your neighbors, and treating members of all groups equally, without discrimination. People are being good citizens when they do volunteer work for places such as a tutoring center, a senior citizens' home, or a museum. This book includes several examples of people who went out of their way to help improve their community, such as the people who started "Neighbors in Need" to help unemployed people in the early 1970's (page 200).

7. Give several examples of good citizenship activities not directly related to government.

What Kind Of Government Does The United States Have?

There are several different kinds of government systems. In the United States, the government is headed by an elected president. The governmental head of other countries may be a king or queen, a dictator, or a prime minister who is elected by the legislature instead of by the citizens.

Here in the United States, voters elect people to run the government and make the laws. This is called a representative government. In this system, all citizens have a role in government, but they do not make laws directly.*

Government in the United States is divided into three levels: federal, state, and local (counties, cities, districts). Each level is responsible for certain areas of government. For example, the federal government is responsible for making treaties with other countries; the state government regulates its own roads and automobile licenses; and local governments provide police and fire protection. The federal government is the highest. No state or local government may pass a law which violates United States laws.

The state and federal governments (and some local governments) are also divided into three parts, or branches. The legislative branch is made up of our elected representatives. It is re-

*The only exceptions are the right to initiative and referendum which exist in some states. See pages 148, 150 for more information.

CHECKS AND BALANCES IN THE FEDERAL GOVERNMENT*

Read across to find out what powers the branch at left has over the other branches of government.

	EXECUTIVE	LEGISLATIVE	JUDICIAL
EXECUTIVE		1. recommends legislation 2. vetoes bills	1. appoints Supreme Court judges 2. grants pardons
LEGISLATIVE	1. overrides vetoes with ⅔ majority 2. must vote to approve some officials appointed by the president 3. can remove president by impeachment 4. sets up executive agencies and programs		1. must approve Supreme Court judge appointments 2. can remove judges by impeachment 3. makes laws to set up courts
JUDICIAL	1. can declare presidential actions unconstitutional 2. reviews cases involving executive agencies	1. can declare a law unconstitutional 2. interprets laws	

*Similar checks and balances exist in Washington State government (substitute "governor" for "president" where state government is concerned). However, there are some exceptions.

1. State Supreme Court Justices are elected, not appointed.
2. The governor may call special sessions of the state legislature.
3. The governor's veto powers are somewhat different from those of the president. (See page 277.)

sponsible for making the laws. The legislative branch of the federal government, and most states, has two parts. These are usually called the Senate and the House of Representatives. The executive branch is headed by the President at the federal level and by the governor at the state level. The executive branch is responsible for carrying out the laws. The judicial branch is made up of our courts and judges. It is responsible for interpreting laws, for deciding exactly what they mean in different cases.

Each branch has certain powers over the other two branches. This keeps any one branch from becoming too powerful. These safeguards are called a system of checks and balances. (See chart on page 269.)

8. What is a representative government?
9. Name the three branches in the federal and state governments of the United States.
10. What is the system of checks and balances?

What Are The Governmental Powers Of Citizens?

Some people suggest that the citizens them-selves should be considered a separate branch of government. Citizens have certain powers and responsibilities, and they participate in the system of checks and balances.

The basic governmental powers of citizens come from their right to vote. If the voters disapprove of the way a President or representative is doing his or her job, they may reject that official at the next election. This fact encourages elected officials to be responsible to citizen opinions. And it gives voters a chance to check or control their elected representatives. The case studies in this unit give some examples of how citizens have used their power to influence government decisions.

Citizens also have an important role in the judicial branch of government. All juries are made up of voters. Anyone who has registered to vote may be asked to serve on a jury, and it is the jury that makes the final decision in many court cases.

11. Why do some people think the voters can be considered a fourth branch of government?

A TREATY WITH CANADA

The formal agreements between the United States government and Washington Indian tribes were called treaties. A treaty represents an agreement between separate nations. The tribes were considered independent nations in 1854, so treaties were needed.

The U. S. government still signs treaties with foreign governments from time to time. One treaty with special importance to this state was the United States-Canada Columbia River Treaty. It was signed in 1964. The treaty deals with dams on the Columbia River.

The Columbia flows through both Canada and the United States, so development of the river affects both countries. In the 1964 treaty, Canada agreed to build three storage dams on the northern part of the Columbia. These would help prevent floods and provide a steady flow of water to the hydroelectric dams on the U.S. part of the river. More electricity could be generated. The two countries agreed to split the extra electricity produced. The U.S. also agreed to pay Canada for flood protection.

This peace arch at Blaine, Washington, marks the peaceful border between the United States and Canada.

Constitutions And Laws

The basic structure of our government is established by a constitution. For example, the United States Constitution tells what officials the voters will elect. It tells how long the officials will serve and what their duties are. It describes the duties and limitations of each branch of government and of the federal government as a whole. The Constitution of the United States makes up our nation's highest laws. No other law may violate the Constitution. The U.S. Supreme Court has the power to strike down any laws which they find unconstitutional.

Constitutions may be changed. But it is a much harder and longer process to change a constitution than to pass a law. For example, an amendment (change) to the U.S. Constitution must be approved by ⅔ of the members of both the Senate and the House of Representatives and also by ¾ of the states. A law requires only a 51% majority of the House and Senate and the signature of the President. In the first 190 years of its existence, the United States Constitution was amended only 26 times.

Generally, a constitution only describes the aspects of government that are most basic and least likely to change. Other governmental decisions are made by laws.

Each state has its own constitution. A state constitution outlines the state government and provides a framework for state laws, just as the United States Constitution outlines the national government.

12. What is the highest law in the United States?
13. What is a constitution?
14. Which are easier to change — laws or constitutions?

How Are Federal Laws Made?

The legislative branch of the United States government is called the Congress. The Congress has two parts, called "houses." They are the Senate and the House of Representatives. Two senators are elected from each state. The number of representatives depends on population. In the 1970's, Washington had seven representatives; Oregon had four; and California had 43. Altogether, there are 100 U.S. senators and 435 members of the U.S. House of Representatives.

A law may be introduced in either house by a member of that house. (The exception are laws

---

POWERFUL SENATORS ON POWERFUL COMMITTEES

In the 1970's, both of the United States senators from Washington were rated among the nation's most powerful and most effective legislators. These senators were Warren G. Magnuson and Henry M. Jackson. Both men had served in the Senate for a long time. Magnuson first became a U.S. Senator in 1944 and Jackson in 1952.

Because of their long service, they attained positions as chairpersons of important and powerful committees. Magnuson became chairperson of the Commerce Committee and of the Appropriations Subcommittee on Health, Labor, and Education. Jackson has been chairperson of the Interior Committee, and he also chairs two subcommittees — one on Armed Services and one on Government Operations.

All legislators have just one vote, but the chairperson of an important committee has much more power than most other senators. This is because so much of the real work of writing laws goes on in committees and because the chairperson can have so much control over how a bill is written, discussed, and promoted.

All bills that involve spending federal funds on health, labor, or education programs would come before Senator Magnuson's committee. As chairperson, Magnuson has often helped get bills passed that affect Washington citizens. For example, he was successful in getting a law passed which gave funds for Seattle's Public Health Hospital, even though Public Hospitals in other American cities were being closed down. Henry Jackson's position on the Armed Services Committee has helped him to get several defense manufacturing programs passed. Boeing has often benefited from these.

Several of the federal programs that benefit people in Washington were passed due to the efforts of Senators Jackson and Magnuson.

---

that deal with taxes. These must start in the House of Representatives.) Such a proposed law is called a bill. In order to become a law, a bill must receive a majority of both houses of Congress and be signed by the President. If the President vetoes a bill (refuses to sign it) the Congress has another chance to pass it. This time, the bill must receive ⅔ of the vote of both houses. If the ⅔ majority is not received after a veto, the bill does not become law. In this way, the legislative and executive branches have certain powers over each other in the lawmaking process. This is an important part of the system of checks and balances.

The President and Congress have other

powers over each other. The Senate has the power to approve or reject cabinet members and other key officials appointed by the President. And the President may recommend that the Congress pass certain laws. Every year, in January, the President gives a "state of the union" message to Congress. In this speech, the President recommends a program of laws and policies for that year.

15. Define the following: Congress, veto, bill.

16. What powers do Congress and the President have over each other?

What Does The Federal Executive Branch Do?

After Congress passes a law, the federal executive branch is responsible for carrying it out. This is often a very complicated process, requiring a great number of people.

For example, suppose Congress decides to spend a billion dollars to build houses for low-income people. The Department of Housing and

CABINET MEMBERS AND THEIR DEPARTMENTS
(FEDERAL GOVERNMENT)

Department	Cabinet Member's Title	Areas of Department Responsibility	Department	Cabinet Member's Title	Areas of Department Responsibility
Agriculture	Secretary of Agriculture	- aid to farmers and rural areas - food inspection - food stamps - soil, forest, and water conservation	Housing and Urban Development (HUD)	Secretary of Housing & Urban Development	- housing programs - urban renewal - natural disaster relief
Commerce	Secretary of Commerce	- promote U.S. business and industry - international shipping and trade - economic assistance to U.S. areas - census and weather bureaus	Interior	Secretary of the Interior	- federally-owned resources (minerals, land, water) - national parks - Indian reservations - fish and wildlife protection
Defense	Secretary of Defense	- all branches of U.S. military - military aid and equipment sales to foreign countries - development and purchase of weapons	Justice	Attorney General	- legal issues involving the federal government - FBI - civil rights - federal prisons - immigration
Energy	Secretary of Energy	- coordinate U.S. energy policy - distribution and price regulation of oil and natural gas - development of new energy sources - nuclear weapons and energy - energy conservation	Labor	Secretary of Labor	- job training - unemployment insurance - worker protection - union/management bargaining
			State	Secretary of State	- foreign policy - ambassadors - foreign aid - treaties
			Transportation	Secretary of Transportation	- federal highways - air traffic - cities' public transportation - coast guard
Health, Education, and Welfare (HEW)	Secretary of Health, Education & Welfare	- welfare programs - health - education - Social Security	Treasury	Secretary of the Treasury	- taxes - making money - secret service - U.S. customs - control of guns, tobacco, and alcohol

Urban Development (H.U.D.) would be given the job of carrying out this law. The workers at H.U.D. must hire planners to decide where the housing is most needed. They must hire architects and construction crews, building inspectors, secretaries, and bookkeepers. They must set up a program to interview people who want to move into the housing. Then H.U.D. must hire building managers, electricians, plumbers, and others to keep the buildings in repair.

The federal government passes a great many laws on a great variety of subjects. The President, as head of the executive branch, needs many helpers and advisors to help enforce the laws. The most important of the President's advisors are the cabinet members. Each cabinet member supervises a large agency which carries out a certain kind of federal law. A list of the cabinet members and their general duties is on page 272. There are a great many other executive agencies and officials, too. Key officials are appointed by the President and approved by the Senate.

The President and Vice-President are elected together for four year terms. The President may be elected no more than twice.

17. What is the job of the federal executive branch?
18. Who heads the federal executive branch?
19. What is the cabinet?

Who Makes Up The Judicial Branch?

The third branch of the federal government is the judicial branch. This is our federal court system. It is responsible for settling disputes between states and for judging people accused of breaking federal laws. The judicial branch may also be called upon to clarify laws or to decide if a law violates the United States Constitution. This is a key part of the judicial role in government checks and balances.

There are several kinds of federal courts. Most federal cases are tried first in District Courts. Each District Court has one or more judges and serves a certain area of the United States. In 1976, there were 91 District Courts in the country. Western Washington is in a different district than Eastern Washington. There are also military courts, territorial courts, and courts that deal with some special kinds of cases.

The highest federal court, and the highest court in our country, is the United States Su-

preme Court. The nine judges of the Supreme Court are appointed by the President and must be approved by the United States Senate. These are checks, or controls, that the executive and legislative branches have over the judicial.

20. Name three levels of United States courts and tell which is the highest.
21. Who decides whether a law is constitutional?

How Is The Federal Government Important To People In Washington?

This is one of the most distant states from the center of national government, in Washington, D.C. Yet the federal government is important in the daily lives of everyone in the Northwest.

For example, federal agencies inspect our food, print our money, license our TV and radio stations, regulate the airports, and deliver our mail. Federal tax money helps pay for public schools and colleges, highways, pollution control, and scientific research. Medicare and Social Security are two of the many public assistance programs sponsored by the federal government. In addition, federal laws help protect many of our civil rights, including freedom of religion, freedom of speech, and the right to equal job opportunities regardless of race or ethnic group.

Here in Washington, the United States government is especially important to our state economy. Much of the electricity we use is produced by hydroelectric power dams built and operated by the federal government. Also, the United States government is the biggest landowner in this state. It owns large national parks and forests, military bases, dams, and some irrigated lands. The federal government also holds in trust all Indian reservation lands.

The government is one of the state's biggest customers and one of its most important employers, too. The Defense Department spent almost three billion dollars here in 1975. The military purchases weapons, transportation equipment, and other manufactured goods and pays salaries to people who work at military bases.

There are thousands of other federal jobs in this state, too, including forest rangers, postal clerks, researchers, secretaries, and administrators. One reason why there are so many federal ''civilian'' (non-military) jobs in this state is that Seattle is the center for many federal

The federal office building in Seattle, where many of the thousands of federal government jobs in Washington are located.

programs located all over the Pacific Northwest and Alaska.

22. What kinds of land in this state are owned by the federal government?
23. Name some kinds of federal jobs in this state.
24. Name several services provided by the federal government.

Voting For Federal Officials

Washington voters help elect the officials of the federal government. Like all American voters, they help choose the President and Vice-President every four years. Washington voters also elect two United States senators and seven representatives. Washington State is divided into seven congressional districts, of about equal population. Voters from each district elect one congressional representative. These congressmen or congresswomen serve two-year terms. All state voters choose the senators who serve six-year terms.

United States senators and representatives from Washington help make important policy decisions for the whole country. They also have a special responsibility to the state or district they represent. One job of Washington's senators and representatives is to look after the interests of their constituents (the people who may vote for them). These officials try to influence Congress to approve laws that will help people in Washington State. They also help to make sure that federal agencies in Washington do their job. Voters with a problem or complaint

about some federal agency can sometimes receive help from a congressperson.

25. What federal officials do Washington voters elect or help to elect?
26. How long are the terms of these officials?
27. How can senators and representatives help their constituents?

What Is The Precinct Caucus?

Washington voters can also help select the presidential candidate of each party. Every four years, before the presidential election, voters here are invited to attend a precinct caucus. (A precinct is the smallest division of government. It includes only about three hundred people who vote at the same place. A caucus is a private meeting of a part of a larger group before a general meeting. For example, you've probably heard of a caucus held by the Black members or the women members of a large organization. The precinct caucus is a private meeting of voters from one political party who live in the same precinct.) In other states, the presidential candidate is chosen in a primary election. See next page.

At the precinct caucus, individual voters from each political party have a chance to vote for the presidential candidate they prefer. At the same time, voters also discuss the important issues of the upcoming campaign. And they choose one of their members to represent them at the district caucus.

Members of the district caucus choose people to represent them at the state convention. Here, the party representatives choose their favorite candidate, and they also write up the party plat-

WASHINGTON'S CONGRESSIONAL DISTRICTS

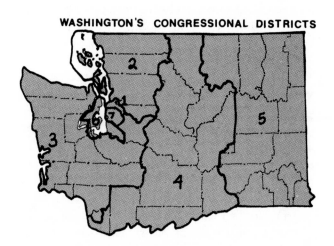

form for the state. (The platform is the party policy on key issues of the election.)

28. Define the following terms: caucus, precinct, party platform.

What Are Primary Elections?

The candidates for all other offices— senator, representative, governor, city council, etc. — are chosen in a separate election, called a primary election. Suppose three different people from the same political party want to run for governor. At the primary election, voters choose the one candidate from each party who will run for governor in the November general election.

This system is called the direct primary, since citizens can vote directly for the candidate of their choice. At the primary election, voters have a choice among major party (Democratic, Republican) candidates for an office. Each voter selects only one candidate. The person who receives the most votes among the candidates from his or her party will represent that party in the general election. Minor party candidates are

---

LAWMAKER LANGUAGE

Several different words are sometimes used to describe members of the legislative branch of government. Sometimes the vocabulary gets confusing. General words for all elected legislative officials are: legislators or lawmakers. We talk about two "houses" of the legislature, the Senate, sometimes called the "upper house," and the House of Representatives, sometimes called the "lower house." Sometimes, the House of Representatives is simply called "the House," even though this can be confusing. Members of the lower house may be called representatives. But members of the United States House of Representatives are usually called Congressmen or Congresswomen. Members of the upper house are called Senators.

---

nominated for public office by conventions. The conventions must be attended by a number of registered voters equal to one for each ten thousand voters who voted in that jurisdiction — city, county, state — in the preceding presidential election or by twenty-five registered voters, whichever is greater. Notice of the convention is published in a county-wide newspaper at least ten days before the convention.

HOW DO I WRITE TO A FEDERAL OFFICIAL?

If you are considering contacting a federal official, here are some points to consider:

— The most effective messages are short and well-informed. A little research on the issue can go a long way in convincing the official that you know what you're talking about.

— Try to let your official know your opinions as early as possible. If you wait until an issue has already been discussed for several weeks or months, the chances are that the official has already made a decision. Early letters, calls, and telegrams are more effective.

— Committees are important. Much of the actual work of writing laws goes on in committees. A voter who wanted Congress to spend more money on schools would probably write to members of the education committee, for example.

— The more letters the better. If you know other people who share your opinion, encourage them to write also. Other people who hold the opposite opinion from your own are probably already contacting the officials.

— Senators and representatives have offices in their districts. It is inconvenient for people in Washington State to call their elected officials in Washington, D.C. But you can call their local office and talk to the official's staff. These staff members can tell you what committees the official serves on and they can pass on information or opinions to the official they work for. These local offices are listed in the phone book.

— It is sometimes useful to write or call other officials in addition to senators or representatives. You can write to the President, for example. You can also write to cabinet members or their staff. Suppose you are concerned about bussing or other federal programs to achieve racial integration in your school district. You could write to the Regional Director of Health, Education, and Welfare in Seattle. This person is in charge of carrying out federal education programs in the Pacific Northwest. To find out the name or title of the best person to write to, you can call United States Government Information in Seattle.

— These same methods can be used to influence decisions by state and local government officials, too.

— Address your letter like this:
   Honorable Joe Doe
   Senate Office Building
   (or House Office Building, 20515)
   Washington, D.C. 20510

— And start the letter: Dear Senator Doe: (or Congressman or Congresswoman).

Washington's primaries are known as blanket primaries, or "wide-open primaries," since voters may select different candidates from different political parties. (In 39 of the other states, voters must register as a member of one political party. At the primary election they may only vote for candidates for their own political party. This is called a closed primary.)

In this state, candidates for city offices and judges are non-partisan. That is, they do not identify themselves with a particular party when they run for office. Therefore, a primary election is held for these offices if more than two people are candidates.

---

29. How many candidates for governor could represent each party at the general election?

30. Describe the difference between the direct primary and the caucus and convention system for choosing candidates.

31. Define the following: direct primary, wide-open primary, closed primary, non-partisan.

Other Ways For Citizens To Participate In Federal Government

Voting for President, senators, and a representative is just one way that citizens can participate in federal decision-making. There are other things that interested citizens can do. If a person or group feels that one particular candidate will best represent their interests, they can try to help that candidate get elected. This might involve talking to friends, donating money for campaign expenses, or volunteering to work at the campaign headquarters.

Between elections, citizens can use various methods to try to influence the decisions that federal officials make. A common way for Washington voters to share their opinions with elected federal officials between elections is to write letters. Voters may also telephone, telegraph, or visit their federal representatives.

Citizens with similar goals may join together for greater political power. For example, people concerned about protecting the environment might join the Sierra Club or the Mountaineers, or start their own ecology group. These organizations can have more effect on policy-making than one individual, since they represent many people.

One way to let federal officials know that there is wide support for a particular issue is to organize or attend a demonstration. This might involve just 20 or 30 people carrying signs. Such groups are often seen picketing the Seattle offices of federal agencies. Other demonstrations may involve thousands of people and require careful planning. The civil rights and anti-war marches of the 1960's are good examples.

In some cases, citizen groups may try to influence federal policy by taking the government to court. The northwestern Indian tribes used this method to make the government honor the 1855 treaties. (See page 106.) Environmental groups often go to court to insure that anti-pollution laws are faithfully followed.

---

32. What may citizens do to try to help a particular candidate get elected?

33. How can citizens share their opinions with federal officials?

WHAT ABOUT THE RESERVATIONS?

Some parts of Washington have their own separate government. These areas are the Indian reservations. Reservation land is held in trust by the U.S. government. The state government may not tax this land or the people who live on it. People who live on the reservations have more contact with the federal government and less contact with the state government than other people in Washington. Reservations also have their own tribal government. Some of the duties of each level of government are listed below:

1. federal — Federal agencies have the main responsibility for health, education, construction, and other tribal services. The federal government may veto tribal laws and financial decisions. It can change the boundaries of a reservation or create a new one. Some cases of crimes on the reservation are tried in federal courts. (Most federal programs are run by the Bureau of Indian Affairs, the BIA.)

2. state — The state government collects no taxes from the reservation, but is responsible for some welfare programs, automobile licenses, etc. Some crimes involving the tribe are tried in state courts.

3. tribal — reservation tribes have the legal power to elect their own government, set up their own courts, pass laws, tax and regulate non-Indian use of reservation land.

Both Indians and non-Indians in this state are sometimes unhappy with this system. Tribal members complain that the federal government has too much control over their lives. They claim that they are not really allowed to govern themselves. On the other hand, non-Indians often complain that Indians receive unfair special treatment from the government.

SECTION 2: WASHINGTON STATE GOVERNMENT

How Is The State Government Similar To The Federal Government?

The Washington State government has a basic structure that is quite similar to the federal government. Both governments have three branches: a legislative branch to make the laws; an executive branch to enforce the laws; and a judicial branch to interpret the laws. Like the U.S. Congress, Washington's legislature has two houses: the Senate and the House of Representatives. (This is called a bicameral legislature.) Laws must be approved by both houses of the legislature and signed by the Governor. This is also similar to the federal system. (The only exceptions are state initiatives and referendums which are laws made by voters.)

The titles, duties, and powers of elected state officials are listed on the chart on the next page. As you can see, the role of the Governor in state government is similar to the role of the President in federal government. The state judicial branch is made up of several levels of courts, with the Supreme Court at the top. This is similar to the structure of the federal court system, although the names and duties of the lower federal courts are different.

34. Describe the three branches of state and federal government.

How Is Washington State Government Different From The Federal Government?

One important difference between state and federal officials is obvious from the chart. Voters elect many more state officials than federal officials. In the United States government, only the President, Vice-President, senators, and representatives are elected by voters. Most other high officials are appointed by the President with the approval of the Senate.

However, here in Washington State, we also elect our judges and several executive officials. This state has what is called a "divided executive," that is, voters elect several executive officials separately.

Although Washington's Governor does not appoint as many officials as the President does, our Governor has a special power not shared by the President. The Governor here may veto just parts of a law, while the President must sign or veto the whole law, as passed by Congress. This special power of Washington's Governor is called the "item veto."

Voters themselves have more powers in Washington State government than in federal government. Voters may make state laws themselves, without approval of the legislature or Governor, by using the initiative or referendum. And the recall allows voters to remove any state official

This set of buildings in Olympia is where the state government is located. It is known as the capitol campus. The large building in the center is the state capitol building.

ELECTED OFFICIALS OF THE WASHINGTON STATE GOVERNMENT

Official	Important Duties	Term of Office
Governor	heads executive branch, appoints many administrative officials, recommends budget and legislation, may veto bills or sections of bills, call out national guard, pardon criminals, call special sessions of the legislature.	4 years
Lieutenant Governor	acts as governor when elected governor is unable to perform duties, presides over state senate.	4 years
Secretary of State	keeps the state seal, files official documents, oversees state elections.	4 years
State Treasurer	manages state money, pays state bills, keeps financial records.	4 years
State Auditor	sees that state funds are properly used, checks financial books of all state agencies.	4 years
Attorney General	acts as state's lawyer: advises state officials on matters of state law, represents the state in some lawsuits, prosecutes some crimes against the state; conducts legal investigations.	4 years
Superintendent of Public Instruction	supervises public schools in the state, carries out policies set by State Board of Education.	4 years
Commissioner of Public Lands	manages state-owned lands, regulates logging and other activities on state lands.	4 years
Insurance Commissioner	inspects and regulates insurance companies in the state, acts as State Fire Marshal.	4 years
State Representatives (98 of them)	the representatives and senators together are responsible for making state laws.	2 years
State Senators (49 of them)	with the representatives, they introduce, study, discuss, get voter opinions on, and pass state laws.	4 years
Superior Court Justices (27 Districts)	judge cases in their district involving serious crimes and large civil disputes.	4 years
Appeals Court Justices (12 of them)	three justices at a time hear cases that have been appealed from lower courts.	6 years
Supreme Court Justices (9 of them)	make up the state's highest court of appeals, interpret the state constitution, hear appeals cases of great public importance.	6 years

IMPEACHMENT

Any elected state official may be removed by impeachment if he or she commits a serious crime while in office. The impeachment process has two parts. First, the House of Representatives must vote to impeach (accuse) the official. Then the Senate conducts a trial. The official is then removed from office if two-thirds of the senators vote for conviction.

A three-quarters majority of the legislature can remove an official for non-criminal reasons, such as illness or incompetence.

meets for a much shorter time than the United States Congress. According to the state constitution, the legislature is only scheduled to meet for 60 days, starting in January of every other year. However, the Governor may call special sessions. In recent years, the state legislature has met almost every year, and the sessions have lasted longer than 60 days.

35. Define the following: "divided executive," "item veto."
36. How are state and federal judges chosen?

What Is The Role Of Political Parties?

Several different political parties may be represented at each state election. But most state and federal officials belong to either the Democratic or the Republican party. These two parties have statewide and national organizations, starting at the precinct level.

Voters elect a precinct committeeperson from each party. The precinct committeepersons of each county meet and elect a chairperson and vice chairperson; one must be a man and one a woman. Each county also elects one man and one woman to the party's statewide committee. Members of this committee elect one woman and one man as state chairpersons.

Each party's goal is to get as many of its members as possible elected to local, state, and national offices. The party organization exists to help select the party's candidates and to help them get elected.

The political party is important in a somewhat different way in the legislature. In Olympia, party members often work together to pass important bills. Individual legislators are often expected to cooperate with other members of their

from office, except a judge of the higher courts. These judges can be removed before the end of their terms by impeachment or by a vote of the legislature. (See pages 148, 150, for more information.)

Another notable difference between state and federal governments is that the state legislature

party. This way, the whole party has more power.

37. Name at least two purposes of political parties.
38. Name the various levels of political party organization in this state.

How Do Political Parties Affect The Organization Of The Legislature?

Before the beginning of each legislative session, all the members of each political party meet together. Each party elects a floor leader and a whip (assistant) for each house. These people are responsible for guiding bills through the legislature. Committee positions are also assigned at the party meeting, or caucus. The chairperson of each committee is selected from the political party with the most legislators. (This is called the majority party.)

Committee assignments are quite important, since much of the actual work of writing laws goes on in committee. A committee chairperson has a great amount of influence on what bills get passed by his or her committee. Therefore, the heads of committees are very powerful people in the legislature.

The most powerful person in each house is usually the chairperson of the Rules Committee. This is because all bills must be scheduled by the Rules Committee before they can be considered by the whole house. (See the chart on page 282 showing how a bill becomes a law.) As a matter of fact, the Rules Committee chairperson is also the chief official of the House of Representatives. This person is called the Speaker of the House. The Speaker is elected by the majority party, and is automatically the chairperson of the House Rules Committee.

39. Why are committee assignments so important?
40. What committee is most powerful?

Constitutions And Other Laws

The United State Constitution sets up the basic structure of our federal government, and it is the highest law of the nation. No federal, state, or local law may be passed which violates the national Constitution. For example, the Washington State government could not make a treaty with Canada, Japan, or any other foreign country. The United States Constitution says that only the federal government may make treaties. The United States Supreme Court has the power to cancel any state law which violates the United States Constitution.

In a similar way, the Washington State Constitution describes the basic structures and responsibilities of state government. The State Constitution is also the highest state law. No state or local law may be passed which violates the State Constitution. For example, no county government could refuse to provide public schools for the children in that county. The State Constitution guarantees that all children in Washington have a right to public education. The state legislature could not pass a law which changed a state representative's term to four years. The Washington Constitution says that state representatives shall serve a two-year term.

Sometimes, the State Supreme Court may decide that a certain law is unconstitutional (prohibited by the State Constitution). When this happens, the Supreme Court has the authority to throw out that law.

41. Why can't Washington State make a treaty with Japan or Canada?
42. What is the purpose of the State Constitution?

How Can The State Constitution Be Changed?

The constitutions of both the state and the nation can be changed. It is sometimes necessary to do this. For example, the original Washington State Constitution said that all voters had to be men. In order for women to vote, the Constitution itself had to be changed, or amended. The State Constitution describes two methods for making such a change. The most common method is the constitutional amendment. An amendment must be approved by two thirds of the members of both houses of the legislature and then by a majority of the voters. (Notice that a constitutional amendment is much harder to pass than a law. A law needs only a majority of the voters or a majority of both legislative houses plus the signature of the Governor.)

An amendment changes only one portion of the Constitution. The second method for changing the Constitution allows much larger and more basic changes. This method is to call a new constitutional convention and to rewrite the whole Constitution. A constitutional convention also needs to be approved by two thirds of the state senators and representatives and a majority

TAXATION IN WASHINGTON STATE

Since Washington became a state in 1889, property tax has been the main source of state and local government funds. The amount of property tax is based on the value of the property owned. This value is determined by the Assessor — an elected official of the county government. Generally, wealthy people with expensive houses and successful businesses pay higher property taxes than poorer people. However, the property tax system does not always divide the tax burden fairly between rich and poor. This is still a problem today. Poorer people — especially senior citizens on small retirement incomes — often pay a greater percentage of their income in property taxes than do wealthier people.

Voters have passed laws to limit the property tax. The first limit was passed by initiative in 1932. Another similar initiative was passed every two years until 1944, when these limits became part of the State Constitution.

Two studies in 1920 recommended a graduated net income tax as a solution to the property tax problems. (Income tax is based not on the amount of property owned but on the amount of money a person or business earns in a year. "Graduated" means that higher incomes are taxed at a higher percentage than low incomes.)

A number of attempts have been made to enact a state income tax in Washington, but they have all been unsuccessful. In 1929, the state legislature passed an income tax on the state's financial institutions. But this law was thrown out by the Washington State Supreme Court in 1930. The court ruled that the United States Constitution made it illegal for state governments to tax national banks. In 1931, the legislature passed income taxes on both persons and corporations, but the governor vetoed them. In 1932, the voters passed personal and corporate income taxes by initiative. (The governor cannot veto an initiative.) These graduated income tax initiatives passed by a 70% majority vote. But they were declared illegal by the State Supreme Court the next year. According to the State Constitution, the court ruled, taxes must be levied at the same rate — not graduated — on all property. (The court ruled that income is property.)

There have been other state taxes in addition to property taxes since the early years of statehood. In 1890, the legislature voted a poll tax of two dollars, but the legislature soon repealed this. (A poll tax is one that must be paid by every voter in order to be eligible to vote. All poll taxes are now illegal in the United States.) In 1891, the state first placed a tax on insurance payments. Some taxes are raised in the form of license fees. Corporation license fees have been charged since 1879 and automobile license fees since 1915. State gasoline tax began in 1921. This was the state's first type of sales tax.

During the worst of the 1930's depression, government expenses for relief programs were high, yet government incomes were low because many people could not afford to pay their property taxes. In 1933, the state legislature adopted the first business and occupation tax and public utilities tax. These two taxes were among the ones started by the 1935 Revenue Act, the most comprehensive tax program yet passed. This act also started the cigarette tax, the 10% liquor tax, the retail sales tax, and several other taxes no longer in existence.

Since then, most changes in Washington's tax system have just been changes in rates or bases of existing taxes. For example, the retail sales tax is now five times higher and applies to more items than at first. The liquor tax, the public utilities tax, and the business and occupation taxes have all increased. In 1972, voters approved a one percent constitutional limit on regular property taxes. A few new minor taxes have been added since 1935. The tobacco products tax of 1971 is an example.

In 1977, an initiative was passed to remove the sales tax on food. It took effect in 1978. Many people had argued that this was the most unfair tax, since food is a necessity.

However, the basic tax structure of this state has changed little since 1935. Property and sales taxes are still the main sources of state and local revenue. Since the 1930's, there have been several attempts to make basic changes such as placing an income tax in Washington's tax system, but the legislature and the voters have resisted major changes.

---

of the voters. Such a constitutional convention has been proposed several times in Washington, but it has never yet been approved.

43. What two methods can be used to change the state constitution? Which method is more common?

The Effects Of Constitutional Amendments: A Case Study

A single constitutional amendment may have very far-reaching effects. After the constitution is changed, old laws may become unconstitutional. The Equal Rights Amendment of 1972 (to the Washington State Constitution) is a good example of how this process works.

The ERA says that women and men shall have equal rights and responsibilities under state law. Many state laws that were passed before 1972 had discriminated between men and women in such areas as jobs, marriage, and care of children. For example, some laws required that certain state jobs be filled by men. The age of retirement was sometimes different for men and women. A woman could collect insurance or retirement payments if her husband died, but her husband did not have the same right. After the Equal Rights Amendment was passed, all these discriminating laws became unconstitutional. More than 100 laws had to be changed. In some cases, officials could not decide how to change a law to make it equal for both men and women. Some of the changes took several years to accomplish. A good example was the issue of laws protecting workers. It is discussed below.

44. What was the ERA?

45. Give examples of some state laws that discriminated between men and women. Why did these laws have to be changed after 1972?

WORKER PROTECTION AND THE E.R.A.

During the Progressive Era of the early 1900's, some important laws were passed that protected women workers. These laws guaranteed women an eight-hour work day with breaks, and other rights. The laws did not guarantee equal rights for men workers.

Most people who supported the ERA believed that these protections should be given to all workers, both men and women. Washington Governor Dan Evans supported this plan. After the ERA became law, the State Department of Labor and Industries had to change the worker protection rules so that men and women would have the same rights. Unfortunately, they took the protections away from all workers. Several women's organizations and other citizen groups in the state began working to get the department to change its decision.

These groups sent lobbyists to Olympia to try to convince the legislature to pass new laws. They also contacted members of the state commission that set the state's labor policy. They asked unions, churches, and other community groups to contact commission members and also to contact the Governor.

At the same time, the Washington Association of Businesses had lobbyists who opposed protective legislation. The association lobbyists and other individual corporation lobbyists contacted legislators and urged them not to support laws that protected workers. The business people opposed many protective laws because they thought the laws were too expensive for businesses. By 1976 the legislature still had not passed any such laws.

Washington's many state parks protect and make public some of the most beautiful and unusual places in the state. This is the Palouse Falls in Eastern Washington. Who decides what state parks will be created?

What Are State Laws?

The State Constitution sets basic guidelines for the duties of state government. But it does not make specific decisions about how to carry those duties out. For example, the Constitution permits a state sales tax, but it does not determine whether to have this type of tax or how much that tax will be. The Constitution allows the state to regulate its natural resources, but it does not create specific state parks. The State Constitution does not suggest how much tax money will be spent in a year on welfare, parks, roads, or office space for government agencies. All of these specific decisions are made by the state legislature.

Each year, many laws passed by the legislature deal with raising and spending money. Other laws might deal with issues such as: legal drinking age, unemployment insurance, state roads and buildings, the minimum punishment for certain crimes, or guidelines for stopping discrimination.

46. *The State Constitution makes basic or general decisions about government duties. Who makes specific decisions?*
47. *Name some issues that might be involved in state laws.*

How Is A State Law Made?

Many of the issues involved in state laws can have a great effect on the daily lives of everyone in the state. Businesses, individuals, and groups will often want to try to influence which laws get passed. In order to do this, it is necessary to understand how state laws are usually made.

The chart below follows a typical bill through the process of becoming a law. Let's say this bill started in the Senate.

48. *Who must introduce the bill?*
49. *What is the role of committees in the legislature?*
50. *What happens after both houses of the legislature have approved the same version of a bill?*

HOW A LAW IS PASSED IN THE STATE LEGISLATURE

1. A senator introduces the bill. (Every bill, or proposed law, must be introduced by a member or committee of the Senate or House of Representatives.)

2. The bill goes to a Senate committee. (Both the Senate and the House of Representatives have several committees to consider different kinds of bills. A bill dealing with schools would go to the education committee, for example.)

3. The committee researches the bill and holds public hearings. Experts may be called to come speak for and against the bill.

4. Within ten days the committee votes. They may recommend that the bill be passed, amended, or vetoed.

5. If the bill calls for spending state money, it must be approved by the Appropriations Committee.

6. The Rules Committee adds the bill to the Senate calendar. (Sometimes, the Rules Committee refuses to do this and succeeds in "killing" the bill.)

7. When the bill comes up on the calendar, Senators debate the issues. They may propose and vote on any amendments to the bill.

8. If passed, the bill is returned to the Rules Committee to be put on the calendar again.

9. A final vote is taken by the full Senate.

After a Senate bill completes all these steps and is approved, then it goes to the House of Representatives. The whole process is repeated in the second house. If a bill starts in the House of Representatives, it must go through the same process in the House first, and then in the Senate.

Sometimes the House and Senate approve different versions of the same bill. Then a committee made up of three senators and three representatives tries to work out a bill that both houses will pass. This is called a conference committee.

After both houses have passed the same bill, the bill goes to the Governor. If the Governor signs it, the bill becomes law.

If the Governor vetoes it, the bill goes back to the legislature. This time both houses must approve the bill by a two-thirds majority in order to pass. (This is called "overriding" the veto.) Otherwise, the bill dies because of the Governor's veto.

Who Are Lobbyists?

Individuals and groups can become involved in the state lawmaking process in several ways. The methods described in Section 1, for influencing federal government policy, can all be used on the state level. Of course, it's much easier to call or visit your state officials than your federal representatives, since the state leaders probably live nearby. While the legislature is in session, you may call your state legislator in Olympia toll-free.

It is also possible for groups to send members to Olympia while the legislature is meeting. These representatives can then have the opportunity to follow a bill from start to finish. They may talk to many legislators in order to win their support. They can try to make sure that good speakers are available for committee hearings. They can do everything possible to help pass laws that the group supports. People who do this are called "lobbyists," because most of their work was traditionally carried on in the lobby outside the official legislative meeting rooms.

Each year lobbyists come to the sessions in Olympia to represent the interests of labor unions, businesses, and citizens' groups. Many of the lobbyists are full-time paid employees of their business or organization, and others are volunteers. In 1976, the largest groups of lobbyists came from educational associations and labor unions. Many big corporations also had several lobbyists. Other lobbyists represented environmental groups, private landowners, business organizations, or cities, for example.

WINNING POWERFUL SUPPORT: A CASE STUDY

To get an idea of how a citizens' group might help get a law passed, let's take a look at a real law that actually was passed. The law guaranteed that all handicapped children in Washington would be able to receive a public education. Before this law was passed, special education classes were not available for everyone that needed them.

The citizens' group that sponsored this proposed law called themselves Education for All. There were only six members: two law students and some parents of handicapped children. Yet these six people managed to gain all the necessary support to get this law passed.

How did they do it? Their main method was to work hard at gathering wide and powerful support. They started by writing to all organizations they could think of that might be interested in the law, such as educational associations, government agencies dealing with the handicapped, and charity organizations. They asked these groups to give public support of the issue. They encouraged group members to write or call their representatives urging them to support the bill (proposed law). A number of groups responded with letters of support, donations of money, and even the help of the groups' regular lobbyists. One of these groups was able to win support for the bill from the Superintendent of Public Instruction, who was an important sponsor.

Next, Education for All talked to the Governor's staff. They convinced Governor Evans to include education for the handicapped in his list of recommended laws for that year, 1970. This gave the bill a strong start. At the same time, the group looked for legislators to sponsor the bill. They were very successful. There were two main sponsors in each house, with extra sponsors in the Senate, and twenty-eight back-up sponsors in the House of Representatives. (In other words, almost one third of all the representatives were sponsoring the bill.)

Education for All prepared a rough draft of the bill with the help of lawyers. They presented it to the Joint Committee on Education. (A "joint" committee means that both senators and representatives are committee members.) Then they held a public meeting to gain wider publicity for the issue.

At one point, a few powerful members of the Appropriations Committee and the Rules Committee tried to stop the bill. (All bills requiring the spending of state funds must go through the Appropriations Committee. All bills must go through the Rules Committee in order to be put on the calendar for consideration. Therefore, members of these two committees have a lot of power. They can sometimes stop a bill even when a large majority of the legislature supports it.)

Education for All used two main methods to move the bill through these committees. They contacted voters from the committee members' districts and asked these voters to write letters. The letters strongly urged those committee members to support the bill. In addition, Education for All decided which committee members could most likely be convinced to change their votes. They concentrated most of their pressure on these particular legislators.

Committee delays made the bill miss the deadline for passage in the regular session. But the group got their sponsors to introduce the bill again the next time the legislature met. This time it passed.

51. List some things a lobbyist might do to help a bill get passed by the legislature.

What Issues Do Legislators Have To Know About?

Senators and representatives are usually very busy while the legislature is in session. Each year, they have to decide how to vote on a great number of different bills. Just keeping informed on the issues takes a lot of time. For example, the following are only a few of the topics that legislators voted on in 1975 and 1976:

— how to raise more taxes in order to pay the rising cost of public schools
— whether to build ''superports'' for giant tankers bringing oil from Alaska
— how much money each state agency may spend
— who should have a right to irrigation water in Eastern Washington
— whether any laws dealing with crimes should be changed
— historic preservation
— sex discrimination
— the legislators' own salaries

Legislators are especially responsible to keep up on the bills that come before the committees they belong to. Committee research may involve such activities as holding public hearings on the bill, listening to speaker opinions, and researching similar laws that have been passed in other states. Each legislator is a member of about three different committees. Sometimes they are so busy with their committee work that they hardly have time to attend the regular legislative meetings!

Remember, too, that being a legislator is only a part-time job. The rest of the year, legislators work as lawyers, educators, farmers, fishers, loggers, doctors, social workers, homemakers, labor officials and so on. Making laws is a demanding second career!

52. About how many committees does each legislator belong to?
53. Why are legislators so busy while the legislature is in session?

Who Carries Out The Laws?

The legislators make our state laws, but they are not responsible for enforcing them or carrying them out. This is the job of the executive branch. For example, suppose the legislature passed a law saying that $10 million of the state's money could be spent to repair bridges in the next year. The actual spending of the money would be done by the Highway Department, which is an agency of the executive branch. Employees of this department would decide which bridges needed repairs. Then they would schedule the construction dates, arrange for

---

IMPROVING WINTER SPORTS OPPORTUNITIES BY LAW: A CASE STUDY

The following case study gives some examples of how the lawmaking process and the law enforcing process are related.

Many winter sports are popular in Washington, including downhill skiing, cross country skiing, and snowshoeing. There are lots of mountain areas that are good for these sports, but most of them couldn't be used until recently. This is because there was almost no place to park a car, except at downhill ski resorts. The rest of the areas were buried deep in snow.

A number of outdoor organizations had tried to talk the state government into plowing more parking spaces, especially for cross-country skiers and snowshoers. But these organizations ran into a problem. There was no particular state agency in charge of winter recreation. No single state agency had the authority, the interest, or the snowplows to do the job. Also, many of the best trails were on federal government property, in national parks and forests. How could all the different state and federal agencies be encouraged to work together to solve the problem?

A citizens' group, made up of members of several different outdoor organizations, decided to try. They asked the president of one of the organizations to write a letter to the Govenor. They asked the Governor to call a meeting of all the different agencies.

In the meantime, the group researched the problem and began writing the rough draft of a proposed law. Under this law, interested people could buy a winter parking permit for $5. Permit fees would pay the cost of plowing out the parking spaces. Group members contacted various outdoor organizations for support, and they got a legislator to introduce a bill. They were successful in getting the legislature to pass the bill. It became a law.

However, the winter parking did not start that year, or the next. It took a long time for the various agencies to coordinate the methods for carrying out the new law. The citizens' group remained active for more than a year after the law was passed. They helped design the road signs and permits, and made sure the agencies were following up on their responsibilities. After a year's delay, the program was in progress.

work crews, pay for materials, and inspect the work after it was finished.

The Highway Department is one of over 100 departments, boards, and commissions that make up the executive branch of Washington State government. The head of the entire executive branch is the Governor. Some individual departments are directed by other elected executive officials. For example, the Department of Natural Resources is headed by the Commissioner of Public Lands, who is an elected official. The State Superintendent of Public Instruction is also elected. (See the chart in this section for the titles and duties of other elected executive officials.)

Other agencies in the executive branch have directors who are appointed by the Governor. These are sometimes called administrative agencies, rather than executive agencies. Some of these agencies are: the Highway Department, the Department of Agriculture, the Parks and Recreation Commission, the Department of Ecology, the Department of Social and Health Services, the Department of Fisheries, the Office of Economic Opportunity, and the Washington State Patrol. There are many more. Some of these agencies provide services. Some enforce state regulations. Some are responsible for the general office work involved in running the state government.

54. Which branch of state government is headed by the Governor and is responsible for enforcing state laws?
55. Who appoints the director of state administrative agencies?
56. Which directors of state agencies are chosen by the voters?
57. Name at least five departments, boards, or commissions that help make up the executive branch of Washington State government.

STATE GOVERNMENT EMPLOYMENT June 30, 1975		
Program Area	Full Time Employees	%
General Government	4,215	8
Human Resources	15,997	30
Natural Resources and Recreation	3,194	6
Transportation	7,552	14
Education	22,325	42
TOTAL	53,283	100

SOURCE: Office of Program Planning and Fiscal Management (Unpublished).

Each level of government contributes some money to support art and cultural events in our communities. This is the Langston Hughes Center in Seattle. It was named after a famous Black poet, and many multi-cultural arts events take place here. It is run by the city government. (The building used to be a Jewish temple, or synagogue.)

How Does The Judicial Branch Make The Laws Clear?

The third branch of state government — the judicial branch — is also involved in the lawmaking process at times. Suppose the Constitution or some other law is not entirely clear, so that different people believe that the law means different things. Who decides exactly what the law does mean in specific situations? This is the responsibility of the judicial branch — the courts.

A good example is the Disclosure Act passed by an initiative in 1972. This law requires elected public officials to disclose (make public) information such as their campaign expenses and contributions and their other sources of income. It requires lobbyists to register and to report their expenses. The law is designed to make our government more open. But some officials have complained that the law is unclear or unconstitutional. Several of them have gone to court so that the judges could decide just what were the exact requirements of the law in different cases. Each court decision gives a clearer definition of what the law really means.

The Superior Courts, Appeals Courts, and Supreme Court must keep detailed records of all court proceedings. These records are referred to by judges who hear similar cases. Usually, judges base their decisions on past decisions made in these "courts of record."

The State Supreme Court meets in this building in Olympia. What are the roles and responsibilities of this court?

58. *Which branch of government is responsible for deciding exactly what a law means?*

What Are The Roles Of The Lower Courts And The Superior Courts?

Each division of the judicial branch has its own structure and responsibilities. The lowest courts (Municipal Courts and Justice Courts) only hear cases involving small amounts of money and short jail sentences.

The Superior Courts have no upper limits on the amount of money or punishment involved in the cases they hear. Serious crimes such as murder, manslaughter, and arson are first tried before the Superior Court.

The cases just mentioned all involve crimes, or broken laws. They are called "criminal" cases. But many cases that are heard in the Superior Courts do not involve crimes. Instead, they involve disputes or differing claims between people. These are called "civil" cases. Some examples are divorces, wills, and broken contracts.

There are 27 Superior Court Districts in the state. Voters in each district elect their judges (or "justices," as they are formally called) for four-year terms.

59. *What courts only hear cases involving small amounts of money and short jail sentences?*
60. *Name several kinds of cases that are first tried by the Superior Courts.*
61. *What is the difference between criminal cases and civil cases?*

What Are The Appeals Court And The State Supreme Court?

Sometimes a person involved in a civil or criminal case feels that a court decision was unfair. When this happens, the person may decide to "appeal" that decision. This means that the person may ask a higher court to hear the case. A higher court has the authority to overturn the decisions of a lower court if the judges believe this is necessary.

Most appeals are heard by the State Court of Appeals. This level of the state judicial branch consists of 12 justices. All are elected for six-year terms. Three justices at a time listen to each case they decide to accept. If the person is still not satisfied, the case may be appealed again.

This time, it would go to the Supreme Court — the highest court in the state. If the Supreme Court justices decided not to consider the case, then the lower court's decision could not be changed.

The Supreme Court also hears cases involving possible violations of the Constitution and appeals cases involving the death penalty, public officials, or issues of extreme public importance.

The Supreme Court consists of nine justices (judges). They are elected for six-year terms. All judges are elected in non-partisan elections. (Candidates do not represent any particular political party.)

62. *Identify the main responsibilities of the Courts of Appeals and the State Supreme Court.*
63. *How many justices listen to a case that comes to the Court of Appeals? How many justices make up the Supreme Court?*

SECTION 3: LOCAL GOVERNMENTS

What Are Counties?

The state government is responsible for passing laws and providing services that affect the whole state. However, some problems and needs are very different in different parts of the state. Some government programs work better when they are controlled on a local level. Examples include police and fire protection, sewage systems, and neighborhood roads. Within Washington State, there are several smaller, local government units. These local governments provide many of the services that we depend on in our daily lives.

The main local government unit in this state is the county. All of Washington is divided into 39 counties, each with its own government. One town in each county serves as the center of government operations. This town is called the county seat. Some duties of county government include:

— issuing some licenses, such as business and pet licenses

— providing police and fire protection

— protecting public health, controlling pollu-

tion, running a county hospital and mental health programs

— operating libraries

— maintaining water, sewage, and waste disposal systems

— other duties not performed by the state government and not in violation of the State Constitution.

Counties have the power to collect taxes to pay for these services.

64. What is the main unit of local government in Washington called? What is the name given to the city that serves as its center of government?
65. How many counties are there in this state?
66. Name some duties of county government.

How Are County Governments Structured?

According to the State Constitution, most Washington counties are run by an elected Board of County Commissioners. The board consists of three commissioners, each elected to a four-year term. Commissioners are both legislators and executive officers. They make regulations — by vote, at public hearings — and

COUNTIES AND COUNTY SEATS

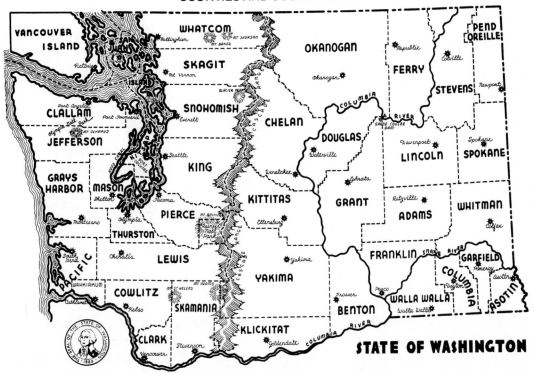

STATE OF WASHINGTON

they also see that the regulations, or ordinances, are carried out. (The word "ordinance," instead of "law" is used to describe rulings by county or city government.) County voters also elect a sheriff, a prosecuting attorney (the county's chief lawyer), a treasurer, an assessor (who determines property values for tax purposes), and some other officials.

Almost all Washington counties have this type of government. However, the Constitution also allows county voters to set up a different kind of county government— if certain requirements are met. The main requirement is that voters approve a county charter. A charter is like a local government's constitution. It is written by "freeholders" who are elected by county voters. A county with its own charter is called a "home rule" county.

King County adopted a home rule charter in 1969. Instead of a Board of County Commissioners, the charter calls for voters to elect a county council and a county executive. The nine members of the council make up the legislative branch of King County government. They are responsible for making ordinances — at public hearings. The county executive has a job similar to that of the Governor. The executive is responsible for enforcing ordinances. He or she may make recommendations to the council, and may veto ordinances. The executive also appoints several county government administrators. The only other elected officials of the King County government are the Assessor and the Prosecuting Attorney.

67. Which elected officials make up the legislative branch in most Washington counties? Who are the legislators for King County?

68. Who heads the executive branch in most Washington counties? How is this different from the King County government?

69. Identify the following: charter, freeholder, home rule.

What Are City Governments Like?

In some parts of the state, some of the county services listed earlier are not provided by the county government. Instead, city governments usually provide these services for the people who live in cities. For example, a city may have its own police and fire departments; water, sewage, and electric systems; parks, libraries, roads, and hospitals. The county government would still provide these services to county residents who live outside a city's limits.

King County Councilwoman Ruby Chow. Chow and her husband have been active leaders of the Northwest's Chinese community for many years. Both of them have been leaders of the Chong Wa Benevolent Assocation. This organization served as a kind of governing body for Chinese Americans in Washington and Idaho. As a council member, Ms. Chow helps make King County's ordinances (laws). What branch of government does the King County Council represent?

According to the State Constitution, cities in Washington may choose one of three basic types of city government. They are mayor-council, commissioners, and council-manager.

The mayor-council system is similar to the King County government structure. The city council acts as the legislative branch. Council members make city regulations and ordinances. The mayor is the chief of the executive branch. He or she has the power to recommend or veto legislation, hire department heads and carry out programs. Council members and the mayor are all elected by voters. Most Washington cities use this type of government.

A second form of government, the city commissioner system, is basically the same as the county commissioner system. Elected city commissioners both make the laws and administer them. Each commissioner has special responsibility for one of the following areas: public safety, finance, streets, and public improvements.

The third city government system is the council-manager system. In this system, only the city council members are elected. The council members select and hire a city manager to administer city programs. The president of the city council serves as mayor on some occasions but does not have veto power or other powers of an elected mayor. The council makes all legislative and policy decisions. The manager sees that these decisions are carried out. Several Washington cities have a council-manager form of government, including Spokane, Tacoma, Yakima, and Vancouver.

70. What other local government may provide some of the same services as a county government?
71. Describe the three basic types of city governments that Washington cities may have.

What Are Districts?

In addition to cities and counties, there are some other local government units called districts. A district may include all or part of one or more counties. It is organized to provide a special service to the people within that district. Port Districts and Sewerage Districts are examples. Usually districts are governed by an elected board of directors who do not receive salaries for their work.

Some district governments pay expenses by charging a user fee. For example, Public Utility Districts sell electricity to residents of the district. The money from electricity sales pays for production and distribution of electric power. Other districts can collect taxes to pay operating expenses. The type of district government that requires the most tax money is the school district. School districts receive money from several sources. Nearly one-fourth of the total state government budget goes toward public schools. The federal government also contributes tax money to local school districts. Other expenses are met by taxing people who live within the school district. For a description of school levies and other funds, see the box on this page.

72. What is a district?
73. What methods may districts use to pay their expenses?

HOW ARE PUBLIC SCHOOLS FUNDED?
Schools are the most expensive service that state and local governments provide. Chart #1 below shows how the state budget is spent and Chart #2 shows sources of education funds.

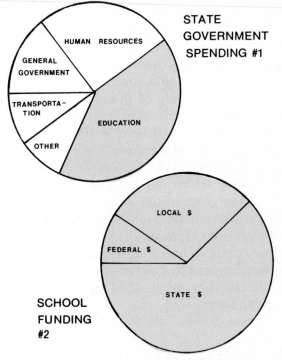

Source: Pocket Data Book 1977, State of Washington

Chart #1 above shows where public schools in this state got their money in 1975-76. The main source of local funds is the school levy. (To levy a tax means to require that it be paid. A levy itself is the tax money raised.) This levy is an extra property tax. People in the district pay a certain amount of tax based on the value of property owned. The amount of a school levy is determined by the local school board, and each levy must be approved by voters.

A levy is harder to pass than an initiative or referendum, since levies must be approved by 60% of those who vote. Also, in order to win, a certain number of voters must participate in a levy election. At least 40% of the number who voted in the last general election must participate in the levy election. If fewer voters turn out, the levy cannot pass unless the number of "yes" votes is at least 60% of the 40% requirement. For example, if 1,000 people voted in the last general election, at least 400 people must vote in a levy election ; 60% must vote for the levy in order for it to pass. If at least 240 (60% of 400) vote for the levy, it will pass even though 400 people did not vote. If the levy fails once, the school board may choose to resubmit it. If passed, the levy applies for one year.

State laws now limit the amount of money that may be raised by a levy. When this book was printed, the state legislature was working on a plan to fully cover the expenses of basic education. This plan would allow limited special levies.

Getting Local Governments To Get Together

Sometimes county governments, plus city governments, plus several different kinds of district governments can add up to confusion. Each of these different governments may have no way of cooperating with the other governments. In a region where there are many cities and many districts, there may be no way to plan and build for the region as a whole. A good example of this problem — and a good solution — can be found in the history of the area around Lake Washington.

In the 1950's, there were 94 separate government units in this area, and Lake Washington was in trouble. Many of the governmental units were letting sewage into the lake. The result was that Lake Washington was becoming filthy, smelly, and unhealthy for fish and people.

In order to clean up the lake, local governments would all have to cooperate. They needed to develop and follow an overall plan. This would require a new kind of government organization for the area.

Private citizens took the lead in creating the new government. A lawyer named James Ellis organized a citizens' group to work on the problem. After years of hard work, Ellis and his supporters succeeded in getting a key law passed by the legislature. This law provided that two or more neighboring governments could set up a "metropolitan corporation" — a government unit with the power to control sewage, water, transportation, garbage disposal, parks, or planning. In September of 1958, the many local governments in the Lake Washington drainage area voted to set up a metropolitan corporation for sewage disposal only. This corporation is called "Metro."

By 1963, tunnels were completed which carried all the area's sewage out to Puget Sound. Within ten years, Lake Washington was clean and beautiful again. Metro's success gained nationwide attention and praise. In 1972, Metro area voters chose to bring the public bus system under Metro control, too.

74. How did the large number of governments affect the pollution of Lake Washington?
75. What is a metropolitan corporation?

GLOSSARY

ADZE — A cutting tool, similar to an axe.

AFL — American Federation of Labor, an organization of trade unions established in 1902.

ABRIDGED — Shortened or limited.

ABANDON — Leave, give up.

ACQUITTED — Discharged completely from an obligation or accusation.

ALIEN — A person of another nation.

AMENDMENT — Addition or change in a law, constitution, or other document.

AQUACULTURE — Farming the sea. Cultivating foods that grow in water.

AUTOBIOGRAPHY — The biography, or life story, of a person told by that same person.

BARRACKS — A large building for housing workers, soldiers, etc.

BICAMERAL — Having two legislative bodies, usually the Senate and the House of Representatives.

BILINGUAL — Having the skill of speaking two languages.

BLACK ROBES — The name that Native Americans called priests or Catholic missionaries.

BOOTLEGGING — Selling liquor illegally.

BOUNTY — Reward. Usually for the capture or killing of a person or animal.

BOYCOTT — A refusal to buy, sell, or use something.

BRACEROS — A Spanish word which means day laborer, or hired hand.

CACHE — A hole lined with wood or leaves to keep out wetness, where goods or supplies are stored until needed.

CALLIGRAPHY — Elegant handwriting.

CAUCUS — A meeting of a small group which is a part of a larger group.

CENSUS — An official count of the population, including such information as age, sex, race, occupations, and annual income. The United States government takes a census every ten years.

COLLECTIVE BARGAINING — Negotiations between employers and organized workers to reach agreement on wages, working hours, benefits, and other working conditions.

CULTURE — The way of life of a race, nation, tribe, or other group of people during a particular period. It includes the system of knowledge, beliefs, skills, customs, and arts.

DIVERSIFIED ECONOMY — An economy based on several important industries.

EBBING — Going away, usually refers to the ocean tide.

ECONOMY — The system that determines how people in a culture produce and distribute goods and services.

EDIBLE — Fit to be eaten, not poisonous.

EQUALIZE — To make equal or uniform.

FINGERLINGS — Salmon at a young age, the size of a finger.

FLOURISH — Become successful, grow or thrive.

EVACUATE — To leave a certain area.

GENERAL STRIKE — The refusal of all unionized workers to go to work.

GEOLOGISTS — Scientists who study how the earth was formed.

GLOSSARY — A collection of terms limited to a special subject or publication.

HISPANIC — Having to do with the people, speech, or culture of people from Spain, Portugal, or Latin America.

HYDROELECTRICITY — Electricity that is generated (created) from the power of running water as it falls over a dam.

I.W.W. — Abbreviation for Industrial Workers of the World. A radical labor union active in Washington in the early 20th Century.

IMMIGRANT — A person who comes to a country to become a permanent resident.

IMMUNITY — Natural protection against disease.

INHABITANT — A resident, a person who lives in a certain region, building, etc.

KLONDIKE — The Yukon River region of Alaska.

LABOR UNION — An organization through which workers unite to improve their wages and working conditions.

LAND BRIDGE — A narrow strip of land connecting larger land areas that are otherwise separated by water.

LAVA — Melted rock that flows over the face of the earth.

LEEWARD — The side away from the wind.

LEGISLATOR — A lawmaker, an elected member of a legislature.

LEGISLATURE — An organized body of people having the power to make laws.

LOCKS — Gates which can be opened and closed to raise or lower water to the level of another body of water.

LOESS — Soil made up of layers of dust carried and deposited by the wind.

MAJORITY PARTY — The political party with the most elected members in the legislature. (The *minority party* has a smaller number of elected members.)

MANGANESE — A grayish-white, hard, brittle mineral that resembles iron but is not magnetic.

MECHANIZATION — The process of adopting machines to replace human labor.

MEDIAN — Midpoint. The middle of a series.

MEGALOPOLIS — A very large urban (city) unit. The word is used for a city that grows far into the surrounding countryside.

MERGE — To become one, unite.

MESTIZO — A Spanish word meaning of mixed racial ancestry.

MIGRANT WORKER — A person who moves in order to find work, especially in harvesting.

MIDDLE LATITUDES — Locations midway between the poles and the equator.

MOLTEN — Melted. (Used to describe melted rock, such as lava.)

ORGANIC — (In reference to the "Organic Act.") Creating a new government.

MONOPOLY — Exclusive ownership, control by one person, group, or company.

PERJURY — Telling a lie in court or in some official, legal situation.

PLAINS INDIANS — The many tribes of Indians who shared similar cultures and were native to the American Midwest. The Sioux, Cheyennes, and Blackfeet are examples.

POLITICAL BOUNDARIES — *Human-made* borders that define different states or countries.

POLLS — Voting places.

PORTAGE — The labor of carrying or transporting, especially used to describe carrying a boat around a part of a river where the boat cannot be safely used.

PRECINCT — The smallest division of government, including only those people who vote at the same place.

PROHIBITIONIST — A person who favors laws denying sale or manufacture of alcohol.

PROSPECTOR — A person who searches for valuable minerals.

PROVISIONAL — Temporary. (In reference to the "Provisional Government of Oregon.")

RANSOM — To pay for someone's release, the money paid.

RATIFIED — Officially approved.

RATION — A standard allowance of food or some other supply, to divide up an item of limited supply.

RECRUIT — To enlist new members into a group.

REFUGEE — One who flees for safety usually from one country to another or from danger.

REMOTE — Located far away, isolated.

RENDEZVOUS — (Ron-day-voo) An appointed meeting, a scheduled place to meet.

"SCABS" — People who work for less than union wages or who work during a strike.

SPARSE — Thin, not thickly grown or settled.

SPAWN — To produce or deposit eggs.

STAMPEDE — A sudden rush of people or frightened animals.

STATISTICS — Facts and figures about a particular topic.

SUFFRAGE — The right to vote.

SUFFRAGIST — One who advocates the right for women to vote.

SURNAME — A name held in common by members of a family.

SURPLUS — More than is needed.

TEAMSTER — One who drives a truck as a trade.

TRADE UNION — A union of workers who share the same job skills or trade. For example: carpenters, truckdrivers.

TRANSCONTINENTAL — Cross-country.

TRUST — A group of companies which together control all, or almost all, of one industry.

VAST — Large.

VERTICAL CLIMATE — A term used to describe temperature change that goes along with change in altitude.

VETO — The power of one branch of the government to prohibit the carrying out of projects by another branch.

VICEROY — A ruler who governs a country or province as a representative of the King.

VISA — An official permit that allows a person to cross into another country. At times a certain visa will allow that person to work in that country.

INDEX

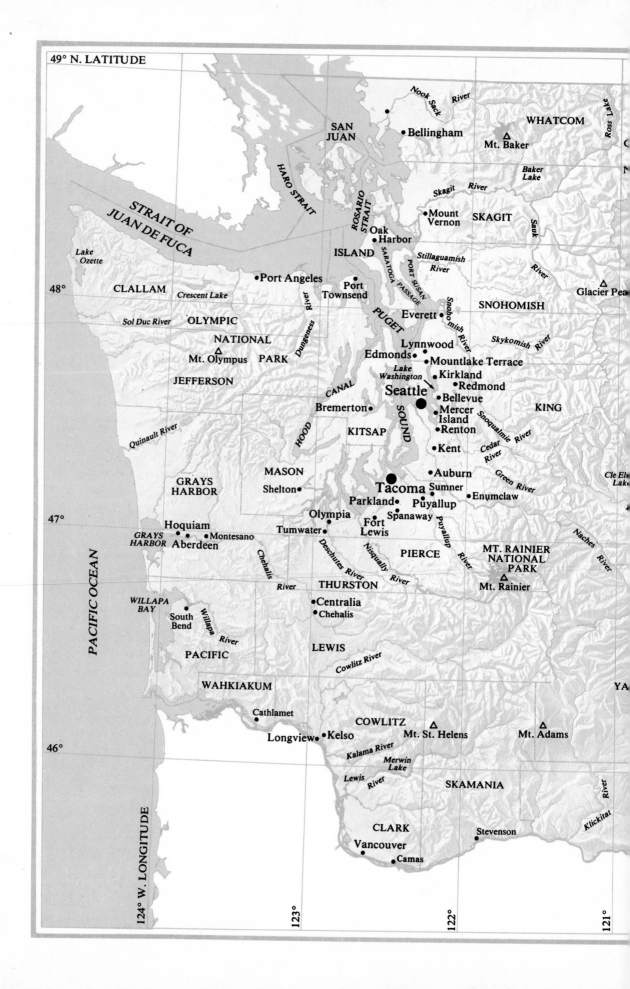

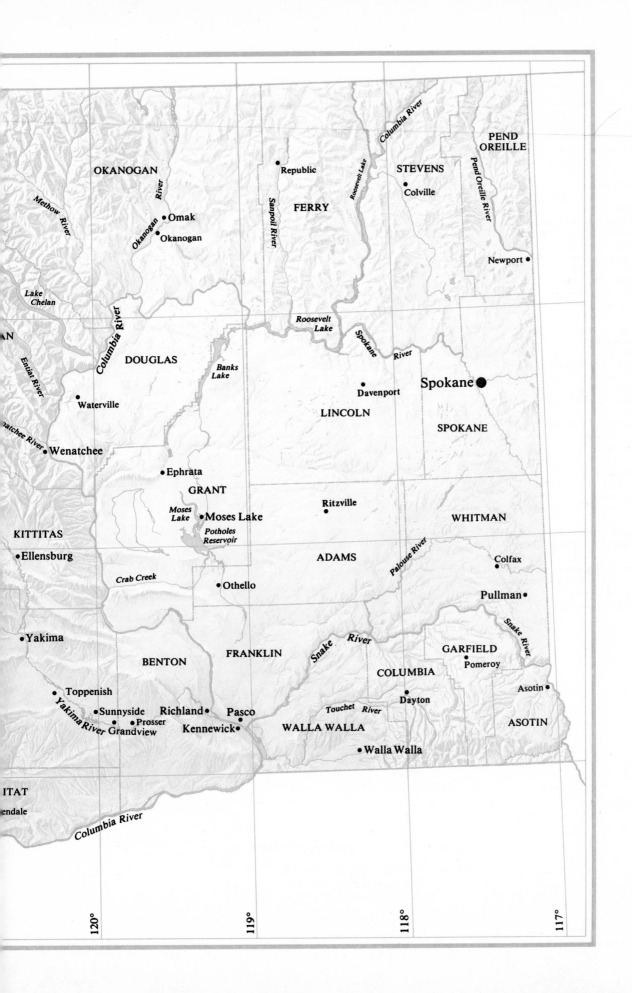

PHOTOGRAPH AND ILLUSTRATION CREDITS

The text of this book was set
in 11/13 English Times. The text
paper is 60 pound bookstock.
The book was typeset and printed
at Murray Publishing Company, Seattle, Wa.
The cover of the softbound edition
is 17pt. Corvon Laflex with binding
by Bindery Services, Inc., Seattle, Wa.
The cover of the hardbound edition
is Roxite cloth stamped with silver
foil with binding by Lincoln and
Allen of Portland, Oregon.

For additional copies of this book contact:

MURRAY PUBLISHING COMPANY
2314 Third Avenue (206) 682-3560
Seattle, Washington 98120